Hawai'i

Moana Tregaskis

Photography by Greg Vaughn, Wayne Levin, and Paul Chesley

COMPASS AMERICAN GUIDES
An imprint of Fodor's Travel Publications

Compass American Guides: Hawai'i

Editor: Paula Consolo
Designer: Tina R. Malaney
Compass Editorial Director: Paul Eisenberg
Compass Creative Director: Fabrizio La Rocca
Editorial Production: Linda K. Schmidt
Photo Editor and Archival Researcher: Melanie Marin
Map Design: Mark Stroud, Moon Street Cartography
Cover photo (Wailea Marriott luau): Greg Vaughn

Sixth Edition
ISBN 1–4000–1482–4

The details in this book are based on information supplied to us at press time, but changes occur all the
time, and the publisher cannot accept responsibility for facts that become outdated or for inadvertent errors
or omissions.

Compass American Guides, 1745 Broadway, New York, NY 10019
PRINTED IN CHINA

10 9 8 7 6 5 4 3 2 1

To the mana of another, brave warrior and man of courage,
that granted me the power to write this book.
Hoʻo manaʻo.

CONTENTS

OVERVIEW 10

HAWAI'I FACTS 12

INTRODUCTION 17

HISTORY & CULTURE 20
Geography 20
Geology 20
Polynesian Voyagers 23
Early Hawaiians 23
Captain James Cook 26
Kamehameha the Great 31
Whalers and Missionaries 35
Rise of Sugar 35
Annexation 36
Growth of Tourism 38
Modern Hawai'i Evolves 40
Hawai'i's People and Culture 44

HAWAI'I—The Big Island 47
History 48
Hilo 53
Puna 56
Hawai'i Volcanoes National Park . . . 59
Road to Kona 65
South Kona Coast 66
North Kona 75
North Kohala Peninsula 83
Waimea and the Parker Ranch 86
Hamakua Coast 89
Mauna Kea 93
Travel Basics 94
Visitor Information Services 95
Food and Lodging 95
Golfing in Paradise 100
Big Island Spas 102
Outdoor Adventures 103
Festivals and Events 104

MAUI—Valley Island 107
History 108
Central Maui 115
West Maui 118
East Maui 126
Upcountry Maui 134
Haleakala National Park 140
Travel Basics 144
Visitor Information Services 144
Food and Lodging 144
Golfing on Maui 149
Maui Spas 150
Outdoor Adventures 151
Festivals and Events 152

LANA'I—Privacy Island 154
History 154
Lana'i City 158
Lana'i High Country 158
North Lana'i 163
South Lana'i 163
Travel Basics 171
Visitor Information Services 172
Food and Lodging 172
Golfing on Lana'i 173

MOLOKA'I—Lonely, Friendly Isle   174
History 174
Central Moloka'i 180
East Moloka'i 188
West Moloka'i 191
Travel Basics 195
Visitor Information Services 195
Food and Lodging 195
Golfing on Moloka'i 196
Outdoor Adventures 196
Festivals and Events 197

HONOLULU AND WAIKIKI . . . 198
History. 198
Waikiki. 201
Diamond Head 211
Downtown Honolulu. 213
The Pali Highway. 230
Pearl Harbor. 232
Travel Basics. 240
Visitor Information Services. 240
Restaurants. 240
Lodging 247
Golfing in Honolulu 248
Waikiki Spas. 249
Recommended Tours 249

GREATER O'AHU 250
History. 251
Southeast O'ahu. 253
Windward O'ahu 258
Central O'ahu 261
North Shore 264
Leeward O'ahu. 267
Travel Basics. 268
Visitor Information Services. 268
Food and Lodging 268
Golfing on Greater O'ahu. 269
O'ahu Spas. 270
Outdoor Adventures 270
Festivals and Events 272

KAUA'I—Garden Island. 276
History. 278
South Kaua'i 284
Waimea Canyon. 293
Mount Wai'ale'ale. 297
West Kaua'i 297
Na Pali Coast 298
East Kaua'i 300
North Shore 304
Travel Basics. 310
Visitor Information Services. 310
Food and Lodging 310
Golfing on Kaua'i. 314

Kaua'i Spas. 315
Outdoor Adventures 315
Festivals and Events 316

FLORA AND FAUNA. 318
Flora. 321
Birds. 326
Mammals. 330

SURFING 340
Surfing on O'ahu 344
Surfing on Maui. 348
Surfing on Kaua'i. 350
Surfing the Big Island. 350
Big Wave Competitions 351

GENERAL INFORMATION 354
Area Code 354
Getting There. 354
Inter-Island Travel 354
Intra-Island Travel 355
Climate 356
Disabled Visitor Information 357
Eating Hawaiian Style 357
Accommodations in Hawai'i 359

RECOMMENDED READING . . 360

LANGUAGE 368

INDEX. 372

ACKNOWLEDGMENTS. 382

Literary Extracts

Captain Cook *from his journal* 27–28
Captain Otto von Kotzebue *on Kamehameha the Great* 32–34
Mark Twain *on Kilauea Volcano* 63
S. M. Kamakau *gives a Hawaiian view of Captain Cook* 72–73
Eric Chock *on mango picking* 90–91
Armine von Tempski *describes ranching on Maui* 135–136
Clara Mitsuko Jelsma *on a Japanese bride* 160–161
Norman Hindley *on Mo'omomi Beach* 164
Robert Louis Stevenson *defends Father Damien* 178–179
Robert Louis Stevenson *on a leper girl leaving for Moloka'i* 184
Thomas Farber *on surfing at Waikiki* 209–210
Mark Twain *on a Honolulu afternoon* 218–219
Captain Mitsuo Fuchida *on bombing Pearl Harbor* 233–234
Isabella Bird *on early Kaua'i* 280–281
Thomas Farber *on dolphins* 339
Jack London *on learning to surf* 346–347

Topical Essays and Sidebars

Pu'uhonua O Honaunau (Place of Refuge) 68–69
Cane Cutter's Journey 112–113
Kaho'olawe 168–169
Dinner with the King 226
Music of Hawai'i 238–239
A Two-Cent Missionary 252
Hawaiian Quilts 286
Ni'ihau—Forbidden Island 308
A Lei for Every Island 324–325
Reef Fish 334–337
Talking Surf 352–353
Hawaiian Fish Found on Menus 358

(following spread) No development is visible from the smooth white sands of Maui's Big Beach.

Hula girl dolls for sale in Waikiki.

Maps

Hawaiian Islands 14–15
Hilo. 52
Hawai'i, the Big Island. 57
South Kona Coast 67
North Kona Coast 75
Maui 109
Lana'i 159
Moloka'i 181
Waikiki 203
Downtown Honolulu 215
Greater Honolulu 221
O'ahu 255
Kaua'i 285

OVERVIEW

■ **BIG ISLAND OF HAWAI'I** *pages 47–106*

Ancient Hawai'i lingers on the Big Island, among Polynesian temple ruins dating from the era of King Kamehameha and legends of the goddess Pele. The island's western coast enjoys sunny weather, fine snorkeling, and warm waters. The rest of the Big Island encompasses every conceivable landscape: rolling pasturelands, tropical forest, the snowy flanks of Mauna Kea—an active volcano to the south—and newly formed black-sand beaches.

■ **MAUI** *pages 107–153*

Western Maui is blessed with clear blue seas, white-sand beaches, and rows of coco palms. Bustling Lahaina, a former whaling town, is filled with historic sights and trendy restaurants. In winter, surfers ride the roaring waves of the weathered north shore. Quieter and more rural areas can be found near massive Haleakala volcano. To the southeast are breathtaking drives through rain forest, seaside parks, and quiet ranch towns.

■ **LANA'I** *pages 154–173*

Rugged and serene, this island invites quiet exploration. Lana'i's one town is in the middle of the island near pine forests, steep gorges, and red-hued mountains. Rural roads through agricultural fields and ironwood forests lead to remote beaches and the eerily eroded boulders of the Garden of the Gods. On the warm southern coast are Manele Bay and Hulopo'e Beach, both known for snorkeling and scuba diving.

■ **MOLOKA'I** *pages 174–197*

Moloka'i offers tranquil isolation and a slow pace. A single highway traverses the length of the island, passing rural villages, mango groves, tropical preserves, and wilderness. On the island's western side Moloka'i Ranch offers luxury camping with cowboy and pastoral adventures. On the northern Makanalua Peninsula, steep cliffs rise thousands of feet above a turquoise sea.

■ HONOLULU AND WAIKIKI *pages 198–249*

On the south side of O'ahu, Honolulu is the state capital and the mid-Pacific's economic center. Part metropolis, part balmy tropical town, it has countless restaurants, hotels, shops, and bars. Rising above the white sands of Waikiki Beach is the dark prow of Diamond Head, with a trail to the crater's summit. Other sights include the 'Iolani Palace, home to Hawaiian royalty; Nu'uanu Pali overlook; and the historic ships USS *Arizona* and USS *Missouri* at Pearl Harbor.

■ GREATER O'AHU *pages 250–275*

The island of O'ahu abounds with natural pleasures. Coral reefs at Hanauma Bay (east of Honolulu) are a favorite spot for snorkeling. Across the island, the north shore is famous for its surf—winter waves at Banzai Pipeline, Waimea Bay, and Sunset Beach often top 30 feet. Inland, spectacular drives loop around the Ko'olau and Waianae mountains and descend into lush valleys and agricultural fields.

■ KAUA'I *pages 276–317*

Kaua'i's spectacular tropical beauty is perhaps best seen on the wild Na Pali Coast, where deep blue waters meet soaring cliffs and deep valleys and waterfalls. The island's central peak, Mt. Wai'ale'ale, receives more than 400 inches of rain a year and is home to rare birds and plants. To the west lies the great Waimea Canyon, 10 miles long and more than 3,000 feet deep. Along Kaua'i's coastline are some of the loveliest beaches in the world, including Lumaha'i Beach on the north shore and Polihale Beach on the west coast.

HAWAI'I FACTS

NICKNAME: Aloha State

CAPITAL: Honolulu

SIZE: 6,425 sq. miles

ENTERED UNION: August 21, 1959

FIRST SETTLED: A.D. 300–600

STATE BIRD: nene (an endangered goose)

STATE TREE: *kukui* (candlenut)

STATE FLOWER: *ma'o hau hele* (yellow hibiscus)

Yellow hibiscus.

ECONOMY:
Major industries: Tourism, defense, finance, retail trade, services, fishing
Chief crops: Fresh pineapple, flowers, macadamia nuts, fruits and vegetables, coffee, seed crops

PER CAPITA INCOME: $25,159

TOURISM: $9.2 billion spent by more than 8 million out-of-state visitors, or $8,400 for each resident (highest ratio in nation)

POPULATION: 1,237,511 (2000 U.S. Census)
Hawaiian/part Hawaiian 31%
White 28%
Japanese 21%
Filipino 12%
Other 8%

COUNTY POPULATIONS (2000):

City and County of Honolulu (O'ahu Island)	876,156
Hawai'i County (Hawai'i Island)	148,677
Kaua'i County (includes Ni'ihau Island)	58,463
Maui County (includes Moloka'i and Lana'i Islands)	160,094

CLIMATE RECORDS:
Lowest Temp ▪ 12° F ▪ 5/17/79 ▪ Mauna Kea, Hawai'i
Highest Temp ▪ 100° F ▪ 4/27/31 ▪ Pahala, Hawai'i
Wettest Place ▪ 460" rainfall per annum ▪ Mt. Wai'ale'ale, Kaua'i
Driest Place ▪ 14" rainfall per annum ▪ Mahukona, Hawai'i

INTRODUCTION

Hawai'i overflows with natural beauty. Piercing up through the surface of the Pacific from the ocean floor, the Hawaiian Islands are ringed by turquoise and purple waters. Each isle is garlanded with strands of soft sand beaches that run from pure white to ebony. On the land lie jagged volcanic cliffs slashed by lush green valleys and deep gorges; there are snowfields and deserts, green palms and red lehua blossoms, black lava, and the heavy scent of tropical flowers.

There is also another kind of natural beauty in Hawai'i. It is her people—everyone is a part of a minority, and we live in extraordinary rapprochement. The islands have absorbed wave after wave of immigrants, each bringing bits and pieces from homelands to create a mixture of taste, sound, and blended ancestry that is unique to these islands. It is her people who have learned from Hawai'i, assimilated the gentle spirit and Hawaiian heritage, and made these islands the Land of *Aloha*. *Aloha* has many definitions and no single one. The Reverend Abraham K. Akaka said it best in his speech on the day Congress granted Hawai'i statehood in 1959:

> *Aloha ke Akua,* God is *aloha* . . . . We do not do good only to those
> who do good to us. One of the sweetest things about the love of
> God, about *aloha*, is that it welcomes the stranger and seeks his good.
> A person who has the spirit of *aloha* loves even when the love is not
> returned . . . the real Golden Rule is *aloha*.

In the coastal cities and rural towns, Hawai'i's people are ingrained from generation to generation with this certain beauty, this spirit named *aloha*. Visitors can experience it today at ancient sites, and through hula, music, and arts and crafts.

It is this real and living culture, coupled with ethnic diversity, that places the Hawaiian Islands apart. It explains the rise of tourism and the large numbers of visitors (52 percent) who return again and again. Honolulu today is the eleventh largest city in the nation and the prime visitor destination in the United States.

Yet the natural beauty remains. With the number of annual visitors passing the 8 million mark, few realize that tourist destination areas are a fraction of the Hawaiian landscape, and that the major portion of the islands is wilderness or rural. On Maui, for example, 75 percent of the land is protected in one type or another of

Carved ki'i, incarnate spirits of the ancient gods, guard Hale O Keawe temple on the Big Island.

wilderness preserve. Mountainous interiors on each island are largely pristine. Hikers may choose from an abundance of trails in unblemished backcountry.

Hawai'i is crowded with polarities and bizarre extremes—the world's highest mountain measured from the seabed, Mauna Kea; the wettest spot on earth, atop Wai'ale'ale; the most active volcano on earth, Kilauea; the largest dormant volcano, Haleakala; the highest sea cliffs, on Moloka'i; and rainfall that may vary by hundreds of inches within a radius of just a few miles. Many thousands of flora and fauna species emerged in these isolated islands and some 90 percent are found no other place on earth. The *po'ouli* is a bird so rare it was not seen until 1975, living in the cloud-shrouded forests of Maui. Some of nature's weirdest mutant changes and diversification of a species from a single ancestor live only here.

Hawai'i's tropical climate is benign due to cooling northeast trade winds throughout the year. The year-round average ocean temperature is nearly constant, fluctuating between 75° F and 82° F. The caressing air of coastal areas is nearly the same; between 66° F and 88° F year-round. Rainbows glistening in sunshine follow brief daylight showers. Hawai'i gave birth to surfing, sport of Pacific kings, and the warm ocean draws windsurfers and bodysurfers, snorkelers, divers, and game-fishing fans.

On the six major islands of Hawai'i, leeward (western and southern) shores are sunny and dry, with soft sand beaches and limpid aquamarine seas, hovering over 400,000 acres of coral reefs. The windward (eastern and northern) coasts are lined with sharp cliffs, waterfalls, lush rainforests, and heavy crashing surf. In the cool and misty highlands are green undulating meadowlands, ranches, and farms.

The Big Island of Hawai'i is the home of Pele, the volcano goddess, and here volcanoes erupt and snow whitens the mountain peaks. On this island that encapsulates every type of climate on earth are orchards growing macadamia nuts and coffee, and farms that cultivate velvety orchids. Astronomers study the heavens, *paniolo* (cowboys) ride herd on cattle, and sport-fishing fans tag leaping marlin. Kaua'i is the island of the most spectacular lush scenery, with a verdant collar, jagged cliffs of the Na Pali Coast, and a Grand Canyon–like gorge (Waimea Canyon). Lana'i, once the Pineapple Island, is newly engaged in tourism, with two luxury hotel-resorts. Maui takes first place in visitor destination development. This island with the vast crater of Haleakala, its twisting drive to Hana, and glitzy megaresorts, is top rated for whale-watching and upland farming. Rural Moloka'i, with the largest percentage of native Hawaiians living on a major island, has just one luxury hotel.

The most populous island is Oʻahu, the capital island, site of government and Waikiki Beach, where one-half of the visitor accommodations in the state are located and nightlife is lively and hip. On this island you can eat many of the world's cuisines at family restaurants or indulge in gourmet Continental wining and dining. Oʻahu is the surfing island of famed international competitions. Traffic in Honolulu and windward suburbs is staggering, yet a mile away lies a quiet rural countryside.

Writers always have been captivated by Hawaiʻi's unique cultural and ethnic mix. Nineteenth-century literary figures captured the Hawaiian magic, creating tales as absorbing today as they were long ago. The vivid descriptions and sensitive, sometimes bumptious tales spun by Jack London and Robert Louis Stevenson, as well as Mark Twain's accounts of his rovings, testify to the seductive witcheries of this chain of Pacific islands.

Newer testaments to Hawaiʻi's magic have come from James Michener and James Jones, and from that storyteller of men in war, Richard Tregaskis, all attesting to the continuing allure of modern Hawaiʻi.

Each island has a separate chapter in this book, beginning with its history and geography. The chapters lead readers to what stood or happened at ordinary places, to sites where Hawaiian gods accomplished fearsome deeds, and to sites where famous writers worked and stayed. With references to these writers' perceptions and observations, I hope the readers' experiences are enhanced. Each island's special qualities, its art and activities are described. Practical information, including lodging, restaurants, outdoor activities, and much more, can be found at the end of each island chapter.

This guide is intended for modern pathfinders, who I hope will sense the voluptuous island magic that courses through Hawaiian culture and myth, its blend of oriental and occidental energy, and fascinating history. It is for those readers and travelers who, like the writers, would go beyond a balmy beach to discover the legend, fabric, and environment that bestow Hawaiʻi's magic.

■ ABOUT GLOTTAL STOPS

You may notice in this travel guide that the names of certain places and historical figures are marked with a glottal stop, or hamza (ʻ), which indicates a pause in a word's enunciation. Keep in mind that these punctuation marks are a relatively recent addition to the written Hawaiian language and may not appear consistently on Hawaiian street signs, maps, institutional names, and other literature about Hawaiʻi.

HISTORY & CULTURE

■ GEOGRAPHY

The Hawaiian archipelago slices through the Tropic of Cancer, extending in a line from southeast to northwest for 1,523 miles, from the island of Hawai'i—known as the Big Island—at 19 degrees north latitude to Kure Island at 28.5 degrees north latitude. All eight main Hawaiian islands are in the tropics. The twenty-eight northwest islands are a National Wildlife Refuge strewn across one thousand miles of Pacific Ocean. With the exception of the five Midway islands (geographically a part of the archipelago but administered by the U.S. Department of the Interior), the entire chain of shoals, reefs, and islands is the State of Hawai'i.

The land area of the main islands and offshore islets is 6,425 square miles. Hawai'i is the biggest and Maui is next, followed by O'ahu, Kaua'i, Moloka'i, Lana'i, Ni'ihau, and uninhabited Kaho'olawe. Mauna Kea on the Big Island rises to 13,796 feet, but when measured from the ocean floor to its summit it is higher than Mount Everest.

■ GEOLOGY

The Hawaiian Islands are more than the land you see. They are peaks of massive volcanoes that began coughing up molten rock some 25 to 40 million years ago from a crack in the earth's seabed mantle. The ocean floor at Hawai'i is part of the Pacific Plate, which stretches out from California and moves northwest some three inches a year. The crack, or hot spot, is stationary. Each volcano was created when a weak spot in the earth's crust moved over the crack. Liquid magma beneath the earth was piled layer upon layer, cooling into rock, until it pierced the earth. The molten rock, known as lava above the earth, continued to mold the peaks and created an archipelago with eight main islands: Hawai'i, Maui, O'ahu, Kaua'i, Moloka'i, Lana'i, Ni'ihau, and Kaho'olawe. As the volcanoes crawled beyond the hot spot, their activities decreased; they finally cooled and became dormant, and later became extinct.

Hawai'i's volcanoes are shield volcanoes, which build up gradually with wide-based gentle slopes, rather than by rapid explosion. There is little gas emitted as the molten rock streams down in flows that may spread over several miles. You can see

Ferns sprout up through Holei Pali lava flow on Chain of Craters Road in Hawai'i Volcanoes

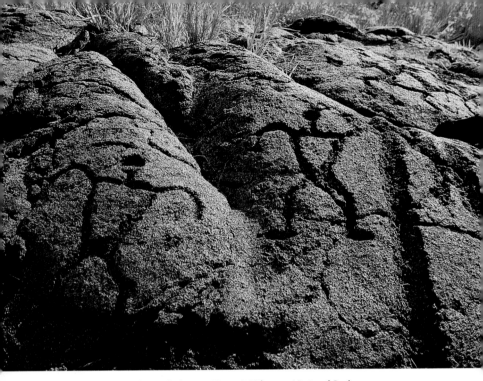

Petroglyphs are carved into the lava in Hawai'i Volcanoes National Park.

this in the tapering slopes dropping down off the summits of Mauna Kea and Mauna Loa on the Big Island of Hawai'i—the youngest of the Hawaiian Islands and still in the process of being created.

Two types of lava pour from volcanoes, and their Hawaiian names are used throughout the world: *pahoehoe* and *'a'a*. You can walk on the smooth surface of *pahoehoe*. It moves in flat billows that wrinkle when the liquid flow beneath a cooling crust drags it forward. The fiery stream forms tubes under the crust, sometimes large enough to walk through, like the Thurston Lava Tube in Hawai'i Volcanoes National Park on the Big Island. *'A'a* lava is rough and knife-sharp. It is cast up in jagged boulders with solid interiors. If you try to walk or climb on it, your shoes and hands may well be cut.

When a volcano stops spewing lava, other forces of nature take hold. Rain, wind, and wave action erode the land. In this way the uninhabited northwest islands, oldest in the Hawaiian chain, have been eroded down from mountains to flat-tops that now barely break the surface of the water. This process is clearly evident on Kaua'i, oldest of the main islands, where the Na Pali cliffs are continuously eroded by wind and rain into sharp, serrated ridges, and where wave-carved caves meet the sea.

The most active Hawaiian volcano is the Big Island's Kilauea, spurting lava directly above the hot spot. Since 1983 more than 2 billion cubic yards of lava have flowed from Kilauea, and the flow shows no signs of abating. The other active volcano in Hawaii is Mauna Loa, also on the Big Island; scientists are tracking new rumblings here. Mauna Kea and Hualalai on the Big Island, and Haleakala on Maui are dormant. All the volcanoes on the other islands are considered extinct.

■ POLYNESIAN VOYAGERS

Hawai'i is the northern point of the triangle of islands spread across the north and south Pacific that is known as Polynesia, or "many islands." The southern point is New Zealand (Aotearoa), home of the Maori. Rapa Nui, or Easter Island (Isla de Pascua, a possession of Chile), is the eastern apex of the vast triangle. The generally accepted theory of the prehistoric roots of Polynesians is that they followed a migration pattern out of South Asia, down into Southeast Asia, moving into Indonesia and across Melanesia to settle in the islands of Samoa and Tonga in about 1000 B.C. Later settlements were formed over the next 1,500 years in the Marquesas, Tahiti, Rapa Nui, and other islands of Polynesia.

The Polynesians crossed the vast empty waters of the world's largest ocean in double-hulled canoes up to 80 feet long and mounted with woven sails. Navigating with extraordinary skill, the voyagers relied on a sort of mental compass point in the sky—the Makali'i, known to Greek stargazers as the Pleiades. By these stars, the equivalent of magnetic north, and by the sun, clouds, ocean swells, and currents, they sought Havaiti, the ancestral home in the sun. (The word also means "the underworld.") In the canoes they brought the food staple taro, dogs, pigs, breadfruit, and the uninvited Polynesian rat. The settlement of the Hawaiian Islands marks the end of the great era of Polynesian exploration and colonization.

■ EARLY HAWAIIANS

Between A.D. 500 and 700, the warring, tattooed Marquesans beached their canoes on Hawaiian shores. Around A.D. 1000 the first Tahitians arrived and probably conquered the Marquesans. By about 1175 a Tahitian priest, or *kahuna* (in Hawaiian), arrived on the Big Island. Named Pa'ao in the ancient oral chants, he founded the *kahuna nui,* or high-priest line, and introduced the institution of a king for each island. From Tahiti he brought Pili, who sired the royal line that led to Kamehameha. These two ruling Tahitian forces formed a dynasty that continued unbroken for 700 years.

Religion centered on four gods: Ku, Lono, Kane, and Kanaloa. Ku was the ancestor of humanity and took many forms—he could be Ku'ula, god of fishing, or Kuka'ilimoku, the war-god-who-snatched-land worshipped by Kamehameha. Lono, the god of peace and fertility, ruled the elements, bringing rain for food plants. Kane made man from dust and gave him life (*kane* is the Hawaiian word for "male"). Kane, Lono, and Ku made the earth and ocean, the moon and stars. Their downfall was an addiction to the alcoholic drink *kava,* and for this they were banished to the underworld, where Kanaloa ruled the dead.

The Tahitian priest Pa'ao hoped to improve upon the way the Hawaiians worshipped their gods *(akua)* by instituting a new order of things. At Puna, Pa'ao built Waha'ula He'iau, the first temple of human sacrifice, and introduced gods and demigods, including the war god Kuka'ilimoku and the fire goddess Pele. He initiated a social order that divided the people into royalty *(ali'i)* and high priests *(kahuna),* commoners *(maka'ainana),* and the lowly outcasts *(kauwa).* The division was enforced by rigid sanctions of the *kapu,* or taboo system that controlled daily life. The ruling chief possessed the greatest degree of *mana,* or supernatural force, and towered over commoners, who were required to fall prostrate when a conch shell hailed his presence.

Commoners could not eat the same food as *ali'i,* walk on the same ground, or cross the king's shadow. Women could not eat with men and were forbidden to take coconut or bananas, pork, and certain fish. Unless the *kapu*-breaker could reach a sanctified place of refuge, or *pu'uhonua,* the penalty always was death. *Pu'uhonua* were used by chiefs and commoners alike, and everyone believed that violating the sanctity of a refuge would bring the wrath of the gods—and retribution in the form of a volcanic eruption or a tsunami. If a pursuer dared enter, he was slain at once by the resident *kahuna* for breaking a *kapu.*

The *kahuna* proclaimed religious laws, or *kapu* (both murder and making distracting noises during religious ceremonies were *kapu*). *Ali'i,* or chiefs, proclaimed the nonreligious laws, or *kanawai*—such as a proclamation sparing the lives of warriors of a defeated chief.

From the twelveth to fifteenth centuries a long list of essentials was brought to Hawai'i from Tahiti: the large *pahu,* or coconut-tree temple drum with a head of sharkskin; the *puloʻuloʻu,* a *tapa* ball on a stick used as a symbol of *kapu;* the *ʻawa,* or *kava* plant for making liquor; the *paʻu,* or *kapa* skirt; the nose flute; and probably the sweet potato.

Life was not all grim. Hawaiians lived in a pleasurable harmony with nature, worshiping gods of lesser rank inspired by the world around them. These included Peleʻs sister Laka, goddess of that paean to nature, the hula. Mitigating the rigid *kapu* system were the pleasures of surfing, kite flying, and most importantly, the concept of *aloha.* Permeating life and meaning "love," *aloha* was a profound sense of compassion, kinship, and friendly spirit. The most important element in Hawaiian life, the spirit of *aloha* imprinted upon Hawaiian culture a communal sense so strong that it has survived into modern times. If human sacrifice and *aloha* seem to derive from antithetical impulses, one can only say that this is typical of human nature and especially typical of Hawaiʻi. The kind nature of early Hawaiians was coupled with ferocious antipathies toward enemies, and terrible, bloody wars, a combination clearly reflected in the way Hawaiians treated Captain James Cook.

Ancient hula combined chanting, dancing, and myth. Painting by Louis Choris, 1812.

■ CAPTAIN JAMES COOK

On his third voyage into the Pacific, in 1778, the English explorer Captain James Cook sailed his ships *Resolution* and *Discovery* into Waimea Bay at Kaua'i. He was welcomed as Lono, the god prophesied to return on a "floating island." Cook recorded in his journal that "all fell flat on their faces, and remained in that humble posture till . . . [I] made signs to them to rise."

Cook is the first Pacific explorer to leave a record of reaching Hawai'i, although he may have been preceded by Spanish galleons on their voyages between the Philippines and Mexico. He found many similarities between Hawai'i and Tahiti in language and culture, and he was welcomed in both places in the same way—with canoe-loads of fresh food. Cook's reciprocal gifts included iron goods, and from the moment Hawaiians saw metal for the first time they were uninterested in trading for beads or trinkets.

English explorer Captain James Cook, who, on his third expedition headed north from Tahiti through uncharted waters, and in January 1778 came unexpectedly upon the Hawaiian Islands. Engraving by Wright.

After spending two weeks reprovisioning at Waimea, Cook set sail for the Arctic, where his mission was to find a northwest passage that might connect the Atlantic and Pacific oceans. Unable to find it, he returned to Hawai'i one year later, discovered the other main islands, and named the group the Sandwich Islands to honor the Earl of Sandwich, First Lord of the Admiralty and patron of the expedition. On this second visit, Cook dropped anchor in Kealakekua Bay, on the Big Island of Hawai'i.

One thousand canoes circled his ships, and again he was welcomed as Lono. What Cook did not realize was that both times he had arrived during the

JOURNAL OF CAPTAIN COOK

Captain James Cook set sail from England on his third voyage to circumnavigate the globe in July 1776. His mission was to find a northwest passage that might connect the northern Pacific and Atlantic oceans. The ships he chose were two converted coal ships, Resolution *and* Discovery. *Together they traveled south of Australia and past New Zealand and Tahiti, trying out the relatively new Harrison chronometer, which made it possible for sailors to find longitude even if they were away from land for more than a month. Cook left Bora Bora in December 1777 and began to head north through uncharted seas.*

Friday 2nd January. We continued to see birds every day of the sorts last mentioned, sometimes in greater numbers than at others: and between the latitude of 10 and 11 we saw several turtle. All these are looked upon as signs of the vecinity of land; we however saw none till day break in the Morning of the 18th when an island was descovered bearing NEBE and soon after we saw more land bearing North and intirely ditatched from the first; both had the appearance of being high land.

Monday 19th January. . . . At this time we were in some doubt whether or not the land before was inhabited, this doubt was soon cleared up, by seeing some Canoes coming off from the shore towards the Ships, I immediately brought to to give them time to come up, there were three and four men in each and we were agreeably surprised to find them of the same Nation as the people of Otahiete [Tahiti] and the other islands we had lately visited. It required by very little address to get them to come along side, but we could not prevail upon any one to come on board; they exchanged a few fish they had in the Canoes for any thing we offered them, but valued nails, or iron above every other thing; the only weapons they had were a few stones in some of the Canoes and these they threw overboard when they found they were not wanted. Seeing no signs of an anchoring place at this part of the island, I boar up for the lee side, and ranged the SE side at the distance of half a league from the shore. As soon as we made sail the Canoes left us, but others came off from the shore and brought with them roasting pigs and some very fine Potatoes, which they exchanged, as the others had done, for whatever was offered them; several small pigs were got for a sixpeny nail or two apiece, so that we again found our selves in the land of plenty, just as the turtle we had taken on board at the last island was nearly expended. We passed several villages, some seated upon the sea shore and other up in the Country; the inhabitants of all of them crowded to the shore and on the elevated places to view the Ships.

... As soon as the Ships was anchored I went a shore with three boats, to look at the water and try the disposition of the inhabitants, several hundreds of whom were assembled on a sandy beach before the Village. The very instant I leaped ashore, they all fell flat on their faces, and remained in that humble posture till I made signs to them to rise. They then brought a great many small pigs and gave us without regarding whether they got any thing in return or no indeed the most of them were present[ed] to me with plantain trees, in a ceremonious way as is usual on such like occasions, and I ratified these marks of friendship by presenting them with such things as I had with me. After things were a little settled I left a guard on the beach and got some of the Indians to shew me the water, which proved to be very good and convenient to come at.

... Our guide proclamed our approach and every one whom we met fell on their faces and remained in that position till we had passed. This as I afterwards understood, is done to their great chiefs.

... No people could trade with more honisty than these people, never once attempting to cheat us, either ashore or along side the ships. Some indeed at first betrayed a thievish disposition, or rather they thought they had a right to any thing they could lay their hands upon but this conduct they soon laid aside.

—Captain James Cook, *The Journals of Captain Cook*, 1778–1779

annual Makahiki—a festival held each January to honor the harvest god Lono. Cook and his crew thought every day in Hawai'i was festive, and after months in the Arctic it's no wonder Hawai'i was paradise. Crewmen were invited to join in sport competitions, and women took them to their beds. Despite Cook's orders that they abstain from sex, the men indulged, infecting Hawai'i's women with venereal disease. The ship's artist John Webber roamed about at will, and today his precise fine-point drawings offer us an excellent visual record of that period.

With his ships replenished and artifacts and idols taken aboard, Cook set sail some three weeks later. Soon afterward, in a violent storm, the foremast of the *Resolution* was cracked, and he ordered the ships back to Kealakekua Bay for repairs. It was a fatal decision. The *kahuna* (priests) were upset: Lono should not have sailed in from an anti-clockwise direction, the timing was not auspicious, and the god's mast was broken.

In their passion for iron, Hawaiians took to absconding with anything metal they could pilfer, which led to a tragic series of misunderstandings, unfortunate diplomatic decisions, and a final confrontation in which Cook was slain on the beach. Enraged, Cook's men rampaged through villages, killing dozens of Hawaiians. As the violence waned, King Kalaniopu'u, aware that a great man had fallen, conveyed belated esteem by returning some of Cook's bones, which had been distributed for their *mana*. The remains were buried at sea while Hawaiians respectfully chanted ashore, and the two ships sailed from Hawai'i in February 1779 under the command of James Clerke, captain of the *Discovery*. At a high price, Hawai'i had entered the modern world.

James Cook is considered one of history's finest explorers. His journals evoke a wise, merciful, and ingenious seafarer who feared European contact with Pacific peoples would bring them disease and forever alter their cultures. Young officers on the Cook expedition would later return to the Pacific with their own ships—the infamous William Bligh in command of the *Bounty*, and Captain George Vancouver, who brought the first cattle to Hawai'i and became a confidante of Kamehameha the Great.

As ship's artist, John Webber documented encounters with Hawaiians during the voyages of Captain Cook.

■ KAMEHAMEHA THE GREAT

Twelve years after Cook's death, the young warrior Kamehameha defeated in battle the heir to the island of Hawai'i and became its ruler. Believing he was the man destined in a prophecy to unite the islands under one king, he waged uncompromising war on the rulers of the other islands. Impressed by Cook's cannon power (which he'd seen as a young man), he shrewdly acquired an armory of western weapons. In 1795, Kamehameha the Great defeated his last enemies in Nu'uanu Valley on O'ahu, and his mission to form a united kingdom was accomplished. Only Kaua'i remained unconquered militarily, and a pact was made with Kaumauali'i, King of Kaua'i, that allowed him to remain governor, while giving up overall power to Kamehameha. After the great king's death in 1819, his son Liholiho, who became Kamehameha II, lured the Kaua'i ruler aboard a ship, kidnapped him, and forced him to marry Kamehameha's widow. With this maneuver the grand design of unification was completed.

Kamehameha I was known for wise decisions and athletic feats. Biographer Richard Tregaskis describes his "strength and grace—surfing in tropical seas, pursuing beautiful women and voluptuousness, living among palms and flowers, mountains, rainbows, volcanoes, tropical lagoons and trade winds." Acting with humanistic and peaceable wisdom, he proclaimed a law still revered:

> Know ye and reverence your God. Have an understanding heart that
> you may regard the small as you would the big man. Love one
> another, lest your affections wither away and die. Let the old man
> and the woman and the little child, traveling, sleep unmolested on
> the King's Highway. Let none disturb them or harm them as they
> walk or sleep. The penalty is death.

Soon after the death of Kamehameha the Great, his favorite wife, Ka'ahumanu, and his sacred wife, Keopuolani, engineered the overthrow of the *kapu* system by convincing the new king, Liholiho (Kamehameha II), to eat with them. Hawaiians were shocked to see that the gods didn't retaliate, and in the ensuing upheaval idols were smashed and the *kapu* system was virtually toppled. With the old beliefs in disarray, the Hawaiians found themselves adrift in a spiritual vacuum.

In Kapa'au, on the Big Island, a statue of King Kamehameha I celebrates the man who unified all the Hawaiian Islands under his rule.

KAMEHAMEHA IN PERSON

In 1816, a Russian brig, the Rurik, *sailed into Kealakekua Bay on the Island of Hawai'i, and its captain, Otto von Kotzebue, visited with Hawai'i's great king, Kamehameha I. It was at Kealakekua Bay that Captain Cook had been killed in 1779, when Kamehameha was a powerful young warrior and nephew to the island's chief. By the time Captain von Kotzebue arrived 37 years later, Kamehameha was not only king of the Big Island, he had conquered all the islands and unified them under his rule. Once a ferocious warrior, he was now a wise older statesman, who had returned to his home island to live out the final years of his life. Not only does von Kotzebue give us an intimate portrait of the king and his family, but the ship's artist, Louis Choris, sketched one of the few portraits in existence of Kamehameha and his favorite queen, Ka'ahumanu.*

The king came to meet us as far as the landing place with some of his most distinguished warriors, and when we got out of the boat he came up to me and cordially shook me by the hand. Curiosity brought the people from all sides, but the greatest order prevailed, and no noise or importunity was permitted. I now stood at the side of the celebrated Kamehameha, who had attracted the attention of all Europe, and who inspired me with the greatest confidence by his unreserved and friendly behavior. He conducted me to his straw palace, which, according to the custom of the country, consisted only of one spacious apartment, and like all the houses here, afforded a free draft both to the land and sea breezes, which alleviates the oppressive heat.

He conversed with a vivacity surprising at his age, asked us various questions respecting Russia, and made observations. Cook [von Kotzebue's translator] was not always able to translate the words that the king used, which were peculiar to the Hawaiian language and so witty that his ministers often laughed aloud.

One of Kamehameha's wives passed by our house, and in a friendly manner wished me a good morning through the door, but she was not allowed to enter, it being the king's eating house. With the king's permission, we took a walk, accompanied by Cook and a guard of honor of five naked soldiers. We visited the favorite queen Ka'ahumanu mentioned by Vancouver; we found her with the two other wives, and were very politely received by all. The house which Ka'ahumanu inhabits is built very neatly, and is very cleanly in the interior; the entrance hall, in which the three wives were seated according to the Asiatic fashion, was covered with fine and elegant mats, and she herself was pretty closely wrapped up in the finest cloth of the country. Ka'ahumanu was seated in the middle, and the two other ladies on either side; and I had the honor to be invited to sit down opposite them, likewise on the ground. They put to me several questions, which I answered to their satisfaction through Cook. Watermelons were brought and Ka'ahumanu was polite enough to cut one and hand me a piece.

The chief employment of the royal ladies consists in smoking tobacco, combing their hair, driving away the flies with a fan, and eating.

■ ■ ■

After we had left the king's wives, we visited his son. Cook informed me that this prince, as successor to the throne, had already begun to exercise the rights of his father, which consist in the fulfilling of the most important tabus. Kamehameha has ordered this from political motives, that no revolution may arise after his death; for as soon as the son fulfills the most important tabu, he is sacred, is associated with the

Queen Ka'ahumanu, who loved surfing, battles, and men, was Kamehameha the Great's favorite wife. Painting by Louis Choris, 1812.

priests, and nobody dare dispute the throne with him. The prince, as soon as he is admitted into the rights of his father, receives the name of Liholiho, that is, dog of all dogs [a mistake; it means fiery]; and such we really found him.

We entered a neat and small house, in which Liholiho, a tall, corpulent, and naked figure, was stretched out on his stomach, and just indolently raised his head to look at his guests; near him sat several naked soldiers armed with muskets, who guarded the monster; a handsome young native, with a tuft of red feathers, drove away the flies from him and from his interesting countenance and becoming behavior, I should rather have taken him for the king's son. Kamehameha, who, by his wise government, has acquired permanent glory, and has laid the foundation for the civilization and improvement of his people, ought to have a successor capable of prosecuting with zeal and judgment the work which he has begun.

■ ■ ■

The dog of all dogs at last rose very lazily, and gaped upon us with a stupid vacant countenance. My embroidered uniform seemed to meet his approbation, for he held a long conversation about it with a couple of naked chamberlains. I could not learn his age, as no account is kept of it. I guess it may be about twenty-two years, and am of the opinion that his enormous corpulency is occasioned by his constant lying on the ground.

Kamehameha's first walk was to the morai; he embraced one of the statues, which was hung round more than the others with fruits and pieces of a sacrificed hog, saying, "These are our gods, whom I worship; whether I do right or wrong, I do not know; but I follow my faith, which cannot be wicked, as it commands me never to do wrong." This declaration . . . indicated much sound sense, and inspired me with a certain emotion.

■ ■ ■

Cook told us that Kamehameha never regarded the rank of his subjects; that he generally chose his confidants from the lower classes, and was seldom deceived in his choice. He behaves to his great men with justice indeed, but with rigor, and as he places little confidence in them, they are obliged to accompany him on his journeys, by which he deprives them of the opportunity to throw off his authority by a conspiracy. They have not forgotten that Kamehameha is the conqueror of their lands, and is now sole monarch, and they would certainly attempt to conquer their property if he did not know so well how to keep them in his power.

—Captain Otto von Kotzebue,
A Voyage of Discovery into the South Sea and Behring's Strait, 1821

◼ WHALERS AND MISSIONARIES

Within a few months the vacuum was rapidly filled by American Protestant missionaries who arrived from New England in 1820, armed with Christian fervor and a plan to rescue the pagans from sin. About this time abundant whaling grounds were being discovered in waters off Japan, whose ports were closed to foreigners. Soon hundreds of whaling ships out of New England put in for replenishment at Lahaina Roads on Maui, and at Honolulu on O'ahu. The whalers' crews also had more personal forms of replenishment in mind and bolted ashore in search of grog and women.

In the space of less than two years fate had thrown the Hawaiians a triple punch. It was just a matter of time until whalers, missionaries, and a kingdom undergoing great change would wear away at the old Hawaiian customs. In the inevitable collision of the two New England factions, the whalers' motto "No God west of the Horn" led to violent confrontations with the missionaries, who were gaining Hawaiian converts. Within an hour of her death in 1823, Queen Keopuolani was baptized a Christian. By 1825, dancing and horseback riding on the Sabbath had been forbidden. Drinking, gambling, and ship visits by women were outlawed. Under a succession of monarchs during the rest of the nineteenth century, the missionaries banished Hawai'i's hula, through which Hawaiians told the great stories and myths of their race; covered the women in baggy *mu'umu'u* gowns; and sermonized against adultery—a previously unknown concept. They convinced Hawaiians that the *haole* (Westerners) were somehow superior. To their credit, the missionaries created a twelve-letter alphabet and put the Hawaiian language on paper, established schools, and began the process of intermarriage, which has culminated in Hawai'i's beautiful part-Hawaiian people.

◼ RISE OF SUGAR

Having done well with the Bible, descendants of the missionaries set about doing well in financial enterprises. They took a sweet route, sugarcane, and it led to the establishment of Hawai'i's five wealthiest *haole* (white) companies. The first of the great sugar plantations was begun on Kaua'i in 1835.

In 1848 Kamehameha III proclaimed the Great Mahele (division), a decree that changed the concept of land ownership. The king, until now the owner of all land, gave up much of it. Before the act, commoners had lived off the land, working it for their personal use and paying chiefs, who controlled lands for the king, in labor or crops. Now chiefs were allowed to buy those lands, and smaller crown plots were offered to commoners. To gain title, all were required to pay a tax and register the land. Although the Mahele was intended to distribute the land, few commoners understood the concept of private land ownership and most failed to complete the registration. Two years later foreigners were permitted to purchase land, and in the 1850s westerners plunged in. Within a couple of generations, 80 percent of all private land lay in large estates, most of them owned by *haole* or the children of *haole* and native Hawaiians. Meanwhile, by the mid-1800s only 50,000 Hawaiians survived, down from the approximately 300,000 reported by Captain Cook in 1778. They had died in droves from imported diseases—venereal disease contracted from Cook's crew, cholera and smallpox from whalers.

When plantation-style agriculture went into full swing in the islands, there weren't enough Hawaiians to work the fields (nor were they enamored of giving up what was left of their traditional life to help those who were destroying it). The sugar companies began bringing in foreign contract laborers. Between 1852 and 1856 many Chinese arrived. In 1885 Hawai'i's king signed a treaty with Japan that allowed large-scale immigration; 70,000 Japanese workers came. Between 1878 and 1887, Portuguese came from the islands of Madeira and the Azores. As most of the workers stayed on and established families, Hawaiians became a landless minority in their own land.

■ ANNEXATION

Hawai'i's last king, David Kalakaua, was elected to the throne in 1874. He was a world traveler known as the Merry Monarch, and his greatest legacy was the revitalization of Hawaiian culture. After years of missionary suppression of the "heathen dance," Kalakaua brought back the hula and compiled ancient legends. However, the moment Kalakaua died in 1891, American planters plunged into plots against his successor and sister, Queen Lili'uokalani. Hawaiian sugar sales to the U.S. had been severely restricted due to a hefty tariff imposed by Congress, and to protect their profits the planters connived for an end to the monarchy and a takeover by the United States. By now the sugar barons, descendants of the missionaries, had taken the land and held key governmental positions. In 1893 the Queen was deposed and replaced by a Provisional Government, which in turn was replaced by the Republic of Hawai'i.

After a series of questionable political maneuvers by prominent Americans, on July 4, 1894, the Kingdom of Hawai'i and the Provisional Government of Hawai'i were replaced by the Republic of Hawai'i, with Stanford Dole as its first president.

The **Republic of Hawai'i** was little more than a governorship controlled by Sanford Dole, the most powerful of the American sugarcane planters. The U.S. president at the time of the coup, Grover Cleveland, called it "not merely wrong, but a disgrace." In 1898, at the urging of Teddy Roosevelt and others, Congress annexed the islands and created the Territory of Hawai'i. That same year, in the aftermath of the Spanish-American War, the U.S. acquired the Philippines and Guam. Since Japan was seen as expansionist, the U.S. Navy set its eye on the finest sheltered harbor in the Pacific, Pearl Harbor, where access had been permitted by Kalakaua. Construction of naval facilities began in 1908.

Meanwhile, the planters increased their profits with the newly arrived pineapple, planted and picked by imported contract laborers. The earlier waves of plantation laborers were augmented by Puerto Ricans who arrived in 1900, Koreans in 1903, and between 1907 and 1931, Filipinos. While working conditions were poor and wages minimal, the planters unwittingly preserved ethnic cultures by setting up plantation camps in native groupings.

■ GROWTH OF TOURISM

Extraordinary events affected the growth of tourism. The roots of the industry took hold well before the 1920s. Just 14 years after the widely publicized annexation of the islands, the Hawaiian swimmer Duke Paoa Kahanamoku (1890–1968) placed Hawai'i again in the international limelight. At the Stockholm Olympic Games in 1912 he shattered the world record in the 100-meter freestyle. In the same year he introduced surfboard riding to Australia, where the Duke is known as the "father of surfing." Kahanamoku brought another Olympic gold home in 1920, and more Olympic medals in 1924 and 1928. With his new fast Hawaiian Crawl style, the Duke's fame spread Hawai'i's name. The popular song "On the Beach at Waikiki" was sung across the mainland at the onset of World War I, implanting the romance and allure of Hawai'i's islands and Waikiki Beach in the public mind.

The development of Waikiki and its tourist industry are tied to Matson Shipping Company in a convoluted web of business and foresight. Matson built the deluxe passenger ship SS *Malolo* (Flying Fish), which entered service on the

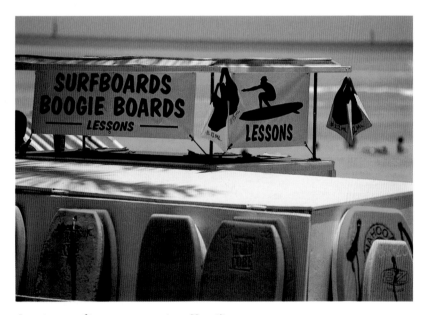

Learning to surf is one way to experience Hawai'i.

San Francisco–Honolulu run in conjunction with the opening of Waikiki's new Royal Hawaiian Hotel in 1927.

Despite the stock market crash of 1929, and the pall that descended across the nation, the business barons of Honolulu continued to flourish in well-heeled bliss. They were prepared to invest in the growth of tourism. Matson contracted for two more ships—placing the new *Lurline* in service to Hawai'i—and bought out the Los Angeles Steamship Company, which had entered the Hawai'i trade in the early twenties. Liner travel flourished until World War II. It did not recover rapidly in following years. Today Matson no longer carries passengers; it plies the waters of the Pacific with giant ships carrying freight, while passengers now arrive on international luxury liners.

■ **PAN AM AND TOURISM**

The most decisive factor in the growth of Hawaiian tourism came in 1936, when a Martin M-130 flying boat, the *Hawai'i Clipper,* soared out over San Francisco Bay with seven paying passengers ($360 one-way). Flying 2,270 air miles, she settled down on Honolulu waters in the amazing time of 21 hours, 33 minutes, introducing an era of luxurious air travel with private compartments and sleeping berths, dining-room tables heaped with gourmet delicacies, and gracious service. The 26-ton giant brought Hawai'i nearer to the mainland by three and a half days. Overnight, modern tourism was born. With the Moana, the Royal Hawaiian, and the new Halekulani hotels, Waikiki in the thirties began to develop into the center of island tourism.

With demand escalating for more and larger aircraft, Pan Am replaced its three Martins with the *California Clipper,* a 74-passenger Boeing B-314. By 1941, with five more Boeings, Pan Am's flying boats were racing the skies on a daily service run from San Francisco to Honolulu.

The great body of lore that fills the logs of aircraft pilots includes an entry for December 7, 1941. While en route from San Francisco and just one hour out from the Pan Am base at Pearl Harbor, the pilot of Pan Am's clipper learned the Japanese had attacked. Diverting to Hilo on the Big Island, instead of laying over, the crew broke every rule for speed, and within two hours had unloaded passengers and mail, refueled the plane by hand, and had taken off as daylight faded. (What the passengers thought of this is unrecorded.) By making a dangerous nighttime take-off, the pilot avoided Japanese patrols and returned the aircraft safely to San Francisco (where he promptly began his government wartime service).

Four years later, on November 16, 1945, commercial flights to Honolulu resumed. North, south, and west from Honolulu, Pan Am flying boat clippers blazed a trail through the Pacific Ocean, prying open faraway Pacific destinations. Now time and progress ordained that the era of the flying boat was coming to an end: by early 1946, land-based aircraft (Douglas DC-4s) entered service on the route to Honolulu.

Pan Am's trail-blazing wasn't finished yet. The dawn of the jet age also belongs to Pan Am. In 1958, just one year before Hawai'i achieved statehood, the airline flew a Boeing 707 to Honolulu, revolutionizing international travel. When its inaugural 747 flight touched down at Honolulu in 1970, Pan Am was first again, and some aircraft historians claim that if Pan Am had not had the foresight to order the 747 in 1966, the modern era of flight would have been delayed.

■ MODERN HAWAI'I EVOLVES

While Pan Am was fostering tourism, two upheavals profoundly altered the political power structure in the Territory of Hawai'i. The clique of Big Five companies was forced to negotiate wages and working conditions with unions, made legal by the National Labor Relations Act of 1935. The other change came after World War II, when the Veterans Act provided education funds for returned servicemen. Men of Hawai'i's highly decorated 100th Infantry and the all-Japanese 442nd Regimental Combat Team enrolled in mainland universities, returned home, and joined the Democratic Party. Labor-supported Democrats swamped Republicans in the election of 1954 and dominated Hawaiian politics for 48 years, until a Republican governor was elected in 2002.

Hawai'i has paid a price for social equality. As wages climbed to acceptable levels, Hawaiian sugar and pineapples could no longer compete with low-cost labor plantations abroad. Both industries began moving out of Hawai'i. Some Hawaiians do not rue their passing. Today there are new ways to earn a living— through large-scale tourism, service industries, and high-tech oceanographic programs. Web-based business ventures are increasing.

■ STATEHOOD AND MASS TOURISM

When Congress granted Hawai'i statehood in 1959 and a 50th star was added to the nation's flag, the islands entered a building boom that shows few signs of abating. New hotels and condominiums stabbed the skyline of Waikiki on O'ahu.

Maui followed, and by the mid 1970s tourism had overtaken the military as Hawai'i's largest industry. Mass tourism flourished in Waikiki, cramming it with restaurants, nightclubs, snack bars, and endless shops. While the giant hotels were expanding, still more construction squeezed into the area between the beach and the Ala Wai Canal. Within the 618 acres of Waikiki, the room count rose to more than 25,000, and now has spilled over the 36,000 mark.

By the 1980s, residents began to wake up, wondering at what they had allowed to happen. Many pointed to the district as an example of what must not be repeated on neighbor islands, and outsiders railed that Waikiki was another Miami Beach. While that comparison is far off the mark, the fact stands that Waikiki *is* overdeveloped. In the nineties, "controlled development" became the watchword of legislators and conservationists. Despite its overdevelopment, Waikiki offers a long list of delights. Amid the ubiquitous concrete, trees and greenery flourish. Though rife with commercialism, Waikiki is clean, the sun is bright, and there are no billboards or neon signs protruding above the street. (They're both banned throughout Hawai'i.) Crowds of visitors stroll the shops clad in beach togs; restaurants abound; and a saunter at night in caressing trade winds delivers the proof that somehow Hawai'i's magic still reigns.

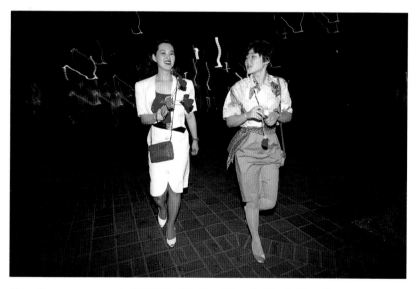

Young Japanese women enjoy Waikiki's nightlife while on holiday in Hawai'i.

■ HAWAI'I'S PEOPLE AND CULTURE

Tourism made the magic of Hawai'i known the world round, yet advertising hyperbole cannot capture its essence. With diverse cultures on islands of great beauty, Hawai'i is a microcosm of the future, and it is her people who make it so. In his novel *Hawaii,* James Michener called Hawai'i's modern people Golden Man. With a population of 1,237,511, Hawai'i is about 28 percent Caucasian, 21 percent Japanese, 31 percent Hawaiian and part-Hawaiian, 12 percent Filipino, and 5 percent Chinese; other Asians and African-Americans make up the remaining 3 percent. Today the most politically powerful group is Hawai'i-born Japanese and part-Japanese.

Hawaiians are the fastest-growing ethnic community in the state. While their culture was vulgarized in the early days of tourism, today few Hawaiians, or visitors, have much interest in imitations. Hawaiians strive to preserve their culture and its traditions, which have always been interwoven with the natural environment. Since 1974, when a *kumu hula* (hula master) led a male troupe through an authentic, vigorous hula, a renaissance of Hawaiian culture has taken root and blossomed. The hula originated, legend says, when the volcano goddess Pele commanded her younger sister Laka to dance. In time, schools sprang up in honor of the goddess of the dance, and temples were dedicated to her. Dancers lived within the confines of the temple grounds, under strenuous training regimes and *kapu* (taboos), for hula was a sacred art; it represented the heart of the people, with its oral tradition carrying history, custom, ceremony, and genealogy. The dancers trained in the classical hula, or *kahiko*—the ancient form of chanting and dance— which tells of knowledge seen, known, and felt; this knowledge travels through generations in oral and dance form.

Some surviving hula chants allow rare glimpses into the past and give clues to the future. In the Kaulilua chant, the unknown composer saw Hawai'i as the homeland of many people fused together in the manner of coral.

To Hawaiians, hula celebrates life. For decades the words of Kalakaua were forgotten; now they are recognized: "Hula is the language of the heart and therefore the heartbeat of the Hawaiian people." Today, *kahiko* is a highly regarded wellspring, and it takes a long stretch of imagination to consider this hula mere popular entertainment. Hula *halau* (house of hula instruction) troupes practice nights and weekends to compete in annual dance contests that are held throughout the islands and followed avidly by the general population. Winners take home a ribbon or a medal, and enormous prestige. Architects, nurses, teachers and attorneys, clerks and artisans—whatever their careers, Hawaiians are eager to study and be a part of this resurgent Hawaiian heritage.

The basic concept of Hawaiian culture is best translated as sharing. It flows from respect and love, which is the hula. And it flows from *ho'opono,* which is communal counseling and problem solving that is nonjudgmental, truth-seeking, and solution-oriented. With the renaissance of the hula, and of *ho'opono,* present-day Hawaiians learn from the wisdom of their ancestors.

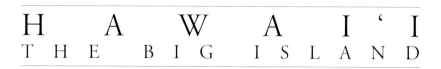

H A W A I ʻ I
T H E   B I G   I S L A N D

Pele, goddess of fire, dominates the heartland of Hawaiʻi, dwelling in her fire-pit home at the summit of the world's most active volcano, Kilauea. Since the ongoing series of eruptions began early in the morning on January 3, 1983, her outpourings of red burning lava have added new acres of black-sand coastline to Hawaiʻi—geologically the youngest, and by far the largest, of all the Hawaiian islands.

Since Hawaiʻi is twice the size of all the other islands put together, you won't be able to see all of its turtlelike shape from your airplane window. Nor is it easy to begin to grasp its great variety. This most diverse island in the Hawaiian chain is something of a miniature planet, enfolding almost all the varieties of topography and climate found on earth. Cool and misty ranch pastures blanket the volcanic slopes of the north at Waimea and North Kohala. In the mountainous center, active volcanoes have shaped arid moonscapes of lava tubes, craters, and volcanic mounds called *puʻu;* smoky plumes rise from rift cracks in the earth. To the south the island swells outward with lava flows spilling into the sea. Beaches run in colors from deep black (formed when lava cinders exploded at the water line), to brilliant white, to green sands laced with olivine and obsidian tossed up by volcanoes.

As your plane approaches, you will see Hawaiʻi's mountains, tallest in the island chain. At nearly 14,000 feet above sea level, they are only the peaks of massive mountains rising 32,000 feet from the ocean floor. Because they create a barrier to wind and rain, the mountains keep the northeasterly trade winds on the windward east flank of Hawaiʻi, watering valleys, pastel-green fruit farms, forests, and the orchid farms of the Hamakua Coast. To the dry west, volcano lands slope down to coffee farms stretching above the sunny beaches of the leeward Kona and South Kohala coasts. Sometimes called the Gold Coast, the landscape here alternates between fields of barren lava and the gleaming emerald grounds and golf courses of luxury hotels. Palm-backed beaches face warm blue snorkeling waters where rainbow-colored fish dart in coral reefs. Beyond the reefs, the cooler navy-blue sea is the domain of game fish—bill fish (also called swordfish or blue, black, and striped marlin); mahimahi (dorado) and ono (wahoo); and skipjack, bluefin, and yellowfin tuna.

Golfers at the Mauna Lani Resort couldn't ask for better views.

Hawai'i is an island that claims time. Within 300 miles of coastline lie centuries of history and the climates of a hemisphere. Beach, volcano, a sunset blue-water sail, game fishing, snorkeling, elegant dining, and trekking through rain forest and cowboy country—all are available. Take time on the Big Island. Hawai'i's magic is here.

■ HISTORY

The history of the Big Island of Hawai'i is very nearly the history of all Hawai'i. Here the Polynesians first beached their voyaging canoes some 1,400 years ago. Following tradition, they built a *he'iau,* or temple of sacrifice, and continued the Polynesian system of social laws, or *kapu.*

Here too Kamehameha the Great was born (probably in 1750) and spent his boyhood. He would have been in his early twenties and may well have been present in 1779 when the strange, high-masted ship of Captain James Cook sailed into Kealakekua Bay—where Cook later was killed. A fearsome warrior, Kamehameha was nephew to Kalaniopu'u, chief of the island, and soon became his most successful general. A pleased Kalaniopu'u made the young warrior the keeper of the god of war—a carved statue of Kuka'ilimoku (Ku). As Kamehameha carried the gory, red-mouthed god into battle, it supposedly emitted horrible screams.

At the death of his uncle, Kamehameha battled with the old king's son Kiwala'o, who had inherited his father's lands and title. After defeating Kiwala'o, Kamehameha emerged as the ruler of the northern half of Hawai'i. This worried his rivals, Kahekili, king of Maui, and Keoua, a cousin, both of whom ruled over southern parts of the island.

Kamehameha had just begun. In 1790, to help fulfill a prophecy that he would rule all the islands, he began construction of Pu'ukohola He'iau, a temple of sacrifice in northwest Kohala. In the prophecy, war would end (and presumably he would dominate) when the *he'iau* was completed and he had sacrificed a major chief. As building progressed, Kamehameha learned that Keoua was sailing a fleet of war canoes up the east coast, planning to come around the top of Kohala to attack him and stop construction. Kamehameha met and defeated the invading forces off the sacred eastern valley of Waipi'o—where he had received his war god Ku. This time, in the Battle of the Red-Mouthed Gun, the war god had the assistance of a cannon manned by two British sailors on the captured schooner *Fair American.*

Construction of the controversial *he'iau* continued. A contingent of Keoua's warriors, returning to south Hawai'i by way of Kilauea Volcano, encountered the goddess Pele near her Halema'uma'u fire pit. Here she came to Kamehameha's aid, heaving rock and cinders in clouds of choking gas in the only explosive eruption known. You still can see the footprints in solidified ash where the warriors tried to run. When the temple was completed in 1791, Keoua, Kamehameha's cousin, was its inaugural human sacrifice.

By the late eighteenth century the warrior king who would be known as Kamehameha the Great filled the horizons with fleets of immense war canoes; with them he subdued and unified the other islands and named the Kingdom of Hawai'i for his home island. When all was secure, he returned to the Big Island, where he died at Kailua in May 1819. After his death his remains were prepared in the ancient way, by separating flesh from bone. To protect the *mana* of his sacred bones, they were hidden in secret—perhaps in a cave; no one knows where. The site never has been revealed, or discovered.

(above) These Hawaiians are dressed in traditional costume at Pu`ukohala He`iau, which Kamehameha built on the North Kohala Coast to fulfill a prophecy that he would rule all the islands and where he made his cousin Keoua its first sacrifice.
(following spread) The sugarcane industry once dominated the fertile lands of the Hamakua Coast.

Six months after Kamehameha's death his strong-minded, favorite wife Ka'ahumanu engineered the breaking of a *kapu* (the rules of social behavior) that forbade women to eat with men. When the gods didn't retaliate against this intrepid woman, the Hawaiians began to doubt both gods and *kapu.* A wave of destruction and violence swept the island as the laws that had long supported Hawaiian social structure came crashing down. Idols were smashed, and one after another the *kapu* were broken, leaving the people bewildered. Into this vacuum sailed the *Thaddeus,* with a shipload of New England missionaries. Landing at Kailua in April 1820, they stepped ashore almost on top of the very spot where the great king had died less than a year earlier. They brought a new god and a new restrictive social system that destroyed much of Hawaiian culture, particularly the hula, heartbeat of the Hawaiian people.

What followed on Hawai'i mirrors the modern history of the Hawaiian Islands: a catastrophic decline in population through disease; domination over Hawaiian culture by the new religion; and the arrival of sugar, ranching, and tourism. Yet the Big Island, steeped in the mythology of the fire goddess, preserves fragments of early Hawai'i and of Kamehameha and the first contacts with foreigners; it is a treasure trove of history and ancient belief.

■ HILO

Visitors landing in Hilo arrive on the lush windward side of the island, where tropical growth is rampant and rain feeds waterfalls, leafy tree ferns, and enough flowers to fill a rainbow. In Hilo the trick is to snare a sunny day—but don't be surprised if it is also hot and humid.

Perhaps named for the first night of the new moon, or for an ancient Polynesian navigator, Hilo is the second largest city (after Honolulu) in the state, and the Big Island's main seaport. The town curves around the broad rim of Hilo Bay and stretches up *mauka* (inland) into lush hills. Rainfall is well over 100 inches annually, making Hilo the wettest city in the United States. Rain usually falls in the afternoon, and is responsible for rich greenery and a slower pace of resort development. Flowers and more flowers are everywhere—orchids, anthurium, and bromeliads bloom in gardens and shops and push up through roadside growth. They are grown commercially as well; Hawai'i's flower industry earns millions of dollars annually from foreign and domestic sales. Two miles from the airport on the road to Kea'au is **Nani Mau Gardens,** an incredibly beautiful 23-acre preserve where you can stroll among a diverse sampling of the island's plants and flowers.

Hilo is a town with spirit. In 1960 a tsunami deluged the waterfront, sweeping an organ console out the stage door of the Palace Theater, depositing fishing boats in streets, and killing 61 residents. Businesses rebuilt, but by 1985 Hilo's downtown was sliding into disrepair. The city responded by turning the old waterfront into a park, but it did not lose its sense of history. Today Hilo retains the aura of a Pacific trading port between 1920 and 1940. Its buildings sport vintage wood and metal roofs, and you still can park your car or tie up your horse at a five-cent meter.

■ DOWNTOWN HILO HIGHLIGHTS

Lyman House Museum *map page 52, B-3*

A good place to delve into the history of old Hilo is this museum in the former home of the Reverend David and Sarah Lyman, who arrived in Hilo from New England in the early 1830s. Half the museum is the home, furnished as though the Lymans still lived there, with clothing, a cradle, quilts, photos, and curios in a Victorian parlor. The other half—extensively renovated in 1997—is a modern museum of Hawaiian natural history, with a 10-foot globe explaining magma and the workings of plate tectonics; a 360-degree mural showcasing Hawaiian flora and fauna; period pieces chronicling the waves of immigrants who came to Hawaii from Japan, China, Portugal, Korea, and the Philippines; and a darkened, fiber optic–lit astronomy center. Look for the *braginha*, Portuguese ancestor of the ukelele, and a Taoist shrine from China. *lymanmuseum.org. 276 Haili Street; 808-935-5021.*

Naha and Pina'o Stones *map page 52, B-2/3*

On a patch of grass in front of the Hilo Public Library lies the **Naha Stone.** This monstrous rectangular block of lava—as heavy as a 40-man war canoe or about three tons—marks the beginning of the career of Kamehameha. It was here, at the age of 14, that he sought to fulfill a prophecy that the man who could move the Naha Stone would be the greatest king of Hawai'i. If he could move it, he would gain fame and status. If he could not, the *kahuna* of the Hilo king might beat him to death for violating a mortal *kapu*. Before high chiefs, a prophetess, and the assembled people, Kamehameha lifted the stone. Appropriately, his star rose.

A round, up-ended stone called the **Pina'o** stands beside the Naha. It is said to have been an entry pillar to the nearby temple Pina'o, where the Naha originally stood. No plaque marks the stones; ask for a flyer at the front desk inside the library. *300 Wai'anuenue Avenue.*

James G. Sawkins painted this view of Hilo in 1852.

Pacific Tsunami Museum *map page 52, B-2*
In 1998 the Pacific Tsunami Museum moved into an abandoned bank building on downtown Hilo's waterfront. The building was designed in 1931 by architect Charles W. Dickey in a uniquely Hawaiian style of architecture: classical with Art Deco motifs. The museum combines public tsunami education with first-hand survivors' accounts recorded in oral histories. *tsunami.org; 130 Kamehameha Avenue; 808-935-0926.*

Mokupapapa: Discovery Center of Hawai'i *map page 52, B-3*
Dedicated to 7,000 species of marine life, including monk seals and green sea turtles, protected in a 99,500-square-mile Ecosystem Reserve, this museum opened in 2003. The islands' royal treasure, its ocean habitats and ecosystems, are featured in exhibits by the National Oceanic and Atmospheric Administration. The museum includes interpretive panels, videos, and a 2,500-gallon saltwater aquarium where tropical fish swim among corals found in the northwestern Hawaiian Islands. Mokupapapa—remote, low-lying islets and reefs—are islands of Hawai'i, the only state with atolls in the U.S. Admission is free. *308 Kamehameha Ave.; 808-933-8195.*

Wai'anuenue Falls *map page 52, A-3*
The name means "Rainbow-Seen-in-Water." The falls drop 80 feet into a large pool. The deep cave behind the falls is a legendary home of Hina, mother of Maui. For the best rainbows and fewest tour buses, go in the early morning. *Located off upper Wai'anuenue Avenue.*

■ EAST OF DOWNTOWN

Suisan Fish Market *map page 52, C/D-2*
Early risers can see varieties of fresh Hawaiian fish brought to market each day by the Hilo commercial fleet. The fish from the Hilo fish auction, which is not open to the public, are rapidly displayed in this retail store. *93 Lihiwai St., a half mile from town at the mouth of the Wailua River; 808-935-9349.*

Wai'akea Peninsula *map page 52, C/D-2/3*
Visitors who stay at the hotels on the Wai'akea Peninsula, which juts out into the bay, will enjoy taking in harbor life and the clear view of Mauna Kea. On the peninsula, ringed by Banyan Drive, are great brooding trees planted by movie stars, athletes, and other celebrities who came here by ship in the thirties. Look for those planted by Amelia Earhart and Louis Armstrong, and note the Babe Ruth plaque in front of the Hilo Hawaiian Hotel.

Also on the Wai'akea Peninsula you will find the **Lili'uokalani Gardens** (Banyan Drive at Lihiwai Street; 808-961-8311). Here you can wander through 30 acres of Japanese gardens, with bridges, lagoons, and stone lanterns. A footbridge leads across to a small island named Coconut, once a place of healing. Facing the bay at the spot known as Waiolama, where Kamehameha once gathered 400 war canoes, stands a new statue of the Warrior King.

■ PUNA *map page 57, D-3/4*

Hawai'i is one of the few places on earth where spectators rush *to* volcanic eruptions instead of running from them. South of Hilo, in the Puna region, you can experience Pele's raw power at close range, as she pours flaming lava from Kilauea Volcano into the sea in loud hissing columns of white steam. Some of this lava, pounded by waves, creates new black sand beaches.

To see this area, take the Volcano Road (HI 11) from Hilo up to Kea'au and turn south on HI 130. The road travels through plantation towns, past orchid

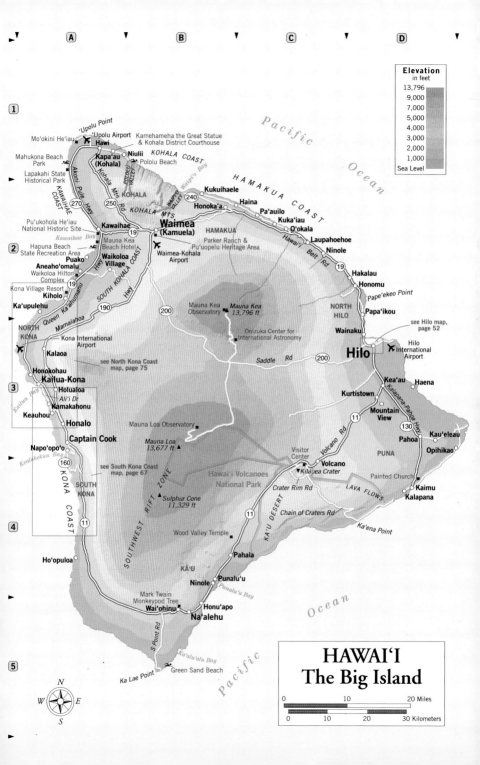

HAWAI'I
The Big Island

Elevation
in feet
13,796
9,000
7,000
5,000
4,000
3,000
2,000
1,000
Sea Level

A B C D

1

Pacific Ocean

'Upolu Point
Upolu Airport
Mo'okini He'iau
Hawi
Kapa'au (Kohala)
Niulii
Kamehameha the Great Statue & Kohala District Courthouse
Pololu Beach
Mahukona Beach Park
Lapakahi State Historical Park
KOHALA COAST
KOHALA
Kohala Mtns Rd
250
KAWAIHAE COAST
Akoni Pule Hwy
270
KOHALA MTS
HAMAKUA COAST
Kukuihaele
240
Honoka'a
Haina
Pa'auilo
Kuka'iau
O'okala
Laupahoehoe
Ninole
Pu'ukohola He'iau National Historic Site
Kawaihae
Kawaihae Bay
Waimea (Kamuela)
HAMAKUA
Parker Ranch & Pu'uopelu Heritage Area
19

2

Hapuna Beach State Recreation Area
Mauna Kea Beach Hotel
Puako
Aneaho'omalu
Waikoloa Village
Waikoloa Hilton Complex
Kona Village Resort
Ka'upulehu
19
Waimea-Kohala Airport
Hawai'i Belt Rd
19
Hakalau
Honomu
Pape'ekeo Point
Papa'ikou
NORTH HILO
SOUTH KOHALA COAST
Queen Ka'ahumanu Hwy
190
Mamalahoa Hwy
Mauna Kea Observatory
Mauna Kea 13,796 ft
Onizuka Center for International Astronomy
200
Wainaku
see Hilo map, page 52

3

NORTH KONA
Kiholo
Kona International Airport
Kalaoa
Honokohau
Kailua-Kona
Holualoa
Ali'i Dr
Kamakahonu
Keauhou
Honalo
Captain Cook
Napo'opo'o
Kealakekua Bay
160
KONA COAST
SOUTH KONA
see North Kona Coast map, page 75
Saddle Rd
200
Hilo
Hilo International Airport
Kea'au
Haena
Kurtistown
Mountain View
11
Kalapana Pahoa Hwy
130
Kau'eleau
Pahoa
Opihikao
Kaimu
Kalapana
PUNA
Painted Church
Kailua Bay

4

Mauna Loa Observatory
Mauna Loa 13,677 ft
see South Kona Coast map, page 67
SOUTHWEST RIFT ZONE
Hawai'i Volcanoes National Park
Sulphur Cone 11,329 ft
Visitor Center
Volcano
Volcano Rd
Kilauea Crater
Crater Rim Rd
LAVA FLOWS
Chain of Craters Rd
KA'U DESERT
Ka'ena Point
11
Wood Valley Temple
Ho'opuloa
KA'U
Pahala
Ninole
Punalu'u
Punalu'u Bay
Mark Twain Monkeypod Tree
Wai'ohinu
Honu'apo
Na'alehu
S Point Rd

5

Ka'alu'alu Bay
Ka Lae Point
Green Sand Beach
Pacific Ocean

N
W — E
S

0   10   20 Miles

0   10   20   30 Kilometers

farms, and down into Puna, the southeastern district of Hawai'i. It continues past old weathered lava flows, but about 25 or 30 miles from Hilo it stops abruptly at a barricade. Now overrun with lava, this road once curved around the southern end of Puna. The barricade is moved from time to time for safety—as Pele hurls her molten cascades downward and wide rivers of fast-moving lava slither over the pavement. The lava moves relentlessly toward the sea, consuming homes and churches, beach parks, whole villages, and sacred Hawaiian sites.

On a small road off the Kalapana-Pahoa Highway (HI 130) stands the **Painted Church,** which has fascinated visitors for nearly 75 years. From the outside it looks like one more little white wooden church in rural Hawai'i, but its interior is dramatically different. Vibrantly colored murals create a miniature European Gothic cathedral.

Upon hitting the ocean, lava explodes into tiny bits, instantly creating wide black-sand beaches. Since the eruption began in 1983, more than 2 billion cubic yards of magma have spewed out of the earth's core—enough lava to bury Manhattan to a depth of 19 feet. Madame Pele's gift is more than 550 acres of new land. The Big Island grows bigger.

■ HAWAI'I VOLCANOES NATIONAL PARK
map page 57, B/C-3/4

In Hawai'i Volcanoes National Park, fire fountains roar, heat radiates from molten *pahoehoe* (smooth, unbroken lava) and *'a'a* (sharp, rough broken, chunks of lava), and cinders laden with olivine and obsidian fall to the ground in fast-rising cones. The air smells of sulphur, and slashes in the earth waft steam. The park was established in 1916 to decipher and give access to the eerie volcanic lands of Mauna Loa and Kilauea; and the place itself is a lesson in geology. Rare plants and birds are carefully protected, and previously unknown species of insects are still being discovered.

Within the park boundaries there are two volcanoes, many scenic drives, 150 miles of hiking trails, campgrounds, an observatory, a visitors center, the Thomas A. Jaggar Museum, and the Volcano Art Center gallery. To visit the park, take Volcano Road (HI 11) from Hilo. (As mentioned above, the alternate road from Puna has been covered over with lava flow.) On the 30-mile drive you'll see a rain forest nourished by volcanic soil; fragrant ginger threatens to smother the roadside pavement. Near the top, a turnoff leads to the tiny village of **Volcano.** The road

Burned 'ohi'alehua trees lie in shreds on volcanic ash along Devastation Trail.

continues through the gate of the national park, bordered in rain forest where *hapu'u* tree ferns, thick-boled and covered in soft red hair, sprout curled fiddle-heads that unfurl to enormous size. A couple of miles past the gate the landscape unfolds in an arid plain of steaming rift cracks. A pervading spiritual presence seems to emanate here—the sacred home of the goddess Pele.

The best way to orient yourself is to drive straight to the **Visitor Center** (808-985-6000) at the park headquarters, a mile from the gate. The free film shown hourly is a fine introduction to volcanoes, and park rangers are available to answer questions. Here you can buy maps and get directions for a multitude of miniexpe-ditions. These include driving the Crater Rim Road (11 miles); circling the sum-mit caldera through desert, rain forest, and past old eruption sites; and walking one of three trails, each about one mile long. They are Thurston Lava Tube, a huge tunnel 400 feet long crossing Devastation Trail—a boardwalk through a cindered moonscape; Petroglyph Trail, which takes one to ancient rock etchings; and the Bird Park Trail. (Bring a jacket to wear in the cooler air of these higher elevations.)

Directly across the road from the Visitor Center are viewing sites for the Kilauea caldera. The Volcano House Inn sits on the rim. Kilauea holds in its caldera the deep fire pit named Halema'uma'u, or "enduring fire-house," home of Pele. From 1823 until 1924 the pit held a bubbling lake of fluid lava, and intrepid travelers once rode horses or mules up from the coast to the burning red-hot hole. Among these travelers were visiting nineteenth- and twentieth-century writers, including Isabella Bird and Mark Twain. The lake vanished in 1924, swallowed whole by a rapid drain-off into a subterranean network of tubes and channels. The pit now lies exposed to a depth of some 270 feet.

Standing at the caldera rim you can look across it and decide if you'd like to take the trail down to the caldera floor to Halema'uma'u fire pit. That trailhead can be reached by driving on Crater Rim Road to the far side of the caldera. If you visit the fire pit, offer a handful of *'ohelo* berries to the goddess Pele—or a few drops of gin. Some claim it's her favorite drink. In ancient times *kahuna* (priests) brought food and flowers here, never human sacrifices. Today offerings still accumulate. The awesome force and beauty of Pele's work inspire respect.

An arid plateau stretches out behind the rim of the caldera. On it, hot steam snakes up from wide cracks (or fumaroles) onto the cool plateau, and ferns drip with moist heat in the fissures. You can drive out onto the plateau, which is well marked with signs. Recently, the foolhardy have taken to steam bathing at the

The curled fiddleheads of the ʻamaʻumaʻu fern, endemic to Hawaiʻi, unfurl into elegant fronds.

MARK TWAIN AT KILAUEA VOLCANO, 1866

We bought horses and bent our way over the summer-clad mountain terraces, toward the great volcano of Kilauea. We made nearly a two days' journey of it, but that was on account of laziness. Toward sunset on the second day, we reached an elevation of some four thousand feet above sea level, and as we picked our careful way through billowy wastes of lava long generations ago stricken dead and cold in the climax of its tossing fury, we began to come upon signs of the near presence of the volcano—signs in the nature of ragged fissures that discharged jets of sulphurous vapor into the air, hot from the molten ocean down in the bowels of the mountain.

Shortly the crater came into view. I have seen Vesuvius since, but it was a mere toy, a child's volcano, a soup kettle, compared to this. . . . Here was a yawning pit upon whose floor the armies of Russia could camp, and have room to spare.

After a hearty supper we waited until it was thoroughly dark and then started to the crater. The first glance in that direction revealed a scene of wild beauty. There was a heavy fog over the crater and it was splendidly illuminated by the glare from the fires below. The illumination was two miles wide and a mile high, perhaps; and if you ever, on a dark night and at a distance beheld the light from thirty or forty blocks of distant buildings all on fire at once, reflected strongly against overhanging clouds, you can form a fair idea of what this looked like.

A colossal column of cloud towered to a great height in the air immediately above the crater, and the outer swell of every one of its vast folds was dyed with a rich crimson luster, which was subdued to a pale rose tint in the depressions between. It glowed like a muffled torch and stretched upward to a dizzy height toward the zenith. I thought it just possible that its like had not been seen since the children of Israel wandered on their long march through the desert so many centuries ago over a path illuminated by the mysterious "pillar of fire." And I was sure that I now had a vivid conception of what the majestic "pillar of fire" was like, which almost amounted to a revelation. . . .

I turned my eyes upon the volcano again. The "cellar" was tolerably well lighted up. For a mile and a half in front of us and half a mile on either side, the floor of the abyss was magnificently illuminated; beyond these limits the mists hung down their gauzy curtains and cast a deceptive gloom over all that made the twinkling fires in the remote corners of the crater seem countless leagues removed—made them seem like the campfires of a great army far away.

—Mark Twain, *Roughing It*, 1872

Lava explodes as the flow reaches the ocean at Hawai'i Volcanoes National Park.

cracks. Don't try it; you could slip in the mud and fall in. Intense heat prevents rescue, so keep behind the safety rails.

Madame Pele frequently shrouds her home in mist and drifting cloud. Covering, then revealing her ghostly works, moving shadows chased by shafts of sunlight float across the caldera. Gnarled or standing tall, Pele's ‘ohi‘alehua trees form matte-green clusters on the plateau. Sometimes their red pompom flowers fly away, inexplicably transformed into small i‘iwi birds.

Hawaiian volcanoes don't blow their tops in the unpredictable manner of Mount St. Helens in the state of Washington. Rather, due to the composition of the lava, the flows are not termed "explosive," and vulcanologists measuring Pele's mood with their high-tech equipment seem to have the leisure of anticipation. Native Hawaiians have their own ways of knowing when an eruption is about to occur: Pele often appears to them in the cloudy night just before an eruption— perhaps on a deserted moonscape, or on the road. She may be an old crone asking for a lift, or a beautiful woman. Sometimes she will send her white dog in the misted moonlight.

On January 3, 1983, Pu‘u O‘o vent opened in the east rift zone on the slope of Kilauea Volcano some 10 miles below the summit. A curtain of red lava shot into the air. Geysering tall one day, spewing steadily the next, the magma came up, and continues to come up, from the earth's core. Vog—volcanic smog—hovers over the vent, and when winds come the vog is carried over the island.

To see flowing lava, take the **Chain of Craters Road,** which begins at midpoint on the Crater Rim Drive and descends 3,500 feet toward the sea. Before Pu‘u O‘o opened its fiery mouth, the Chain of Craters Road looped down from the summit of Kilauea to the sea, where it continued along the shore northeasterly into Puna. Now the road is cut by a vast undulating plain—as far as you can see—of new lava thrust from the depths of Pele's home. Currently, 375,000 cubic meters of lava spew out every 24 hours, enough to pave the Chain of Craters Road 15 times a day. A national park barricade alerts drivers.

Rangers of Hawai‘i Volcanoes National Park are stationed at the barricade to provide travelers with information—including daily updates on the state of the lava flow—and to direct them toward areas that can be reached safely on foot, a long walk from the barricade. Out on newly cooled lava, park rangers (outfitted, of course, in sturdy boots) walk around to determine its condition. At no other place on earth can you safely come so close. Accompanied by a park ranger, you can walk right on top of *pahoehoe*—the smooth, unbroken lava. Below the gray, slightly cooled crust, the lava is still molten. Often there are places—if you can stand the heat—where you can stir it with a twig and the flow will consume the twig in a sudden brief spurt of flame. Above the sound of the molten river you hear the sharp pops and bangs of bushes and trees exploding in the heat.

If you look up from the road barricade toward the high ridge above, cloud cover often confuses the view, and visitors sometimes wonder whether they are looking at Kilauea Volcano or Mauna Loa Volcano. Nearest to you is Kilauea, rising to 4,093 feet. It is Kilauea that is erupting from Pu'u O'o vent on its slope to pour lava down into Puna. The tall peak you see actually is behind Kilauea. Often shrouded in cloud, this is the much taller mountain of Mauna Loa, towering to 13,677 feet. Mauna Loa and Kilauea are the two active volcanoes that make up Hawai'i Volcanoes National Park.

When vulcanologists determine that the eruption is surely done, the barricades will be taken down and the road reconstructed. Until then, the traveler must return to park headquarters and the main highway (HI 11).

When you leave Pele's region, it's unwise to take away pieces of lava rock. Tradition has it that bad luck will hound you. Park rangers say that parcels of rocks arrive in the mail every day. Enclosed are notes telling of dire events that have plagued the lives of visitors since they took rocks away with them, and they implore the rangers to give them back to Pele. (If you find yourself having inadvertently made off with a piece of Pele's rock, and you want to send it back, the address is: Headquarters, Hawai'i Volcanoes National Park, Volcano, HI 96785.)

■ **ROAD TO KONA** *map page 57*

The Hawai'i Belt Road (HI 11) descends southwest from Hawai'i Volcanoes National Park to loop down around the southern tip of the island and turn north along the west coast. In this 101-mile journey toward Kailua-Kona the road travels first through the uninhabited Ka'u Desert on the southwest rift zone, then passes Pahala, a tiny plantation colony leading to **Wood Valley Temple,** a Tibetan Buddhist retreat where visitors are permitted. It continues past Na'alehu, the most southerly town in the United States (its 19-degree latitude is the same as Mexico City's), to the village of Wai'ohinu, where the canopy-shaped **Mark Twain Monkeypod Tree** stands at the roadside. The original tree, planted by the author in 1866, was felled long ago by strong winds, and the present tree rose from the roots. At the South Point (or Ka Lae Point) turnoff, South Point Road leads 11 miles through pasturelands to the nation's southernmost jut of land, rocky **Ka Lae Point,** where fishermen drop ladders off sheer cliffs to reach baited pots or to board boats that pull up below. Veins of the clear green mineral olivine run through the bedrock of South Point. Lava flows broke these open eons ago, leaving green streaks in the near-black earth and layers of color in the wind-sculpted cliffs of Ka Lae. **Green Sand Beach,** a three-mile hike east from South Point, was formed when a cinder cone of olivine collapsed close to shore. To enjoy the beach you'll need to scurry down the cinder face, but on a calm day you can enjoy a refreshing dip in the water.

Bending around the bottom of the island, the Belt Road crosses an ancient lava plain at the southwest shores of Ka'u district.

■ SOUTH KONA COAST   *map page 57 and opposite*

The west side of the island is lush with tropical vegetation, but the sun always shines on the golden Kona Coast. From the macadamia nut orchards of South Kona to Kawaihae to the north, there are more than 80 miles of sun-soaked coastline. Even afternoon showers in the coffee fields seldom reach the shore a short two miles away. Sometimes called Kamehameha's Coast, the Kona Coast is lined with some of the most important sites in Hawaiian history, and it boasts the best watersports activities on the island.

■ HO'OKENA BEACH   *map opposite page, A/B-5*

Ho'okena Beach Park is north of Ka'u and about 22 miles south of Kailua. A sign marks the Ho'okena paved road, and it is two miles to the beach. The soft black sands of Ho'okena are rimmed by sheer lava walls. Its wide strand, lined with coco palms, opens a broad view of the south Kona coastline. Straight out from a wave-battered landing once used to ship cattle to market in Honolulu, there's good swimming and deep-water snorkeling above coral groupings. Look for spectacled angelfish and silvery wrasses that bump sea urchins upside down to eat their meat. Sometimes schools of dolphins swim into the bay.

It was toward this tiny fishing community that Robert Louis Stevenson headed in a whaleboat from Kailua in 1889, arriving in a heavy squall and disembarking near a point of reef in knee-deep water. Drenched by rain and sea, Stevenson waded ashore where he was met by D. H. Nahinu, a former judge who "with a hat band of peacock feathers, a face like an old trusty dog's, no eyes, and no English," was to be his host. He led the writer to an open shed that served as the village store. No one paid the slightest attention to Stevenson, and while Nahinu shopped the writer waited, talking and "flirting with a little maid of seven." Stevenson stayed alone here for a week, in comfortable quarters, with no interruptions, enjoying the solitude, and writing at the end of the stay that he no longer felt "oppressed with civilization." His journal entries later were integrated into his book *Travels in Hawaii*.

While he was in the Ho'okena store, Stevenson heard a story of Hawaiians who were buying 60,000 acres in the mountains for $4,000. As Hawaiians seldom bought land, Stevenson wanted to see the site, and the next day the writer, despite his poor health, endured five hours on a mule riding to the land in "the place of the mist" and reaching "the region of the gods and goblins." On the descent, Stevenson rode a tortuous path above the sea through forest dappled with lichens, dripping with vines, and dotted with mysterious cave entrances. Since this was sacred territory, where bones of chiefs were interred and could not be disturbed, he did not tarry.

SOUTH KONA COAST

PU'UHONUA O HONAUNAU (PLACE OF REFUGE)

map page 67, B-4

The Pu'uhonua O Honaunau, or "place of refuge at Honaunau," was a site of absolution for *kapu-* or lawbreakers—if they could reach it. If not, they met with immediate death. A stone wall built in 1550 marks the refuge boundary. Dry-laid and held in place by friction, it is 1,000 feet long, 10 feet high, and 17 feet wide. Tide pools built of *pahoehoe* lava meet the L-shaped wall and form the 12-acre refuge into a triangle.

Adjacent to the north wall lay the palace grounds. If a *kapu*-breaker was on the run from the north, he had to skirt the grounds and swim through stiff currents and shark-haunted waters to reach the sanctuary. If making a dash from the south, and if the king's pursuers didn't grab him, he entered by land.

Hale O Keawe temple was built about 1650 in honor of chief Keawe. It is located at Pu'uhonua O Honaunau, or Place of Refuge at Honaunau Bay, in South Kona. Kapu- and lawbreakers could escape the death penalty by swimming through stiff currents to this sanctuary.

Along the ocean side of the north wall, Hale O Keawe, the *he'iau*, or temple, of Keawe, still stands—built about 1650 in honor of ruling chief Keawe. Because the *mana* of a chief continued to be associated with his remains after death, the wrapped bones of Keawe were carefully stored in the *he'iau*. Over succeeding generations, the bones of 23 chiefs were interred, adding spiritual force to the sanctuary.

Robert Louis Stevenson recounted a tale of these bones in *The Eight Islands:*

> . . . Since his death he [Keawe] has wrought miracles. As late as 1829 Ka'ahumanu sent messengers to bring the relics of the kings from their long repose at Honaunau. First to the keeper's wife and then to the keeper the spirit of Keawe appeared in a dream, bidding them prevent the desecration. They rose trembling . . . exchanged the bones of Keawe with those of some less holy chieftains; and were back in bed . . . before the messengers arrived. So it comes that to this hour the bones of Keawe . . . sleep in some unknown crevice of that caverned isle.

Hale O Keawe, carefully reconstructed in 1985, is flanked by towering carved images called *ki'i*, incarnate spirits of the ancient gods.

At the visitors center near the entrance, pick up a brochure describing a self-guided walk passing Hale O Keawe, the ruins of two older *he'iau*, a petroglyph, lava tree molds, thatched huts, and a hand-carved koa-wood canoe. Beside the center a "story wall" with audio messages describes the migration of Polynesians to Hawai'i. As some of the park rangers are Hawaiian, you may see them garbed in *kapa* cloth while demonstrating thatch, *haku hulu* (featherwork), or canoe or *ki'i* carving; they present 20-minute orientation talks six times a day. On the weekend nearest July 1, a three-day cultural festival features ancient hula, *hukilau* (community net fishing), crafts and games, food, and processions led by a royal court.

Pu'uhonua O Honaunau National Historical Park can be visited by taking the *makai* (seaward) turnoff at the 104-mile marker on the Belt Road for 3.5 miles, or on the secondary Middle Ke'ei Road from Kealakekua Bay, four miles to the north.

■ **KEALAKEKUA BAY** *map page 67, B-3*

The small town of **Captain Cook** edges the Belt Road above Kealakekua Bay about 12 miles south of Kailua. At its mouth, Kealakekua (Pathway of the God) Bay is a mile wide. Napo'opo'o town and Hiki'au *he'iau* lie at the south end. It was into this bay that the English explorer Captain James Cook sailed in January 1779, as the Hawaiians were holding feasts in honor of the god Lono. Thinking Cook might be Lono himself, the Hawaiians welcomed him joyously and honored him with a great feast. After an initial period of welcome, however, the Hawaiians began to suspect that the Englishmen might not be gods after all. (Kamehameha the Great, not yet king but a trusted warrior to his uncle the chief of Hawai'i, most likely was at the feasting and saw Cook.) The Englishmen, reprovisioned, set sail, but were soon caught in a storm, found their foremast broken, and were forced to return. Cook's reappearance convinced Hawaiians that the English were mere mortals. Goodwill degenerated into thievery, tempers rose on both sides, and Cook was killed on Kealakekua Beach.

The actual place where Cook was killed, at the north end of the bay, is enclosed by steep cliffs and is accessible only by water or trail. (The little-used trail starts from a dirt track off Napo'opo'o Road. It takes about an hour and a half each way through tall grass to travel the trail. It's uphill all the way back.) Here, when the main bay is roiled by storms, the northern cove offers calm waters in one of the best natural boat shelters on the Kona Coast. Deep waters, dark blue and sparkling over coral reefs, glint with tropical fish, drawing snorkelers and divers. Glass-bottom boats cruise the cove, and tour operators bring snorkelers to some of the best viewing waters of Hawai'i.

The entire Kealakekua Bay is a state underwater park and marine life conservation district. Underwater caves, sunken lava flows, and coral reefs shelter parrot fish and goatfish and night-swimming big-eyed reddish squirrel fish. In clear blue waters 30 feet deep, they flash rainbows on the sea bed.

From the beach at Napo'opo'o you can see the **Captain Cook Monument** in the northern cove, a 27-foot white obelisk surrounded by a single-chain railing. Its plaque reads: "In memory of the great circumnavigator Captain James Cook, RN, who discovered these islands on the 18th day of January 1778 and fell near this

Captain Cook Monument, on the spot where Cook was killed, is accessible only by water or trail. The most popular way to visit is by kayak.

HAWAIIAN VIEW OF CAPTAIN COOK

More than eighty years after the arrival of Captain Cook, the native Hawaiian writer S. M. Kamakau described events leading to the explorer's death at the island of Hawai'i in 1779. Kamakau, who was educated at a school established to train young Hawaiians as Congregational ministers, reflects both the way native Hawaiians remembered Cook and a nineteenth-century Christian view of why Cook was implicated in his own death.

When Captain Cook went ashore at Kealakekua, the kahuna, believing him to be a god [Lono], led him to the he'iau, and seated him above the altar where sacrifices were offered. . . . Now it is doubtful whether Captain Cook consented to have worship paid to him by the priests. He may have thought they were worshiping as in his own land. But he was a Christian and he did wrong to consent to enter an idolator's place of worship. He did wrong to accept gifts offered before idols and to eat food dedicated to them.

■ ■ ■

On February 4, Lono [Cook] sailed away in his ship and had got beyond Kawaihae when he discovered that one of the masts was decayed and he had to put back to Kealakekua to repair it. The natives saw him return, and the women took up once more their association with the sailors, but not in such numbers as before. The natives had begun to be suspicious, and some said, "these are not gods; these are men, white men from the land of Kukanaloa." . . . One man said, "The woman who was on the ship says that they groan when they are hurt."

After one of Cook's longboats was stolen, a series of misunderstandings occurred, and an English sailor shot a chief named Kalimu. The Hawaiians were outraged by this and a warrior named Kalanimanookahoowaha tried to block Cook's way with a club.

Captain Cook struck Kalanimanookahoowaha with his sword, slashing one side of his face from temple to cheek. The chief with a powerful blow of his club knocked Captain Cook down against a heap of lava rock. Captain Cook groaned with pain. Then the chief knew that he was a man and not a god, and, that mistake ended, he struck him dead together with four other white men.

■ ■ ■

When the strangers on the ship knew that their chief was dead, they shot their guns from the ship while the natives tried to ward off the shots with sleeping mats.

The bodies of Captain Cook and the four men who died with him were carried to Kalaniopuu at Manualoia, and the chief sorrowed over the death of the captain. He dedicated the body of Captain Cook, that is, he offered it as a sacrifice to the god with a prayer to grant life to the chief (himself) and to his dominion. Then they stripped the flesh from the bones of Lono.

■ ■ ■

Captain Cook . . . had been but a short time in Hawaii when God punished him for his sin. It was not the fault of the Hawaiian people that they held him sacred and paid him honor as a god worshiped by the Hawaiian people. But because he killed the people he was killed by them without mercy, and his entrails were used to rope off the arena, and the palms of his hands used for fly swatters at a cock fight. Such is the end of a transgressor. The seeds that he planted here have sprouted, grown, and become the parents of others that have caused the decrease of the native population of these islands. Such are gonorrhea, and other social diseases; prostitution; the illusion of his being a god [which led to] worship of him; fleas and mosquitoes [erroneous]; epidemics. All of these things have led to changes in the air which we breathe; the coming of things which weaken the body; changes in plant life; changes in religion; changes in the art of healing; and changes in the laws by which the land is governed.

—S. M. Kamakau, *The Floating Islands and the Return of Lono,* [about] 1865

spot on the 14th day of February 1779. This monument was erected in November 1874 by some of his fellow countrymen." In later times the Commonwealth of Australia erected a jetty and plaque in front of the monument in memory of Cook, "the discoverer of both Australia and these islands."

At six-acre **Napo'opo'o Beach Park,** four miles down the winding road to Kealakekua Bay, the beach is strewn with bits of lava and rock, yet it is a popular spot, with facilities and excellent deep-water swimming. While fishing is restricted, the boat ramp receives heavy use. Tour buses bring visitors to **Hiki'au (Moving Current) He'iau** in the park, and the whole area has quite a lot of traffic.

Around Palemano Point at the south end of Kealakekua Bay, the white sand of tiny **Ke'ei Beach,** speckled with shreds of lava, draws water-sports fans. At night, torch fishermen congregate. During the day, snorkelers find medium-sized grey snapper *(uku)* and perhaps a black-tailed snapper (introduced from Tahiti) swimming in the clear waters of a broad shallow reef. Surfers are drawn to some of the longest surfing rides on this part of the Kona Coast. Mark Twain once paused here and wrote with characteristic ebullience: "We came upon a large company of naked natives, of both sexes and all ages, amusing themselves with the national pastime of surf-bathing."

Ke'ei is the site of the Battle of Moku'ahai, Kamehameha's first offensive in his bid to dominate the Big Island. By devious measures, Kiwala'o—the weak son who had succeeded Kalaniopu'u as ruling chief—had taken temple lands belonging to his cousin, Kamehameha. Insults mounted, and the two young chiefs soon were riding a collision course. After the land and sea battle at Ke'ei, with Kiwala'o slain and his forces on the run, Kamehameha ruled over the northern half of Hawai'i.

■ **KONA COFFEE COUNTRY** *map page 67*
From Ke'ei, the Hawai'i Belt Road cuts north past small upland towns. This is Kona coffee country, some 3,000 acres, and the only place coffee is grown commercially in the U.S. These coffee trees were brought to Hawai'i via Brazil, and they thrive in the fertile volcanic earth of the Kona Coast. Tropical evergreens do not do well in direct sunlight, and in other coffee-growing parts of the world shade trees are planted to protect them. In Kona, however, afternoon clouds that form on the slopes of Hualalai protect the coffee plants. They are kept pruned to a height of 12 feet for ease in hand-picking. An average plant yields about five pounds of coffee cherries a year, or one pound of roasted coffee from the beans contained in the cherries. The berries turn from green to red from September until mid-December. If you are on Napo'opo'o Road driving toward the bayshore, you might stop at the **Kona Pacific Farmers Cooperative and Museum** (Mamalahoa Highway, Captain Cook; 808-328-2411), where you can taste flavored blends of Kona coffees, tour the museum, and purchase freshly roasted coffee.

At the south end of Captain Cook town, on Mamalahoa Highway, **Royal Kona Coffee Company** (808-328-2511) operates a visitors center where you can sample a fine cup of Hawaiian Joe, view a video explaining coffee processing, and check out some old coffee plantation equipment. An adjacent area offers a walk among the coffee plants to see the berries up close.

■ NORTH KONA

■ KAILUA-KONA

map this page, A-4

The hub of activity on the Kona Coast is at mid-point, in Kailua-Kona town. Surrounding Kailua Bay at the foot of Hualalai mountain, eight miles south of Kona International Airport, Kailua-Kona is a still-quaint old village smothering under the onslaught of souvenir shops and a mall in the vicinity of moderate- to budget-priced hotels. Stacks of condos and larger hotels follow a five-mile strip of secondary coast road (Aliʻi Drive) directly south to Keauhou. Near the end of this road, lifeguards offer daily surfing lessons at the largest white-sand swimming beach in the area, Kahaluʻu Beach Park.

The town is famous for its proximity to deep-sea sport fishing; the Hawaiian International Billfish (Marlin) Tournament takes place out of Kailua every summer. You've probably seen photos of catches taken at the hanging scales on Kailua Pier: a Pacific blue marlin may weigh more than 1,000 pounds. Every October, Kailua-Kona hosts the **Ironman Triathlon World Championship,** which includes a

NORTH KONA COAST

| 0 | 1.5 | 3 Mi |
| 0 | 1.5 | 3 | 4.5 Km |

Swimmers begin the first leg of the Ironman Triathlon World Championship on the Kona Coast. After a 2.4-mile swim, participants face a 112-mile bike ride, then a 26.2-mile run.

2.4-mile swim, a 112-mile bike ride, and a 26.2-mile run. It's arduous, some say the world's most arduous. Luc Van Lierde of Belgium set the men's record in 1996 at 8 hours, 4 minutes, 8 seconds; and Paula Newby-Fraser, a naturalized U.S. citizen from South Africa, set the women's record in 1992 at 8 hours, 55 minutes, 28 seconds.

Kailua-Kona, or Kailua for short, overflows with history. When Kamehameha returned from Honolulu to Kailua in 1812, the kingdom was secure and at peace. In his last years, Kamehameha wanted to come home—to the Kona coast. He lived at Kamakahonu, a town on Kailua Bay, until his death on May 8, 1819.

When the first batch of Congregational missionaries stepped ashore at Kailua Bay in April 1820, almost a year after Kamehameha's death, they could not know that the ancient religion of the Warrior King of Hawai'i, based in part on the *kapu* system, had been battered, denied, and broken at this same place just six months earlier. They lost no time in making converts among a bewildered people who had come to doubt the power of ancient gods. It was not long before a series of thatched churches arose on the site, in what is now the center of town.

In 1836 the Big Island's governor, John Adams Kuakini, decided to tear down the last of these weathered thatch structures and build the first stone church in the islands, **Mokuaikaua Church.** To accomplish this task, he sent every male in the district into the mountains to cut and haul *'ohi'a* trees, which were to serve as beams. These spanning beams were cut 50 feet long, and the name of the church is probably taken from the forest where they were cut. The walls of the stone church were held in place by mortar made from coral dragged ashore and burned for its lime. Built with intensive labor, primitive tools, and massive effort, the church was dedicated in February 1837.

Mokuaikaua Church is notable for its simple, well-proportioned mass, and it was soon to be imitated by missionaries on the other islands—Kawaiahao Church in Honolulu takes advantage of this engineering design. Modern architects note with admiration that the roof was designed so as to require no trusses. Still in service, Mokuaikaua Church marks the influence of pioneer missionaries in Hawai'i, and in 1978 it received a National Historic Landmark designation. *75-5713 Ali'i Drive.*

Governor Kuakini not only built a fine house of worship, but he also issued laws for the so-called betterment of its congregation. Women were to wear bonnets to service; dogs were not permitted inside; and anyone caught sleeping received a rap on the forehead with a long cane.

In 1838, Governor Kuakini built **Hulihe'e Palace** across from the church. Meant to be his home, it became instead a royal summer residence. Built of the same lava block as the church, this two-story home was plastered smooth by King Kalakaua in 1885. By 1916 it had been abandoned, and it was left to deteriorate until the 1950s, when the state-owned palace was leased to the Daughters of Hawai'i (read, daughters of missionaries) who have since guided its restoration. Now a somewhat stuffy museum, it displays furniture and antiques acquired by Hawaiian royalty on visits to Europe, and Hawaiian pieces such as Kamehameha's war spears, a table inlaid with 25 varieties of Hawaiian woods, and an armoire of Hawaiian sandalwood. *75-5718 Ali'i Drive; 808-329-9555.*

The **Blue Ginger Gallery** offers a more upbeat, modern museum option in Kailua. It features 80 local artists whose works range from painted silk scarves and jewelry to hand-carved furniture and stained glass. *79-7391 Kainaliu (Mamalahoa Hwy.); 808-322-3898.*

Near Hulihe'e Palace, at the northern end of Kailua Bay is **Kamakahonu (Turtle Eye) Beach,** which fronts the King Kamehameha Kona Beach Hotel and is

(following spread) Luahinewai Pond hides behind the trees along Luahinewai Beach on the North Kona Coast.

the only swimming strand in town. Calm, shallow, and usually safe for children, it was named for a turtle-shaped *pahoehoe* lava formation, now buried under Kailua Pier, onto which the first missionaries stepped ashore. It is also the same sandy little cove where Kamehameha made his last home and dealt with affairs of state; the beach was his canoe landing.

■ HOLUALOA TOWN *map page 75, B-5*

Five miles upslope from Kailua sits the village of Holualoa. At 1,400 feet, it is cooler than the beach, and the lifestyle here still is rural, with a slowed pace and few tourists. The art galleries and shops are evidence of a small colony of artists who call this home. **Studio 7 Gallery** (Mamalahoa Highway; 808-324-1335), with its eclectic collection, is one of the best.

■ UP THE COAST ON HI 19 *map page 75*

From Kailua-Kona, HI 190 leads straight inland to the cool upland ranches of Waimea, while HI 19 leads north to the luxury hotels of the South Kohala coast.

Stop at Honokohau for a visit to **Kaloko-Honokohau National Historic Park,** a living monument to pre-contact Hawaii, demonstrating how Hawaiians lived and practiced sophisticated fishpond aquaculture. Drive down to the Honokohau Small Boat Harbor to reach the park, where you can swim, surf, snorkel, enjoy the white-sand beach, or hike along the coast to view archaeological sites. *73-4786 Kanelani Street, #14; 808-326-9057.*

Seven miles north of Kailua-Kona, at the airport, is the **Ellison S. Onizuka Space Center,** a museum/monument dedicated to the astronaut and Holualoa resident who died in the 1986 *Challenger* space shuttle explosion. *Kona International Airport, between the Aloha and Hawaiian airline terminals; 808-329-3441.*

Four miles north of the airport and one mile from HI 19 is **Makalawena Beach,** one of the island's best. Take the paved road down to **Kekaha Kai State Park** (no phone) and follow the foot trail across Kawili Point. Curving white sand slopes into shallow swimming coves separated by small points of water-worn lava. In the high surf conditions of winter, the waters are perilous. While this beach is just a mile from the highway, it is a remote, untouched area without lifeguards.

The coast road cuts across ancient lava flows where megaresorts lie in the distance like green sequins on a cloth of barren brown. Along its 35-mile length from the airport north to Kawaihae, the road passes several *makai* (seaward) turnoffs.

One leads down to the luxurious Kona Village Resort, where *honu* (green sea turtles) swim and sunbathe. The road contnues on to the Waikoloa complex, where Hilton operates a popular theme-park type of hotel. An ancient site, fishponds, petroglyph trails, and golf courses lie here. In the Hilton lagoon you can swim with silky-skinned dolphins—if you're lucky enough to win a spot in the daily drawings and willing to spend $50 for the privilege.

Continuing north across ribbons of razor-sharp '*a'a* lava, the drive passes roadside plantings of bougainvillea, flowering a brilliant crimson against the stark and arid landscape. Because the road is smooth and well-engineered, speeding is a temptation. Beware! Unmarked police cars monitor this part of the highway.

Four miles south of Kawaihae, upscale tourism on the Big Island arose from the lava flows in the 1960s. Here Laurence Rockefeller leased lava-covered land, and after much bulldozing, building, and watering (the lava turns to soil so rich that anything can grow here), he opened the **Mauna Kea Beach Hotel** in 1965, adorning it with an impressive collection of Asian art and artifacts. The first luxury hotel outside O'ahu, the Mauna Kea's atrium-centered design became a model for many luxury hotels in Hawai'i and around the Pacific. Other world-class hotels blossomed on the naked lava of South Kohala, in resorts at Waikoloa and Mauna Lani, but for many years the Mauna Kea has reigned as the area's elegant, understated doyen.

■ **HAPUNA BEACH STATE RECREATION AREA** *map page 57, A-2*
Just north of the Mauna Kea Hotel is Hapuna Beach, one of the most beautiful beaches in all Hawai'i. The beach is divided in half by a tongue of lava, and the recreation area occupies the southern portion, where a smooth lawn dotted with cocos, hala, and kiawe trees unfolds down to a half-mile strand of soft white sand some 200 feet wide. Hapuna (Spring) is the widest white-sand beach on the Big Island. This is the island's most popular beach and is often crowded with body-surfers, snorkelers, and sunbathers. Board surfing is not permitted. During the summer the surf is generally tame, and it is usually a good, safe water-play area for children.

If Hapuna Beach is calm throughout the spring and summer, it is pounded by heavy waves from October to April. There is no lifeguard, and it is not advisable to swim at Hapuna during high surf periods. Hapuna's six A-frame cabins may be reserved from the Division of State Parks in Hilo, but there is no tent camping. *Off HI 19; 808-974-6200.*

■ PU'UKOHOLA HE'IAU NATIONAL HISTORIC SITE

map page 57, A-2

A mile above Kawaihae Harbor, the Pu'ukohola (Hill of the Whale) temple was the focal point of a dramatic final confrontation between Kamehameha and his rival and first cousin Keoua Ku'ahu'ula. After battling Keoua for years, Kamehameha was advised by a prophet that success would come after he built a high temple to Ku at this site and sacrificed an important chief. Temple construction was undertaken by hundreds of Hawaiians who passed heavy, water-smoothed stones from hand to hand for a distance of up to 14 miles, to be dry laid, without mortar. Down south in Ka'u, Keoua and kings of the other islands heard of the prophecy and believed they must stop the construction to prevent Kamehameha from acquiring unbeatable *mana*.

Once the massive temple platform (224 feet by 100 feet) was complete, it required a human sacrifice. Kamehameha thought Keoua would be a good candidate, and he invited his cousin to attend ceremonies at the *he'iau*. Believing all the signs pointed toward Kamehameha as the leader chosen by the gods, and knowing it would mean his death, Keoua accepted Kamehameha's invitation. As he stepped

Hapuna Beach is one of the most beautiful and popular beaches in all Hawai'i.

from the canoe a spear was thrown. Keoua and 11 of his men were killed, their bodies sacrificed at the consecration. With Hawai'i under his control, Kamehameha turned toward his ultimate goal—uniting the islands under his rule. Stop at the visitors center to pick up a brochure on the 77-acre park. Set aside an hour to walk the trail to the temple, or you may drive the beach road to the *he'iau* towering above the trail. *HI 270 at HI 19; 808-882-7218.*

■ **NORTH KOHALA PENINSULA** *map page 57, A-1/2*

Visitors tend to skirt right past the North Kohala peninsula, but this is a mistake. The cool uplands of Kohala are the one place in the islands where a feeling of ancient Hawai'i is all-pervasive and rural Hawai'i is still natural, not contrived. Continue north on the rising coast road, here called Akoni Pule Highway (HI 270). You can loop back down to Waimea on the inland route, HI 250.

■ **LAPAKAHI STATE HISTORICAL PARK** *map page 57, A-1*
Old Hawai'i is re-created at Lapakahi State Historical Park. Extending four miles inland and a mile along the shore, the long chunk of land is called an *ahupua'a*—a land division from the mountains to the sea. From 1968 through 1970, the state conducted archaeological studies here, discovering settlements dating back to the fourteenth century. Despite its being a somewhat bleak place of little rain or vegetation and brackish drinking water, its main village, called Koai'e, carried on successfully until late in the nineteenth century. A highway sign marks the park entrance. There, pick up a self-guided trail brochure for a walk past reconstructed ruins of canoe shelters, animal enclosures, *hale* (houses), and salt pans. The park shoreline was designated a Marine Life Conservation District in 1979. *HI 270; no phone.*

■ **MAHUKONA BEACH PARK** *map page 57, A-1*
Mahukona Beach Park is an insider's secret. Despite its name, there isn't any beach here, yet Mahukona has some of the best swimming and snorkeling on Hawai'i. Long ago this was a harbor, where a railroad brought in raw sugar from Kohala plantations to be loaded onto ships and sent to O'ahu. The harbor fell into disuse in 1956, when bulk-sugar trucks began making the 90-mile run to Hilo Harbor. Structural relics of the port are still visible in the lucid blue water. These railroad wheels, cables, and slabs of metal have become fish havens ideal for snorkelers and scuba divers. There's an anchor chain adorned with sea growth out to a sunken

boiler and ship in about 25 feet of water, and visibility is excellent. At the concrete landing, boats can be launched with the chain hoist and winch. In winter a heavy surge prevents all water activities. Camping is allowed at a grassy area bordered by small tide pools and swaying cocos, and there is now a golf course in the park. *HI 270; no phone.*

Beyond Mahukona the road veers east around the top of the island and away from miles of rugged coastline, a wild area where wind and heavy seas pound the shore year-round and no beaches beckon. Yet long ago Hawaiians lived here, and they left evidence of villages and canoe landings.

■ KAPANA'IA *map page 57, A-1*
Near 'Upolu Point, at the northernmost tip of the island, Kamehameha was born in secret at Kapana'ia, probably in 1750. Because there had been a prophecy that this infant would become a killer of kings, Kamehameha's mother Kekui'apo'iwa (of royal Kona lineage), went in the night to the cave of birthing stones. She then gave the baby to a trusted servant, probably named Naeole, with instructions to hide him. Raiding parties sent out by King Alapai of Hawai'i and Kahekili, a prince of Maui, tried to find and kill the newborn child. As his *kahu*, or tutor, Naeole reared the boy in the remote and mountainous district of Kapa'au.

To reach the birthplace, take the almost-deserted paved road to 'Upolu Airport (used infrequently by commuter aircraft), and turn left onto the jeep trail. About a mile down the trail the sacred site of Kamehameha's birth ritual, the 1,500-year-old **Mo'okini He'iau,** rises on a stark and windy plain. The stunningly large temple—250 feet by 125 feet, about the size of a football field—is bathed in an aura of calm and silence.

■ POLOLU VALLEY *map page 57, B-1/2*
Before looping down to Waimea from the small old plantation town of Hawi, continue east on HI 270 for another six miles to discover a surprise. Through green and cool rolling countryside where horses graze in front yards, the road dips down and then up again. As you come up over the rise, suddenly, like a curtain lifting, the horizon fills with a sweeping line of verdant, purple-shadowed cliffs and valleys, falling away before an expanse of blue ocean: this is the Pololu Valley. At the end of the road the lush valley stretches out below the remote scarps of the Hamakua Coast. A steep, convoluted old Hawaiian trail leads down from the

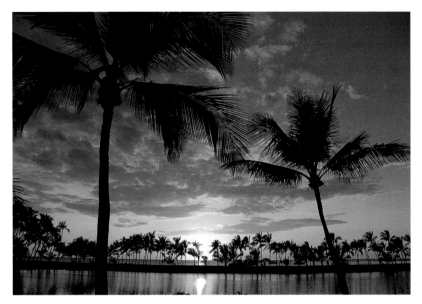

A spectacular sunset over Anaehoomalu Bay on the Kohala Coast.

lookout to inky black sands at **Pololu (Hardwood Spear) Beach.** Because the waters are always rough, Pololu is not for swimming; remote and isolated, it is a place to savor the ancient tranquillity of Hawai'i. From the restored old mule station near the lookout you can ride a mule down the 1,000 feet of winding trail to the valley floor. *Call 808-331-8505 for reservations.*

■ **KOHALA DISTRICT COURTHOUSE** *map page 57, A-1*
Backtrack on HI 270 to the tiny plantation community of Kapa'au (Kohala) and stop at the Kohala District Courthouse. A single-story frame building with a corrugated iron roof, an eight-foot wraparound lanai, and ornamented elliptical arches, the building is a good example of late nineteenth-century plantation architecture. Built in 1889 under King Kalakaua, it is one of fewer than six surviving monarchy period courthouses. Since 1975 it's been used as a civic center.

In front of the courthouse stands a bronze **statue of Kamehameha the Great,** the warrior king who has been called the Napoleon of the Pacific and the George Washington of Hawai'i for his brilliant strategy in war. The 8½-foot statue depicts the king in his *a'ahu* (feather cape), *malo* (loin cloth), and *mahiolo* (feather helmet).

One arm is outstretched and the other holds an upright spear. The statue was commissioned by the Hawaiian legislature in 1878, oddly enough to commemorate the centennial of Captain Cook's discovery of the islands. The Boston sculptor Thomas R. Gould was chosen to undertake the work, and for a fee of $10,000 he set about forging it in Italy. In 1880 the statue was shipped to Honolulu from Germany aboard a vessel that was lost at sea off the Falkland Islands. Those who commissioned it must have congratulated themselves for taking out a $12,000 insurance policy to cover the casting of a second statue from the original mold. This statue at the courthouse isn't that second casting. It's the first and was "found" by a sea captain familiar with Hawai'i who came face to face with it while strolling in the streets of Port Stanley, capital of the Falkland Islands. Captain Jervis inquired if he might buy the statue and was able to do so for $500, whereupon he took it off to Hawai'i and sold it at a profit. The Hawaiian government replaced the statue's damaged arm, and the original Kamehameha statue was unveiled here in 1912. The bronze and gold monument to Kamehameha that stands fronting Ali'iolani Hale (the Judiciary Building) in Honolulu is the second casting, installed in 1883.

■ **KOHALA MOUNTAIN ROAD** *map page 57, A/B-1/2*
The route from Hawi to Waimea is one more reason to visit Kohala. HI 250, or Kohala Mountain Road, passes through the eroded Kohala Mountains, where cattle and horses graze on meadows undulating over knolls and *pu'u* (mounds), and where sighing ironwood trees cluster in pastures and tower at roadside. At the highest point, 3,500 feet, stop at a lookout to enjoy the crisp air and a panoramic view stretching from the high green meadows, down across sloping parched mountainsides to the Kona-Kohala coast and out to a sparkling sea.

■ **WAIMEA AND THE PARKER RANCH** *map page 57, B-2*

In the cool, sometimes cloudy, mist-laden uplands 15 miles above the sunny luxury hotels of South Kohala is Waimea, cowboy country and home of Parker Ranch—the largest family-owned ranch in the United States. From a two-acre site purchased by John Parker for $10 in 1847, the Parker Ranch has burgeoned into a swath of 225,000 acres, ranging from 3,000-foot elevation uplands to a long coastline. Its 700 miles of fence encloses forests, pastures, 50,000 head of cattle, and 400 working horses. Kekuya grass, a bright almost electric green, forms clumps and unrolls like a gigantic sculpted carpet on the pasturelands.

The original homestead site served as a payment in 1847 to John Parker for rounding up feral cattle and horses. The cattle had been running around since Captain George Vancouver gave a bull and cow to King Kamehameha in 1793, and the horses were offspring of a mare and foal given as gifts to the king in 1803. (The mare, frightened, rolled her eyes, and Hawaiians called this startling behavior *lio,* or wild-eyed, and it became the Hawaiian word for "horse.") More animals followed, and the king issued a *kapu* around 1835 that none might be killed for ten years. When the kapu ended, the cattle were rounded up and became the first stock to graze at Parker Ranch. The development of the ranch required cowboys, so men were brought in from the Azores to join Mexicans already in Hawai'i. To Hawaiians they all were *espagniolos,* or *paniolo,* Hawaiian cowboys. Today the 27 *paniolo* who herd cattle at the Parker Ranch ride horses that are a special breed developed here from Spanish California and local stock. While the horses are the main ranch tool, the *paniolo* also use motorized all-terrain vehicles known as Japanese quarterhorses.

In recent years the Parker Ranch has opened to the public for riding tours. Visitors to the Parker home, called **Pu'uopelu Heritage Area,** follow a guided route through many rooms. The main house contains a surprising collection of fine Venetian art, Chinese jade, and luminous, sunflower-yellow Peiping glass. Evenings and on weekends the home and extensive grounds are busy with weddings and parties. The home is located in town, off the belt road, less than a mile south of the intersection with HI 190. *Parker Ranch Office, 808-885-7311; Pu'uopelu Heritage Area, 808-885-5433.*

Waimea town is known as **Kamuela,** Hawaiian for Samuel (Parker). The ranch town offers wagon rides, polo, hot-air ballooning, and an elegant theater. The town's visitors center hosts a museum, the Parker Ranch Store, a food court, and a wonderful restaurant. During the past 25 years the area around Waimea has grown dramatically with a mix of artists, wealthy transplants from the mainland and Europe, retirees, and Honolulu part-timers.

If you are lucky enough to be in Kamuela during a parade, you will see *pa'u* riders draped in elegant satin. This tradition traces back to 1880s modesty. Hawaiian women adored racing horses. To ride astride they covered up in 12 yards of fabric fastened with six kukui nuts. Today's parades follow a strict protocol and etiquette and always include a poop scoop brigade.

East of Kamuela the Hawai'i Belt Road crosses the island and veers south, down the windward Hamakua Coast 54 miles to Hilo.

■ HAMAKUA COAST *map page 57, B/C-2*

The sugarcane industry once reigned supreme on the Hamakua Coast, lording over tens of thousands of rain-fed acres where ancient lava flows have weathered into fertile soil. From the late 1800s well into the twentieth century, the area was locally known as the Scotch Coast, in tribute to the many Scots who came to work as managers, or *lunas,* on the sugar plantations.

Today a new wave of agriculture is spreading through the area. Small-scale farmers raise unusual crops sought by the islands' gourmet chefs. Check local markets for exotic fruits such as the bright red furry rambutan, relative of the lychee; starfruit; brown sapodillas tasting like a pear with spice and sugar; round, grapelike jaboticabas; and the bumpy, greenish-brown jackfruit that can weigh up to 80 pounds. Look for Japanese mizuna lettuce, baby romaine, and green tango.

Above these fertile lands, the slopes of Mauna Kea tumble down to the sea in emerald valleys ridged by volcanic cliffs. Extravagant tropical growth fills the valleys and no road intrudes. Under leafy canopies rare birds chirp, the beauty of their calls vying with the musical sound of the water coursing through. In the distance rushing waters crash down into pools. Only one valley in this area is accessible, and just barely: Waipi'o.

■ WAIPI'O VALLEY *map page 57, B-2*

For generations the pristine beauty of Waipi'o (Curved Water) Valley has inspired Hawaiian legend and song. It is the largest valley on the island; its sheer 2,000-foot lava walls are blanketed in green and ribboned with waterfalls. Waipi'o stretches back six miles to the double falls of Hi'ilawe, which drop more than 1,200 feet to a stream that wanders down the lush flat valley floor and meets a mile-wide black-sand shore fronting perilous surf over a sandbar.

Rich in tradition, Waipi'o, the Valley of the Kings, was once Hawai'i's religious and political center. Here Kamehameha received the blessing of his war god and defeated his cousin and rival, Keoua. Thousands lived here, cultivating Hawai'i's staple crop, taro, fishing, and harvesting breadfruit. Many were lured from Waipi'o by western lifestyles and driven off by devastating inundations from tsunamis. Today a few remaining families still cultivate smaller patches of taro and lotus.

To visit the Waipi'o Valley lookout from Honoka'a town, take the secondary paved road HI 240 nine miles north to its end. The only way into Waipi'o is little

Nanue Falls tumbles down the steeply forested mountains of the Hamakua Coast.

THE MANGO TREE

"One old Chinese man told me," he said, "that he like for trim his tree so the thing is hollow like one umbrella, and the mangoes all stay hanging underneath. Then you can see where all the mangoes stay, and you know if ripe. If the branches stay growing all over the place, then no can see the mango, and the thing get ripe, and fall on the ground."

And us guys, we no eat mango that fall down. Going get soft spots. And always get plenty, so can be choosy. But sometimes, by the end of mango season when hardly get all ready, and sometimes the wind blow em down, my mother, sometimes she put the fall down kind in the house with the others.

I was thinking about that as I was climbing up the tree. The wind was coming down from the pali, and I gotta lean into the wind every time she blow hard. My feet get the tingles cause sometimes the thing slip when I try for grip the bark with my toes. How long I never go up the tree! I stay scared the branch going broke cause too small for hold me, and when the wind blow, just like being on one see-saw. And when I start sawing that branch he told me for cut, the thing start for jerk, and hard for hold on with my feet. Plus I holding on to one branch above my head with one hand, and the fingers getting all cramp. My legs getting stiff and every few strokes my sawing arm all tired already, so when the wind blow strong again, I rest. I ride the branch just like one wave. One time when I wen look down I saw him with one big smile on his face. Can tell he trying not for laugh.

He getting old but he spend plenty time in that tree. Sometimes he climb up for cut one branch and he stay up for one hour, just looking around, figuring out the shape of the tree, what branches for cut and what not for cut. And from up there can see the whole valley. Can see the trees and the blue mountains. I used to have nightmares that the thing was going erupt and flood us out with lava, and I used to run around looking for my girlfriend so she could go with our family in our '50 Dodge when we run away to the ocean. But I never find her and I got lost. Only could see smoke, and people screaming, and the lava coming down.

The nightmare everytime end the same. I stay trapped on one trail in mountains, right on one cliff. Me and some guys. The trail was narrow so we walking single file. Some people carrying stuff, and my mother in front of me, she carrying some things wrapped in one cloth. One time she slip, and I grab for her, and she starting for fall and I scream "Oh no!" and then I wake up. And I look out my window at the mango tree and the blue mountains up the valley. The first time I wen dream this dream I was nine.

Since that time I wen dream plenty guys falling off the trail. And plenty times I wen grab for my mother's hand when she start for fall. But I never fall. I still stay lost on the cliff with the other guys. I still alive.

And my father still sitting in the mango tree just like one lookout, watching for me and my mother to come walking out of the mountain. Or maybe he stay listening to the pali wind for the sound one lady make if she falls. Or maybe he just sitting in his mango tree umbrella, rocking like one baby in the breeze, getting ripe where we can see him. And he's making sure no more extra branches getting in the way.

—Eric Chock, "The Mango Tree," from *The Best of Bamboo Ridge,* 1986

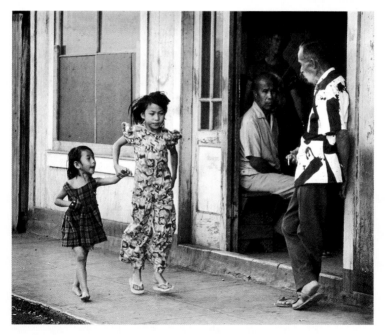

Small Hawaiian towns have an easy, friendly ambience.

changed since writer Isabella Bird's time. In 1873 she wrote: "We were at the top of the Waipi'o *pali* and our barefooted horses, used to the soft pastures of Waimea, refused to carry us down its rocky steep, so we had to walk." Today the bumpy, very steep track with its hairpin turns is passable only with four-wheel drive; downhill vehicles must yield to uphill. The walk down is arduous and takes about 25 minutes, but you can ride one of the shuttle tours based at the top, including one by mule-drawn wagon (P.O. Box 5086, Honokaa, HI 96727).

Through rain forests, spanning deep green gorges, the Belt Road to Hilo passes small sugar towns and unmarked turnoffs to isolated beaches, waterfalls, and botanical gardens. If you just zoom through, at least take time for the majestic Waipi'o Valley lookout. The other route between the Kona Coast and Hilo, the risky Saddle Road (HI 200), heads over the 6,600-foot pass between the Mauna Loa and Mauna Kea volcanoes. Rental cars are not permitted.

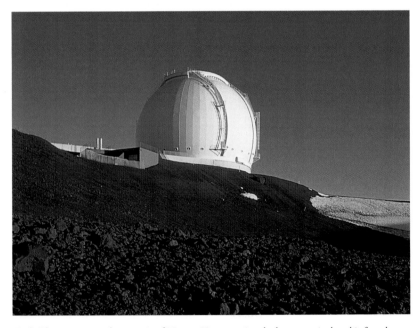

Keck Observatory, on the summit of Mauna Kea, contains the largest optical and infrared telescopes in the world.

■ MAUNA KEA *map page 57, B/C-2/3*

Mauna Kea (White Mountain) stretches up into the island heartland behind Kamuela and rises to a snow-capped 13,796 feet. Winter skiers come with rented four-wheel-drive vehicles to drive up and then ski down the volcano's immense treeless slopes. Located above 40 percent of the earth's atmosphere, a cluster of observatories on the chill summit benefit from the flawless clear air that makes it the world's premier location for astronomers. Eleven nations have come here to build 13 of the boldest telescopes in the world: infrared from NASA (U.S.), Canada, the U.K., Japan, and France; submillimeter from the U.K. and Cal Tech; optical from the University of Hawai'i; and Uncle Sam's Keck I, a 10-meter super-scope, and Keck II, with unique segmented mirror systems that make them look like the sci-fi eyes of a giant bug. The Kecks are the largest optical and infrared telescopes in the world. In 2003 the Submillimeter Array debuted atop Mauna Kea. This telescope's new technology is called interferometry. Eight 20-foot antennas are hooked up to function as one giant telescope and can be moved among 24 pads to organize data into images. Able to detect objects 30 times smaller than earlier telescopes, the Array is suited for peering into "nurseries," clouds of cold gas and dust where planets and stars are formed.

You will need four-wheel drive to make the trip up to the **Onizuka Center for International Astronomy,** at the 9,300 foot level, where star-filled films are shown every night. On weekends, free guided tours of the telescopes are conducted during daylight hours. *808-961-2180.*

On the eastern face of Mauna Kea, above the rugged Laupahoehoe area, a cairn protected by Douglas fir trees surrounds the **Doctor's Pit.** The trees are named for David Douglas, the noted Scottish botanist who discovered more than 200 species of plants in the Pacific Northwest and Hawai'i and whose name is a part of many scientific names. Mystery haunts the grounds of the Doctor's Pit, originally dug for trapping wild cattle. In 1834 Douglas's body was found here, and to this day his death remains shrouded in controversy. One theory has it that he fell in and was trampled by a trapped bull; another, that he was murdered by an escaped English convict. Coming upon the nearly eight-foot-tall memorial pyramid built of dark basaltic stones is a surprise in this wilderness. Its brass plate is inscribed to the doctor's memory, July 12, 1834. Douglas was buried in the graveyard of Kawaiahao Church in Honolulu (precise location unknown), and inside the church a plaque rather oddly describes Douglas as a *victima scientiae,* a victim of science.

■ TRAVEL BASICS

The Big Island is so big you can drive all day without encountering a megaresort. Hawai'i Belt Road outlines the island's contour, yet some areas remain untouched. While tourism is well established, it blends into the landscape most successfully on Hawai'i, and there are miles and miles of pristine wilderness. Whether you arrive at Hilo, the county seat in the wet tropical east, or at Kailua-Kona in the dry volcanic west, it's well to realize these two main towns are far apart. One hundred thirty-one miles stretch between them when you drive up into the middle and down around the southern end of the island. By the northern route, the drive is 116 miles.

Public bus service on the Big Island is available between Hilo and Kailua-Kona, and to Volcanoes National Park, but service is infrequent. The Hele On bus operates between Kohala Coast hotels and the Lanihau Shopping Center. This privately operated bus also services the area in and around the Hilo city limits; call 808-961-8343.

Climate: In the tropical climes of Hawai'i, northeasterly trade winds prevail most of the year. From summer to winter, average temperatures vary slightly. Coastal areas average between 65° F and 85° F. The average year-round temperature of ocean swimming areas is 74° F, and in summer the waters are around 80° F. In winter the summits of Mauna Kea and Mauna Loa are white-capped with snow. Mauna Kea, the tallest mountain in the islands, is also the coldest spot. A record low of 12° F has been recorded at the summit observatories; the highest record there is 66° F.

Winter is the rainy season in the Hawaiian Islands, with the heaviest rains expected between December and March. It might rain all day for several days, or only at night. Rainfall, however, varies more by location than with the season. It's an old story in Hawai'i that you can cross to the other side of the street to avoid a shower. In the verdant valleys, daily showers fall in the afternoon. The windward shores receive more rain than leeward coasts. Volcanic peaks seize the trade winds and block rain clouds from pouring down on the leeward sides. In Hilo, on the windward side, the average annual rainfall is 130 inches, making it the rainiest city in the U.S. Conversely, in Kona, on the leeward shore, you can sunbathe nearly all year long and watch rain clouds drench the slopes just two miles away. Because the volcanic peaks capture the rain, the leeward sides also are the sunniest and driest, with placid ocean waters and an average annual rainfall of 10 to 25 inches.

■ Visitor Information Services

Big Island Visitors Bureau. 800-648-2441.
Division of State Parks. Hilo; 808-974-6200.
Hawai'i Visitors Bureau-Hilo. 250 Keawe St., Hilo 96720; 808-961-5797.

■ Food and Lodging

On the Big Island driving distances are great, so you may want to base part of your trip in Kona or Kohala in the west and part in Hilo in the east. Better still, if you are adventurous and want to see Hawai'i thoroughly, drive your rental car all the way around, staying in the small inns of country towns. Before statehood, jet planes, and resort complexes, family-operated lodging houses catered to traveling salesmen who brought their wares into rural towns. While only a few remain, they are strategically located, the rates are low, the rooms basic and clean, and the old-time island atmosphere is relaxed and friendly. These lodgings are not for everyone—there may or may not be a TV in the room, and probably there is only one telephone. Neither are there mai tais, room service, or movie moguls as fellow guests, although you might meet a tractor or feed salesman. Some inns have cavernous restaurant-bars where you can hear the lilting inflections of local pidgin.

☷ For agencies offering listings and booking services for bed-and-breakfasts, hotels, and condominiums on all islands, see page 359.

$ For room and restaurant price designations, see page 359.

■ Captain Cook *map page 67, B-3*
✕ **Kona Theater Cafe.** HI 11 in town; 808-328-2244. Friendly café where locals gather for coffee. Full breakfast and lunch menus. Greek and veggie specialties. $
✕ **Manago Restaurant.** Manago Hotel, HI 11; 808-323-2642. Local favorite serving simple Japanese and American food; delicious fresh fish. $
☷ **Manago Hotel.** HI 11 in town; 808-323-2642. Family-managed, with old island atmosphere. Views of Kealakekua Bay. The Japanese Room is the nicest and has an *ofuro* (Japanese bath). $

■ Hilo *map page 52 and 57, D-3*
✕ **Cafe Pesto Hilo Bay.** 308 Kamehameha Ave.; 808-969-6640. Fresh seafood, exotic wood-fired pizzas; local microbrews; espresso bar. Heavenly desserts. $

✕ **Ken's Pancake House.** 1730 Kamehameha Ave.; 808-935-8711. American coffee shop open 24 hours. Omelets and pancakes, sandwiches and steaks. Good Belgian waffles. **$**

✕ **Panda Express** 111 Pua'inako St.; 808-959-1277. Traditional Chinese stir-fry preparations of fresh meat and vegetables. Good take-out. **$**

🏨 **Dolphin Bay Hotel.** 333 Ili'ahi St.; 808-935-1466. In residential area four blocks above downtown; TVs, fans, kitchens, sunken baths. **$**

🏨 **Hawai'i Naniloa Hotel.** 93 Banyan Dr.; 808-969-3333 or 800-367-5360. Modern high-rise; largest hotel in Hilo. **$$–$$$**

🏨 **Hilo Bay Hotel–Uncle Billy's.** 87 Banyan Dr.; 808-935-9861. Oceanfront Polynesian; some rooms with kitchens. Shops and restaurants. Weekly rates. **$**

🏨 **Hilo Hawaiian Hotel.** 71 Banyan Dr.; 808-935-9361 or 800-367-5004. Modern highrise overlooking Coconut Island. **$$**

🏨 **Shipman House.** 131 Ka'iulani St.; 808-934-8002 or 800-627-8447. Comfortable and quiet B&B gem; elegant former home filled with the ambience and art of old Hawai'i. Listed on national and state historic registers. **$$$**

■ HOLUALOA *map page 75, B-5*

🏨 **Holualoa Inn.** Mamalahoa Hwy.; 808-324-1121 or 800-392-1812. B&B in large cedar home. Six rooms, private baths. Pool, billiards. Nice views. **$$**

■ HONOKA'A AND ENVIRONS *map page 57, B/C-2*

✕ **Tex Drive Inn and Restaurant.** HI 19; 808-775-0598. Famous for delicious *malasadas* (Portuguese donuts). Local-style food; low on atmosphere, but you can take out. **$**

🏨 **Hotel Honoka'a Club.** Honoka'a; 808-775-0678. Family-managed, old-style island lodging popular with the *paniolo.* Ten basic rooms with mountain views. Cavernous restaurant and bar. Book rooms well in advance. **$**

🏨 **Waipi'o Ridge Rental.** Kukuihaele; 808-775-0603. Modern bungalow above Waipi'o with fine view. Kitchen, fireplace, sunken tub. Often rented by the month. **$$**

■ KAILUA-KONA *map page 57 and 75, A-4*

✕ **Don Drysdale's Club 53.** Kona Inn Shopping Village, Ali'i Dr.; 808-329-6651. Fresh fish, sandwiches, salads, and buffalo burgers. Try Peggy's peanut butter pie. **$**

✕ **Huggos'.** 78-5828 Kahakai St.; 808-329-1493. Long-time favorite for grilled American food; beside the shore in town. **$$–$$$**

✗ **Jameson's by the Sea.** 77-6452 Ali'i Dr. at Magic Sands Beach; 808-329-3195. Wonderful seafood in tasteful, airy room; varied menu. Oceanfront. **$$**

✗ **La Bourgogne.** 77-6400 Nalani St., Kuakini Plaza South; 808-329-6711. Blue-velvet booths, dark wood, and flowery decor. French food is served from an à la carte menu. Dinner only. **$$**

✗ **Sam Choy's Keauhou.** 78-6740 Ali'i Dr.; 808-322-2469. Overlooking the ocean in the Keauhou Beach Resort. Sam Choy, pioneer of Kona cuisine, offers fresh island-grown vegetables and herbs in his distinctly "local" dishes. **$–$$**

✗ **Tante's Restaurant.** Palani Rd., inside Kona Bowl; 808-334-1555. A great find. Owner won a 2004 national award for Asian entrepreneurs. This is not your everyday bowling alley eatery; the Continental menu is a favorite of locals and guests of upscale North Kona hotels. **$**

⌂ **Four Seasons Resort Hualalai.** 100 Ka'upulehu Dr.; 808-325-8000 or 888-340-5662. Glamourous hotel with lanai set around natural anchialine (brackish) ponds famed in the area. Great ocean views; three pools; PGA golf course. Don't miss Pahu I'a, the Hawaiian restaurant with reef-fish aquarium; menu includes a plethora of island fish. **$$$**

⌂ **Hale Maluhia Bed & Breakfast.** 76-770 Hualalai Rd.; 808-329-5773 or 800-559-6627. On an upcountry Kona plantation close to Holualoa; rooms range from small bungalows to a huge treehouse. Spa, large lanai, and pool table; wheelchair friendly. **$$**

⌂ **Kanaloa at Kona.** 78-261 Manukai St.; 808-322-2272. Deluxe 1-, 2-, and 3-bedroom suites. **$$$**

⌂ **King Kamehameha's Kona Beach Hotel.** 75-5660 Palani Rd.; 808-329-2911 or 800-367-2111. Large hotel on the only beach in town; historic Kamehameha the Great site; excellent exhibit of artifacts. **$$–$$$**

⌂ **Kona Seaside Hotel.** 75-5646 Palani Rd.; 808-329-2455 or 800-560-5558. Modern 6-story wing and an older wing; pool. **$**

⌂ **Kona Village Resort.** 808-325-5555 or 800-367-5290. Inter-island: 800-432-5450. On a beautiful beach at the foot of old lava flow. Elegant bungalows, gardens, famous buffets. Exclusive and expensive. **$$$**

⌂ **Royal Kona Resort.** 75-5852 Ali'i Dr.; 808-329-3111 or 800-774-5662. This large hotel was designed to resemble an early Hawaiian *holua* slide dropping toward the sea. Tasteful interior. Great pool. **$$–$$$**

■ **KOHALA COAST** *map page 57, A-1/2*

✕ **Bamboo Restaurant & Kohala Koa Gallery.** HI 270, Hawi; 808-889-5555. Fresh Pacific Rim cuisine. Old Hawai'i atmosphere. Sip a *liliko'i* margarita while browsing in the art gallery. **$**

✕ **The Batik.** Mauna Kea Beach Hotel, 62-100 Mauna Kea Beach Dr.; 808-882-7222. European cuisine influenced by Provence. Nightly entertainment. Jackets required. **$$$**

✕ **Cafe Pesto.** Kawaihae Center, Wharf Rd. and Makahona Hwy.; 808-882-1071.Gourmet pizzas; Italian pastas; seafood with island ingredients. Casual atmosphere. **$$**

✕ **Canoehouse.** Mauna Lani Bay Hotel, 1 Mauna Lani Dr.; 808-885-6622. Enormously popular. Menu emphasizes seafood and Pacific Rim cuisine and includes such dishes as wasabi lobster tempura on a stick! Oceanfront with fine views of the coast. **$$$**

✕ **Coast Grille.** Hapuna Beach Prince Hotel, 62-100 Kauna'oa Dr.; 808-880-1111. Elegant dining beneath high ceilings or outside on the lanai. Lobster, rack of lamb, and island fish. Oyster bar. **$$$**

✕ **Gallery Restaurant.** Mauna Lani Resort Racquet Club; 808-885-7777. Casual fine dining in glass-walled small room with fine views. Fresh seafood, American sauces, Hawaiian plate, and wide selection of fruit desserts. **$$$**

✕ **The Pavilion.** Mauna Kea Beach Hotel, 62-100 Mauna Kea Beach Dr.; 808-880-1111. Mediterranean/Italian cuisine. Casual, open-air restaurant. Open all day; music nightly. **$$**

✕ **Roussels Waikoloa Village.** Waikoloa Village Golf Club; 808-883-7674. Hearty French Creole cuisine. Overlooking the golf course. **$$**

✕ **Tiara Room.** Royal Waikoloan Hotel; 808-886-6789. Elegant and romantic; ocean views. Good poached oysters, venison, and rabbit. Dinner only. **$$$**

🏨 **Hapuna Beach Prince Hotel.** 62-100 Kauna'oa Dr.; 808-880-1111 or 800-882-6060. Business-oriented hotel in Mauna Kea Resort; lush gardens; artwork by native Hawaiians. Overlooking the island's best beach. **$$$**

🏨 **Hilton Waikoloa Village.** 69-425 Waikoloa Beach Dr.; 808-885-1234 or 800-445-8667. This sprawling resort setting resembles a theme park, with minitrams and a man-made lagoon where you can swim with dolphins. **$$$**

🏨 **Mauna Kea Beach Hotel.** 62-100 Mauna Kea Beach Dr.; 808-882-7222 or 800-882-6060. The first of the sumptuous Kohala Coast hotels, renovated in 1996. Wide-ranging collection of Hawaiian and Pacific art throughout; notable art gallery. The chef uses fresh local ingredients; low-fat selections. In-room TV by request. **$$$**

⊡ **Mauna Lani Bay Hotel and Bungalows.** 68-1400 Mauna Lani Bay Dr.; 808-885-6622 or 800-367-2323. Luxury accommodations. Most rooms are spacious and elegantly decorated in white and beige; ocean views and sunny lanais. Beautiful golf courses overlooking the ocean, 10 tennis courts, pool. **$$$**

⊡ **The Orchid at Mauna Lani.** 1 N. Kaniku; 808-885-2000 or 800-782-9488 Jungle plantings have been pruned away to expose the ocean view. Former Ritz-Carlton is now a Sheraton property. Spa facility. Showcase of island arts and crafts. Tennis and golf. **$$$**

⊡ **Waikoloa Beach Marriott.** 69-275 Waikoloa Beach Dr.; 808-886-6789 or 800-922-5533. Operated by Outrigger Hotels at Anaehoomalu. Hawaiiana dominates the decor. Set on a white-sand beach. Tennis, 2 golf courses, pool, petroglyph park, and trails. **$$–$$$**

■ NA'ALEHU AND PUNALU'U *map page 57, B/C-4/5*

⊡ **Colony One at Sea Mountain.** Hawai'i Belt Rd.; 808-928-8301 or 800-488-8301. On a black-sand beach at Punalu'u. Spacious and comfortably furnished condominium units with standard amenities and full kitchens. There are 76 units, some of them time-shares. Adjoins golf course. **$$**

⊡ **Shirakawa Motel.** Na'alehu; 808-929-7462. Southernmost lodging in the United States; run by the same family since 1921. Thirteen motel-type lodgings set amid hibiscus. Some units have cooking facilities. Near Mark Twain Monkeypod Tree. **$**

■ VOLCANO *map page 57, C-4*

⊡ **Chalet Kilauea–The Inn at Volcano.** Wright Rd.; 808-967-7786 or 800-937-7786. Comfortable B&B with six rooms (including a treehouse suite) and six off-property sites. Cozy library and a garden hot tub. French and Spanish spoken. **$$–$$$**

⊡ **Kilauea Lodge.** Old Volcano Rd.; 808-967-7366. One mile from Hawai'i Volcanoes National Park. Hawaiian décor; fireplaces in most rooms. ✘ Commendable country-style restaurant. Dinner only. **$$**

⊡ **Volcano House.** Hawai'i Volcanoes National Park; 808-967-7321. Memorabilia-filled hotel on the rim of Kilauea caldera, across from park headquarters. The only large hotel in a Hawaiian national park. Room decor is standard; request one with a crater view. The inn's large restaurant, ✘ **Ka Ohelo Room,** is large and often packed with tours at lunchtime; best is the cozy fireplace lounge. **$$–$$$**

■ **WAIMEA (KAMUELA)** *map page 57, B-2*

✕ **Edelweiss.** Kawaihae Rd. (HI 19) entering Kamuela; 808-885-6800. Owner/chef Hans-Peter Hager draws diners island-wide for sophisticated food at terrific prices. Varied menu popular with meat-eaters. Swiss chalet–like decor with *koa* wood and high ceilings. **$$**

✕ **Maha's. Cafe.** 1 Waimea Center; 808-885-0693. In Kamuela's historic Spencer House. Island-style cuisine; huge sandwiches at lunch. Collection of Hawaiian handcrafted housewares for sale from Cook's Discoveries. **$**

✕ **Merriman's.** Opelo Plaza II, Kawaihae Rd. (HI 19); 808-885-6822. Favorite spot for fresh fish and Pacific Rim cuisine. Fresh local produce; game in season. **$$**

✕ **Paniolo Country Inn.** 65-1214 Lindsay Rd.; 808-885-4377. American coffee shop with *paniolo* decor. Exceptional breakfast menu. **$**

✕ **Tres Hombres Beach Grill.** Kawaihae Shopping Center; 808-882-1031. Traditional Mexican dishes. Crab and shrimp poblanos, fish tacos. Excellent shrimp fajitas. **$**

⊡ **Kamuela Inn.** Kawaihae Rd.; 808-885-4243 or 800-555-8968. Located in the cool uplands. Nice third-floor penthouse for up to 6 people; full kitchen, cable TV. Private lanai, no telephone. Complimentary Continental breakfast. **$–$$$**

⊡ **Waimea Country Lodge.** 65-1210 Lindsey Rd.; 808-885-4100. Mainland-style motel-type lodgings; 20 rooms with kitchenettes, AC, telephones, and large TVs. In town, next door to Paniolo Country Inn restaurant. **$$**

■ GOLFING IN PARADISE

Golf in the Hawaiian Islands is an addictive endeavor. Once you drive a fairway where bordering palms march down to the sparkling blue Pacific while trade winds caress you in bright sunshine, the image will be imprinted deep in your mind. You'll yearn to come back and play under the sapphire sky where even a blown shot has its compensations. The scenery and views surrounding the layouts are so compelling that even golf widows and widowers are content to just ride along, watching rainbows paint the mountains and humpback whales cavorting in the sea.

Hawai'i has some of the world's most beautiful and challenging courses. There are more than 70 courses on the six main islands, and no two are alike. Each island's unique geology contributes to the character of each course.

Standards are high here. Hawaiian courses include several PGA Gold Medal resorts. All resort courses offer PGA professionals at layouts created by every top course designer you can think of: Jones Sr., Jones Jr., Nicklaus, Norman, Palmer, Weiskopf, Robinson, and Nelson. The islands draw more professional tournaments than any other state. The pros come to play the Sony Open, Seniors Skins, Kapalua International, PGA Grand Slam, Women's Kemper Open, and many others. You can test your skills on these same courses; almost all of them are open to the public.

The cost for enjoying the Hawaiian golf experience runs from well over a hundred dollars for a round at a luxury resort to as little as $20 for 9 holes on a municipal course. Be sure to set a tee time.

■ GOLF COURSES ON THE BIG ISLAND

Seventeen golf courses flow across most of the Big Island's climes, plunging through lava flows and coco palm barriers and over undulating volcanic mounds. One course is inside a national park. Big Island courses include four of the top ten in Hawai'i named by the Professional Golfer's Association.

Hilo Municipal Golf Course. Hilo; 808-959-7711. An 18-hole county course with four sets of tees; par 71. With a flat layout and extensive views of Hilo Bay and Mauna Kea, this course is lush green with tall banyans, coco palms, and flowering monkeypods. You can walk this course for $5.

Hualalai Four Seasons Resort. Kohala Coast; 888-340-5662. Site of the Senior PGA Masters tournament each January, the course varies according to wind conditions. Known as a match play course with a putting emphasis; there are many sand traps, and hole 12 has a trap in the center of the green. Hole 17 is considered a triumph of Jack Nicklaus design.

Kona Country Club. Keauhou Bay, Kona; 808-322-2595. Two 18-hole courses, Ocean and Mountain, with majestic views and low wind; at one hole the ocean spurts up in a geyser through rugged lava.

Mauna Kea Beach Resort. Kohala Coast; 808-882-5400. An 18-hole course with four sets of tees; par 72. The grande dame of Hawaiian courses set, and continues to maintain, the standard for resort golfing throughout the state. Set between black lava and the sparkling blue sea. The famed third hole is situated on an ocean inlet, with the tee box on one side and the green across the long stretch of water on the other.

Mauna Lani Resort/Ritz-Carlton. Kohala Coast; 808-885-6655 or 800-845-9905. Two world-class courses here, Francis H. I'i Brown North and South

Courses, each with 18 holes and three sets of tees; par 72. Amid vast lava fields stretching to the horizon, bright ribbons of green are laid to form the courses. The 17th hole of the north course plays from an elevated tee to a green surrounded by walls of lava; it is one of the most photographed holes in Hawai'i. Balls shanked or sliced from the fairway into the sharp lava are lost forever.
Volcano Golf and Country Club. Hawai'i Volcanoes National Park; 808-967-7331. One of the world's most unusual courses in that it is located within the national park. Golf balls travel a little farther in these cool 4,000-foot uplands. Laid out amid pine and *'ohi'a* trees and ancient lava flows.
Waikoloa Village Golf Club. Kohala Coast; 808-883-9621 or 808-886-7888. Two 18-hole courses adjacent to two oceanfront hotels; the par-72 Kings' Course is favored by pros as a shot-maker. You play around, over, and sometimes into the lava—in the latter case, forget your ball; it is either gone or battered by sharp *'a'a* lava. Holes six through eight border a field of Hawaiian petroglyphs. Don't miss a glance at the clubhouse, where a 14-carat gold-plated crown sits atop the weathervane. These courses are topographical wonders, with rock formations plopped down in the middle of fairways, lakes with greens behind them, and broad views of Mauna Kea and Mauna Loa. Howling sea winds are always a challenge.

■ BIG ISLAND SPAS

Kohala Spa. Hilton Waikoloa. Waikoloa Beach Dr.; 808-885-1234. Separate saunas for men and women, steam room, cold baths, whirlpool. Massage; full beauty salon; nutrition and meditation training.
Mauna Lani Hotel Spa. 68-1400 Mauna Lani Bay Dr.; 808-885-6622. Separate saunas for men and women, steam and workout rooms. Massage and loofah scrubs. Full beauty salon. Stress-relief program features the Moor Back Treatment.
Paradise Spa. Naniloa Hotel. 93 Banyan Dr., Hilo; 808-969-3333 or 800-367-5360. Small spa beside the swimming pool. Workout room (no classes), whirlpool, cold baths, wet and dry saunas. Swedish, shiatsu, and *lomilomi* (Hawaiian) massages.

■ OUTDOOR ADVENTURES

■ BIKING

Kona Coast Cycling Tours. Waimea and Captain Cook; 808-327-1133. Kohala downhill, the old highway, coffee country, and North Kohala guided rides.

■ HIKING AND RIDING

Captain Cook Trail. Department of Land and Natural Resources; 808-961-7200. This 2.5-mile trail drops 1,400 feet from the bluffs to the spot where Captain Cook met his end, when the Hawaiians figured out he was not a god but a mere mortal. The trailside is choked with tropical fruits, and the bay at the bottom is one of the best snorkling sites on the island. The trailhead is off HI 11 in the town of Captain Cook.

Crater Rim Trail. Hawai'i Volcanoes National Park; 808-985-6000. The 11.6-mile loop trail completely encircles the Kilauea caldera, passing through stunning scenery. Maps are available from park headquarters.

Horseback Waipi'o. Waipi'o Ridge Stables; 808-775-1077. Guided Valley Rim and Hidden Waterfall rides take 3-5 hours and offer spectacular views.

Waipi'o Valley. Department of Land and Natural Resources; 808-961-7200. This is one of the holy grails of Hawaiian hiking. A strenuous three-mile trail snakes through the verdant jungle, passing tumbling waterfalls and succulent fruits free for the picking on its way to the sea. It takes about three hours to walk the looping trail back to the bottom of the uphill road; no stops.

■ SKIING

Ski Guides Hawaii. Kamuela; 808-889-6747. Skiing in Hawai'i? Yes! Between December and May, Ski Guides Hawaii rents gear and provides lifts to the top of Mauna Kea. Snowboards are available too.

■ WATER ACTIVITIES

Atlantis Adventures. Kailua-Kona; 808-329-6626. A 65-foot submarine has room and views for 48 passengers. It's great for kids, and night rides are available.

Captain Zodiac. Kailua-Kona; 808-329-3199. This outfitter offers raft expeditions on the Kona Coast and snorkeling in Kealakekua Bay and lava tubes.

Dolphin Discovery Tours. Kealakekua Bay; 808-322-8000. Guided, interpretive boat trips to swim with the dolphins in Kealakekua Bay.

Fluming Da Ditch. Hawi; 808-889-6922 or 877-449-6922. Starting above Polou

Valley, guided tours kayak down old sugar plantation irrigation ditches and flumes. This is not a white-water trip, but there is some fast water and you will get wet. **Sandwich Isle Divers.** 75-5729 Ali'i Dr., Kailua-Kona; 808-329-9188. Instruction, certification, and six-passenger diving charters are all offered. The dive shop carries a variety of rentals, including boogie boards, dive equipment, underwater cameras, and snorkel gear.

■ Festivals and Events

■ January
31-Mile Volcano to Hilo Marathon & Relay. 808-965-9191.

■ April
100K Saddle Road Relay & Ultramarathon. Hilo; 808-961-3415.
Merrie Monarch Hula Competitions. Largest hula contest in the Islands. Hilo; 808-935-9168.

■ May
Big Island Bounty Festival. Three-day showcase of regional cuisine featuring demonstrations, samplings, and wine pairings. Mauna Lani in Hilo; 808-885-2000.
Keauhou Kona Triathlon. Endurance event equal to one-half of the Ironman: 2.3-mile swim, 56-mile bike race, 13.1-mile run. Keauhou Bay, Kona; 808-329-0601.
Old Hawai'i on Horseback. An elaborate horseback pageant, races, traditional Hawaiian cowboy music, a ranching memorabilia auction, line dancing, and plenty of food. Kamuela; 808-885-9691.

■ June
King Kamehameha Statue Draping. Statues draped in long lei. King Kamehameha Celebration Commission, Kapa'au, North Kohala; 808-586-4333.
King Kamehameha Holua Ski Tournament. Dependent on availability of snow. Mauna Kea; 808-329-7787.
Waiki'i Music Festival. Celebrates Hawaiian music and culture during Father's Day weekend. Waimea; 808-885-0538.

■ July
International Festival of the Pacific. Parade, athletic tournaments, music, and dances of the multiethnic people of the Pacific. Hilo; 808-961-5797.

Orchid Society Show. Hobbyist and commercial growers present thousands of orchid varieties. Hilo; 808-961-5797.

Parker Ranch Fourth of July Rodeo & Horse Races. Paniolo Park, Kamuela; 808-885-7311.

■ **AUGUST**

Hawaiian International Billfish Tournament and Pro-Am. The oldest big game–fishing tournament in the Pacific. Pro/Am begins late July. Kailua-Kona; 808-329-6155.

■ **SEPTEMBER**

Aloha Polo Match. Waiki'i Ranch, Waimea; 808-885-0538.

Big Island International Marathon. From Pepeekeo to the old scenic route of HI 19 to Hilo Bayfront. 808-969-7400.

Hawai'i County Fair. Old-time country fair with music, food, and rides. Hilo; 808-961-5797.

Outrigger Canoe Race. On Labor Day weekend, men and women race 18 miles in six-person single- and double-hull canoes between Honaunau and Kailua. There's a torchlight parade in Kailua on the second night. Call the Waikoloa visitor's bureau, 808-886-4915.

■ **OCTOBER**

Ironman World Triathlon. 2.4-mile swim, 112-mile bike ride, and 26.2-mile marathon. Kailua-Kona; 808-329-0063.

■ **NOVEMBER**

Annual Kona Coffee Cultural Festival. A Kona coffee cupping and picking contest, parade, recipe contest, arts and crafts, ethnic foods, tours of coffee mills. Kailua-Kona; 808-326-7820.

Mauna Kea Invitational Golf Tournament. 54-hole men's and 36-hole women's tournament. South Kohala, Aloha Section PGA; 808-593-2230.

M A U I
V A L L E Y   I S L A N D

Maui is named after the prankster son of Hinaakeahi (Hina of the Fire), a demigod revered through the Pacific for his superhuman feats, including lifting the sky so people no longer had to crawl on all fours, and lengthening the day by lassoing the sun. Maui enjoyed wrapping his good deeds in trickery, and when he sought the gift of fire for mankind he employed his usual tactics. First Maui captured the mud hen, who knew the secret of fire, and told her he'd wring her neck until she told him how to make it. After he'd wrung her neck a few times, the mud hen directed him to rub sticks together, and tricky herself, she advised him to use the wrong kind of sticks. Maui kept on wringing her neck, and when at last she told him how to make fire, Maui said he had one more thing to rub. Grabbing the bird once more, Maui rubbed the top of her head with a fire stick until all the feathers fell off. To this day the Hawaiian mud hen has a bald head—and Hawaiians have the secret of making fire.

From the air, Maui the island seems to have a human shape—a head, neck, and torso floating on the blue waters of the Pacific. In fact Maui is two dormant volcanoes joined by an isthmus, and it is on this neck that you're most likely to arrive, at Kahului airport. The mountainous center of the head is cloaked in tropical rain forest, and on the torso an immense brown and green volcano, Haleakala, rises into cloud cover. Ringed by more swimming beaches than any other island, Maui's cream-colored sandy bays curve before sapphire blue and indigo waters.

Leaving the airport, the majority of visitors cross the neck of Maui, passing through agricultural flatlands. To the northeast, on the nape of Maui's neck, are the two towns Kahului and Wailuku (the county seat), where residents conduct everyday business. To the west, above Lahaina town, coffee trees carpet mountainsides in deep matte green. This is picture-postcard Maui, where coco palms line gleaming white-sand beaches, humpback whales breech and sing, and touring sailboats ply the waters of Lahaina Roads. Here, beneath the surface of seas colored pink and purple by the setting sun, bright-red and butter-yellow reef fish drift in the currents, much as do the sea birds floating on air currents of the sky. Inevitably,

Hikers take a break to gaze out on one of Maui's many valleys.

this also is where the bulk of Maui's megaresorts, condos, restaurants, and nightlife are concentrated. At Kapalua, Ka'anapali, and Lahaina, at Kihe'i, Wailea, and Makena, where Hawaiian villages once thrived, tourism now is an exploding, almost devouring force.

Yet there is another Maui, and it doesn't take long to find. Seventeen miles by road from busy Lahaina, on the highest peak of the West Maui Mountains, 400 inches of rain fall each year and waterfalls cascade down the verdant 'Iao Valley. The road up the windward northern side of Maui's torso brings you to the laid-back ambience of nineteenth-century tropical Hana. Along the way, you meet head-on the astonishing diversity of Maui, passing through lush coastal rain forest high above the turquoise sea.

At the heart of the island, clothed in brown desert at its soaring summit, Haleakala, the largest dormant volcano in the world, reaches into the clouds. Flanked on the west by "Upcountry" cattle ranches and flower farms, Haleakala's barren crater and lush eastern valleys offer a phenomenal variety of flora, fauna, and spectacular scenery.

Although there is concern about overdevelopment, tourist areas hugging the western shores stay clear, so far, of an island mass that is 75 percent wilderness. Still, old-timers worry, as tourism has replaced the once-thriving industries of sugar and cattle. Fortunately, large areas are protected in one kind of preserve or another, residents understand the fragility of tourist destinations, and the golden goose is unlikely to die of overfeeding. At its best, which is to say almost anywhere you go, Maui is a haven from modern stress, enameled with enough sophisticated glamour to delight rather than overwhelm.

■ HISTORY

Maui the demigod pulled up the island from the sea with his fishing hook. Delighted, he hauled up the other islands and claimed Maui for his own.

In the fourteenth century, high chief Pi'ilani of Hana built the largest temple on Maui—Pi'ilanihale He'iau. It still stands. He built a royal road around Maui, in itself an engineering feat, and today half the island's highways still are called Pi'ilani.

It was a time of battling kings and war canoes, as wars raged until nearly the end of the eighteenth century. Strict *kapu* (taboos) were enforced, and the penalty of

(following spread) A young couple carefully negotiates the rocks below Wailua Falls, near Kipahulu.

CANE CUTTER'S JOURNEY

In the early 1900s, Hawaiian sugar companies posted handbills in Spanish, Portuguese, and Italian towns near Mediterranean ports, advertising for sugarcane workers. In exchange for working a certain number of years for very low wages, they would receive free passage to Hawai'i and the New World. This account was written in 1992 by a California attorney, Manuel Abascal.

My mother's family knew of the opportunity because my grandmother was able to read and write, a rare ability for a woman at that time. In Spain, schools admitted only boys. However, my great-grandmother, a truly wise woman, had traded the only teacher in town, "El Professor," all the goat milk his family could ever use in exchange for teaching her daughter. So, in 1911, when my mother was five years old, her family decided to make the journey to Hawai'i. They walked for many days along the beach, from Malaga to Gibraltar, carrying all of their belongings. They were not too sad to leave the soil they had tilled for landowners.

Everyone on the ship was filled with hope for a better life even though they traveled in cramped, squalid quarters, headed for soil to till for others. Whenever my mother recounted the journey she became sad that she saw many people take ill not long after it began. Some suffered from frailty and the strain of the voyage, others from a measles epidemic for which there was nothing, not so much as an aspirin, to ease the pain. My mother and her three-year-old sister were kept under their mother's long petticoats for most of the trip, in hopes that they would offer protection from the epidemic. It worked. Those large ships came to be known as "coffin boats," although the travelers that perished were buried at sea.

The moment everyone, including the brave young ones, most feared was not the discovery that one or another malady was "in their cards." Rather, it was that moment when their very large ship suddenly seemed to become so very small in the raging seas of Cape Horn at the tip of South America. Everyone on board prayed like they never had before. Once they passed Cape Horn, my mother remembered smooth sailing to the Islands.

After they landed in Lahaina, Maui, families from the same country who had come at different times were grouped together, because of common language and culture, as well as for the convenience of the landowners in organizing work crews. There were different villages for the Italians, Portuguese, and Spanish who had shared the same large ship and different villages for the Chinese and Japanese. Not far away were the villages of the native Hawaiians.

The house assigned to my mother's family is still standing, one of several which have been preserved in Lahaina. In the back is the earthen oven that she, her younger sister, and many other children from their camp anxiously watched as her grandmother baked the bread for the family and the treats for little ones. It was also in the backyard that my mother's lifelong appetite for fruit was born. Every fruit she ever ate started her talking about how good it was as a child on Maui, when she quenched her thirst with mangos, papayas, and pineapples.

The work was very hard. The people got along. For the first time for each of them, there was not only hard work, but also housing, enough food, even a doctor to see if need be. There was a school not far from the work camps, one tiny room under a huge tree. Both the school and the tree are still standing. Such close living conditions brought the mutual understanding that everyone should cooperate. There was competition between the best workers, but not to discourage one another.

Sundays were the days they did not have to work, and the villages became crowded by all of the adults who were in the fields during the week. Young men courted blossoming women, my mother's elder sisters among them. They were watched very closely, not only by their mother's stern eyes, but also by the children who were trying to understand. Getting away meant a walk, followed by others. Sundays also meant that many people came to my grandmother's house to have their letters written, or to have read what was written to them.

The hard work, long hours, and low pay did not make life in Maui worse than the life they had left behind. None of the adults regretted the decision to till the soil on Maui rather than till the soil of the Old Country. All the children attended school, boys and girls together.

---

death fell on any commoner unfortunate enough to cast his shadow on the king. The last ruling chief of Maui was Kahekili, lifelong enemy of Kamehameha the Great (and probably his father). Ruthless and powerful, in the 1780s Kahekili brought O'ahu and Moloka'i under his rule.

While Kahekili was on O'ahu in 1790, Kamehameha sailed a fleet of double war canoes to attack Maui. Making use of a cannon acquired from a British ship, and the mastery of two British seamen, John Young and Isaac Davis, Kamehameha massacred Kahekili's forces at 'Iao Valley. Returning to confront battles on his home island of Hawai'i, Kamehameha fought on-again, off-again battles for Maui that continued for another three years. In 1793 Kahekili died on Oʻahu and his realm was divided. In a masterstroke of strategy, Kamehameha landed a fleet of war canoes at Lahaina and brought Maui under his rule in 1795. About 1800 he transferred the royal court to Lahaina, a favored residence of Maui chiefs, and made it his capital.

Two very different forces originating in New England arrived on Maui soon after Kamehameha's death and the demise of the *kapu* system on the Big Island in 1819. (*See* "History" in the Hawaiʻi chapter.) By this time, European ships had reported whales in the Pacific, and as whales in the Atlantic were nearly depleted, hundreds of ships headed around Cape Horn and into the then little-known Pacific Ocean. Many of them dropped anchor in the little port of Lahaina on the northwest shore. At the same time that rowdy whalers arrived, another group of New Englanders disembarked: Protestant missionaries—a moral bunch eager to mend the Hawaiians' sensual ways. They wanted to protect the Hawaiians from themselves, and from the whalers who were infecting Hawaiians with syphilis, precipitating a radical decline in fertility.

Missionary strictures destroyed a way of life. After Chief Hoapili, governor of Maui, was converted to Christianity, new laws were instituted against drinking and womanizing, engulfing the capital in dissent. Whalemen rioted and missionaries sermonized. Native Hawaiians found their traditional way of life threatened by opposing forces from New England.

King Kamehameha III grew to manhood under the influence of missionaries, and to their dismay he was fond of drinking, gambling, and carousing with women. Reared under the regency of Queen Kaʻahumanu, when he took the throne at age 18 Kamehameha III declared guerrilla war on Christian morality. The king and his clique opened the first sally by drinking 32 barrels of liquor in a single week, and urged a return to the hula, surfing, gambling, and racing. Big, vibrant Hawaiian women, who traditionally had surfed and taken lovers, found few attractions in following the example set by the missionary wives, and many thought Kamehameha III was on the right track. Schools and churches emptied.

The king and his sister Princess Nahiʻenaʻena presented the missionaries with a dilemma. Reared in the old ways, in which it was normal practice, if not a duty, for a royal brother and sister to marry in order to produce a high-caste heir, they were forbidden by the Christians from doing so. The king's sister, struggling between a lifelong love for her brother and her adopted Christian conscience, lived a double life, marrying a prince from the Big Island while continuing to sleep with her brother. In 1836 Nahi'ena'ena gave birth to a son who died within hours, and she herself died a few months later. Chastened, Kamehameha III conceded defeat, shut down his distilleries, and turned to kingly duties.

By mid-century, Lahaina was the whaling capital of the Pacific. In 1846 nearly 400 whalers laid anchor at the little seaport and brought prosperity to Maui. By the 1860s, as whale oil was being replaced by petroleum, fewer and fewer whaling ships were dropping anchor in Lahaina, and it reverted to a sleepy town.

Sugarcane, first planted at Haiku in 1870, began to flourish after 1876, when an irrigation ditch was dug to channel water onto the dry, central Wailuku plains. As the neck of Maui turned green with fields of cane, sugar led Maui's economy until tourism blossomed at Ka'anapali in the 1960s. Today, as more than 2 million visitors a year flock to Maui, both locals and the more responsible developers struggle to preserve Maui's beauty.

■ CENTRAL MAUI

A narrow, flat neck joins Maui's mountainous head and torso. Kahului and Wailuku hug the north shores and slopes at the nape of Maui's neck, at Maui's center. Serving as the island's urban center, the twin towns are good spots for local-style plate lunches or *saimin* (noodle soup). The Maui Arts & Cultural Center in Kahului is a magnet for international music and dance performances (808-242-7469).

■ KAHULUI ATTRACTIONS *map page 109, B/C-2*

Kahului Airport
During World War II, the U.S. Navy built the Air Station Kahului to serve as a supply and maintenance depot for the Pacific fleet. Today it is the site of the airport—and for some visitors not much more than a place to alight before rushing off to east or west.

Kanaha Beach Park
A part of the Navy area included a park with a mile of sandy beach. Now called Kanaha Beach Park, it offers white sands separated by rock groins built to reduce erosion. The bottom is shallow, and it's the best place in the two-town area for swimming. Although the waters are smoke-colored, the Kahului shore is the epicenter for kite-boarding (also called kite-surfing), the hottest new water sport.

The beauty of Hawai'i shines in the faces of young boys in Wailuku.

Developed here as a blend of surfing, wakeboarding, and parasailing, kite-boarding involves a sail of light fabric that harnesses the wind for soaring aerial maneuvers. To the chagrin of diehard sailboarders, the older sport of bulky gear is being abandoned to lightweight kiting. Dirt roads used by shore fishermen cross the park; Kanaha Beach has picnic facilities. *Behind the airport; take Keolani Road.*

Kanaha Pond Wildlife Refuge

Hawaiian stilts and gallinules breed and wintering birds fly in from Alaska. You can watch the pond's birdlife from an observation pavilion at the junction of HI 36 and HI 380, where there's a parking lot. In 1971 the refuge was registered as a National Natural History Landmark. *Inland from the west end of Kanaha Beach Park.*

Alexander & Baldwin Sugar Museum

The museum takes its name from the sugar company founded by Samuel Alexander and Henry Baldwin in 1869. The former plantation manager's home, built in 1902, is filled with period artifacts and exhibits that describe the history of sugar on Maui—including Alexander & Baldwin's battles with Claus Spreckels, the so-called king of sugar, over water development for the irrigation of cane fields. There are old photographs of immigrant Japanese laborers, and a typical contract: $15 a month for 10-hour work days, 26 days a month, $2.50 banked toward return passage. The planters were innovative, constantly experimenting with new methods of growing, harvesting, and milling the cane. On the museum grounds you can watch a working scale model of a cane-crushing plant. *Near the intersection of Pu'unene Avenue and Hansen Road; 808-871-8058.*

■ **WAILUKU** *map page 109, B-2*
The county seat of Wailuku, with its hilly streets and easygoing atmosphere, is coming out of a long slumber. With new cafés and boutiques, galleries, and cultural festivals, it is undergoing a revitalization. Mingling old and new, the old plantation town is developing into one of Maui's hippest places.

Bailey House Museum
In the foothills of Wailuku, overlooking the harbor, a missionary complex is laid out in tartuffian splendor: Bailey House Museum, standing on land given to the American Board of Commissioners for Foreign Missions by King Kamehameha III and the governor of Maui. Built in 1840 and maintained by the Maui Historical Society, it was the home of Edward and Caroline Bailey for 45 years. The house is stuffed with quilts, dolls, and china that came out of Boston and around Cape Horn to the Islands, and its Hawaiian collection is a little treasure. On display are stone and shell implements; *kapa* cloth; wood, feather, and bone pieces; gourds; and a hand-hewn *koa*-wood canoe. Outside on the grounds lie vestiges of an ancient Hawaiian irrigation system used for taro, and growing among rare plants are some of the original varieties of Hawaiian sugar cane. *'Iao Valley Road, one block from the intersection of High and West Main streets; 808-244-3326.*

■ **'IAO VALLEY STATE PARK** *map page 109, B-2*
Driving south from Wailuku town you're on flat terrain, the flanks of the west Maui mountains to your right. These hills are the remains of a volcano that spewed up the head of Maui and once towered some 7,000 feet above the sea. Now eroded down to 5,788 feet, the diminished summit, Pu'u Kukui, is deluged each year with some 400 inches of rain, making it the second wettest spot in the island chain. Radiating from the summit, remote, untamed, and inaccessible gorges rip open the mountainside. **'Iao (Cloud Supreme) Valley** is the best known—and the only one

where visitors may drive up to its mouth. The turnoff is seven miles west of Wailuku—take 'Iao Valley Road (West Main Street, or HI 320). From the parking lot, where there's a new nature center, a well-traveled trail with innumerable steps climbs a loop that opens onto glorious views of the valley. Cloud streams waft through 'Iao, alternately obscuring and revealing misted, steep canyon walls. Punctuating the valley and towering like a stele is **'Iao Needle,** a 2,250-foot green-carpeted cinder cone.

It was here in 1790 that Kalanikupule, son of Kamehameha's archenemy the ruthless Maui King Kahekili, sought to stem the tide of the Warrior King's onslaught. At this battle Kamehameha brought over to Maui a weapon new to Hawai'i, a *haole* (foreign) cannon. Kalanikupule put up a fight but was forced, along with his chiefs, to flee through a mountain pass. Victors chased vanquished warriors scrambling up the steep valley walls, and bodies fell mangled into the bloodied waters of 'Iao stream until pyramids of the slaughtered dammed the flow.

Kepaniwai (Damming of the Waters) gives its name to the **Kepaniwai Heritage Gardens,** in 'Iao Valley State Park. Here, a Hawaiian grass shack, a missionary salt-box house, a Japanese tea house, and a Chinese pagoda stand amid manicured gardens honoring Hawai'i's multicultural past. *'Iao Valley State Park, follow Route 320 west from central Wailuku; 808-984-8109.*

■ WEST MAUI

Across the 14-mile neck, three highways link east Maui to west Maui's famous beaches and hotels. The finest beaches for swimming or sunbathing are along the 18-mile stretch from Olowalu to Kapalua. At the south end of the neck, Honoa Pi'ilani Highway (HI 30) splits north and south. To the north it follows the face of Maui through Lahaina, Ka'anapali, and Napili along the west coast. The road continues around the crown of the head in a narrow, single-lane paved surface. Frequent passing shoulders are located on this curving mountain road and four-wheel-drive vehicles are recommended.

■ MA'ALAEA *map page 109, B-3*

Ma'alaea Bay is a major wintering spot for humpback whales, and a prime place to watch them calve, breech, and spout in somewhat shallow waters. After summering in Alaska, more than half of all humpbacks travel down the Hawaiian island chain to spend the winter in waters between west Maui and Lana'i. As they are sensitive to noise, the whales stay farther out to sea off Lahaina and Kaʻanapali. Fortunately, jet-skiing is off-limits in winter, and you may see more than one bumper sticker proclaiming "Save the Whales—Harpoon a Jet Ski."

As awareness of the vital need to protect ocean environments grew, the **Hawaiian Islands Humpback Whale National Marine Sanctuary** expanded in 1998 to include waters around all the major islands, and the sanctuary headquarters are located in Maʻalaea. It is one of only 12 national marine sanctuaries strewn across the Atlantic and Pacific, from Samoa to Cape Cod. The **Education Center** has interesting displays and offers whale-watching from October to April. *726 S. Kihei Road, Kihei; 808-879-2818.*

The **Maui Ocean Center** at Maʻalaea Harbor Village features a "walk through" aquarium, where visitors stroll through an acrylic tunnel in the center of a 750,000-gallon tank for face-to-fin views of spotted eagle rays, tiger sharks, blue-green mahimahi, and myriad other indigenous sea life. There's a touch pool for the kids and excellent exhibits that entertainingly describe some unusual mating habits and defense mechanisms of local marine life, as well as a wonderful explanation of certain sea creatures in Hawaiian mythology. *Enter from Route 30, Maʻalaea; 808-270-7000.*

Visitors walk with the fish at the Maui Ocean Center.

Facing a complex of restaurants and shops, **Ma'alaea Harbor** is the boarding point for boat trips out into the 'Au'au Channel for snorkeling at Molokini Island and Turtle Arches, where protected green sea turtles cavort amid scenic lava formations. While snorkeling you may hear ringing in your ears; probably it's a couple of humpback whales singing somewhere in the area.

■ LAHAINA *map page 109, A-2*
No other town in the islands preserves the nautical flavor of a mid-nineteenth-century Hawaiian seaport so well as does Lahaina—in fact, the entire town has been declared a National Historic Landmark. The refurbished and energetic little seaport retains much of its lusty whaling past in a tourist mode. Along Front Street, the main artery facing the harbor, old wooden buildings lean over the water, their ships' chandleries and grog shops metamorphosed into clothing, gift, and jewelry boutiques. Interspersed are T-shirt shops and a fistful of art galleries heavy on the marine theme. (You may not want to see another breeching whale on canvas for the next 20 years.) Resident artists attend the galleries on Friday nights.

Adventurous visitors will find a panoply of appealing trips offered by tour companies lining the harbor front. On-the-spot temptations include parasailing,

Boaters dock at Lahaina, an energetic seaport with a whaling past.

rain forest hikes, undersea viewing trips, day tours to Lana'i, bike rides, helicopter tours, dinner cruises, golf, sport fishing, or a ride on a little steam train. From December until April, whale-watching excursions sail from the harbor. In Lahaina, you can walk around dressed in shorts and a T-shirt, gobbling fast food, or go out in elegant garb for champagne dining. Nightlife in the little town dances to a fast beat.

All day long Lahaina manages to bustle and relax at the same time. Yet somehow its old charm percolates through. The time to find it is in the early morning—before mobs of sightseers and traffic clog the narrow streets. In the cool hours following dawn, the few people seen walking may actually be residents. To sense the "charming, drowsy, and dreamy village" Charles Warren Stoddard found in 1885, stop beside the sea wall at Front Street. Harbor waters are clear and calm, the air free of diesel bus fumes, and fishermen are out on the breakwater. Bring along a copy of the free booklet *Lahaina: A Walking Tour of Historic and Cultural Sites,* published by the Maui County Historic Commission; old sites in a concentrated area centering along and near Front Street are marked on a small map. The sites are woven through a Lahaina teeming with activity.

■ LAHAINA'S FRONT STREET

Front Street, the main street of Lahaina, follows the shoreline. A good walking tour begins at the south-central end of town.

Stuck in Irons House.

Two blocks *mauka* (inland) from Front Street, at the intersection of Prison and Wainee streets, stands Hale Pa'ahao, the Stuck in Irons House. Built in 1852, Lahaina's old wooden prison housed Hawaiian inmates who broke missionary moral code, and brawling whalemen who broke the Sabbath, drank, swore, and bolted down Front Street racing horses. The building was restored in 1988, using guidelines from old photographs. Plaques describe prison life; one is taken from the journal of a visitor in 1855: "10 dozen kanakas, male and female, all had the freedom of the prison yard and mingled promiscuously with each other." *Prison and Wainee streets; 808-661-3262.*

Baldwin House Museum.

One block north of Prison Street is the two-story, white-washed Baldwin House Museum. Built of coral block between 1834 and 1835 and restored in exacting detail, the oldest standing building in Lahaina was originally the home of Reverend Dwight Baldwin, and is full of New England items as well as Hawaiian artifacts. A

Dedicated to Hawai'i's first Japanese immigrants, this huge Buddha in Lahaina looks out to sea toward Japan.

Harvard-trained physician, Baldwin is credited with curbing a smallpox epidemic in 1853—a disease brought to Hawai'i by westerners. Opening their home to Hawaiian nobility and influential guests, the Baldwins lived in the house from 1836 until 1868. The prime land of the house is the seed that grew into the extensive holdings of Maui's H. P. Baldwin Estate. *696 Front Street; 808-661-3262.*

The bookstore next door retains something of the building's original purpose. It was the **Masters' and Mates' Reading Room,** a rudimentary library and quiet lair where ships' officers wrote letters. The second floor houses research materials and offices of the Lahaina Restoration Foundation, the town's guiding beacon.

Pioneer Inn

Across the street, on the waterfront, you'll find the heart of old Lahaina—the old, two-story Pioneer Inn. Built in Victorian style in 1901, with verandas railed in lacy woodwork facing the sea, it still accepts guests in a newer annex and in the old green-and-white-painted frame building. Eating breakfast on its lanai looking out onto the harbor is a tradition among locals. In the adjacent bars the nightly din might call to mind a whaling crew embroiled in a drinking bout. *658 Wharf Street; 800-457-5457.*

At the south side of the hotel, **the largest banyan tree in the U.S.** sprawls across the courthouse square. Planted in 1873, its rooted aerial vines are so huge that the tree provides enough shade for more than 500 people.

Hauola Stone

On the north side of the hotel and *makai* (seaward), ruins of Hale Piula, the unfinished royal residence of Kamehameha III, face the Hauola Stone. Large and flat, it is an ancient Hawaiian stone of healing. A Hawai'i Visitors Bureau signpost marks the spot in the breakwater.

Lahaina Heritage Museum

This new attraction offers three hands-on exhibits each year. Such themes as canoes, the royal family, and pineapple plantation life are covered. *648 Wharf Street; 808-661-1959.*

Buddha

As you walk north on Front Street, the coastline veers seaward at the north end of town. Here the jutland is landscaped in greenery surrounding the largest Japanese Buddha statue outside Japan. It was dedicated by the Jodo Mission to Hawai'i's first Japanese immigrants; its bronze face looks out to sea, toward Japan.

■ **KA'ANAPALI** *map page 109, A-1*

Five miles north of Lahaina is Ka'anapali Bay, where a long curve of wide, white sand faces deep, radiant blue seas, and swimmers can see down to the bottom 30 feet below the surface. Soon after statehood in 1959, a single low-rise hotel and golf course arose before the bay—the Royal Lahaina Resort, which still rests regally amid lawn-covered knolls. Separating the bay into halves is a volcanic spatter cone, **Pu'u Keka'a** (Rumbling Hill), also known as Black Rock, said to represent the vanquished form of a demigod who taunted Maui. Not long after the Royal Lahaina was built, another hotel, the Sheraton, put down roots here. It was a unique structure then—its lobby is on the top floor, and the building cascades down the cliff. These two hotels, forerunners of the Ka'anapali complex, maintain a measure of calm in the eddying swirl of resort tourism.

At the southern end of this bay is the Ka'anapali complex. Some 30 years ago American Factors, an old sugar company in search of diversification, changed its name to Amfac and pioneered "master-planned tourism" on still out-of-the-way Maui. Along three miles of beach extending south of the bay toward Lahaina is a mega-complex of gleaming, manicured hotels, golf courses, and a shopping village named Whalers. A free shuttle service to Lahaina runs all day and most of the night.

Side-by-side high-rises line the shore of the Ka'anapali complex. At this section of shoreline, swimming is dangerous; the reef is near, the sands narrow, and the waters turbulent. Stroll along the paved beachside path fronting the resorts.

■ **NAPILI BAY AND KAPALUA** *map page 109, A-1*

HI 30 and the Lower Honoa Pi'ilani shore road run up the coast. The lower road slides past a miles-long string of moderately priced hotels and condominiums following a shore of nonstop beaches, some of them projecting right into a reef. The **Napili Bay** beach of white sands, crowded with tenants from the chock-a-block condos looping the cove, has good swimming and snorkeling. The benign surf makes it a good place for beginning surfers.

Snorkelers drift over warm turquoise waters along this strip, looking down onto a magical kingdom of coral heads and reef. Mushroom corals loll on the white sand bottom. The three-inch brighteye damselfish swims here. Colored golden-olive, the damselfish likes surge areas where it can make a home in the holes and cracks of the reef. Slightly larger and found only in Hawai'i, tight clouds of white-spotted damsels with snub faces and bright white dominoes on their black bodies swim over coral

The white-sand beaches of Ka'anapali Bay front the Royal Lahaina Resort.

fingerheads. Here are Hawaiian surgeonfish *(palani),* with golden fins and gold-blue tails. You wouldn't want to sniff this beauty out of the water—it's smelly, because, we are told, a goddess being ferried by the fish lost control and urinated on it.

Kapalua Bay, the next cove north, is a beach much like Napili, minus the mob. With white-white sands, fine and soft, the crescent-shaped pocket of Kapalua is protected by rocky side-croppings that subdue the blue-green waves. Sparkling in the northwest curve of the island, the tasteful complex of the Kapalua Bay Hotel & Ocean Villas resort is a golfers' paradise, with a championship course and international tournaments, fashionable shops, and elegant surroundings. Originally developed by a subsidiary of Maui Land & Pineapple, it sits in pleasant contrast to the uninspired condos of the Napili stretch.

Immediately north of Kapalua is **D. T. Fleming Beach Park** at Honokahua Bay, a broad strip of white sand backed by an undulating lawn and dappled with palm and ironwood trees. Picnic here and swim in the summertime. In the winter, when waters roil and turn furious, swim instead at **Oneloa Beach** a fraction of a mile south, where one end of the slight cove is protected. Few find this lovely little sand patch rimmed by sea cliffs; the path down to Oneloa is short and steep.

■ **KAHAKULOA COAST** *map page 109, B-1/2*
Past Oneloa, curving northeasterly around the top of the island, the Maui coastline leaps and turns like tight curling hair. This "women's head" is unknown Maui country; go slowly. Passing grassy meadows, the road is potholed and isolated, with stunning ocean views. Stop at the art galleries in tiny **Kahakuloa village.** Surfers' havens slice the shore. Down steep cliff paths to secluded Honolua Bay lies Pohakupule (Prayer Rock) Beach, also known as Windmill or Punalau Beach. Experienced surfers gather here when enormous winter swells are running, but the beach is not recommended for swimming.

Beyond, the road (HI 30) becomes a winding, extremely narrow paved track (four-wheel-drive vehicles recommended), making a loop around west Maui to Kahekili Highway and Wailuku at the neck of the island.

■ **EAST MAUI**

Dominating the torso shape of east Maui is Haleakala Volcano. HI 360 (better known as the Hana Highway) twists up the northern (windward) shore and follows the island contour to the eastern slopes. Here lie Hana and the lush, rain-forested southeast coast. The western slopes rise from the neck of Maui into Upcountry ranchlands and, higher up, the misted summit. To the southwest, the coast of the torso is lined with beaches and resorts.

From the throat of Maui at Ma'alaea Bay, Pi'ilani Highway (HI 31) takes you to the southwest shores, where one beach park after another faces the sea. These beaches are most enjoyable before the daily wind rises at noon.

■ **KIHE'I AND WAILEA BEACHES** *map page 109, C-3*
At the ancient fishing village that grew into the little town of **Kihe'i,** the beaches run for miles in an unbroken line, a jogger's paradise. Small hotel-condos ranging from luxury to budget cluster near the stretch of open, flat sands. Shopping complexes rise in the burgeoning town. Three beach parks south of Kihe'i at Kama'ole are excellent swimming strands.

Farther south, the megaresort at **Wailea** fronts a mile-and-a-half strand of white-sand crescents and good swimming. Nearly a billion dollars have been spent at the 1,500-acre resort, where once there was only space and *kiawe* scrub. Now Wailea's upscale shops complement a total of five hotels and four condominium villages, each offering from 250 to 550 rooms, suites, or villas. Designers have gone for the Greek. The hotels neither look nor feel Hawaiian, and the only Hawaiians you'll meet are on hotel staffs. Yet the hotels *are* basking in Maui sunshine, and the trade winds are kind to the skin—no desert dryness here. Take a saunter on the 1.5-mile paved beachside walkway from Wailea Beach Resort south to Polo Beach.

Winter whale-watching, good from vantage points down the length of the leeward shore, is a special treat off the Wailea beaches. Sometimes, just 100 yards from shore, a 40-foot humpback may be seen breeching in the ocean, perhaps with a newborn beside it. Often an entire family group, or pod, can be seen spouting farther out to sea.

Four miles south of Wailea, approaching the end of the paved road, is **Makena Beach State Park**, where the Maui Prince resort sprawls behind two beaches. Lumped together and often called simply Makena Beach, Little Beach and Big Beach are considered by many to be the most beautiful on Maui.

Little Beach, or Pu'u Ola'i (Earthquake Hill), lies in a little cove at the tip of a cinder cone bulging the shoreline out into the ocean south of Makena Bay. Swim here in lucid turquoise waters lapping over a sandy shallow bottom. Body and board surfers come for the gently breaking waves, and snorkeling is excellent around the point to the south. A popular spot, Little Beach also is known as a nudist sanctuary—its enthusiasts mildly alert to punishment by law, or sun.

Big Beach lies directly south of Little Beach. (The proper name of Oneloa [Long Sand] is seldom used because the name is the same as the beach in the northwest.) No development is visible from the long half-moon of smooth white sand, nearly hidden from the road by *kiawe* trees. Green sea turtles laid their eggs in the sands here until the turn of the twentieth century. Big Beach really is big— more than 100 feet wide and half a mile long, all of it open to the ocean with a steep drop-off and heavy waves. If the pounding surf doesn't keep you awake, this makes a good place to camp.

You can drive down to a paved parking lot at the beaches. Turn at the highway sign marked "Shoreline Access No. 101," less than a mile past the intersection of Makena Alanui and Makena roads. Or park off the highway and walk through the trees to the beach. The two beaches are linked by a foot trail. There are no lifeguards.

Beyond the paved road, off a dirt track at the point of land where the island curves south, is a deep bay named for Comte de La Perouse, the French navigator

(following spread) Visitors walk through a lava tube to reach this beach at Wai'anapanapa park.

who dropped anchor in its calm waters in 1786. La Perouse, who had come to verify Cook's findings on behalf of the French crown, took in a landing party and became the first westerner to step ashore on Maui. Two years after his visit to Maui, La Perouse visited Australia and was never heard from again. The sunken wrecks of his two ships were discovered off the Solomon Islands 40 years later. Commemorating La Perouse today is an imposing, eight-foot-tall stonework standing on arid lava at the end of the paved road. The monument was unveiled by the navigator's great-great-grandnephew, Philippe de La Perouse, in 1994.

■ **HANA HIGHWAY** *map page 109, C to F-2/3*
To reach the wild north shore of east Maui's torso, take HI 36, the Hana Highway (also known as HI 360). Depart from Kahului before 8 A.M. to elude tour traffic. Following the north shore, the 52-mile road is a rising, dipping, slithering mass of 600 curves through jungle-clad cliffs, past plunging waterfalls, and over 54 bridges. This smooth, paved road to Hana is sometimes called the "narrow escape to paradise." It's a half-day trip if you allow no stops, and that's hard to do—this is one of the most scenic drives in the state. (Start with a full gasoline tank; there are no service stations.) You'll want to stop (lock your car) for picnicking, and for breathtaking views of white-foamed shorelines and of jungled valleys backed with misty cascades, and cold, clear pools. Guavas, mountain apples, passion fruit, and red and fragrant yellow ginger thickets frame the road. You can buy a cassette tape to play in your car while traveling this road. (Stop at the Shell Service Station in Kahului on HI 380 before it joins HI 36; 808-572-0550.) A 50-mile section of the Hana Highway—from Pa'uwela to Kaupo—is listed in the federal directory of Millennium Legacy Trails.

Curving past valleys enclosing old vine-draped villages, the road offers constantly changing views. At the halfway mark, the road descends near Ke'anae (Mullet) Point and offers a glimpse of an old Hawai'i when life centered on the sea and soil. Coco palms border wet taro patches behind bungalows. The flatland lies before a rocky shore.

■ **WAI'ANAPANAPA STATE PARK** *map page 109, F-3*
About three miles before Hana the road rises slightly at east Maui's finest treasure, Wai'anapanapa (Glistening Water) State Park. A short walk leads to a lava tube,

which you can walk straight through to the waters of a black-sand beach. The heavy surf is only for powerful swimmers and scuba divers—who think they've reached Nirvana, swimming through lava arches and underwater to a cave believed to be a place where lovers once met secretly. *Hana Highway, near mile marker 32; 808-984-8109.*

■ **KAHANU GARDEN AND PI'ILANIHALE HE'IAU** *map page 109, F-3*
On the outskirts of Hana, just west of Wai'anapanapa State Park, lies the **Kahanu Garden,** one of several gardens run by the National Tropical Botanical Garden (headquartered on Kaua'i). The garden features plants that have significance to Hawaiian and Polynesian cultures, including the world's largest collection of breadfruit. On the grounds of the garden is **Pi'ilanihale** (House of Pi'ilani) **He'iau,** Hawai'i's largest temple, built about A.D. 1400. Pi'ilani, a famed Maui chief who managed to wield power for an unprecedented 40 years, built the terraced stone platform giant-size, 415 feet long by 340 feet wide. Today visitors who stand beside a cliff overlooking a vertical plunge to foaming shoreline often sense otherworldly forces here, the powerful presence of ancient gods eternally inhabiting sacred ground. *Off Hana Highway, at mile marker 31; 808-248-8912.*

■ **HANA** *map page 109, F-3*
Until the road from Kahului was completed, Hana, at the extreme east end of Maui, remained isolated from the rest of the island. It remains a quiet place where the sounds heard are those of soft wind, of seas crashing or lapping ashore, and the chirps and drips of the rain forest. Frequent rains pelt rich agricultural lands, and rolling hills are verdant pastures. Only about 10 people per square mile call Hana home, and of those more than half claim descent from native Hawaiians. Heavenly Hana, as it's known, is in a world apart from the resorts of west Maui. Clinging to the foot of the volcano's eastern slopes that slide gracefully down to the deep curve of Hana Bay, Hana is a pretty ranch town swathed in pandanus and banana trees. Frame homes are set amid flowering trees clustered in small lanes.

Activities around Hana are oriented to the outdoors. You don't have to be a guest at the town's small inns or hotel to arrange horseback riding at sunrise or sunset, picnics, swimming, and hiking excursions. If you do stay at the luxurious bungalow hotel called Hana-Maui, bring a hefty wallet.

Hugging Maui's north coast, the Hana Highway is sometimes called the "narrow escape to paradise."

Hana Cultural Center and Museum

Hana's museum exhibits an astounding variety of Hawaiian brooms made from coconut fibers, as well as war clubs, carved stone idols, *kapa,* and quilts. The old courthouse, other historic buildings, and some ethno-botanical gardens are now owned by the museum. *Ukea Street; 808-248-8622.*

Hana Beach Park

At the foot of town, calm waters lap at the sandy shore in the broad, deep curve of Hana Bay. Hana Beach Park lies at the southern end. The beach has an older name—Kapueokahi, "the Single Owl." A *kupua,* or ghostly being, he was capable of changing himself from owl to man. The brown-sand beach, formed from eroded cinders, is 700 feet long and 100 feet wide, with gently sloping sands at the water's edge. When heavy surf pounds the coast, this is the safest beach for swimming and snorkeling in the Hana district. (Stay inside the bay. Outside, currents flow out to sea.) The park facilities are popular, and local residents often gather here for impromptu music-making.

Hana Bay

Hana Bay claims an illustrious history, and a bloody one. Since the bay was remote, chiefs from Hawai'i gathered fleets of double-hulled war canoes here to assault Maui, and in 1802 when Kamehameha landed, it is believed he dedicated several *he'iau* to Kuka'ilimoku, the war god whose sacred idol was entrusted to his guardianship. Because King Kamehameha the Great succeeded in uniting the islands, he was the last chief to take strategic advantage of Hana Bay.

Ka'uiki Head

Marking the south end of the bay, Ka'uiki Head is a 386-foot eroded cinder cone. Legend tells us that Ka'uiki, a gift from the *menehune,* fell in love with Noenoe, daughter of the demigod Maui, who forbade their union. The two lovers defied him. Enraged, Maui turned Ka'uiki into a hill and Noenoe into the mist caressing it each day. The cone-hill once held a cave—the birthplace of Queen Ka'ahumanu in about 1773. Kamehameha first saw her near Hana when she was seven years old. She grew to be six feet tall and imperially beautiful, an ardent surfer and swimmer. A lover of battles, she was also partial to intrigue, and to men. When she was 16, she was married to Kamehameha and became his favorite wife. On the east side of Ka'uiki Head, **Red Sand Beach** (Kaihalulu, or "Roaring Sea Beach") is a pocket of red-cinder sand facing a deep rough-swimming cove. Nestled beneath high sea cliffs, it is the only red beach in the islands, and one of the few in the world. The trail begins near Hotel Hana-Maui's Sea Ranch cottages; tread carefully on the loose cinders. There are no lifeguards.

■ BEYOND HANA

Hana Highway, at this point Route 31, curves southwest around the east flank of Maui to its end at Kipahulu on the south coast. Along the way, overlooked beaches appear to crouch beneath cliffs and can be reached only by risky sea-cliff trails where loose volcanic cinder material breaks free. These eroded cinder beaches face roaring seas, and their red, brown, black, and white colors fill up half a rainbow.

Pools of 'Ohe'o *map page 109, F-4*

Near the road's end are the Pools of 'Ohe'o, where 'Ohe'o Stream plummets into 22 clear and icy pools. Bounding down the southern slopes of Haleakala volcano like a liquid stairway, the stream carves its way through lush greenery into a wide mouth and roiling sea. While slippery boulders require caution, swimmers find the pools hard to resist. A hiking trail into the jungle starts at the parking lot.

Haleakala Rain Forest *map page 109, E/F-3*
High above the 'Ohe'o Stream the Haleakala Rain Forest is a biological treasure, a realm populated with strange creatures found nowhere else—fish that climb 200-foot waterfalls, flightless moths, carnivorous caterpillars, and giant picture-wing fruit flies. Between the Haleakala crater and the rain forest, bogs support miniature bonsai-like *'ohi'a* trees, and floral sprays three feet across sprout from native lobelias. Unfortunately, the forest is inaccessible and officially closed to visitors; however, near this northeast corner of Haleakala National Park is the Nature Conservancy's **Waikamoi Preserve** (808-587-6220), an area that has been virtually untouched for 2,000 years. You can join small groups on walking tours into the gnarled, loamy forest.

Lindbergh Country *map page 109, F-4*
The tiny green village of **Kipahulu,** on the southern foot of Haleakala, is where the famed aviator Charles A. Lindbergh (1902–1974) lived out his last years. In 2003 his cottage was moved one mile to a site within Haleakala National Park, where it rests beside the Kipahulu Visitor Center (808-248-7375). In the village, **Palapala Ho'omau Congregational Church** stands in lava rock on a headland above the sea. The church was restored by Lindbergh and now watches over his grave, which is covered with smooth beach stones.

The Pools of 'Ohe'o and Kipahulu mark the southern boundary of Haleakala National Park. Beyond here the Hana Road dissolves into a bumpy potholed dirt track that crosses the southern limits of Kaupo Gap, an abruptly arid lava zone. Car-rental companies do not allow their vehicles to be driven through this area, so to reach the southwest coast, or the Upcountry slopes and the volcano summit, visitors must backtrack to Kahului.

■ UPCOUNTRY MAUI

The heartland of the island's torso is Upcountry Maui, where artists come to live and paint, where sweet Kula onion, potato, lavender, and flower farms pattern the hills, and where horses trot in pastel green meadows. No one remembers who coined the label "Upcountry." However it happened, it is *up,* up into the grassy mountainous waistband that girds the central slopes of Haleakala Volcano. To get

RANCHING ON MAUI, 1905

Most of the stock raised on the ranch was slaughtered locally, but four or five times a year surplus steers were sent to Honolulu to be marketed. Shortly after my fifth birthday Daddy announced that I was old enough to go with him when the next shipment of beeves was made, and not until I went on this expedition did I realize that Daddy and the *paniolos* often risked their lives when they jogged out of my secure world every morning.

For days after I knew I was to go I spent most of my time leaving offerings before *akua* stones, praying to Christ, burning incense before Tatsu's image of Buddha, and lighting candles before the shrines of Portuguese saints to make certain that all the Great Forces would be solidly ranged about me to prevent any possible disaster which might interfere with my going.

The afternoon the steers were due to come down the mountain Makalii took me out to meet them. We spotted the cattle and riders swooping down a green hill. The Herefords reminded me of a swift red river foaming at its edges where their white legs and faces showed. The afternoon shook as they bellowed their fury and bewilderment at being driven from the high grasslands they knew.

Makalii opened the gates into the holding pasture. Daddy galloped ahead of the herd, sitting his saddle in the straight-legged fashion of Hawai'i—a beautiful, poised seat suggesting a winged centaur about to take flight and sail off into space. As he passed he brandished his coiled lasso and smiled. Owing to the steep pitch of the land it was impossible to prevent the wild mountain cattle from running. Daddy raced through the gates, maneuvering so the stock would not collide with the posts and bruise themselves.

When they were safely through, he pulled out of their way. They surged across the pasture, belly-deep in grass, slowed up, wheeled around, and collected in a tight knot facing the riders. Holomalia followed Daddy into the pasture and they conferred for a few moments. The rest of the men halted at the gates which Makalii was closing, slacked girths, and shook saddles to cool their horses' hot backs.

Wind scurried down from Haleakala; the sharp sweet whistle of plover sounded overhead. Across the green isthmus joining the two halves of the island, the West Maui mountains stood out distinctly, golden mists hanging in their deep valleys. A sort of elemental excitement, brewed by animals, wind, grass, and drifting clouds, flowed toward me. Makalii had trained my ears to hear the minute sounds of rocks, soil, and vegetation worked on by changes in the atmosphere. I could listen in the dark, and by the sound of the wind name the point of the compass from which it was blowing. I could sense the imperceptible change of one season sliding into the other: a sort of vast, muted rustle in earth, sky, and sea—an instant of altered vibrations, then a great peace, like a sigh, when the transition was completed. In a dim instinctive way I was conscious now of the majestic rhythm of Nature's machinery moving behind tangible objects and, reaching out, I grabbed Makalii's hand.

"What is it?" he asked in Hawaiian.

I looked at Haleakala, at the men and cattle, listened to the majestic dissonances of the Pacific. How could I express even to my old Makalii what I was feeling? But with the amazing intuition of his race he knew. Wrinkles gathered up the outer corners of his eyes.

"Today you feel like an *akua* walking on earth," he said, smiling.

I nodded. He had it exactly. In that moment, I felt immortal, I was a lesser god with a small niche in the huge swoop of living.

—Armine von Tempski, *Born In Paradise,* 1940

here, take Haleakala Highway (HI 37) from Kahului, beginning at the intersection stoplight at HI 36 on the east side of the airport. (There are only two stoplights in Upcountry. The other one is eight miles up.)

■ RANCHES, GARDENS, AND VINEYARDS

Makawao *map page 109, D-2*

This is cowboy country, and it all started in the 1820s, when whaling ships' cooks started asking around for meat. By 1830, Mexican cowboys were brought here to teach Hawaiians cattle ranching. The cattle industry still flourishes, and every year on the Fourth of July the town erupts in a rip-roaring rodeo. Makawao is also home to polo on Maui. The town, two miles east of HI 37, has a sort of contrived Old West atmosphere, with worn wooden buildings and new galleries and boutiques that retain the nineteenth-century false-front look.

Kula Botanical Garden *map page 109, D-3*

Five miles south of the Makawao turnoff is the vast Kula Botanical Garden, where jacaranda trees take on their lavender plumage and fat blue hydrangeas blossom in the cool mountain air. Maui onion and protea flower farms flourish on the undulating landscape. *638 Kekaulike Highway; 808-878-1715.*

Church of the Holy Ghost *map page 109, D-3*

The turn-of-the-century octagonal building on the road near Kula is the Church of the Holy Ghost. Debate continues over Father James Beissel's 1897 design; it is generally agreed that he chose an octagon because it was a familiar shape to his Portuguese parishioners. Nearly 100 years later, the carefully restored spire-topped church looks like an elfin pastry in Kula town, and the parishioners still are mainly Portuguese.

Tedeschi Vineyard *map page 109, C-4*

Hawai'i's only vineyard occupies 20 of the 20,000-acres of 'Ulupalakua Ranch, located south of Kula on Route 37. While cattle munch in the adjacent pastures, the winery manufactures both conventional wine and a unique wine made from pineapple. The winery is housed in a lava jailhouse built in 1857, where a stone-carved rain god stands sentinel. To try these wines, visit the tasting room. *Kula Highway; 808-878-6058.*

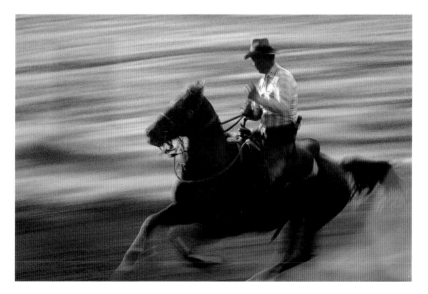

(above) Hawai'i's cowboys (paniolo) *have been overseeing the cattle industry since the mid-nineteenth century. (following spread) The Hotel Hana-Maui, with its beautifully appointed bungalows and upscale dining room, has been an exclusive resort for more than 50 years.*

■ HALEAKALA NATIONAL PARK *map page 109, D to F-3/4*

Maui's "highway to heaven," rising up into the misty cloud hovering on Haleakala (House of the Sun), is the world's most rapidly ascending road. It makes you realize that eastern Maui really is a mountain, and you're driving up the slopes of the largest dormant volcano in the world. From Kahului to crater rim, over a distance of 37 miles, the smooth, well-angled road ascends from sea level to 10,023 feet—past eucalyptus and cactus plants, above the tree line into an undulating, dry-brown, alpine desert clustered with lava boulders, where wide vistas sweep under passing billows of cloud. Because of the altitude, the temperature (especially at dawn and dusk) can drop to nearly freezing, around 33° F. Depending upon the weather, it also can be in the 80s. In these rarefied heights, you'll want to be prepared for anything.

To reach Haleakala National Park from Kahului, take the Haleakala Highway (HI 37). Turn onto HI 377 just past the Makawao turnoff, continuing another six miles to Haleakala Crater Road (HI 378), which takes you up sharply curving switchbacks to the volcano's crater rim. En route, watch for caravans of helmeted bicycle riders coasting down to sea level, and stop at the **Haleakala National Park headquarters** (808-572-4400), one mile from the park entrance, for brochures and general information. There are a number of overlooks. At the crater's rim, 11 miles farther up, a good place to stop is at the round, glass-paneled **Visitor Center** near the end of the road. It stands to the side of a cinder cone hovering on the rim. This is Pu'u 'Ula'ula (Red Hill), the highest point on the mountain and 28,000 feet above the ocean floor.

When you look down, the immense 3,000-foot-deep crater of Haleakala lies before you, often swathed in velvety cloud. A moonscape rolls down and away from the rim into a distant veil of fog—coagulating and dissolving like an ephemeral beast. Pink and gray cinder cones, swirled streams of barren red sands, and eerie, windworn lava formations emerge from shadows to fill the horizon. Blobs of lava called bombs, and spatter cones—islets in a mist-sea—are associated with gods and goddesses. Directly below the visitors center is Kalu'u O Ka O'o, home of Pele's brother, a god of mist and steam. The single, powerful presence enfolding all who gaze on the crater is silence. By some unknown force the awesome view seeps soundless into the consciousness, and you feel the power of the gods. Here, at the gods' ancient home, Hawaiian *kahuna* (priests) performed sacred rites of initiation.

The oval-shaped crater, an astounding 27 miles in circumference, is 7½ miles across, 2½ miles wide, and 3,000 feet deep—19 square miles formed by the action of rainwater percolating through porous layers of cinders and ash. Two massive gaps slash the crater rim, formed by an eons-long geological battle of volcanic outpourings versus erosions by wind, torrential rains, and streams. Kaupo Gap cuts south from the crater's eastern end, and on the northern side, Ko'olau Gap opens down onto the Ke'anae flatland.

The best times to see the crater are early morning, when dawn slips over the rim, and at sunset. During these moments you can visualize the demigod Maui slowing the path of the sun to make the day longer by lassoing it "with the loop of Maui's snaring rope." According to the creation chant, *The Kumulipo,* Maui harnessed each ray of the sun. When he released the fiery ball, Maui left some of the ropes dangling, and every evening at sunset you may see them slipping off into darkening sky. If clouds cooperate, you too may gaze at a glimmering horizon of pink, red, gold, and orange colors, that has awed writers for nearly two centuries. In 1866 Mark Twain described the crater's dawn:

> A growing warmth suffused the horizon, and soon the sun emerged and looked out over the cloud-waste, flinging bars of ruddy light across it; staining its folds and billow-caps with blushes, purpling the shaded troughs between, and glorifying the massy vapor-palaces and cathedrals with a wasteful splendor of all blendings and combinations of rich coloring. It was the sublimest spectacle I ever witnessed, and I think the memory of it will remain with me always.

Protecting and preserving Haleakala occupies the prime efforts of park authorities, and with more than one and a half million visitors each year, it is a formidable goal. The enormous preserve stretches from the summit area down the slopes eastward to the coast, joining the volcano crater with the rain forests of the Kipahulu coastal area. In order to protect fragile ecosystems, no road has been built to connect the two sections, and most of the area in between is closed to the public. In 1980, Haleakala National Park was given the status of an International Biosphere Reserve by UNESCO.

The complexity of resources in the 30,183-acre Haleakala National Park requires careful management. Dry forests, considered the richest in plant species of all Hawaiian forests, once rimmed the lower mountain flanks. Rain forest flourished

on the eastern slopes. Arriving in Hawai'i in their voyaging canoes, colonizing Polynesians brought pigs that soon multiplied and roamed the wet forests. Later came European goats and pigs, the gifts of Captain Cook and Captain Vancouver some 200 years ago. These, added to the existing feral population, ravaged the dry forest and turned vast areas into weed-strewn rocky pastures. Only a few patches of native trees and shrubs survive, and in the diminishing rain forest tender flowers are smothered by muddy pig wallows. As plant cover is eaten away, irrevocable erosion of the mountain slopes progresses rapidly, and some scientists say that the silt carried into the ocean by rain and wind is responsible for killing fish and coral.

By 1986 the nearly impossible goal of fencing in part of Haleakala was completed. A 32-mile perimeter fence now controls animals within the park and keeps feral goats and pigs from the crater. A massive removal program of thousands of animals was undertaken by park authorities, and today no feral goats remain inside the barrier section of the park.

Perhaps the best-known examples of conservation on Haleakala are the native silversword *('ahinahina)* plant and the Hawaiian *nene* goose. Some 50 years ago, fewer than a hundred plants grew on the western rim of the crater. Today, more than 50,000 delicately rooted silverswords stand tall on the mountain. The *nene* population, once down to 30 birds, now numbers in the hundreds.

■ HALEAKALA TRAILS

Hiking and horse trails cross the 3,000-foot deep crater of Haleakala, and three rental cabins built in 1937 are available through the park superintendent (808-871-2521). Hikers use three main trails: **Sliding Sands** and **Halemau'u** trails descend four miles to the crater floor through loose cinder surfaces and down steep switchbacks. The nine-mile **Kaupo Gap** trail exits the park and continues on private ranchland; it is also rocky and steep. The recently opened five-mile **Lahaina Pali** trail is a historic route that zigzags up and down the hot, arid slopes of southwest Maui, running through gulches and over high ridges to Ma'alea. An interpretative guide, called *Tales from the Trail*, is available at the state forestry office in Wailuku (808-572-4400).

Silversword, unique to the Hawaiian islands, thrives on the sunbaked slopes of Haleakala.

■ TRAVEL BASICS

Most visitors to Maui arrive by plane at the Kahului Airport, but those with a west side resort destination may choose to fly directly into the smaller Kapalua West Maui Airport. There is also a small airstrip on the eastern side of the island, near Hana. The island's first intraisland public transportation began operating in 2004. **Holo Ka'a Public Transit** (808-879-2828) serves central Maui and the destination areas of west and south Maui from 5:45 A.M. to 10:55 P.M. daily. In addition, there is a free shuttle that runs between Ka'anapali and Lahaina.

Climate: Maui, like all the Hawaiian Islands, enjoys a comfortable tropical climate influenced for most of the year by the northeasterly trade winds. From summer to winter, average temperatures vary slightly, though in winter atop Haleakala the mercury can drop below freezing. Coastal areas average between 85° F and 65° F. The average year-round temperature of ocean swimming areas is 74° F, and in summer the waters are around 80° F. The heavy rains come between December and March, but rainfall can vary more by location than by season. Windward shores receive more rain than leeward coasts. Volcanic peaks seize the trade winds and are often drenched with rain while the leeward sides remain sunny and dry, with placid ocean waters and an average annual rainfall of 10 to 25 inches.

■ VISITOR INFORMATION SERVICES

Chamber of Commerce. 176 Hinanao St., Wailuku 96793; 808-871-7711.
Hawai'i Visitors Bureau. 1727 Wilipa Loop, Wailuku 96793; 808-244-3530.
Ka'anapali Beach Operators Assoc. 2530 Keka'a Dr., Lahaina 96761; 808-661-3271.

■ FOOD AND LODGING

While most visitors come to enjoy Maui's full-service beach resorts, interesting alternative destinations such as Hana, the 'Iao Valley, and the slopes of Haleakala provide a glimpse of life in Maui before tourism became the major industry.

⌗ For agencies offering listings and booking services for bed-and-breakfasts, hotels, and condominiums on all islands, see page 359.

$ For room and restaurant price designations, see page 359.

■ HANA *map page 109, F-3*

✕ **Hana Ranch Restaurant.** Across road from post office; 808-248-8255. One of two restaurants in Hana. Local plate lunches and take-out counter. Good ocean view from outdoor tables. **$$**

▥ **Hana Plantation Houses.** 808-923-0772. Fully equipped houses; private hot tubs and sun decks. Try the Cafe at Hana Gardenland for good organic meals and local art. **$$$**

▥ **Heavenly Hana Inn.** 808-248-8442. Japanese themed suites. Elegant and moderately priced. Two-night minimum. **$$**

▥ **Hotel Hana-Maui.** Hana Ranch; 808-248-8211 or 800-321-HANA. An exclusive resort for 50 years, the ranch offers beautifully appointed bungalows with standard amenities and many outdoor activities. ✕ The upscale **dining room** has garden views. Fresh fish; local ingredients; game in season; Continental and Pacific cuisine. Prix-fixe dinners. **$$$**

▥ **Wai'anapanapa State Park Cabins.** State Parks Division, 54 S. High St., Wailuku 96793; 808-984-8109. Twelve rustic cabins with full facilities. The best lodging deal on the island, and many know it. Make reservations up to six months in advance. Five-night maximum. No credit cards. **$**

■ KA'ANAPALI AND LAHAINA *map page 109, A-1/2*

✕ **Bubba Gump Shrimp Company.** 889 Front St., Lahaina; 808-661-3111. Casual, fun, and the best view in town. Theme patterned after the Forrest Gump movie. Southern shrimp by the bucketful. **$**

✕ **David Paul's Lahaina Grill.** 127 Lahainaluna Rd., Lahaina; 808-667-5117. Old Lahaina atmosphere in restored Lahaina Hotel; owner-chef David Paul offers wonderful New American cuisine with Southwestern accents. **$$$**

✕ **Gerard's.** Plantation Inn Hotel, 174 Lahainaluna Rd., Lahaina; 808-661-8939. Owner-chef Gerard Reversade creates nouvelle and classic French cuisine with fresh local ingredients and game in season. Quaint, intimate surroundings. Dinner only. **$$$**

✕ **Hula Grill.** Whalers Village, Ka'anapali; 808-667-6636. Casual, beachside bistro with Hawai'i regional seafood. Its Barefoot Bar is popular. **$**

✕ **Kimo's Restaurant.** 845 Front St., Lahaina; 808-661-4811. A landmark on the main drag. Whaling decor upstairs and a waterfront lanai downstairs. Seafood fare and other island favorites. **$–$$**

✕ **Lokelani.** Maui Marriott Resort, 100 Nohea Kai Dr., Ka'anapali; 808-667-1200. Understated, pleasant Hawaiian decor. Serving seafood specialties with homemade bread, using fresh local ingredients. **$$**

✕ **Longhi's.** 888 Front St., Lahaina; 808-667-2288. A Lahaina institution; some love the bustling atmosphere, others find it irritating. Oceanfront dining on noisy main drag. American-Italian menu. **$$**

✕ **Nikko Japanese Steakhouse.** Maui Marriott Resort, 100 Nohea Kai Dr., Ka'anapali; 808-667-1200. Japanese decor with teppanyaki service—tableside grills and chefs who wield knives like kung fu masters. **$$$**

✕ **Old Lahaina Cafe.** 505 Front St., Lahaina; 808-667-2998. Reliable local coffee shop; on the main drag. **$**

✕ **Outback Steakhouse.** Kahana Gateway Center, 4405 Honoapiilani Hwy., West Maui; 808-665-1822. Down Under favorites and Aussie decor. Large, luscious steaks, lamb, and baked potato with heaping condiments. Don't miss the flowering onion appetizer—one is enough for four. Dinner only. No Reservations. **$$**

✕ **Royal Ocean Terrace.** Royal Lahaina Resort, Ka'anapali; 808-661-3611. Beautiful garden setting minus the flashy Ka'anapali megaresort atmosphere. Continental and American menu. **$$**

✕ **Sound of the Falls.** Westin Maui Hotel, 2365 Ka'anapali Pkwy., Ka'anapali; 808-667-2525. A somewhat flashy restaurant on the seafront, surrounded by waterfalls. **$$$**

✕ **Spats Trattoria.** Hyatt Regency Maui, Atrium Tower, 200 Nohea Kai Dr., Ka'anapali; 808-667-4727. Posh decor; dress code (elegant casual). Mediterranean and Northern Italian menu; well-known for veal. Dinner only; dancing. **$$$**

✕ **Swan Court.** Hyatt Regency Maui, 200 Nohea Kai Dr., Ka'anapali; 808-667-4727. Shoreside setting with large windows overlooking swimming swans and flamingos. Continental menu. **$$–$$$**

▦ **Embassy Suites Resort Ka'anapali.** 104 Ka'anapali Shores Pl.; 808-661-2000. Over 400 spacious suites, each with wet bar, stereo, 2 phone lines, and kitchen appliances. Landscaped oceanfront; health spa, pool, tennis, golf. Rates include breakfast. **$$$**

▦ **Hyatt Regency Maui.** 200 Nohea Kai Dr., Lahaina; 808-661-1234 or 800-233-1234. Premier hotel on the strip for those who like Greco-Roman design. Over 700 rooms with standard amenities, shops, restaurants, and health club. Pool has curving waterslide, grotto, and bar with seating in the water. **$$$**

⊞ **Ka'anapali Beach Hotel.** 2525 Ka'anapali Pkwy., Ka'anapali; 808-661-0011 or 800-262-8450. Over 400 rooms with standard amenities, shops, and restaurants, but with an accent on Hawaiiana: classes offered on the hula, lei-making, and playing the ukelele. **$$–$$$**

⊞ **Maui Islander.** 660 Waine'e St., Lahaina; 808-667-9766 or 800-542-6827. Over 370 rooms and condos in gardens about 3 blocks inland from Front St.; standard amenities, pool. **$$**

⊞ **Pioneer Inn.** 658 Wharf St., Lahaina; 800-457-5457. A smaller inn facing the harbor. Features a second-floor veranda. The outdoor covered restaurant and bar, with live music, is noisy, but there's plenty of local color. **$–$$**

⊞ **Plantation Inn.** 174 Lahainaluna Rd., Lahaina; 808-667-9225. Nicely appointed B&B, with 19 rooms, decorated with antiques. Downstairs is Gerard's French restaurant. **$$**

⊞ **Royal Lahaina Resort.** 2780 Keka'a Dr., Ka'anapali; 808-661-3611 or 800-447-6925. The only Ka'anapali hotel that's not boxed in by other hotels. Over 500 rooms and bungalows with kitchens. Broad grounds; beach; 3 pools; 11 tennis courts (6 lighted). **$$$**

■ KAHULUI AND WAILUKU *map page 109, B/C-2*

✗ **Mama's Fish House.** 79 Poho Pl., Paia; 808-579-8488. In Paia town, on the Haleakala Road. A slice of Old Hawai'i featuring Hawaiian dishes. **$$**

✗ **Picnics Maui.** 30 Baldwin Ave., Pa'ia; 808-579-8021. The menu is a map showing every good picnic location on the island. Drop in to pick up a box lunch from the extensive selection. **$–$$$**

✗ **A Saigon Cafe.** 1792 Main St., Wailuku; 808-243-9560. Reasonably priced Vietnamese cuisine in a homey atmosphere with the TV always on and punkha fans whirring. Make yourself a Vietnamese rice-paper wrap-up and dip it in sweet-sour garlic sauce. No sign outside. **$**

✗ **Siam Thai Cuisine.** 123 N. Market St., Wailuku; 808-244-3817. Generic decor, but delicious Thai standards. **$–$$**

⊞ **Maui Seaside Hotel.** 100 Ka'ahumanu Ave., Kahului; 808-877-3311 or 800-367-7000. Town hotel with standard amenities, pool. Car packages available. **$–$$**

■ KAPALUA *map page 109, A-1*

✕ **Kapalua Bay Club.** Kapalua Bay Hotel, 1 Bay Dr.; 808-669-5656. Understated elegance with wonderful views of Moloka'i and Lana'i. Favorite haunt of film stars and dignitaries. International menu. **$$–$$$**

⊞ **Kapalua Bay Hotel & Villas.** 1 Bay Dr.; 808-669-5656 or 800-367-8000. Elegant luxury resort complex; 194 rooms and condos, 2 pools, 3 restaurants; 3 beaches, shops, and golf course. **$$$**

⊞ **The Ritz-Carlton Kapalua.** 1 Ritz-Carlton Dr.; 808-669-6200 or 800-262-8440. Luxury resort on 37 acres; 558 rooms and suites, most with wide ocean views. 1,000 square-foot, 3-level pool. **$$$** ✕ **Anuenue Room.** International menu with Provençal and Hawaiian accents; focus on light sauces with herbs from the hotel garden. **$$–$$$**

■ NAPILI *map page 109, A-1*

⊞ **The Mauian Hotel.** 5441 Lower Honoapi'ilani Rd.; 808-669-6205 or 800-367-5034. A quaint, two-story condo-hotel on the beach. A rarity, it is owned and operated by a Hawaiian family who preserve an Old Hawai'i ambience. Daily service, pool; no TVs or phones. **$$**

⊞ **Napili Shores Resort.** 5315 Honoapi'ilani Hwy.; 808-854-8843 or 800-688-7444. Beachfront resort with 152 units, featuring lanais and full kitchens. **$$**

■ OLOWALU AND MA'ALAEA *map page 109, A/B-2/3*

✕ **Chez Paul.** Olowalu Village, HI 30; 808-661-3843. A casual, stylish bistro in a country village on the road to Lahaina. The French and Continental menu has gained a loyal following. Prix-fixe dinner only. **$$$**

✕ **The Ma'alaea Waterfront.** Ma'alaea Harbor, 50 Hauoli St.; 808-244-9028. Innovative local seafood. A beautiful view of the harbor and lanai seating; excellent service. **$$**

■ UPCOUNTRY *map page 109*

✕ **Casanova Italian Deli.** 1188 Makawao Ave., Makawao; 808-572-0220. *Paniolo* atmosphere and clientele. Deli menu, homemade pasta, espresso, pastries. Live music and dancing. **$–$$**

⊞ **Kula Lodge.** RR1 Haleakala Hwy., Kula; 808-878-1535 or 800-233-1535. Reminiscent of a Swiss chalet, this cozy lodge is set on 3 wooded acres. Two wooden cabins containing 5 units, 2 with fireplaces. **$$** ✕ The **restaurant** has broad mountain views and wood-panel chalet decor. Light and airy with basic American menu. **$$**

■ WAILEA, MAKENA, AND KIHE'I *map page 109, C-3/4*
✕ **Five Palms Beach Grill.** 2969 S. Kihe'i Rd., Kihe'i; 808-879-2607. Hawaiian regional cuisine; fresh local fish specials. Superb ocean and sunset views. **$$**
✕ **Pacific Grill.** Four Seasons Resort Wailea, 3900 Wailea Alanui, Wailea; 808-874-8000. Flashy dining room with ocean views. Pacific Rim international cuisine. **$$$**
✕ **Prince Court.** Maui Prince Hotel, 5400 Makena Alanui, Makena; 808-874-1111. Lovely views. Creative Sunday brunch; American cuisine with nouvelle emphasis; fresh fish, and local ingredients. **$$$**
✕ **Raffles.** Wailea Beach Resort, 3550 Wailea Alanui, Wailea; 808-879-4900. Asian decor with good ocean views. Continental menu. Dinner only. **$$$**
✕ **Seasons.** Four Seasons Resort Wailea, 3900 Wailea Alanui, Wailea; 808-874-8000. One of Maui's finest dining experiences; contemporary Hawaiian cuisine. Romantic open-air setting with sweeping ocean views. **$$$**
☷ **Maui Prince.** 5400 Makena Alanui Dr., Kihe'i; 808-874-1111 or 800-321-6284. At Makena, near end of the paved road. Japanese style. Heavy walls surrounding tropical courtyard; 300 rooms with standard amenities, some with ocean views. **$$$**
☷ **Wailea Marriott Outrigger Resort.** 3700 Wailea Alanui; 808-879-1922 or 800-688-7444. Sprawling oceanfront resort on 22 acres with seven low-rise buildings and an eight-story tower. Polished native woods gleam in the decor of the
✕ **Hula Moons Restaurant**. **$$$**

■ GOLFING ON MAUI

The Dunes at Mauna Lani. Inland from Kahului; 808-873-0422. Designed by Robin Nelson and conjuring Scottish vistas, this course on wooded sand dunes is as close to an authentic links as can be built in the islands. Golfers' prime assets here are good shot-making and their own brain power. With blind shots, you won't see the clubhouse until the memorable 588-yard, par-5 18th hole. A large pond remains in play to the finish, where the slope and trade winds will nudge your ball toward the water.
Kapalua Bay Hotel & Ocean Villas. 300 Kapalua Dr.; 808-669-8044. Three championship resort courses in natural terrain—lush gorges and sloping green hills with big views, big bunkers, and big challenges. The Plantation Course, sprawling over former pineapple fields in the lower West Maui mountains, is home to the PGA Tour's Mercedes Championships. Designed by Ben Crenshaw and Bill Coore, it has

views from every hole that take on a spectacular panorama of Moloka'i and Lana'i islands. Pros have said this course allows you to use every club in your bag; choices are available that make the course playable for the average golfer. The Bay and Village courses at Kapalua, designed by Arnold Palmer, wind through forests and mountain ravines. Hole Number 5, signature hole on the Bay course, plays across the sparkling blue water of Oneloa Bay; its winds are tricky. The Village course has many elevated shots.

Pukalani Country Club. Pukalani; 808-572-1314. A public 18-hole course in the cool heights of Upcountry Maui. Par 72. Expansive views of the sparkling Pacific Ocean.

Royal Ka'anapali Golf Courses. Lahaina; 808-661-3691. Two 18-hole resort courses, both par 71. North Course roams into the highlands above Ka'anapali. The 18th hole is said to be one of the most difficult in the state. The South Course is more forgiving, but like the North it ascends upward and offers the same stunning views.

Wailea Golf Club. Wailea Resort; 808-875-5155. Three courses serve the complex of posh hotels. The Blue course is an Arthur Jack Snyder layout; the Emerald and Gold courses were designed by Robert Trent Jones, Jr. The Gold course, incorporating lava swaths and clumps, and *kiawe* growth of the lower Haleakala hills, demands accuracy as well as length. Spectacular open ocean views, flowering trees around tee areas, and massive Haleakala looming in the background.

■ Maui Spas

The Health Centre at Four Seasons Resort Maui. 808-874-8000, ext. 53. Private massage cabanas tucked into beachside greenery. Many options in massage and body treatments; excellent workout area.

Hotel Hana-Maui Wellness Center. Hana, 808-248-8211. Programs for physical and spiritual well-being. Water exercises in a 25-meter lap pool. Gym, planned hiking. Massage.

Mandara Spa. Outrigger Wailea Resort; 808-879-1922. Surrounded by gardens, the spa features plunging pools, a full salon, and a fitness center. At open-air oceanview massage pavilions the massage oils, spices, and extracts used are derived from Asian and Polynesian traditions.

Spa Grande. Grand Wailea Resort Hotel & Spa, Wailea; 800-772-1933. Hawai'i's largest spa with 40 treatment rooms and 5,000 square feet devoted to the best of an

Old World spa (Roman and Greek themed decor), ancient Hawaiian treatments, a Japanese traditional bath, and Ayurvedic and Siddha treatments from India. Five kinds of speciality baths, a Swiss jet shower, a Roman tub, waterfall showers, and marble steam rooms. Good fitness center, and the only color light therapy capsule in the state.

■ OUTDOOR ADVENTURES

■ BIKING
Cruiser Bob's. Paia; 808-579-8444. **Maui Downhill.** Kahului; 808-877-8787 or 800-535-2453. The Haleakala Downhill, a 40-mile, rip-roaring downhill plunge from the crater rim to the sea, is a Maui must-do. Cruiser Bob's and Maui Downhill are two outfitters that will pick you up at your hotel room before first light, feed you, shuttle you to the top, and, in the glow of the sunrise, send you on your way. They also rent bikes.

■ HIKING
Haleakala National Park. 808-572-4400. Pick up the interpretive guide *Tales from the Trail* at the state forestry office in Wailuku.
Maui Cave Adventures. Hana; 808-248-7308. A spelunker's delight, passing through a two-mile underground passage of Ka'eleku Caverns; dark crawl spaces and cathedral-high rooms lit by open-air skylights. Hard hats, lights, and gloves provided.

■ HORSEBACK RIDING
Adventures on Horseback. Makawao; 808-242-7445. Horseback treks along the beach and through the jungle to hidden waterfalls and inviting swimming pools.
Rainbow Ranch. Lahaina; 808-669-4991. Full-day and half-day excursions into the West Maui Mountains.

■ PARAGLIDING
Proflyght Paragliding. 808-874-5433. Launch from the lofty heights of Haleakala and float effortlessly to the valley below. Tandem flights available.

■ WATER ACTIVITIES
Dive Maui. 900 Front St., Lahaina; 808-667-2080. Scuba lessons and gear.
Maui Moloka'i Sea Cruises. 831 Eha St., Ste. 101, Wailuku; 800-468-1287. Motorboat charters, snorkeling, and whale-watching tours.

Maui Windsurfing Company. 520 Keolani Pl., Kahului; 808-877-4816. Learn to windsurf or just rent equipment.

Ocean Activities Center. 1325 S. Kihe'i Rd., Suite 2212, Kihe'i; 808-879-4485. Snorkeling trips, including Molokini Crater; whale-watching, deep-sea fishing.

Pacific Whale Foundation. Kealia Beach Plaza, Kihe'i; 808-879-8860. The pioneers in humpback whale-watching; you can watch for dolphins too. Have a look in the Marine Science Education Center; send the children to outreach programs, attend naturalist classes, or take a snorkeling tour.

South Pacific Kayaks. Kihe'i; 800-776-2326. A variety of guided sea-kayak tours, including whale-watching and sea-turtle trips with knowledgeable guides.

■ FESTIVALS AND EVENTS

■ JANUARY

Hula Bowl. Maui's sunny skies brighten up mainland TVs every winter. The college all-star football game is played the first Saturday of each new year. War Memorial Stadium, Wailuku; 808-947-4141.

■ MARCH

Maui Marathon. Ka'ahumanu Center, Kahului, to Whaler's Village, Ka'anapali; 808-871-6441.

■ APRIL

Maui County Agricultural Trade Show. Mauians call it "the 'Ulupalakua Thing." An annual event showcasing Maui products. Try a sandwich of beef cut from sides of roasting meat on a spit; Kula strawberries, and Tedeschi wines. Look for fruit-bright Namoeata soaps—almost good enough to eat. 'Ulupalakua Ranch, Upcountry; 808-875-0457.

■ MAY

International Festival of Canoes. Master carvers from Pacific nations showcase their hand-built canoes (and surfboards). Front St., Lahaina; 808-667-9194.

■ JUNE

Maui County Slalom Championships. Pro-Am windsurfing series. Also in July and August. Kanaha Beach Park; 808-877-2111.

■ **JULY**

Bon Odori Festivals. Buddhist evening ceremonies honoring souls of the dead; lantern boat ceremonies, Bon dances. Jodo Mission; 808-661-4304.

Kapalua Wine and Food Symposium. Weekend of culinary delights featuring executive chefs and winemakers from the world over. Kapalua; 808-669-0244 or 800-527-2582.

Makawao Fourth of July Rodeo. Makawao.

Polipoli Mountain Bike Race. Professionals and amateurs; cross-country and downhill races. Polipoli Forest; 808-878-1850.

Wailea Tennis Open. International players. Wailea Resorts Tennis Club, Wailea; 808-879-1958.

■ **AUGUST**

Maui Onion Festival. An annual event featuring celebrity chef demonstrations, onion-eating contest, fresh produce, and entertainment. Also a gala 5-course dinner by 5 chefs. Reservations: 808-661-4567.

■ **SEPTEMBER**

Annual Hana Relay. A 52-mile run from Kahului Airport to Hana. 808-243-9636.

Earth Maui Nature Summit. Five days of fun and education at the Kapalua Resort designed to provide a new look at how we use natural resources. Bring the kids; plunge beneath waves and walk in rain forests. Sponsored by Kapalua Nature Society. Kapalua; 808-669-0244 or 800-527-2582.

Kapalua Open Tennis Tournament. Annual Labor Day grand prix is the state's largest tennis tournament. Kapalua; 808-669-5677.

■ **OCTOBER**

Maui Roughwater Swim. Kawekapu Beach, Wailea; 808-875-9066.

Maui Triathlon. A swim-bike-run event. Choose your catagory: Ironman, Half-iron, Olympic, or Youth sections. 808-579-9502.

L A N A ' I
P R I V A C Y   I S L A N D

Shaped like an oyster shell and formed by a single volcano, tiny Lana'i is rugged, wild, and austere. Steep, eroded gorges and red lava mountains fall away to the east from a central rolling tableland, and to the west 2,000-foot cliffs drop to the sea. Remote beaches nestle untrammeled on northern shores, and in the northwest, eerie piles of red earth and ancient lava mold a barren moonscape. From a trail winding up through Norfolk pine forests above the only town (Lana'i City), five of Hawaii's other islands can be spotted—every island except Kaua'i.

Nine miles across the 'Au'au Channel from the glamorous shops and nightlife of west Maui, Lana'i remains serene, relaxing, and a fine place to stargaze. At one time there was only one hotel, the 10-room Hotel Lana'i, set on a grassy hill overlooking town, where wind ruffles pines on cool evenings and there's a single TV set in the front lounge. Most travelers, upon learning that the smallest island was a huge plain of pineapples with few paved roads, left Lana'i to its wild sheep and goats. Today Lana'i has awakened to elegant tourism. Two luxurious and pricey hotels rise on the island. Built in the early 1990s by the real-estate arm of the Dole Food conglomerate, the hotels diffuse a stylish grace into Lana'i's country charm.

It takes stamina to see the rugged beauty of Lana'i. From the unpaved roads and jeep trails that crisscross the island, visitors can see Axis deer, mouflon sheep, goats, partridge, and pheasant in the wild. If you go hiking in the mountains, you may see a ram—one of the most beautiful sights on the island—his great horns curving down around his head and standing in silhouette against azure sky. Yet there's a paradox here. Game birds and feral animals, all introduced in the past two centuries, lack natural predators, rapidly reproduce, and ravage the native ecosystem. For this reason, hunting has long been allowed on Lana'i, making the island popular with sportsmen.

■ HISTORY

Fearing Lana'i's reef-studded shores, ancient Polynesian and Hawaiian voyagers often bypassed the island. Later it had a reputation as the home of terrifying man-eating spirits, and it remained uninhabited until the son of a great Maui chief was

A sunset stroll along Polihua Beach is worth the extra effort taken to reach it.

banished here. Named Kaulula'au, he was something of a juvenile delinquent, breaking *kapu* by chopping down breadfruit trees. His father exiled him to Lana'i and probably expected him to die there, yet people kept seeing his campfires on the shore. Before long, word filtered back to Maui that Kaulula'au had slain the odious spirits, and his father, no doubt rejoicing, declared Lana'i safe for habitation. Controlled by Maui chiefs, it soon supported a population of some 3,000 people, who farmed the tableland until the island was decimated by war at the end of the eighteenth century. By the time European mariners were steering clear of the reefs, the rich central tableland lay fallow. Although Lana'i played only a small role in Kamehameha the Great's surge to unite the islands, its name means "day of conquest."

In the 1860s Lana'i was settled by Mormons under the leadership of the charismatic Walter Murray Gibson, who bought the island with Mormon funds and registered it to himself. For this, he was promptly excommunicated. Gibson's followers stayed. They established a sugar plantation, mill, and cane railroad at

Hawai'i's pineapples are legendary as evidenced by this joking photograph from 1950.

Palawai Basin in the south-central part of the island. Crops had to be irrigated, as Lana'i receives scant rainfall—35 inches annually in the highlands, and in the lower levels barely a foot. Difficulties increased, and the Mormon farming and ranching operations failed. In 1901 they sold the island.

By 1922 businessman James Dole, a descendant of missionaries, envisioned planting Lana'i's rolling fields with pineapple. For $1.1 million the island was his. Dole planted fruit, brought workers from the Philippines, built a plantation town, and forever changed life on Lana'i. His 15,000 acres represented the agricultural effort of the entire island, and it soon became the world's largest pineapple plantation.

An island with only one town, dominated by one company, and planted in one crop now faces striking changes. In the late 1980s Lana'i (and Dole Food) embarked on a new era: tourism. Elegant, Rockefeller-style tourism for the super-rich replaced pineapple cultivation as the island's main economy. Dole (merged with Castle & Cooke, and renamed Dole Food Company) radically cut pineapple production, and in 1993 the last Lana'i pineapple for the canning market was shipped aboard a barge from Kaumalapau Harbor on the west coast.

Palm-tree shadows on the beach at Manele Bay.

A single hotel, built by Dole and operated by Castle & Cooke's Lana'i Company subsidiary, altered the gritty soul of Lana'i. Opened in 1990, the Lodge at Ko'ele in the cool 1,700-foot central highlands above Lana'i City marked the dawn of the new era. On its grounds, amid tall, old pines on 21 acres of lawns and gardens, stands Hawai'i's original Norfolk pine tree—the towering shaft that inspired the planting of similar trees and brought a piney atmosphere to Lana'i. Ko'ele has the air of a Victorian country estate, with a broad view over land where decades ago a cattle ranch stood; the hotel's reflecting pool was once a stock watering hole. A major sister hotel, the Manele Bay, above a beach six miles south of Lana'i City, is the other luxury enclave for the very wealthy. Along the rugged coastline, luxury vacation homes are cropping up next to the Manele Bay Hotel's top-rated golf course.

Family ties are strong on Lana'i, whose 2,900 residents are 51 percent Filipino, 18 percent Japanese, 11 percent white, and the rest Hawaiian or Filipino-Hawaiian. Children of recent generations have gone away from the fields, some to universities. Those who want to return no longer come home to back-breaking jobs planting 6,000 to 10,000 seed sprouts a day.

There may be irony in trading dirty work in the earth for clean work in the hotels. Yet residents recognize opportunities for youth in tourism and express confidence in its stability. As Lana'i swaps its main crop of pineapple for tourists, the legacy Dole Food bequeaths the island is controversial—islanders want the old lifestyle and tourism jobs as well. While Dole seems to be accomplishing that blend, residents still worry about the possible sale of the land to foreign interests.

■ LANA'I CITY

A mile from the small airport, the island's only town, Lana'i City, sits precisely in the center of the island at a cool elevation of 1,645 feet—perhaps the most isolated settlement in all of Hawaii. Almost all the residents of this plantation town still live in frame houses clustered near its main street. The town is little changed. Stores still close at lunchtime, and no traffic light, movie theater, or disco mars its tin-roofed, quiet, ambience. After living accommodations were built for hotel employees, a new mood prevailed, and the tired atmosphere has received a jolt of energy. Old plantation buildings have been renovated into little shops, cafés, and brave boutiques.

■ LANA'I HIGH COUNTRY

■ MUNRO TRAIL TO MOUNT LANA'IHALE *map opposite, C-2/3*

The seven-mile Munro Trail, a jeep road and hiking trail, begins behind Lodge at Ko'ele and winds up through pine forests to the summit of Mount Lana'ihale, the island's highest point (3,370 feet). Here is a lookout with a view of the other islands. About a third of the way up the trail, a hiking path leads to an overlook above Lana'i's deepest gorge, Ha'uola Gulch, which drops 2,000 feet before it meets the sea on the island's east coast.

The trail was developed by George C. Munro, a New Zealand naturalist, who stepped ashore on Lana'i in 1911. For the next three decades, while Dole cultivated pineapple on the rolling mesas, Munro trudged the highlands, planting Norfolk pines to capture moisture and reduce erosion. On the lower slopes of western Lana'i several unique and scattered patches of dryland forest survive.

■ KANEPU'U PRESERVE *map below, B-1*

One of George Munro's forests is Kanepu'u Preserve, six miles northwest of Lana'i City. At this site in 1918, Munro, by now a ranch manager, erected fences and removed stray cattle to preserve a grove of *lama* (native persimmon) and *olopu'a* (a native olive), together with dozens of less common native plants. For 30 years he worked to protect the site, and his dedication reminds us that long before the modern concept of ecology evolved, visionaries like Munro understood its precepts and tried their best to preserve the land.

In 1935, when the eminent botanist Raymond Fosberg visited Kanepu'u, he described it as "the last place in Hawai'i where one can witness the forests that must have once covered vast areas of the dry lowlands." By the 1970s several plants were gone; however, the groves and 48 native species remained, including *ili'ahi*, the endangered Lana'i sandalwood, and wild specimens of *nanu*, the Hawaiian gardenia. In 1989 Dole, now owner of 98 percent of the island, made a gift of a conservation easement over 462 acres at Kanepu'u to the Hawai'i chapter of the Nature Conservancy. *Polihua Road; 808-537-4508.*

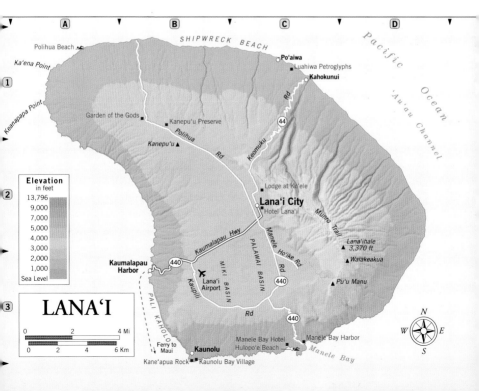

JAPANESE BRIDE

The author of this piece, Clara Jelsma, recorded her mother's memories of being an immigrant homesteader in Hawai'i between 1905 and 1925.

About this time Father's older brother, Soske, received a letter from his half brother, Umetaro, who had emigrated to Hawai'i 16 years before. He had written that he had purchased 200 acres of land there and would like to have Soske find a wife for him and send her to Hawai'i. He specified that she should be a country girl, but educated, and not too ugly.

Soske found this to be a very big order. Country girls were not very educated, and the pretty girls were in the city. Also, it seemed hard to believe that Umetaro, who had always been the black sheep, could really be doing so well that he could have bought 200 acres of land.

Since he was not sure whether it was true or not, he felt he could not ask for a bride from the village or from among strangers. So, he decided that it would be best to find a bride from among the kinfolk.

Thinking over the qualifications which had been specified Soske thought about Umetaro's first cousin, Iku Hayashi. She was not too homely and was a country girl. But she could be considered educated since she had studied in Tokyo and had been travelling around trying to be a nurse.

Soske wrote to Umetaro asking what he thought about his choice. Umetaro wrote back that he would trust in Soske's judgment and accept whoever he decided was best. If he considered Iku to be a suitable bride for him, that was fine with him.

So, Mother was notified.

If you want to go to Hawai'i as a bride, come home immediately, she was told in the letter from Soske.

As she read the letter, Mother was not very much excited by the prospect of marriage. But the thought of going to Hawai'i was enough to entice her to head home immediately. No one from her little village had ever travelled abroad.

Soske was only a farmer, but because the government had run a highway through his rice field and rebated him 20,000 yen, he furnished Mother liberally with money for her trousseau.

"If you're going abroad, you should go in good style. Buy the very best," he advised her.

So, Mother went shopping in Nagoya and bought the best of everything she thought she needed. She purchased her kimono, her *montsuki* (bridal garment with the beautiful *obi* or sash, her *haori* or outer garment, and her *jiban* or slip), her gold wedding ring, her Wittnauer gold watch, her umbrella, her *zori* (slippers), and her *geta* (clogs). She had never owned or worn such fine things in Japan. . . .

Finally the day of departure came. It had been about two years since she had decided to go to Hawaiʻi. She was thirty years old, and felt fully prepared for the life before her. Of course, she envisioned Hawaiʻi to be a place like Nojiri where you could buy all the things you needed.

She was handed a three pound Crisco can of *ume* by Umezo Kongaki, a well travelled friend of Umetaro. The sour pickled plums were from his trees and were given to soothe the sea sickness en route. "Give the extra ones to Umetaro," he told her.

Umezo accompanied Soske and Mother to Yokohama harbor where she boarded the *Taiho Maru*. Last words were exchanged and a few tears shed. Then the men returned home. Mother was on her way.

The ship was full of other brides on their way to Hawaiʻi. Most of them were women in their thirties. They were from various places and backgrounds, and all hopeful about a new life in Hawaiʻi.

■ ■ ■

The disembarking from the *Taiho Maru* in Honolulu was one of relief for the weary, sea sick passengers. The immigration center has been a place of confusion and loud activity.

Very prominent there was a large, talkative man of about sixty from Niigata by the name of Katsuno-san who was a sort of manager for the immigrants coming in and had some official position at the immigration office. Katsuno-san was loud and spoke very coarsely, joshing the women with his crude remarks.

The identification time at the immigration center was a joyful time for some and a shocking crisis to others. Some brides who knew their husbands only by the photographs sent them, many of which were very deceptive, were so shocked at seeing their mates that they fled from their husbands.

When Mother's name was called, she was startled to see a tall, ferocious looking man with overgrown hair and an unkempt, bushy beard coming toward her. Could this man really be her cousin, Umetaro, she wondered. She had not seen him for over sixteen years.

—Clara Mitsuko Jelsma, "Teapot Tales," from *The Best of Bamboo Ridge,* 1986

■ **GARDEN OF THE GODS** *map page 159, B-1*

In the northwest quadrant of the island, an unpaved road and jeep trail lead to the Garden of the Gods. Here, boulders are piled in eerie, tottering, eroded heaps permeated with earthy colors, which change hues at dawn and sunset. The boulders are set upon red-sand hills that sweep down to the north shore, and the scent of sage hovers in the wind.

■ **KA'ENA POINT** *map page 159, A-1*

Ka'ena Point, at the foot of a jeep track on the northwest corner of Lana'i, was once a penal colony where, between 1837 and 1843, women subsisted in misery. "Thou shalt not sleep mischievously" wrote the missionaries in their translation of the Seventh Commandment in 1825. Baffled by the new concept of adultery, astonished Hawaiian women found themselves shipped off to Lana'i on the schooner *Ho'okaika* out of Maui. At Ka'ena they were confined to a sort of environmental prison—without walls or guards, and with little food. Furious winds and perilous currents kept them isolated within sight of their homes on Maui or Moloka'i.

Swimming is dangerous at Shipwreck Beach, an eight-mile stretch of Lana'i's north coast.

■ NORTH LANA'I

■ SHIPWRECK BEACH *map page 159, B/C-1*

The eight-mile stretch of Lana'i's north coast, from Polihua in the west to Kahokunui in the east, is rimmed with sand punctuated by points of rock. The entire portion is named Shipwreck Beach. The thread of sandy plots is fine for beachcombing and shore fishing, but swimming is dangerous, as the waters are murky, the seabed rocky and shallow. The section most easily accessible is reached from the end of HI 440 (also known as HI 44 and Keomuku Road). Take the north branch dirt track to the lighthouse ruins at Po'aiwa

Hulks of ships torn by sharp, wave-shrouded coral lie rotting on the reef off Shipwreck, scourge to mariners since the days of whalers. Beside the beach lies the rusting wreck of a World War II Liberty Ship. Islanders and sculptors track the sands for mangled shapes of driftwood or old hand-blown glass balls used by Japanese fishermen as floats.

■ POLIHUA BEACH *map page 159, A-1*

Wide, windy, and remote Polihua (Egg Nest) Beach, a mile and a half long and the largest white-sand beach on Lana'i, follows the island's contour at the west end of the north coast. Once this was a green sea turtle *(honu)* nesting beach. Tragically, this endangered, federally protected species has not been seen since 1954. The beach can be reached only by four-wheel drive. Check with the rental agency for road conditions before taking the dirt tracks northwest from the end of the inland paved road at the Garden of the Gods. A sign points the way to the shore.

Although it is possible to hike the north shore all the way from Shipwreck west to Polihua, not even a jeep track connects the two. Each is reached by widely separated tracks.

■ SOUTH LANA'I

■ MANELE BAY AND SURROUNDS *map page 159, C-3*

Manele Bay Hotel

Six miles south of Lana'i City by paved road (HI 440), the second of Dole's luxury hotels, the Manele Bay, opened in 1991. This elegant pile of concrete stands on a low cliff above the island's best and most accessible beach. The resort is pricey: up to $600 per night, and there are butlers to draw your bath water for you.

Water Born

Mo'omomi Beach, narrow and hooked like a horseshoe
From centuries of wear, is reefless. Seas pound it
And strong currents often cut through
Carving pockets and cleaning stations out
Of the lava. I brought you there to dive,
To spear ulua, fish with an approach like a spaceship.
We moved easy, consumed,
Flippers never breaking the surface,
Drawn into an unnoticed current, and carried
Out to deep, purpling water.
Alerted by the color I turned to you
But you knew, your mottled eyes filled the window
Of your mask like a single bruise.
We pumped hard for shore
Burning our lungs up, making no headway,
I turned again, you'd fallen far behind,
All timing gone from your stroke.
I felt death by drowning
And went to hold you, taste the last water in your hair,
To slip under with you, and await the coming sharks,
Their fins dipped, bodies arched,
The beautiful pewter of their tails,
To accept death and be finally brave for us,
Bellow like an old hero
Into a deafening white mouth.
It lasted less than seconds
And I remembered about a current,
Go with it, ride till it slows and lets you off.
Panic lifted, order rose out of my chest
Like smoke, we breathed and were limp.
We hadn't gone far, and a steady swim brought us in
East of the beach. Through it all you'd held on
To your 3-prong and stringer of poked fish.
We rested on a pile of warm stones
One of many that speckles Mo'omomi
And marks the ancient fallen.
You asked about them, their weapons and deaths,
Putting our scrape into perspective.
Picking up the spear and fish
We headed back,
Renewed, heroic, or as close as we'd ever get.

—Norman Hindley, "Water Born," from *The Best of Bamboo Ridge,* 1986

Manele Bay Harbor

At the far end of Hulopo'e Beach, a volcanic spatter cone rears up like an eroded sculpture. On its far side is Manele Bay, a small inlet beneath lava cliffs. Manele once held a curve of black sand. Then in 1965, construction of a small boat harbor engulfed the west end of the beach. On the shore, ruins of old native Hawaiian houses stand like a painted backdrop to yachts anchored in waters of the harbor. Boat anchoring is not permitted outside the designated harbor, and the types of fishing allowed, or not allowed, are clearly posted.

Harbor construction left a patch of white sand at the eastern corner of Manele Bay, where calm waters offer fine snorkeling and diving. It is wise to watch for small-boat traffic. A Marine Life Conservation Area since 1979, the two crescents of Hulopo'e and Manele beaches teem with sea life.

Hulopo'e Beach

The quarter-mile crescent of smooth sands at Hulopo'e (White) Beach is framed in *kiawe* trees. Fronting waters are locally famed for snorkeling. You can plunge into the scuba site called Cathedrals, where coral pinnacles rise from 70-foot depths, creating chasms alive with slipper lobsters, striped convict fish, and three-foot-long zebra moray eels *(puhi)*.

With good deep-water swimming, a picnic area, the only beach park facilities on the island, Hulopo'e has been a traditional favorite of residents. Years ago, a wide tidal pool was blasted out of shoreline rock to make a safe swimming section for children in the east arm of the bay. A resident pod of spinner dolphins is known to make regular morning visits. Now that a luxury hotel rises on the unspoiled and largely unknown shore, the easygoing atmosphere of Hulopo'e and the pleasure of the locals are fated to be joined by the sleeker sophistication of wealthy pleasure-seekers.

Luahiwa Petroglyphs

A sunset stop at Palawai Basin on Manele Road (HI 440), halfway between Lana'i City and Manele Bay, rewards visitors with fiery red earth caught in the evening light. You can hike in to Luahiwa from Ho'iki Road to the east side of the basin, where 20 boulders on the hillside are carved with some 400 petroglyphs. Most are linear and triangular human figures; others, dogs or horses.

(following spread) Kiawe trees frame the smooth white sands of Hulopo'e Beach, known locally for great snorkeling.

Kaho'olawe

Known as Kanaloa in ancient times, Kaho'olawe is the only Hawaiian Island named for Kanaloa, one of the four major gods of Polynesia. It is the smallest, driest, windiest island in the Hawaiian chain, and is uninhabited. Brown and brooding and without natural barriers, it lies in the shadow of Maui's great volcano, Haleakala. By the time trade winds have raced around that immense volcano, they have spilled their rain and hit nearby Kaho'olawe bone dry and at near-gale force.

Kaho'olawe probably was settled later than the other islands. Archaeologists date the earliest known site around A.D. 1000, some four to six centuries after the settlement of O'ahu and Moloka'i. At inland sites, amid evidence of sweet-potato cultivation, fishing artifacts have been found. It is thought these early Hawaiians lived inland and visited the coast, making offerings to the fish god 'Ai'ai at Haki'oawa, where an altar faced the sea on a rise above the northeast shore. At an inland basalt quarry they hacked out a fine quality of adze stones that were traded across the channels to other islands. In traditional migration chants Keala'ikahiki, on the island's western tip, is mentioned as a place where ancient navigators set out on voyages to Tahiti.

No archaeological evidence of settlement on the island after the early 1600s has been found, suggesting Kaho'olawe's population may have been radically reduced in the mid-seventeenth century—a time of inter-island warfare.

For a brief time in the mid-1800s Kaho'olawe served as a penal colony established by missionaries. Ranching followed—a move that brought dire consequences to the land as sheep and cattle destroyed most of the vegetation, and up to 15 feet of topsoil blew off in the wind.

In 1875 King Kalakaua's *kahuna* (spiritual advisor) sent him to Kaho'olawe to exorcise his spirit of dark influences. His *mana* had been tarnished by contact with the body of King Lunalilo, his predecessor who died in 1874. Preparation for internment of the remains, and the nearness of Lunalilo's new tomb to Kalakaua's new palace put the king at risk. Arriving on the island in the morning, Kalakaua rode up to Kaho'olawe's highest peak, Ulapu'u, where he performed ritual prayers and subjected himself to an intense purification ceremony. The newly sanctified king did not spend the night on the rugged island though, and in a more majestical than mystical fashion he boarded the luxury steamer *Kilauea* and returned to Honolulu in time for dinner.

After the Japanese attacked Pearl Harbor in 1941, the War Department leased the island for target bombing and shelling practice. When World War II ended in 1945, the wartime status lingered, and in 1953 an executive order transferred jurisdiction of Kaho'olawe to the Navy. Aerial target practice blanketed the ground in unexploded, dangerous ordnance, and civilians were not allowed on the island.

For years the fate of Kaho'olawe simmered on a back burner. With the renaissance of Hawaiian culture in the 1970s, protesters began to demand the return of the island to the Hawaiian people. Civil suits followed, and soon the Navy was required to submit environmental impact statements—an almost laughable requirement for land so impacted with ordnance that some military experts believe it can never be cleared.

No one can live on bomb- and projectile-strewn Kaho'olawe. In 1976 an agreement between the Navy and the state permitted a group of Hawaiians to step ashore at Haki'oawa, but the effect could be no more than symbolic. In 1990 a presidential directive halted bombing practice on Kaho'olawe and mandated a joint body of the Department of Defense, State of Hawai'i, and the Kaho'olawe Island Conveyance Commission "to examine the future status of Kaho'olawe." Findings and recommendations were compiled. On May 7, 1994, Hawaiians celebrated Kaho'olawe's historic homecoming to their state with solemn rituals. The Navy was authorized to spend $400 million on clearing and revegetation over a 10-year period.

On November 12, 2003, control of the island was formally transferred from the Navy to the state's Kaho'olawe Island Reserve Commission. Charged with managing the island's 45 square miles, the commission was given $30 million in federal funds to continue removing unexploded ordnance and to develop water storage. Access to the island remains limited.

Nobody can live on battered Kaho'olawe.

■ PALAOA POINT   *map page 159, B-3*

At Kaunolu, where cliffs descend to the southwest tip of the island, the ruins of ancient **Kaunolu Bay Village** stand like silent sentinels in the wind. **Halulu He'iau** stood on the west side of the small bay. Inland from the *he'iau*, petroglyphs are etched on boulders above the west side of a stream bed. The figures are triangular muscled humans and goats. At the eastern side of the bay Kamehameha the Great built a home and fishing retreat. A jeep track, off the Kaumalapau Harbor paved road, bumps and bounces south to the ancient village, a National Historic Landmark archaeologists consider to be one of the finest preserved Hawaiian ruins in the island chain. Grave markings, 86 houses, and 35 stone shelters have been identified.

In 1868 Kamehameha V visited his grandfather's fishing retreat here, and it is said he hid a stone image of Ku'ula, god of fishermen, somewhere nearby. A plaque set into a stone in 1963 tells this story.

To the west of the bay at **Kane'apua Rock,** warriors of Kamehameha the Great courted death to prove their loyalty to the king. From a patch of lava 60 feet above the sea, they plunged out as far as possible to clear a 15-foot outcropping before dropping into 12 feet of water. It is known as **Kahekili's Leap,** and perhaps Kamehameha bestowed the name to honor an old foe. In his youth Kamehameha had fought Kahekili on Lana'i—and lost.

North of Kaunolu at more than 1,000 feet is **Pali Kaholo,** the highest sea cliff on Lana'i. It is unusual to find a sea cliff on a southwest shore in Hawai'i—normally they rise on north coasts, where wind and waves batter and erode them. Lana'i, shielded on the north by west Maui, is an exception, and here it is the south shore that is most vulnerable to wind and waves.

In ancient songs the island of Lana'i was noted for its *kauna'oa,* a strange ground-running plant that thrives on leeward beaches. A parasite rooted in the sand above the high-water mark, *kauna'oa's* thread-like stems rest on the sand and reach out to attach themselves to host plants. The smooth, peach-colored tendrils are gathered in handfuls and twisted or braided to make a thick lei. Small pieces of greenery add contrasting color. The lei requires no tie; after a few hours the tendrils bind themselves together.

■ Travel Basics

The best way to see Lana'i is to rent a four-wheel-drive vehicle, take a map, and explore. There are 30 miles of paved road, but many more unpaved roads and jeep trails crisscross the island. Most visitors arrive by plane at the Lana'i Airport, but one can also arrive by the passenger ferry that operates five times a day across the 'Au'au Channel from the town of Lahaina on Maui, to Manele Bay on Lana'i's south coast. The trip takes only 40 minutes.

Climate: Lana'i, like all the Hawaian Islands, enjoys a comfortable tropical climate influenced for most of the year by the northeasterly trade winds. Temperatures vary between 85° F and 65° F. Water temperatures range from 74° F to around 80° F in summer. Winter is the rainy season, but weather can be affected more by location than by season.

The Munro Trail winds up through pine forests to the summit of Mount Lana'ihale.

■ Visitor Information Services

Destination Lana'i. P.O. Box 700, Lana'i City 96763; 808-565-7600.
Hawai'i Visitors Bureau (Maui County). 800-525-6284.

■ Food and Lodging

Two luxury resorts, the Lodge at Ko'ele and Manele Bay Hotel, are the modern centerpieces of tourist Lana'i, but the Hotel Lana'i captures the heart of Old Lana'i.

⊞ For agencies offering listings and booking services for bed-and-breakfasts,
hotels, and condominiums on all islands, see page 359.

$ For room and restaurant price designations, see page 359.

✗ **Blue Ginger Cafe.** 409 7th Ave. Lana'i City; 808-565-6363. Casual eatery
with good burgers. **$**

✗ **Ihilani.** Keomoku Hwy., Manele Bay Hotel; 808-565-7700. A sophisticated,
elegant restaurant. The chef here uses fresh local ingredients and changes his
menu nightly. **$**

The Lodge at Ko'ele has the air of a Victorian country estate.

⊡ **Hotel Lana'i.** Lana'i City; 808-565-7211. Cozy mountain lodge built by Dole in the early 1920s. Eleven basic rooms, some with lanais; one cottage; TV in lounge. **$–$$**

⊡ **The Lodge at Ko'ele.** Keomoku Hwy; 808-565-7300 or 800-321-4666. A charming mountain retreat just a 10-minute walk from Lana'i City. Designed like a plantation manor with fine woodwork. Luxurious rooms and suites. Golf course set amid pines. Horseback riding, pool. Spa facilities available at Manele Bay Hotel (free shuttle). **$$$**

⊡ **Manele Bay Hotel.** Keomoku Hwy.; 808-565-7700 or 800-321-4666. Seaside villa with modern, airy rooms, atop a cliff overlooking Hulopo'e swimming beach and marine preserve. Spa with exercise gym, whirlpools, and beauty treatment rooms. A free shuttle operates between the Manele Bay and the Lodge at Ko'ele hotels. **$$$**

■ GOLFING ON LANA'I

Cavendish Golf Course. Lana'i City. No telephone. No power carts, no cashier, no reservations, and no starter. This is Old Hawai'i, a nine-hole, par-36 public course built in 1947 and operated on the honor system. Put your $5 in the mailbox next to the first tee and walk out to play—all day if you like.

The Challenge. Manele Bay; 808-565-2222. Jack Nicklaus has said this course is one of the most beautiful pieces of land he has ever built on; it is one of Hawai'i's top ten. Built along sea cliffs in hilly terrain, all 18 holes have wide-ranging ocean views; the finishing holes play on the cliffs. A shot-maker's course, no water hazards—except for the unending ocean—are at play.

The Experience. Ko'ele Lodge, Lana'i City; 808-565-2222. Designed by Ted Robinson and Greg Norman, this is the island's first luxury course. Stunning setting high at the island's center, with sweeping vistas of pine valleys and upper Lana'ihale Mountain slopes. You can see out across the channel to Moloka'i and Maui. Deer and pheasant wander the course.

MOLOKA'I
LONELY, FRIENDLY ISLE

Moloka'i lay like a homely sway-backed whale on the water.
—Mark Twain

Rural Moloka'i retains a distinctive, nineteenth-century charm, perhaps because nearly 50 percent of its population is native Hawaiian and keeps alive the real Hawai'i's mood and culture. Living in tiny towns studded with fruit-packed, flowering gardens, the island's 7,800 residents see few tourists, and because Moloka'i has dangerous reefs and no natural harbors, development has come slowly. Though the glamorous hotels lighting up west Maui can be seen just eight miles away across the Pailolo Channel from Moloka'i's rugged eastern shore, visitors who prefer a natural Hawai'i rather than the megaresorts of larger islands are in the right place.

In geographically diverse Moloka'i, lush tropical preserves flourish on the eastern shore. Most of the north shore is a line of soaring valley-slashed sea cliffs, among the tallest in the world, falling 2,000 feet to meet wild ocean waters below. The western section of the north shore tapers down to remote fishing beaches, and the western interior is a dry plain clad in the bright green color of seed-corn fields growing in rich red earth, and scrub plains that drop into shallow ravines where brown-green *kiawe* trees grow tall. At the western end, Hawai'i's largest beach, Papohaku, stretches along the Kaiwi Channel. Outlined in the shallow waters of southern shores are ancient fish ponds, some restored and used as they were long ago, for farming fish.

■ HISTORY

In ancient chants, Moloka'i is the child of Hina in her embodiment as goddess of the moon. It has always been something of an outpost. Called the Lonely Isle in olden times, it was a haven for *kapu*-breakers and the vanquished, and associated with mystical practices of the *kahuna* (priests) and sorcery. The power of the *kahuna* was

A Hawaiian man in a traditional ti-leaf rain cloak blows a conch shell on the north shore of Moloka'i at the mouth of the Wailau Valley.

feared throughout the archipelago, for it was believed they could pray a person to death. The sacred hula associated with ceremonial rites was born on this island.

In 1786, eight years after Captain Cook first saw the islands, the British sailor George Dixon anchored off south Moloka'i, and Hawaiians on the island took their first look at foreigners.

Four years later Kamehameha the Great came here to negotiate a marriage, then sailed from south Moloka'i to the Big Island in a double war canoe, accompanied by the young bride-to-be Keopuolani, her mother, and her sister. The little girl was the daughter of a chieftess and her brother—the prescribed marriage if its issue were to be a child of the highest caste *(Niau'pio)*. This caste was so exalted that if the shadow of a *Niau'pio* caste member fell on someone of inferior caste, that person had to be killed and the body burned. By the age of eleven, Keopuolani was betrothed to Kamehameha, who already had a roster of wives, including his favorite—the beloved, wise, and childless Ka'ahumanu. As young Keopuolani was capable of bearing Kamehameha a *Naiu'pio* son, and because this was a religious and political necessity, she became his "sacred wife."

Father Damien poses with girls from Moloka'i's leper settlement, circa 1880.

The strategy of the Warrior King called for conquest of his most important targets—the largest islands and populations—before he mopped up the smaller isles. In his final year of conquest, 1795, a line of war canoes four miles long appeared in waters off Molokaʻiʻs southern shore, and soon the island was his. In the same year Kamehameha married Keopuolani, now 16 years old, in Waikiki.

When explorers, whalers, and sandalwood traders arrived in the islands they found no natural harbor at Molokaʻi and steered clear of its reef-strewn muddy south shores. British Captain George Vancouver lowered his anchor here in 1792. Though he remained aboard, he estimated the population at 10,000, including large numbers of people in the remote and lush north-shore valleys.

By the 1830s missionaries had arrived, and cattle and sheep ranches began to flourish on the island. In 1848, during the reign of Kamehameha II, the Great *Mahele* became law. The greatest land revolution Hawaiʻi had ever known, it ended the Hawaiian system of communal land tenure. With the intent of giving native Hawaiians an opportunity to possess land, the new law divided and reallocated the kingʻs land. (See History & Culture chapter) In the 1850s, Kamehameha V acquired nearly 40 percent of the island and formed the 60,000-acre Molokaʻi Ranch, which was, for a time, the second-largest cattle station in the islands. Sold after his death, it was acquired by Honolulu businessmen in 1897.

In the 1860s a gift arrived with consequences no one could foresee: axis deer, from the emperor of Japan to Kamehameha V. From the point of view of the deer, this must have seemed like a fine, predator-free environment. They began to propagate rapidly, and were soon a blight on native plant and birdlife. Feral cattle and sheep added to the ravage of the ecosystem.

In 1866 the nickname Lonely Isle took on a new meaning for Molokaʻi. The dreaded disease leprosy, believed to have entered Hawaiʻi with the immigrant waves from China, had spread throughout the islands, and Kamehameha V decided to isolate lepers on Molokaʻi. He established a leper colony at **Kalawao** on the islandʻs lonely north peninsula. Lepers were wrenched from their homes, taken by ship to Molokaʻi, and tossed into the seas near the windy peninsula—doomed to survive, if they could, without support on a wave-lashed projection of land.

To this broken-hearted, lawless scrubland, Father Damien (Joseph Damien de Veuster), a Belgian priest, came in 1873. For the next 16 years the "Martyr of Molokaʻi" worked and lived among the tormented, wrapping superating sores, banging coffins together, and praying over graves. During Damienʻs last days the

THE DAMIEN LETTER

Few people have inspired such admiration as Father Damien, the Belgian priest who in 1873 went to care for Moloka'i's lepers. Perhaps inevitably, less saintly humans soon were itching to point out his flaws. One of these was a Dr. C. M. Hyde, who wrote this letter about Damien to a fellow minister and allowed it to be reprinted in several newspapers.

Honolulu
August 2, 1889
Rev. H.B. Gage.

Dear Brother,—In answer to your inquiries about Father Damien, I can only reply that we who knew the man are surprised at the extravagant newspaper laudations, as if he was a most saintly philanthropist. The simple truth is, he was a coarse, dirty man, headstrong and bigoted. He was not sent to Moloka'i, but went there without orders; did not stay at the leper settlement (before he became one himself), but circulated freely over the whole island (less than half the island is devoted to the lepers), and he came often to Honolulu. He had no hand in the reforms and improvements inaugurated, which were the work of our Board of Health, as occasion required and means were provided. He was not a pure man in his relations with women, and the leprosy of which he died should be attributed to his vices and carelessness. Others have done much for the lepers, our own ministers, the government physicians, and so forth, but never with the Catholic idea of meriting eternal life.—Yours, etc.,

C. M. Hyde

Hyde's letter was reprinted in Australia in the Sydney Presbyterian, *where Robert Louis Stevenson, author of* Kidnapped *and* Treasure Island, *happened to read it. Stevenson had only recently left Hawai'i and had spent a week at the Moloka'i leper colony just a few days after Damien's death. His reply, also published in the newspapers, was as follows:*

An Open Letter to the Reverend Dr. Hyde of Honolulu
Sydney,
February 25, 1890
Sir

. . . Your Church and Damien's were in Hawaii upon a rivalry to do well: to help, to edify, to set divine examples. You having (in one huge instance) failed, and Damien succeeded. . . .

■ ■ ■

. . . Of Damien I begin to have an idea. He seems to have been a man of the peasant class, certainly of the peasant type: shrewd, ignorant, and bigoted, yet with an open mind, and capable of receiving and digesting a reproof if it were bluntly administered; superbly generous in the least thing as well as in the greatest, and as ready to give his last shirt (although not without human grumbling) as he had been to sacrifice his life. . . .

■ ■ ■

. . . [You say] Damien was *coarse*. It is very possible. You make us sorry for the lepers, who had only a coarse old peasant for their friend and father. But you, who were so refined, why were you not there, to cheer them with the lights of culture? Or may I remind you that we have some reason to doubt if John the Baptist were genteel; and in the case of Peter, on whose career you doubtless dwell approvingly in the pulpit, no doubt at all he was a "coarse, headstrong" fisherman! Yet even in our Protestant Bibles Peter is called Saint. . . .

. . . [You say] Damien was *dirty*. He was. Think of the poor lepers annoyed with this dirty comrade! But the clean Dr. Hyde was at his food in a fine house.

. . . [You say] Damien *was not a pure man in his relations with women.* How do you know that? Is this the nature of the conversation in that house on Beretania Street which the cabman envied, driving past?—racy details of the misconduct of the poor peasant priest, toiling under the cliffs of Moloka'i.

Many have visited the station before me; they seem not to have heard the rumour.

■ ■ ■

But I fear you scarce appreciate how you appear to your fellow-men; and to bring it home to you, I will suppose your story to be true. I will suppose—and God forgive me for supposing it—that Damien faltered and stumbled in his narrow path of duty; I will suppose that, in the horror of his isolation, perhaps in the fever of incipient disease, he, who was doing so much more than he had sworn, failed in the letter of his priestly oath—he, who was so much a better man than either you or me, who did what we have never dreamed of daring—he too tasted of our common frailty.

—Robert Louis Stevenson, *Scots Observer,* 1890

colony was moved to the western (and more protected) side of the peninsula, called **Kalaupapa** (Flat Plain). In 1889, at the age of 49, Father Damien died of leprosy, contracted from the people he'd strived so hard to help. He was buried at the settlement. In 1937 his remains were exhumed and reburied at Louvain in Belgium, where he had trained for the priesthood. In 1995 Damien was beatified by Pope John Paul II, who presented a reliquary containing the right hand of Damien to be interred at the original gravesite in Kalaupapa.

By 1921 a significant number of Hawaiians were settling on 40-acre Moloka'i homesteads acquired under the Hawaiian Homestead Act. With them came a gracious heritage and the spirit of *aloha*—and Moloka'i acquired its present label: the Friendly Isle. When pineapple was introduced in the 1920s, the companies imported laborers from the Philippines and Japan to work the fields. Many homesteaders leased their lands to the pineapple companies. While that put them in a position of dependency, it offered a measure of security. Some 60 years later, in the late 1980s, Dole and Del Monte closed their pineapple operations on Moloka'i, and the realities of lost lease rent and unemployment dealt residents a mighty blow. Diversified agriculture and labor-intensive seed-corn may someday replace the single crop, but a majority of Moloka'i's residents prefer an economy based on limited tourism—confined to "master-planned" beaches on the western coast. The island has just one small hotel and a few condos and vacation rentals, so the availability of rooms is limited.

■ CENTRAL MOLOKA'I

Moloka'i's small airport lies at the island's narrow mid-point, eight miles from Kaunakakai, which hugs the south-central shore. In addition to regularly scheduled inter-island flights, there is quite a lot of private plane traffic. One time when we landed here, my husband asked the tower where to park and was told to head for an apron vaguely located under the tower. Taxiing there, he asked if we were in the right spot. The tower voice replied: "Tarreefick!" The car-rental agencies were closed. No one was around. When a pickup truck drove in, we asked for a lift. No problem. We climbed into the open truck and were taken straight into town. The Friendly Isle really is *friendly*.

MOLOKA'I

Pailolo Channel

Cape Halawa
Halawa Bay
Halawa Beach
HALAWA VALLEY
Halawa
Waialua

Pu'u Lua
3,202 ft
Pukoo
Ili'ili'opae He'iau

Hwy 450
'Ualapu'e Fishpond
'Ualapue

WAIALU VALLEY
Kamakou
4,970 ft
450
St. Joseph's
Kamalo

Oloku
4,602 ft

Moloka'i Forest Reserve

Kalaupapa Point
Moloka'i Light Station
Kalaupapa
Kalaupapa National Historic Park
Kaunako Crater
Kalawao

WAIKOLU VALLEY

Kamakou Preserve

Sandalwood Boat
Nene O Moloka'i Sanctuary
Pakuhiwa
Kamehameha
Kawela

Kalaupapa Airport
KALAUPAPA PENINSULA
Kalaupapa
Phallic Rock
Kalaupapa Lookout
470
Kualapu'u
480
470

Church Row
Kaunakakai
Kamiloloa Beach

Umipaa
460
Kiowea Park

Mo'omomi Beach
Mo'omomi Bay
Mo'omomi

Mokio Point

Ho'olehua
Ho'olehua Airport
460
Rd

Ilio Point
Kaluakoi Rd

Maunaloa Hwy
Pu'u Nana
1,381 ft
Ranch Lodge
460
Palaau

Kepuhi Beach
Papohaku Beach
Moloka'i Ranch Headquarters
Maunaloa
Kaupoa Beach Village
Hale o Lono Beach

Laeu Point

Kaiwi Channel

Kalohi Channel

Ferry to Maui

N
W — E
S

0   3   6 Miles
0   3   6   9 Kilometers

④

A B C D E F
1 2 3 4

■ **KAUNAKAKAI** *map page 181, C/D-3*

Moloka'i's largest town, flat and treeless Kaunakakai, looks like an Old West movie set, with false-front buildings lining the single street. Its three commercial blocks offer a couple of old-fashioned general stores, two grocery markets, an all-purpose drug store, and a bakery-restaurant. No traffic light, movie house, or elevator; no disco or boutique, bus line, or fast-food emporium intrudes in the sleepy port town.

Kaunakakai, an abbreviated form of Kaunakahakai, means "beach landing." If you stroll down to the shore of the tiny port town, you'll see a concrete wharf extending out over coral and mud into deep ocean. This modern pier replaced an old coconut-log pier onto which, in early days, passengers disembarked from ships. They then boarded a rail car which was pulled by a mule up to the beach.

As Moloka'i lacks a natural deep-water harbor, the Army Corps of Engineers dredged a channel adjacent to the pier in 1934. It can service only barges, and even today deep-draft ships cannot be accommodated at Moloka'i. In a corner of the man-made harbor is a marina that provides the only public boat ramp on the island. (At other areas of the island, residents launch over the beach.) On the west

It is said that if a women strokes Phallic Rock reverently, she will become more fertile.

side of the wharf, behind the thatched canoe club, lie the ruins of Malama, a vacation home and compound built by Kamehameha V. Today only a stone platform of the royal residence remains.

A couple of miles to the west of Kaunakakai is **Kiowea Park,** famed for its coconut grove named in honor of the island's high chief, Kapua'iwa. In 1863 Kapua'iwa (Prince Lot) became Kamehameha V, and it is said he planted the trees himself here at his place of birth. Due to erosion, some of them now lean directly over the water, and at low tide you can see freshwater springs that once were on land, burbling in the ocean. (Watch out for plummeting coconuts. If there's strong wind, it's not advisable to walk here.) With its muddy waters and a rock-strewn beach, Kiowea is better for picnics than swimming.

Across the highway from Kiowea, marching in line like a band of troops, are seven small chapels belonging to seven different denominations. Known as **Church Row,** it stands in silent testimony to the arrival of fervent Protestant missionaries upon the sacred ground of ancient Hawaiians.

■ **KALAUPAPA LOOKOUT AND PHALLIC ROCK** *map page 181, C-2*
Beyond Kiowea, travel north and *mauka* (inland) from Kaunakakai on HI 460 and turn onto HI 470 just before the rural village of Kualapu'u. The land rises gently up to its highest point where there is a parking lot. A quarter-mile walk through a pine wood brings you to **Kalaupapa Lookout.** Here, atop 1,664 feet of sheer cliff, an incomparable view of the sheer north coast *pali* stretches before you—14 miles of the tallest sea cliffs in the world, 1,000 feet or more high, weeping with waterfalls, and another 15 miles of lesser heights. Directly below lies a sweeping view of a fin-shaped projection jutting out from beneath the wall of *pali*—the Makanalua Peninsula (also known as the Kalaupapa Peninsula), site of the Kalaupapa leper settlement. About a quarter-mile walk from Kalaupapa Lookout, **Phallic Rock** protrudes immodestly from the pine-needled floor of a dense ironwood grove. It is said that if a woman strokes this worn six-foot outgrowth reverently, she'll become more fertile.

■ **KALAUPAPA LEPER COLONY** *map page 181, D-2*
Jutting out midway on the north coast lies the fin-shaped Makanalua (Kalaupapa) Peninsula, site of the Kalaupapa Leper Colony. The isolated flatland, belted with wind-whipped waves on three sides and cut off at its back by the sheer bulkhead of

LEPER GIRL

This story was inspired when Robert Louis Stevenson witnessed a group of lepers leaving their home at Kona, on the island of Hawai'i, to join Moloka'i's leper colony.

Between nine and ten of the same morning, the schooner lay-to off Hookena and a whaleboat came ashore. The village clustered on the rocks for the farewell: a grief perhaps—a performance certainly. We miss in our modern life these operatic consolations of the past. The lepers came singly and unattended; the elder first; the girl a little after, tricked out in a red dress and with a fine red feather in her hat. In this bravery, it was the more affecting to see her move apart on the rocks and crouch in her accustomed attitude. But this time I had seen her face; it was scarce horribly affected, but had a haunting look of an unfinished wooden doll, at once expressionless and disproportioned; doubtless a sore spectacle in the mirror of youth. Next there appeared a woman of the middle life, of a swaggering gait, a gallant figure, and a bold, handsome face. She came, swinging her hat, rolling her eyes and shoulders, visibly working herself up; the crowd stirred and murmured on her passage; and I knew, without being told, this was the mother and protagonist. Close by the sea, in the midst of the spectators, she sat down, and raised immediately the notes of the lament. One after another of her friends approached her. To one after the other she reached out an arm, embraced them down, rocked awhile with them embraced, and passionately kissed them in the island fashion, with the pressed face. The leper girl at last, as at some signal, rose from her seat apart, drew near, was inarmed like the rest, and with a small knot (I suppose of the most intimate) held some while in a general clasp. Through all, the wail continued, rising into words and a sort of passionate declamatory recitation as each friend approached, sinking again, as the pair rocked together, into the tremolo drone.

—Robert Louis Stevenson, *The Eight Islands,* 1893

ominous cliff, seems laden with melancholy. Lepers, once forcibly banished to this desolate flatland, lived here in despair and violence until the arrival of Joseph Damien de Veuster—Father Damien—in 1873.

Since Father Damien's time, great strides in medicine and support have come to Kalaupapa. With the introduction of sulfone and other antibiotic drug therapies, the disease can now be arrested, and those taking the drugs are no longer contagious. In the 1960s, some 100 years after the first shipload of lepers stood off the eastern side, admission of new residents at Kalaupapa ended. The settlement is destined for gradual phase-out, although Kalaupapa will continue to operate so long as any resident wishes to stay. Today some 49 elderly people still choose to live in the drowsy compound. In 1980 Kalaupapa became a National Historical Park, including a modern hospital, historic sites, wooden churches, and dusty lanes with small and tidy homes.

Unless you visit the colony on a guided tour, visitors must hire local guides and make arrangements in advance. Starting from "topside," you can walk or ride a mule down the Kalaupapa trail, descending 1,664 feet in 3 tortuous, breathtaking miles through 26 switchbacks; your guide will meet you at the bottom. Kalaupapa also can be visited by air.

Most tours stop at Kalawao, the first settlement on the east side; Father Damien's church, St. Philomena; and the monument and grave of Mother Marianne, who spent 30 years at Kalaupapa and was beatified by the Pope in 2004. Artifacts collected by patient and tour operator Richard Marks include specialized tools for

(above) A mule train carries visitors down 1,664 feet in three miles to the Kalaupapa leper settlement. (following spread) A mule train walks below the Kalaupapa cliff, on a desolate flatland where some elderly people still live.

everyday living such as a spoon that wraps around the wrist for patients who had lost fingers. While some of the tour is on foot, you'll also ride in a car—it will be an old car; there are no new ones at Kalaupapa. Unless you are on the mule-train tour, bring a pack lunch; no meal facilities are available. Photography is permitted of everything you see except patients. While the peninsula is a tourist attraction, its residents are not. *Contact Damien Tours, 808-567-6171, or Moloka'i Mule Ride, 800-567-7550.*

■ **MOLOKA'I LIGHT STATION** *map page 181, D-2*
Built in 1909, Moloka'i Light Station stands above ferocious seas on the northern tip of the Kalaupapa Peninsula and acts as a critical navigational guide for ships approaching O'ahu from the east. It was here that in 1946, following an earthquake in the Aleutian Islands, a 55-foot tsunami—equal to the highest recorded in the Hawaiian islands—swept ashore. The 138-foot concrete lighthouse remains unchanged since its construction and is one of the few original structures still in use in Hawai'i. The light atop the tower is visible 28 miles out to sea, and serves vessels bound from the west coast of the United States and the Panama Canal. For 57 years the isolated tower was operated by lighthouse keepers. When automation came in 1966, the colorful history of their tenancy came to an end.

■ **EAST MOLOKA'I**

The words *makai* (toward the ocean) and *mauka* (toward the uplands) apply as they do on all the islands, and on Moloka'i there is another: *mana'e*, meaning toward the east end. Here, especially on the northern shore, remote rain-forested valleys undulate down to the sea like great green cracks in the sea cliffs. They are accessible only in calm seas of the summer months, when small boats can run up close to the wide sandy beaches that fill the valley mouths. Only the easternmost Halawa Valley can be reached by road. This district lies apart in wilderness, untouched, or barely so, by civilization.

From Kaunakakai, a single road (HI 450) runs east along the southern shoreline. About three miles out from town a small hotel wreathed in red and yellow hibiscus trees hugs the shore. The fringe of the south shore, studded with coco and mango groves (some with picnic facilities), fronts muddy waters silted by the runoff of rain-forest streams. No swimming beaches here. Occasionally surfers may be seen far offshore standing on their boards in low waves. Along the way, ancient fishponds, piled with lava boulders in semicircles of varying size, can be seen in the shoreline waters.

Just before the four-mile marker, a turnoff leads up ten miles to **Kamakou Preserve** and the highest point on Moloka'i—Kamakou, at 4,970 feet. The road rapidly dissolves into a muddy and dangerous jeep track. The 2,774-acre sanctuary, managed by the Nature Conservancy, is a boggy rain forest where 219 species of endemic plants and endangered native forest birds are protected. Among tree ferns, 'ohi'a trees, and wild orchids live two bird species found nowhere else: the 'olomao (Moloka'i thrush) and the kakawahi'e (Moloka'i creeper). Hawaiian owls (pueo) and brilliant red 'apapane flash in the forest. Hiking trails here are very muddy, and the best way to go into the preserve is under the guidance of the Nature Conservancy, which conducts hikes once each month. *Contact the Nature Conservancy in Honolulu at 808-524-0779.*

Farther along the crest is the **Moloka'i Forest Reserve.** Here lies Lua Na Moku Iliahi—the **Sandalwood Boat.** In the 1830s, Hawaiians sought a way to gauge the quantity of sandalwood required to fill the hold of a trader. To do this, they sized and shaped an earthen pit in the shape of a sailing ship's hull and heaved in cut sandalwood until the pit was filled. Within just a few years the fragrant sandalwood forests were wiped out; some say the workers ripped out saplings so that their children would be spared the backbreaking labor. Now you find dark green cypress and eucalyptus, kuku'i (candlenut) trees, and wild berries to pick—as well as a lot of mud.

For a face-to-face encounter with the nene goose, Hawai'i's state bird, stop at the **Nene O Moloka'i sanctuary,** 4.2 miles east of Kaunakakai on HI 450. Visits are free, by appointment (808-553-5992). Please don't feed the birds.

Back on the highway, eight miles east of Kaunakakai, at Kawela Village, a Hawai'i Visitors Bureau sign marks **Pakuhiwa,** an early battleground and canoe-launching site used by Kamehameha the Great. Near the 10-mile marker stands **St. Joseph's,** a tiny, Gothic, white-frame chapel built by Father Damien in 1876.

Kamalo village marks Moloka'i's southernmost point. Just beyond, a monument locates the Smith & Bronte Landing—a bleak spot where the first civilian aircraft to fly the Pacific crash-landed in 1927, the same year Lindbergh flew across the Atlantic.

Three miles past Kamalo the road curves slightly eastward. Here you come to the 18-acre **'Ualapu'e Fish Pond,** which has been restored and restocked with 'ama'ama (mullet). A mile and a half farther, on the far side of Mapulehu Stream, a

Hawaiian boys walk through fields on north Moloka'i.

gate beside the highway leads to the largest and oldest *he'iau* (temple) on Moloka'i, the **Ili'ili'opae He'iau.** It is a short easy walk into Mapulehu Valley. The ancient, mossy stone platform—dated to between A.D. 1100 and 1300—is immense: up to 22 feet high, 87 feet wide, and 286 feet long. Legend says it was built in a single night by *menehune*—mythical elves who carried stones in the dark from a valley across the island. Here, where gods demanded human sacrifice and the *kahuna* trained novices, visitors sense their power. It is said the *kahuna* of Moloka'i possessed a force and mastery of power far surpassing the *kahuna* of other islands. The *he'iau* is on private land; visitors take a wagon-ride tour to the site. *Contact Moloka'i Horse and Wagon Ride, 808-558-8132.*

■ **HALAWA BAY** *map page 181, F-2*
As you continue *mana'e* (east) on HI 450, you'll see that the land becomes lusher, and the road begins an easterly climb with hairpin turns above cliffs, passing **Whispering Stone,** where fishermen once prayed for a good catch. The road then curves inland at the eastern tip of the island, through rolling cattle lands to reach an overlook above the white sands of Halawa Bay. Halawa is the easternmost valley on Moloka'i, and the only one accessible by car.

As you approach Halawa Valley, the *pali* backdrop seems part of a vivid watercolor painting, framing a tiny green-painted wooden church. At a sharp bend, stop to look down onto the beach before hairpinning down to the valley floor. A wandering stream wends through pastel shades of green to the beach. You may wish to swim at **Halawa Beach;** take care, the sea can be treacherous. The left cove is somewhat protected. The sea here was a favorite surfing spot of Molokaʻi's chiefs and is still locally popular. Opposite the valley mouth lie two rocky islets where booby birds gather.

Halawa means "curve," and in the curve of the valley, taro, staple of the Hawaiian diet, once was heavily cultivated. The area was settled as early as A.D. 650, and by the 1800s some 500 people still lived here, supplying the entire island with taro. The 1946 tsunami destroyed the homes and fields of the few remaining commercial taro farmers and fishermen in Halawa, and waves of another tsunami again flooded the valley in 1957. While the old taro fields now are sunk under rampant tropical growth, a few residents still choose to live in the isolated valley.

■ West Molokaʻi

West of Kaunakakai, the Maunaloa Highway (HI 460) bisects western Molokaʻi. Past lands where pineapple once flourished, the road twists and rises gently through dry grassy plains. As pineapple production was phased out on the island, severe unemployment set in. Today coffee bushes thrive at the 800-foot level. Try the Molokaʻi Coffee Plantation Company's espresso bar (808-567-9023).

■ Molokaʻi Ranch *map page 181, A/B-2*
The Molokaʻi Ranch—sprawling from the mountains to the sea across 35,000 acres (almost one-third of the island)—has made substantial investments to open a unique, ecologically sensitive beach camp and a ranch lodge. Beside the ocean, Kaupoa Beach Village fronts two crescents of white-sand beach and offers snorkeling, tide-pool exploration, and fishing. The Ranch Lodge, in Maunaloa town, stands atop a mountain bluff at a cool 1,000-foot elevation and has expansive views of the ocean. Here rustic plantation days are recaptured in historic photos and a wraparound veranda. Take in the stunning big-sky view of pasturelands and unending blue Pacific Ocean. Activities at the camp and lodge are close-to-nature experiences; knowledgeable ranch hands will accompany you while mountain biking and horseback riding, cattle roping and kayaking. You can take a nature walk

with a local ethnobotanist, or just laze like a pasha, eating fresh tropical fruits and listening to the surf pound. *Maunaloa town and Kaupoa Beach; 888-627-8082, or in Honolulu, 808-534-9561.*

■ MAUNALOA *map page 181, A/B-3*

About 15 miles out of Kaunakakai on the Maunaloa Highway, the road forks. The northern route heads west to western beaches, the southern road winds upward for two miles to Maunaloa (Long Mountain) village, where bright bougainvillea and mango trees front frame and stucco homes, dogs sleep on the front steps, and a *mo'a* (chicken) may scratch at the ground near a fishing dory parked on a trailer.

Like Tombstone after the West was won, this old plantation town has revived to become the island's version of trendy craft shops and art galleries. One is unique— the Big Wind Kite Shop. In windy Maunaloa, at Hawai'i's only kite factory, designer-owner Jonathan Socher flies hula dancers in the wind; heavenly palm trees sway, painted clouds ruffle by, and mythical beasts gallop the skies.

■ WESTSIDE BEACHES

Hale o Lono Beach *map page 181, A/B-3*

South from Maunaloa town at a rocky point on the west side of Lono Barge Harbor lies narrow, sandy Hale o Lono (House of Lono) Beach. Every year in October, the **Moloka'i to O'ahu outrigger canoe race** starts from this patch of sand. Canoe-paddling clubs throughout Hawai'i, and world-wide, practice year-round for this race. The crossing of the perilous Kaiwi Channel is considered one of the most challenging open-ocean competitions in the world. Spectators gather at Hale o Lono the morning of the race.

Kepuhi Beach *map page 181, A-2*

About five miles west from the main fork above Maunaloa, HI 460 reaches the western shore. Kepuhi Beach, far from everywhere, is long and wide, and its white sands drop off sharply into deep water. Swimming here is safe only on the calmest of days; otherwise it's treacherous. This beach is best for sunbathing and viewing the profile of O'ahu, which rises in brown and purple colors across sparkling blue white-capped waters.

The white sands of Kepuhi Beach drop off sharply into deep water. Swimming is safe only on the calmest of days.

■ **Papohaku Beach** *map page 181, A-2*

Separated from Kepuhi by a hill, Papohaku (Stone Fence) Beach is three miles long and 100 yards wide, the largest, whitest beach on the island. Backed by sand dunes and *kiawe* trees, it is beckoning and picturesque, and like Kephui, it is best as a viewing beach. Powerful currents of Kaiwi Channel thunder onto the shore unbroken by a protecting reef, and the strong backwash is perilous to beach strollers. From the early 1960s until 1972, the beach sands were mined to feed O'ahu's construction boom.

Inland from the dunes at the north end of the beach, Papohaku Beach Park is equiped with facilities and camp sites.

Hairy little plants called *'ena'ena* (hot), found only in western Moloka'i, grow on the hot coastal sand dunes behind the beaches. This Hawaiian cudweed differs from other cudweeds in its thick covering of delicate hair that casts the leaves in a silvery blue color. *'Ena'ena* grows about a foot high and bears tight clusters of tiny muted yellow flowers.

■ THE DESERT STRIP *map page 181, B-2*

The northern coast of western Moloka'i is all but inaccessible. One place, **Mo'omomi Beach,** is well worth the effort. Long ago, Hawaiians came by canoe to catch and dry fish at a place on the shoreline called Mo'omomi (pearl lizard). Bashed by wind and pounding surf, this stretch is known as the Desert Strip, or Keonelele (Wind-Blown Sands). It is a storm beach. Sands are steep at the water line, the ocean bottom abruptly deep. At the eastern side, called Kawa'aloa (Long Canoe), a shattered reef gives mild protection, and experienced surfers sometimes paddle over from Mo'omomi Bay. This area is exposed to almost constant wind that picks up shoreline sand and carries it inland, sometimes as far as four miles, to form sand dunes that continually pile up, reform, and evolve into weirdly shaped wind-carved stone. The fragile native ecosystems thriving at Mo'omomi are managed and protected by the Nature Conservancy. Driving in is not permitted, and the gate is locked. Under special circumstances you can arrange to drive in for trail walks. *Call the Moloka'i offices of the Nature Conservancy at 808-553-5236.*

To reach Mo'omomi Bay Beach, take HI 470 from central Moloka'i. At Kualapu'u turn northwest onto HI 482. After a few minutes turn west on HI 480, a narrow paved road passing through Ho'olehua village and continuing for a couple of miles to the bay. Here the Hawaiian Home Lands Recreation Center fronts a tiny, protected, white-sand beach on the east side of the bay that is popular and safe for swimming.

■ TRAVEL BASICS

A single highway travels the length of Moloka'i. From Kaunakakai, Moloka'i's main town, the road heads east, following the south shore and curving along the eastern flank of the island to end at the north shore sea cliffs. In the west it ends at a wide, white beach. There is no public transportation on Moloka'i, and car-rental agencies are located only at Ho'olehua Airport, eight miles west of Kaunakakai.

■ VISITOR INFORMATION SERVICES

Chamber of Commerce. P.O. Box 515, Kaunakakai 96748; 808-922-1786.
Hawai'i Visitors Bureau, Maui. 808-244-3530.
Moloka'i Visitors Association. P.O. Box 960, Kaunakakai 96748; 808-553-3876. From U.S. and Canada, 800-800-6367.
Moloka'i Visitors Bureau. 800-800-6367.

■ FOOD AND LODGING

⊞ For agencies offering listings and booking services for bed-and-breakfasts, hotels, and condominiums on all islands, see page 359.
$ For room and restaurant price designations, see page 359.

■ KAUNAKAKAI *map page 181, C/D-3*

✕ **Kanemitsu Bakery & Restaurant.** Kaunakakai town; 808-553-5855. Old island-style Japanese restaurant and bakery. Breakfast and lunch only. **$**
✕ **Kualapu'u Cook House.** Kualapu'u village; 808-567-6185. In a converted plantation residence, this is the only eatery within miles of Kualapu'u village. American diner and Hawaiian plate lunch menu. Entertainment some nights. Owned by local artist Nannette Yamashita. **$**
⊞ **Hotel Moloka'i.** Kamiloloa Beach.; 808-553-5347 or 800-535-0085. Reopened after renovations, this 35-room waterfront hotel is a cluster of A-frame bungalows just outside of town. Dining room, lounge, and pool. **$–$$**

■ WEST END *map page 181, A/B-2/3*

⊞ **Moloka'i Ranch Lodge & Beach Village.** Maunaloa town and Kaupoa Beach; 888-627-8082, or in Honolulu, 808-534-9561. The flavor of old ranch-style Hawai'i is everywhere on the island, and the ambience at both Moloka'i

Ranch sites is luxury in far places. The Lodge, constructed of wooden beams, offers gourmet dining, country-themed rooms, and old-fashioned claw-foot bathtubs, as well as an outdoor heated pool and nightly entertainment. The Beach Village is the ultimate in yuppie camping. Its "tentalows" are tents mounted on wooden platforms, with wide decks and lounge chairs, solar-powered lights, showers, and ceiling fans. A pavilion on the beach serves buffet meals, and there is nightly entertainment under the stars. Ranch transportation is provided; access to diverse activities is offered from both locations. **$$$**

■ **WAIALUA** *map page 181, F-3*

▦ **Aloha Beach House.** Waialua Beach; 808-828-1100 or 888-828-1008. On a 7-acre estate, this Hawaiian-style two-bedroom house on a white-sand beach is ideal for families (up to 5 people). Complete kitchen, VCR, and library; close to the Neighborhood Store for shopping or eating out. Horseback riding is available. **$$$**

■ **GOLFING ON MOLOKA'I**

One golf course graces this island. Once discovered, it quickly becomes a favorite.
Ironwood Hills Golf Course. P.O. Box 182, Kualapu'u; 808-567-6000. This public 9-hole course built by Del Monte Corporation in 1928 and 1990 is the most affordable course in the state. It's hidden away and hard to find but lots of fun, with Bermuda fairways, few hazards, and sometimes flat and sometimes steep, hilly terrain. There are bunkers at nearly every hole; wind is the player's main consideration. Pro shop, putting green, snack shop, and carts. Take HI 470 northwest for 3.3 miles from the junction with HI 460; course is on the left. Reservations suggested.

■ **OUTDOOR ADVENTURES**

Bill Kapuni's Snorkel and Dive. 808-553-9867. Moloka'i native Bill leads you to the island's hottest dive and snorkel spots. Rental gear and dive certification also available.
Moloka'i Horse and Wagon Ride. 808-558-8132. Take a wagon tour to Ili'ili'opae He'iau.
Moloka'i Mule Ride. Kaunakakai; 800-567-7550. A perilous yet exhilarating trip on sure-footed mules that drops almost 1,700 feet down a narrow trail to the former leper colony on the Kalaupapa Peninsula.

Molokaʻi Plumerias. 1342 Maunaloa Hwy; 808-553-3391. The state's largest plumeria farm. Tour the orchard and come away with a fragrant lei you've strung yourself.

Molokaʻi Ranch. Maunaloa; 808-552-0184 (or 808-553-5926 in Kaunakakai). Offers horseback riding, mountain biking, sea kayaking, snorkeling, and more.

■ **KALAUPAPA TOUR**

The most informative pilgrimage around the Kalaupapa Peninsula is the tour operated by Richard Marks, a third-generation Kalaupapa resident. Marks is a walking library of Kalaupapa history and an accomplished storyteller with a light touch. He also arranges overnights at the lighthouse. *Contact Damien Tours, 808-567-6171.*

■ **FESTIVALS AND EVENTS**

■ **MAY**

Molokaʻi Ka Hula Piko. Celebrates birth of hula with storytelling, performances. Molokaʻi Visitors Association; 808-553-3876 or 800-800-6367.

■ **JUNE**

Kamehameha Day Celebration. Crafts, food, royal court. Mitchell Pauole Center, Kaunakakai; 808-586-0333.

■ **NOVEMBER**

Molokaʻi Ranch Rodeo. Annual rodeo and stew cook-off brings top rodeo professionals to compete for cash prizes at the arena. Favorite contests include bareback and saddle bronco riding and bull riding. There's a barn dance too. Molokaʻi Visitors Association; 808-553-3876 or 800-800-6367.

Ultramarathon. A 100K (62-mile) race and a 42K (25.2-mile) race. The 100K starts in Kaunakakai and traverses the southeast side of the island to Halawa Valley, the halfway point. Runners retrace the course; stations every 5K. For the shorter race, runners are transported to Halawa Valley to begin. Contact Lani Sahagun, 808-553-5471, or P.O. Box 408, Kaunakakai, HI 96748.

HONOLULU & WAIKIKI
DIAMOND HEAD AND PEARL HARBOR

Nine miles east of O'ahu's main airport, skirting downtown Honolulu on the Nimitz Highway, lies Waikiki, undeniably among the most exquisite, lively, and overdeveloped tropical beaches in the world. It is also the Hawaiian Islands' most famous beach resort, and it lies at the base of an O'ahu landmark known the world round—the volcanic profile of Diamond Head, or Le'ahi (Brow), shaped some 400,000 years ago. In downtown Honolulu, an important business and economic hub of the Pacific, stands the symbol of the only monarchy in the United States—'Iolani Palace. Its history is the history of the last days of Hawaiian royalty.

High-rises stab the skylines of Waikiki and downtown Honolulu, and their detractors bemoan the island's commercialism—its ostentatious homes, glitzy boutiques, and clogged freeways. Honolulu's admirers tell you to use your *maka* (eyes) and look around you. Waikiki Beach is one and one-half miles of exquisite white sands, and nearby Ko'olau mountain waterfalls, hiking trails, and forest reserves are only minutes from Honolulu's urban centers. At the same time, Honolulu offers gourmet dining and a glamorous nightlife, Japanese Noh theater and Broadway plays, performances of ancient and modern hula, ballet, and symphony concerts. Then there is the shopping—spacious open plazas brimming with shops and designer boutiques straight from Paris, Milan, London, and New York.

Honolulu (Protected Bay) is the mid-Pacific's business and economic center, Hawai'i's state capital, and the eleventh most populous metropolitan area in the United States.

■ HISTORY

In 1907, when the Great Lady of Waikiki, the Moana Hotel, was just six years old, the shortest way from Honolulu to the beach was the King Street electric trolley. With open-sided cars and flop-over seat backs, it trundled along McCully Street and out onto a wooden trestle mounted over a swamp. Passing over rock and soil mounds, the trolley ran through small, mosquito-infested, malodorous islands with Chinese-owned duck farms and an assortment of chickens, cows, mules, and horses, before it turned onto Waikiki Road (now Kalakaua Avenue).

The trolley rolled past a dense growth of trees and shrubs on the ocean side. Landward from the Moana was Ainahau (Cool Place), where the young Princess Ka'iulani (1875–99) once lived. Nearby, the palms of the Royal Grove enclosed the summer homes of royalty; up Ke'alohilani (Glow of Heaven) Street, were the homes of King Kalakaua and his queen, Kapi'olani. Kamehameha V built his summer place where the Princess Ka'iulani Hotel now stands. The summer home Queen Lili'uokalani described as her "pretty seaside cottage" faced onto Ohua Avenue, and her own pier reached out into the water along the shore of the present Kuhio/Queen's surf beaches.

Beside the open ocean, past long white threads of breaking surf, the trolley line ended near the base of Diamond Head. Spectator stands for the race track and polo field of Kapi'olani Park stood on the plain nearby.

Hawaiians continue to enjoy live music and hula dancing.

The sun sets on the quiet waters of Ala Wai Yacht Harbor.

At the beginning of the century the beach at Waikiki (Spouting Water) was a narrow strand of sand that ran from the Moana pier to the western end of the present Royal Hawaiian Hotel. In those days, every time a heavy rain fell, swollen streams sped down nearby valleys, flooding the Royal Grove, Ainahau, and parts of Waikiki Road. Inundated swamps spewed water through a culvert under the road, and water settled into a pond next to the Moana Hotel, cutting overflows across the beach. Often, it took as long as a week for the water to abate.

The accessibility to Waikiki brought by the trolley line gained popularity for the Moana, and soon more seaside hotels and homes of influential or wealthy families were built along the shore. Concrete seawalls spread in both directions from the little beach—built by landowners in a time before people realized that, rather than preserving the beaches, walls can cause their erosion. Access to the beach and surf grew increasingly limited for common folk. One person who noticed this was the writer Jack London, who sailed into Honolulu in 1907 aboard his barely seaworthy though celebrated ketch, the *Snark*.

An apocryphal story relates that London was walking on the beach one day with an acquaintance, concerned that Waikiki was less accessible to ordinary Hawaiians than previously. Remarked London, "It's a damn shame that the royal sport of surfriding is dying out." The other gentlemen replied, "Something can be done and we will do it." The outcome of this was the Outrigger Canoe Club, founded in 1908. It continues to thrive as a haven on the beach for surfers, canoeists, and swimmers. The haven works wonderfully for those who can afford it, though many water enthusiasts are discouraged when club membership swells and a moratorium is put on new members. The club's oral histories are a rich stash of early Waikiki Beach water sports.

By the mid-1920s the marshes and duck ponds around Waikiki were soon to become history. In 1930 the 250-foot wide Ala Wai Canal was completed. Built to channel speeding rainwaters from the valleys, it runs the length of Waikiki several blocks inland from the main road. Its brackish, tidal canal waters now undulate into the Ala Wai Yacht Harbor fronting the Ilikai and Prince hotels. On summer evenings you can watch canoe teams bolting down the canal in paddling practice for state and international competitions.

■ WAIKIKI

Under the modern assault of concrete and glass, the mile-and-a-half Waikiki resort strip moves to a fast beat. About 31,000 permanent residents call Waikiki home, and some 70,000 visitors converge on Waikiki every day, strolling along its stretch of white sands and through the shops of Kalakaua Avenue. With about half the accommodations for visitors in the state, Waikiki hosts planeloads of conventioneers, package tourists, and honeymooners from the U.S. mainland, Japan, and Europe. In its roughly 450 restaurants you can taste many of the world's cuisines. There are hundreds of bars and more shops and designer boutiques than can be found on New York's Madison Avenue. It's a vibrant crowd scene, and despite the noise of construction and rebuilding, people smile in the benign climate, and you hear laughter in the street.

If the beaches draw tourists all day long, the streets come alive at night as discos boom, bars blare, and ladies of the night parade. The more exclusive hotels provide another side to Waikiki, where gourmet dining, Hawaiian music and the hula, and popular dance music are featured.

Waikiki sunsets are an antidote to the clatter and clutter. A great orange ball surrounded in brilliant pink sinks into a sea studded with sailboats, leaving crimson and rust-colored skies that dim to smoky blue. Twilight lasts but a moment in these climes, so look quickly, and don't miss the high-rises glowing like sheets of gold in the fading light.

Holding the whole show together are the fabled white sands and surf of Waikiki Beach. With its gradually sloping seabed and softly lapping waves, Waikiki can be enjoyed by every level of swimmer or surfer. Recent construction of groins and sea-walls has altered the offshore sea bottom, and the lines of breaking surf are some-what different than when royalty surfed here. Fortunately for Waikiki's visitors and residents, jet skis and other thrillcraft are prohibited.

Each section of Waikiki—from the Colony Surf Hotel west to Duke Kahanamoku Beach at the Hawaiian Village Hotel—has its own name, often that of the facing hotel. At the east toward Diamond Head, the beach is fronted by an arbor grown thick with gnarled branches of *hau*. Tall coconut trees grow amid open lawns. These same trees, now sheltering visitors, were planted in the 1870s by the Scotsman Archibald Cleghorn, father of Princess Ka'iulani. Known as Honolulu's "father of parks," Cleghorn also planted two banyan trees that have grown large in front of the zoo across the street.

■ **SANS SOUCI BEACH** *map opposite, D-2*
The east-end beach was once home to the Manuia Lanai, a beach bungalow where Robert Louis Stevenson stayed in January 1889. Eventually, a small hotel named the Sans Souci was built here, and prior to the overthrow of the monarchy in 1893, loyalists met at the hotel. The Sans Souci became infamous after arrests were made on the premises, including that of Prince Jonah Kuhio Kalaniana'ole. In a later five-week stay at the hotel, Stevenson extolled its delights in his writings. Today the **New Otani Kaimana Beach Hotel** stands on the site, and its patch of sand still is known as Sans Souci. Safe and shallow, with a sandy bottom, the beach is a good spot for children to swim. (The *hau* tree that sheltered Stevenson still pre-sides over the hotel terrace.)

■ **WAIKIKI AQUARIUM** *map opposite, D-2*
It was at the aquarium, west of the Kaimana, that Jack London was heard to exclaim, "I never dreamed of so wonderful an orgy of color and form." It is the only aquarium in the U.S. located on a live coral reef, and the first facility to breed

(following spread) Visitors claim a small piece of paradise on the beach at Waikiki.

and maintain living coral in captivity. It pioneered methods of raising large quantities of *mahimahi* (dolphinfish, or dorado), whose snubnosed male resembles a small iridescent sperm whale. Unlike reef fish, *mahi* are fast swimmers accustomed to open ocean and are kept in a specially designed tank.

The aquarium is the world center for information on the chambered nautilus and was the first in the U.S. to display the living creatures. It also holds the record for successfully breeding them. Although deep-sea mollusks have existed for more than 500 million years, the chambered nautilus has never been reared outside its natural environment; it lives only in deep water—at depths up to 2,000 feet. No one has found baby nautilus or their eggs in nature.

Here also are the endangered Hawaiian monk seals, giant 100-pound clams, and galleries of Hawaiian and South Pacific sea life. Deep-swimming, newly discovered butterfly fish are on display. Also look for the rare sight of bigfin reef squid, which can change color almost instantaneously. Established under the aegis of the University of Hawai'i in 1919, the aquarium is operated by the School of Ocean and Earth Science Technology. *2777 Kalakaua Avenue; 808-923-9741.*

■ **KAPI'OLANI BEACH PARK** *map page 203, C-2*

Swim, board-surf, snorkel, and dive here. The best swimming area is Queen's Surf Beach, named for a nightclub and restaurant that once stood on the site of a former private home. Today the area is all beach, backed by lawns. At the eastern side, in front of the aquarium, residents often pole-fish for tiny goatfish called *'oama*. These waters are laced with a shallow reef that drops off abruptly. Snorkelers should come in high tide, to see red- or yellow-striped goatfish poking in the coral for small crustaceans and worms. At the opposite end, near a groin called the Wall, beginning surfers practice in the small surf, and swimmers should be on the lookout for the new initiates.

The finish line of the Honolulu Marathon, held each December, is in Kapi'olani Park. The event has grown from small beginnings to an international race that brought more than 22,000 runners and thousands of spectators to the city in 2004. Records held since 1986 were broken: Jimmy Muindi of Kenya won the men's race in 2 hours, 11 minutes, 12 seconds, shattering the race record by 31 seconds. Russia's Lyubov Morgunova broke her own previous course record by a full minute, setting a blistering pace to come in at 2 hours, 27 minutes, 33 seconds.

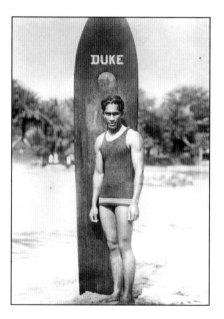

Duke Kahanamoku (1890–1968), winner of Olympic gold medals in swimming in 1912 and 1920, became an international celebrity who introduced surfing to the world.

■ **KUHIO BEACH PARK**
map page 203, C-2

Named for Prince Kuhio, Hawai'i's second (nonvoting) delegate to Congress at the turn of the century, Kuhio Beach Park is a good place to dive, snorkel, body- and board-surf. Swimming at Kuhio is wonderful. With a sandy bottom inside a parallel groin, it's like a deep pool. The sea pours into the pool over the groin known as Slippery Wall. Don't jump off into the sea side—there is shallow reef below.

Even now if you look *mauka* from this beach, straight up Pa'o'akalani (Perfume of Heaven) Street, the view Queen Lili'uokalani once had of the Ko'olau Mountains from her summer home remains unobstructed. On the Kuhio sands facing Kalakaua Avenue stands the statue of a man who in his quiet way spread the name of Hawai'i worldwide. His Olympic feats introduced the Hawaiian Crawl to international swimming. Unveiled in 1990, one hundred years after his birth, the **statue of Duke Paoa Kahanamoku** (1890–1968) stands with a bronze version of his 24-foot koa-wood surfboard. Swimmer, surfer, and sheriff of Honolulu for 26 years, Duke is still held dear in the memory of Hawai'i's people.

Beside the statue are four huge volcanic boulders. A plaque in these **Stones of Kapaemahu** describes a legend of four *kahuna* who long ago came to Hawai'i from Tahiti. The four priests, famed for their healing powers, transferred their powers to these stones, and then vanished. Pick up a map of the self-guided **Waikiki Historic Trail,** a paved beach path along which sites are well described on plaques shaped as surfboards.

■ MOANA-ROYAL HAWAIIAN BEACH *map page 203, B-2*
Next to Kuhio Beach Park is the Moana–Royal Hawaiian Beach, the heart of Waikiki Beach and home to the Moana-Surfrider Hotel, the Great Lady of Waikiki. Wide, soft white sand fronts coral-free ocean. The beach is packed with sun-worshippers slathered in lotion, introverts with their heads in books, children building sandcastles, honeymooners, and eye-roving singles. Here you can ride an outrigger canoe, sail on a catamaran, board-surf, snorkel, and swim in clear, turquoise waters that deepen gradually. The highest concentration of beach rental concessions along the length of Waikiki is in this area.

Offshore are the two most famous surfing lines in Waikiki: Queen's (not to be confused with the patch of beach with the same name) and Canoes. The waves at **Queen's,** named for Queen Lili'uokalani's beach home, are steep. **Canoes,** which has a longer roll and was well-suited to the old canoes of heavy koa-wood, joins Queen's at its *'ewa* side. (*'Ewa* is a term peculiar to O'ahu meaning "west toward the 'Ewa Plain.") Canoes is also popular with board surfers. Sometimes in summer, when there are many beginners in the water, together with outriggers and swimmers, it can be frantic, and lifeguards are busy untangling the mix.

Waikiki even now hides glimpses of her past. On the lawns of the **Royal Hawaiian Hotel** are tall coconut palms, descendants of those growing in the old Royal Grove. It was from this beach that Kamehameha the Great once paddled out to surf the long white-foaming ocean crests. And it was here that he married his sacred wife, Keopuolani, chieftess of the highest rank, who later gave birth to the sons who became Kamehameha II and III.

On the Royal's sands, Kamehameha presided over Hawai'i's version of the Olympic games—great competitions called the Makahiki. They were held between September and January, a sacred time of the year when temples closed, crops were planted, taxes collected, and war put on hold. The Makahiki served as the high point of this period, when Hawaiians stopped everything to compete in sports, various types of chants spoken or sung, and specialized thanksgiving hula. The king's sacred altar dedicated to Lono, god of the Makahiki, lay approximately in front of what is now the Sheraton-Waikiki Hotel. The sacred status of this *he'iau* (Po'okanaka) was removed in 1860, when the site was dismantled and returned to crown land. The sands adjacent to the *he'iau* on the west side were a healing area where *kahuna* practiced Hawaiian sports medicine on injured Makahiki participants.

■ **GRAY'S BEACH** *map page 203, B-2*
Old-timers still call the next patch of sand, in front of the **Halekulani Hotel,** Gray's Beach, as it was once the site of Mrs. Gray's by the Sea Teahouse. The original building was a hut owned by Robert Lewers, who allowed fishermen to beach their canoes in front of his hut at a time when access to Waikiki was limited for the common folk. Grateful fishermen named Lewers's house Halekulani (House Befitting Heaven). The property later became an estate and was acquired by Clifford Kimball, who converted the home into a hotel and named it the Halekulani.

In the 1930s author Earl Derr Biggers stayed here and wrote a murder mystery called *The House Without a Key,* at a time when Honoluluans never locked their doors—a time long gone. The main character was the detective Charlie Chan. In honor of Biggers and his novel, Kimball named the hotel terrace the House Without a Key. The terrace and lawns facing the sea at the hotel still are known by this name.

Residents and distance swimmers migrate to Gray's for its water—a long and wide, warm and calm channel running from the beach out a quarter of a mile to a protruding rock. The seabed is soft white sand, fresh water springs bubble

SURFING WAIKIKI

Call me Queequeg. Out once more to surf at Tongg's, the lineup perhaps two hundred and fifty yards offshore. Storm clouds above the Ko'olaus and over past the cathedral-like mass of Diamond Head, rain beards—gray, grayer—dropping from the low sky, and then suddenly a squall is on us, boards and riders blown down wind, paddling hard into the chop and spray just to hold position. A simultaneous abrupt absence of light: furrows, folds, flanks, buttresses, and crevices of Diamond Head obliterated, waves almost black. Wai and kai, fresh and salt. Song of the water planet (Earth-the misnomer). But then, faster than we can adjust to the change, the sun's reappeared, the water's jade green, and saying he has to get home, Wendell paddles ewa towards Sans Souci beach.

Wendell. "Local" Chinese, in his late fifties/early sixties. Former airline mechanic, grew up in Honolulu. The year before, Wendell arrived one morning—spontaneously generated as if summoned by the waves—out at Tongg's riding high on his massive ten footer, paddling easily, surgical tubing around his waist as a leash. Unorthodox, but effective. No one else there that day, we sat bobbing on the swell, shafts of the boards erect before us, thick plume of smoke rising from the cane fields

Waikiki surfers get a view of high-rises towering over the famous beach.

down toward the Wai'anae range. Watches and clocks irrelevant mechanisms of measure here, time organizing itself into sets and lulls, sets and lulls, Wendell speaking of the change in the color of the water since he was a kid, the loss of clarity/kelp/shellfish. We sat silent for a while, gently rising and falling, Diamond Head always again compelling our attention, like the landform obsessing Richard Dreyfuss in Close Encounters. Sometimes, clouds scudding behind the volcano's vast bulk as we lifted and dropped, sometimes it seemed we were the fixed point, Diamond Head that must be moving.

■ ■ ■

Glassy, that state of grace: no wind, no noise, board shooting along, waves perfectly defined, absolutely themselves, their shape not affected by any other force, a realm of clarity and ease. Water thick as milk, as cream. As porridge.

A windless winter day, after a month of cold. Very heavy rain, each drop making a small crater on the ocean surface, but despite the cumulative impact of so many minute explosions the net effect is to calm the water, to eliminate all other normal movement or pattern—ripple, chip, groove, rill. In the torrential downpour, each successive incoming wave seems smooth, sheer, immaculate, pure as the formula of the textbook curve.

Poet Philip Larkin: "If I were called in/To construct a religion/I should make use of water." Not to think of believing in the Almighty or not believing in the Almighty one way or the other, but then to hear the words on one's lips after two hours in the surf: "Thank you, God."

For what? Oh, for this pulsing, undulating, shimmering, sighing, breathing plasma of an ocean. For the miracle of warm water. For rideable waves and no wind.

—Thomas Farber, *On Water,* 1994

beneath it, and no coral grows. Swim two round-trips and you've done your daily mile. On either side of the channel are the surfing breaks called **Paradise** and **Number Threes.**

■ FORT DeRUSSY BEACH *map page 203, A/B-2*
Fronting the **Hale Koa Hotel,** this safe, wide, sandy strand is a military facility and has unlimited public access. On the spacious lawns of the Hale Koa is the **U.S. Army Museum** (808-438-2822). It is undervisited and deserves better. The

dioramas of American soldiers in war are lifelike, and its memorabilia heartwrenching. Exhibits describe Hawaiians in early warfare and their modern participation in the nation's defense.

The museum is housed in Battery Randolph, one of six coastal implacements built on O'ahu between 1908 and 1915 by the U.S. Army Corps of Engineers. Made of steel-reinforced concrete and designed in low silhouette, it contained its own ammunition magazines and powder rooms. By 1969 Battery Randolph lay on the Army's demolition list, and a wrecking ball was sent to knock it down; however, the battery was built to withstand direct hits, and its concrete sides broke the ball. As a consequence, impregnable Battery Randolph opened as a museum on December 7, 1976.

A new monument on the Kalakaua Avenue green lawns of Fort DeRussy honors Hawai'i's Americans of Japanese ancestry and Medal of Honor soldiers who volunteered in World War II. The Brothers in Valor centerpiece holds four soaring bronze spires representing the famed 100th Infantry Battalion, the 442nd Regimental Combat Team, Military Intelligence Service, and the 1399th Engineers. Four plaques detail the units' histories.

■ **DUKE KAHANAMOKU BEACH**   *map page 203, A-2*
A walkway between the Hale Koa Hotel's lawns and sands reaches Kahanamoku Beach and Lagoon fronting the extensive **Hilton Hawaiian Village Hotel.** Both beach and lagoon are man-made extensions of Waikiki Beach constructed by Henry J. Kaiser in 1955, when he built the original Hawaiian Village hotel. Before that time the area was known as Kalia, family home of the Kahanamoku clan and the place where the fabled Duke learned to swim. (Referring to swimming power, Duke once said, "It's all in the legs.")

■ **DIAMOND HEAD**   *map page 221, E/F-4*

Diamond Head, Hawai'i's volcanic profile recognized around the world, lifts its face at the eastern end of Waikiki. Named Le'ahi (Brow) by Hawaiians, it was first called Diamond Head in 1825, when British seamen saw calcite crystals twinkling in sunlight and thought they'd found gems. At the base of the cone on the inland side are the film studios that played home to "Hawaii Five-O," "Magnum P. I," and "Baywatch-Hawaii." Also on this side of Diamond Head is the former Army facility of Fort Ruger, built in 1909. From it a web of bunkers and tunnels

penetrates into the crater. In World War II cannons were placed on the volcano's rim. They were never fired. The best way to see Diamond Head is to climb it. If you stop by the New Otani Kaimana Beach Hotel in the shadow of Diamond Head and buy a small hiker's kit, the hotel staff will issue a certificate on your return, proof that you trudged to the summit. Take Diamond Head Road to the crater entrance. The trail to the 760-foot crater rim is steep, though less than a mile in length; plan on a 45-minute climb. It's a good idea to bring water for the open, hot part of the trail, and a flashlight for the long curving tunnel. Once you're through the tunnel, there are 99 stairs to climb, another short tunnel, and some more steps. The 360-degree view is worth it—you can see the entire leeward coast, below to Kapi'olani Park, and out along the blue Pacific east to Koko Head. Place a dollar in the fee box at the trailhead ($5 to park a car).

The bowl-shaped, 175-acre crater is dry, its vegetation scrub *kiawe* trees and tiny orange *ilima* flowers. Landscaping surrounds the parking lot. At the brow of Diamond Head facing the sea, a small temple once stood. It was dedicated to the fish god Ku'ula and received offerings from fishermen. Near the base stood a *he'iau* piled with bodies of the dead at the time of Kamehameha's onslaught. Below, a ribbon of sand beach is accessible on foot.

Leaving Waikiki along Kalakaua Avenue travelling *'ewa,* you'll encounter the **Hawai'i Convention Center,** a soaring glass structure opened in 1998. With 1.1 million square feet of space, pillars that look like gigantic palms, and leafy plantings throughout the corridors, it is a place for state-of-the-art telecommunications, meetings, and technology amid tropical splendor. *808-943-3500.*

■ DOWNTOWN HONOLULU *map page 215 and 221, B/C-2*

Physically only six miles west of Waikiki, downtown Honolulu is about as far from the hum of tourism as you can get on southern O'ahu. It is bounded by Beretania, South, Nimitz (called Ala Moana Boulevard here), and River streets, and its restored older buildings retain much of Honolulu's early merchant spirit. Beside them rise graceful glass and concrete office towers and cumbersome great piles of government buildings. Winding through its core of historic structures is open space—greenery protected in a "mountains to the sea" concept—which affords views of historic buildings from the top of Punchbowl Crater down to Honolulu Harbor.

Diamond Head lifts its face on the eastern sweep of Waikiki.

Honolulu's **Chinatown,** designated a National Historic Landmark in 1973, is one of the more appealing parts of downtown. Located between Maunakea and River streets, its herbal stores and produce shops, contemporary art galleries, and noodle shops are reminiscent of central Hong Kong—a crammed jumble of the old and new. Its restaurants serve excellent Cantonese and other Asian foods, and its customers tend to be Honolulu professionals.

There was a time when rabble-rousers, rogues, and drunkards ruled the streets. Whaling ships dropped anchor and sailors hurried ashore looking for grog and women. Central downtown's Fid Street area was named Fid after the carrot-shaped, six-inch steel or wooden tool used to open strands of rope when splicing lines. Three hotels dedicated to drinking and prostitution, all named Blonde, operated on Fid Street. (They took their name from the HMS *Blonde,* which in 1825 carried back to Hawai'i the bodies of Kamehameha II and his queen, Kamamalu, both of whom had died of measles in London.)

Soon after their arrival in 1820, missionaries built a church right in the middle of saloonville—and the church gave its name, Bethel, to another street of bars and bawdy houses. At the O'ahu Follies, Honolulu's wildest bar, drinkers swilled down 33 barrels of whiskey every week, while the missionary Hiram Bingham stood outside loudly praying for the sinful guzzlers. Among them may have been the author of *Moby Dick,* Herman Melville, who found temporary employment setting pins at the Globe Hotel.

While sailors brought venereal disease, the missionaries brought the concept of sexual sin, and instituted laws requiring adulterers to pay for their sins in roadwork. Consequently, the streets of Honolulu rapidly improved.

If anyone symbolized the contradictions of Honolulu's culture at this time it was Princess Victoria Kamamalu (1838–66), younger sister of Kamehameha IV. She became involved in a love affair with the photographer Charles Monsarrat. When they were discovered, Monsarrat was banished by the king. The princess, however, went on to become the monarchy's last *kuhina nui,* a position akin to prime minister and perhaps even more powerful. When Victoria Kamamalu died, the black-clad missionaries who attended her Christian royal funeral found themselves listening to chants praising her amorous escapades.

Central downtown's **Fort Street Mall,** the main cross street, now meets Nimitz Highway where the Hawaii Tower rears skyward. The fort built here by Kamehameha the Great in 1816 was used by the missionaries as a prison. The mission

DOWNTOWN
HONOLULU

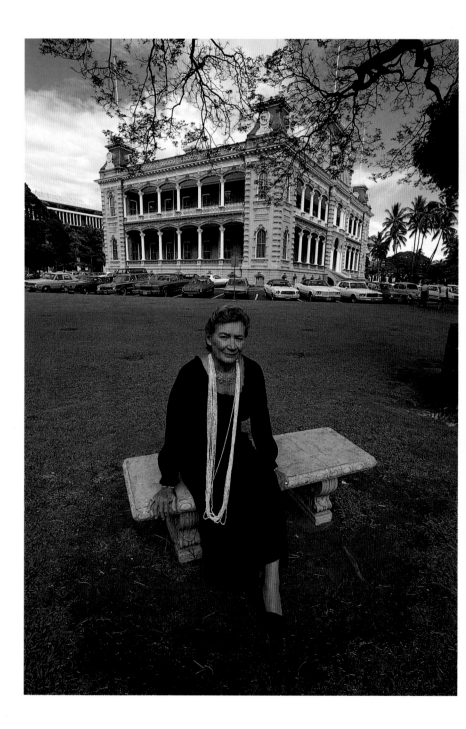

had decreed that no divorced person could remarry as long as the original spouse remained alive. Reasoning that the way around that law was to dispose of the former spouse, a Hawaiian named Hamanawa poisoned his wife. His was the first murder trial held in the Hawaiian Islands. After being found guilty, Hamanawa was hanged by the neck over the side of the fort. The hanging was watched by Hamanawa's young nephew, David Kalakaua, who later became king. Kalakaua never forgave the mission.

By 1870, in the reign of Kamehameha V, the fort was torn down to fill in a new section of the harbor. Across the highway and over the edge of Pier 12, the blocks that were once part of Kamehameha's fort can be seen poking out of the water.

■ 'IOLANI PALACE *map page 215, C-2*
'Iolani Palace, built for King Kalakaua from 1879 to 1881, stands at the eastern end of downtown Honolulu on South King Street. Now lovingly returned to its former dignity and grandeur by a volunteer society and the state, the palace is Hawai'i's paean to, and museum of, its monarchy. Missing pieces of art and furniture have been tracked down and recovered from around the world. The Grand Hall staircase is a gleaming spiral of *koa* wood with *kamani* and walnut trim. In the State Dining Room a table is laid with china from France, crystal from Bohemia, and silver from England, France, and the U.S. In the Throne Room are escutcheons showing the orders of the Crown of Hawai'i, the Order of Kamehameha, and other Hawaiian, European, and Asian honorific orders.

On the second floor the king's bedroom, the library, the music room, the upper hall, and the queen's apartments contain chandeliers, draperies, and furniture either meticulously restored or duplicated. Photographs and gifts from royal European houses decorate walls and tables. Queen Lili'uokalani's chamber recreates the sparse furnishings of her nine-month imprisonment after the overthrow of the monarchy in 1893. In that lonely time she wrote music, including "Aloha Oe":

> Though I was still not allowed to have newspapers or general litera-
> ture to read, writing-paper and lead-pencils were not denied; and I
> was thereby able to write music, after drawing for myself the lines of
> the staff . . . I found great consolation in composing . . . .

Princess Kawawanakoa, here seated before the 'Iolani Palace, is one of the few remaining collateral descendants of Hawaiian royalty.

MARK TWAIN'S HONOLULU

Mark Twain sailed into Honolulu in 1866 as a correspondent for a California newspaper, the Sacramento Union. *He was on assignment to write 25 articles about the Sandwich Islands.*

Passing through the market place we saw that feature of Honolulu under its most favorable auspices—that is, in the full glory of Saturday afternoon, which is a festive day with the natives. The native girls by twos and threes and parties of a dozen, and sometimes in whole platoons and companies, went cantering up and down the neighboring streets astride of fleet but homely horses, and with their gaudy riding habits streaming like banners behind them. Such a troop of free and easy riders, in their natural home, the saddle, makes a gay and graceful spectacle. The riding habit I speak of is simply a long, broad scarf, like a tavern table cloth brilliantly colored, wrapped around the loins once, then apparently passed between the limbs and each end thrown backward over the same, and floating and flapping behind on both sides beyond the horse's tail like a couple of fancy flags; then, slipping the stirrup-irons between her toes, the girl throws her chest forward, sits up like a Major General and goes sweeping by like the wind.

■ ■ ■

Moving among the stirring crowds, you come to the poi merchants, squatting in the shade on their hams, in true native fashion, and surrounded by purchasers. (The Sandwich Islanders always squat on their hams, and who knows but they may be the old original "ham sandwiches?" The thought is pregnant with interest.) The poi looks like common flour paste, and is kept in large bowls formed of a species of gourd, and capable of holding from one to three or four gallons. Poi is the chief article of food among the natives, and is prepared from the taro plant. The poi root looks like a thick, or, if you please, a corpulent sweet potato, in shape, but is of a light purple color when boiled. When boiled it answers as a passable substitute for bread. The buck Kanakas bake it under ground, then mash it up well with a heavy lava pestle, mix water with it until it becomes a paste, set it aside and let it ferment, and then it is poi—and an unseductive mixture it is, almost tasteless before it ferments and too sour for a luxury afterward. But nothing is more nutritious. When solely used, however, it produces acrid humors, a fact which sufficiently accounts for the humorous character of the Kanakas. I think there must be as much of a knack in handling poi as there is in eating with chopsticks. The forefinger is thrust into the mess and stirred quickly round several times and drawn quickly out, thickly coated, just as if it were poulticed; the head is thrown back, the finger inserted in the mouth and the delicacy stripped off and swallowed—the eye closing gently, meanwhile, in a languid sort of ecstasy. Many a different finger goes into the same bowl and many a different kind of dirt and shade and quality of flavor is added to the virtues of its contents.

■ ■ ■

In old times here Saturday was a grand gala day indeed. All the native population of the town forsook their labors, and those of the surrounding country journeyed to the city. Then the white folks had to stay indoors, for every street was so packed with charging cavaliers and cavalieresses that it was next to impossible to thread one's way through the cavalcades without getting crippled.

At night they feasted and the girls danced the lascivious hula hula—a dance that is said to exhibit the very perfection of educated motion of limb and arm, hand, head and body, and the exactest uniformity of movement and accuracy of "time." It was performed by a circle of girls with no raiment on them to speak of, who went through an infinite variety of motions and figures without prompting, and yet so true was their "time," and in such perfect concert did they move that when they were placed in a straight line, hands, arms, bodies, limbs and heads waved, swayed, gesticulated, bowed, stopped, whirled, squirmed, twisted and undulated as if they were part and parcel of a single individual; and it was difficult to believe they were not moved in a body by some exquisite piece of mechanism.

Of late years, however, Saturday has lost most of its quondam gala features. This weekly stampede of the natives interfered too much with labor and the interests of the white folks, and by sticking in a law here, and preaching a sermon there, and by various other means, they gradually broke it up. The demoralizing hula hula was forbidden to be performed, save at night, with closed doors, in presence of few spectators, and only by permission duly procured from the authorities and the payment of ten dollars for the same. There are few girls now-a-days able to dance this ancient national dance in the highest perfection of the art.

—Mark Twain, *Roughing It,* 1872

Although trappings of royalty and Christian mores had been brought by Europeans to the Hawaiian court, the heart and spirit of what it meant to be Hawaiian remained clear in the minds of all Hawaiians. The spirit of *aloha*, which is love, never was damaged. The palace tour is perhaps the best way to understand later Hawaiian royalty. *South King Street; 808-522-0832 (tour reservations required).*

Today the restored grounds of 'Iolani Palace and 'Iolani Barracks (built in 1870) are public areas where office workers picnic at lunchtime. The Royal Hawaiian Band regularly performs in King Kalakaua's 1883 coronation pavilion. A Korean-Vietnam War Memorial recessed into a fern-top berm stands on the palace grounds.

■ KAWAIAHAO CHURCH *map page 215, C-3*

Across South King Street from the palace, at the corner of Punchbowl Street, is Kawaiahao Church, where Hawai'i's later monarchs were baptized, wed, eulogized, and interred. Three thatched churches preceded the present stone church, which was designed in 1837 by the Reverend Hiram Bingham (1789–1869) in New England colonial style complete with Gothic embellishments. Deeded to the people and the mission by King Kamehameha III in 1842, Kawaiahao, or Water of Ha'o, takes its name from a spring at the site.

The Kawaiahao Church was designated a National Historic Landmark in 1962.

GREATER HONOLULU

Honolulu is an important business and economic hub of the Pacific.

Kawaiahao's construction is an epic tale of mountains climbed, wood hewn, and logs hauled. Hawaiians dived, dragged ashore, chopped, shaped, and smoothed coral into stone blocks to build the church. They burned broken coral pieces to make lime for mortar. A cornerstone of Wai'anae sandstone, laid in 1839, arrived at the site as a great uncut slab, brought by sea, lashed to canoes.

In 1865, when the royal graveyard was moved from what is now the grounds of 'Iolani Palace to a new royal mausoleum in Nu'uanu Valley, a controversy arose over one of the graves. The result is a tomb at Kawaiahao. The tale of how this came about is a haunted one:

Kamehameha V, who ruled from 1863 to 1872, refused to allow the bones of High Chieftess Kekaulei'ohi, mother of Prince William Charles Lunalilo, to be reburied at Nu'uanu when the royal graveyard was moved. Her indignant son, who in 1873 became the first elected king, vowed that he would have no part of the new royal mausoleum. Four days before his death in 1874 he approved a codicil to his will, providing for a tomb at Kawaiahao for himself and his father, Charles Kana'ina. There is some question whether the bones of Lunalilo's mother remained in the old 'Iolani burial place. According to some accounts, the family secretly carried them away for burial at sea many miles off Diamond Head.

On the night Lunalilo's casket was carried into the tomb at Kawaiahao, a loud clap of thunder startled the retinue. Hawaiians claimed it a heavenly royal salute—the salute denied Lunalilo by the new king, Kalakaua, on the premise that 21 guns could not be fired for a man who was no longer king. Each year on January 31, Lunalilo's birthday, the tomb is opened ceremonially to the public. The royal crypt, shaped in the form of a Greek cross, stands regally fenced and in need of a good scrubbing at the main entrance to Kawaiahao.

Behind the church an arched gate and sign at the end of a walkway marks the **Alanui** (Pathway), which "since ancient times . . . had been trodden by feet entering the village from the Waikiki area." Kawaiahao, a member of the United Church of Christ Congregational, the largest Protestant denomination in the islands, was designated a National Historic Landmark in 1962. *957 Punchbowl Street; 808-522-1333.*

■ **MISSION HOUSES MUSEUM** *map page 215, C-3*

Directly across Punchbowl Street from Kawaiahao is the Mission Houses Museum. Here the missionary incursion that forever changed the islands began in earnest when a small band of American Protestants armed with the Bible, a printing press, and the stiff-necked spirit of their Lord, came face to face with Hawai'i's native people.

Three buildings served as headquarters for the Sandwich Islands Mission—the Mission frame house built in 1821, the Levi Chamberlain House (1831), and the smaller Printing House (1841). These houses make clear that the missionaries intended to cast the destiny of the island people in a New England mold. Islanders were meant to become Christians clothed in stiff New England garb, to pray in a building of colonial architecture, and to sit on New England furnishings. Lumber for the main house, cut in Massachusetts, was shipped from Boston in 1819—the same year the missionaries departed on their hardship voyage around Cape Horn. Only the Printing House, originally a storage vault, is built of coral block. The museum's reading room is a treasure trove of materials from the libraries of the Hawaiian Mission Children's Society and the Hawaiian Historical Society.

This King Kamehameha statue is decked out with lei in celebration of Kamehameha Day.

The restored mission houses, complete with original furnishings and curios, contain the antique rocking chair of Queen Ka'ahumanu and a *koa*-wood crib for missionary infants. A living-history program re-creates the Honolulu of 1831—with missionaries, Hawaiians, merchants, and even rowdy seamen. The museum also sponsors a walking tour of Honolulu's historic core. *553 South King Street; 808-531-0481.*

A few steps from the museum stands the bronze and gold **statue of Kamehameha the Great,** in front of Ali'iolani Hale (the judiciary building). Surrounded by stately trees, it is a popular attraction and on Kamehameha Day (June 11), Hawaiians place hundreds of long, long lei on the statue, covering Kamehameha with flowers from neck to toe. This statue, installed in 1883, is the replica of the original statue positioned near his birthplace in Kohala on the Big Island. Another copy of the statue represents Hawai'i in Statuary Hall on Capitol Hill in Washington, D.C.

■ **HAWAI'I STATE CAPITOL** *map page 215, C-2*
Across a broad walk lined with flowering purple bougainvillea, just *mauka* (inland) of 'Iolani Palace facing Beretania Street, stands Hawai'i's State Capitol. State law keeps this downtown area green and open so that the vista from mountains to sea remains unhampered. The capitol, designed by architect Carl Warnecke, is open-roofed at its center, and curves outward like the rim of a volcano's crater. The building soars above a central courtyard, and sun and rain fall on its reeflike mosaic. From a distance the open roof resembles a crown.

Two-story-high, rounded-glass legislative chambers rise like smaller cones on two sides of the courtyard. The House of Representatives is decorated in the blue of sea and sky, and earthen hues complete the Senate chamber. Sixty-foot columns suggesting tall royal palm trees gird the five-story capitol building. Surrounding ponds evoke tropical lagoons.

On the seaward side of the building, facing the palace where she was imprisoned, stands the stately **bronze figure of Lydia Kamaka'eha,** Queen Lili'uokalani (1838–1917), last ruling monarch of the Hawaiian kingdom. Greatly esteemed by the people in her time, she is revered to this day. The statue, unveiled in 1982, is always adorned with a lei or flowers placed there by admirers.

At the opposite side of the capitol, facing Beretania Street, stands the bronze **statue of Father Damien** (1840–1889), the Belgian priest who devoted his life to the care of lepers confined on Moloka'i. The statue, which depicts Damien with a cane, priest's hat, and eyeglasses on his leprous face, is an angular, modern impression by the Venezuelan sculptress Marisol (Escobar).

The Aloha Festivals Royal Court poses on the steps of 'Iolani Palace.

DINNER WITH THE KING

Robert Louis Stevenson, famed author of *Kidnapped* and *Treasure Island,* sailed into Honolulu on January 24, 1889. The following week a luau was given in honor of the Stevenson family, and Hawai'i's last king, David Kalakaua, and Princess Lili'uokalani were in attendance. Stevenson's wife, Fanny, presented the king with a gold-filmed double oyster shell cradling an attached gold pearl, given to her in the Tuamotu Islands, and Stevenson read aloud an accompanying sonnet dedicated to the king. On this occasion the Stevensons were served roast dog, which they had the good grace to eat and apparently found delicious.

During the next five months Stevenson became a popular figure in Honolulu, befriending the king and frequently walking to the estate of Archibald Cleghorn, fellow Edinburgh Scotsman and father of Princess Victoria Ka'iulani. When the princess, then 13 years old, greeted Stevenson, she'd often ask him to sit with her beneath a tall banyan or in a little grass shack and tell her tales of Scotland and the South Pacific.

Stevenson's stories of Hawai'i include a journal and story of the Kona Coast, a tale of Queen Ka'ahumanu, the "lazaretto" stories of Moloka'i, a steady stream of letters and poems, and one of the most furious denouncements in the English language (see "The Damien Letters" in the Moloka'i chapter).

Robert Louis Stevenson (seated in background) dined with Hawai'i's last king.

■ **HAWAII STATE ART MUSEUM** *map page 215, C-2*
This museum is in the Capitol District Building, which has a varied past and has been extensively up-scaled. Visit here to find diverse and provocative expressions of Hawaiian identity culled from a 5,000-piece collection of the State Foundation for Culture and the Arts. Most of the works are by Hawaiian artists and date from the 1960s to the present. *250 South Hotel Street; 808-586-0900.*

■ **ALOHA TOWER AND HONOLULU HARBOR** *map page 215, A-3*
Landmark of downtown and beacon for arriving ships, the Aloha Tower stands at the foot of Fort Street, at the entrance to Honolulu Harbor (Pier 8). Once the tallest building in Honolulu, it is now dwarfed by the sleek pillars of business. The tower is the focal point of a large-scale waterfront array of shops and restaurants, and passengers on ocean liners board at a facility in front of the tower. Walkways, open malls, condos, and more shops are planned. The first increment, Kakaʻako Waterfront Park (reached from Ohe Street *makai* of Ala Moana Boulevard), opened in 1993.

The **Honolulu Fish Auction** is a teeming sight for early risers. Its starting bell at 5:30 A.M. is muffled by the sounds of trucks and walkers placing pallets of shiny fish piled on mounds of ice in the auction room. It's a flurry of activity as fish are bought for local and offshore consumers; buyers huddle around the auctioneer, pallets are sold and quickly moved out. Wear a jacket, closed shoes, and old clothes; it's cool and wet. *United Fishing Agency, 117 ʻAhui St.*

Next to the tower is Pier 7, site of the **Hawaiʻi Maritime Center.** It includes the Kalakaua Boat House, which takes its name from a sailing club captained by King Kalakaua. Here he played poker, drank whiskey, and swapped stories with Robert Louis Stevenson. Museum exhibits describe voyages of early Polynesians and Hawaiʻi's relationships with other island groups in the Pacific. An enormous whale skeleton, Hawaiian objects carried at sea, and oceangoing canoes also are displayed. Riding at the end of the pier is the *Hokuleʻa*—modern replica of an ancient voyaging canoe—which sailed with a crew of 16 for more than two years in the mid-1980s, navigating by the stars from Hawaiʻi to New Zealand.

Also tied to the pier and part of the maritime center is the *Falls of Clyde,* a 266-foot, iron-hulled, four-masted sailing ship. Built in Glasgow in 1878, she plied the Pacific trade for many years. A restoration made her clean and gleaming, but a tour of the crew's and officers' quarters still makes evident the cramped and practical lifestyle aboard traders. *Ala Moana Boulevard; 808-536-6373.*

Honolulu was a busy seaport at the beginning of the twentieth century.

■ **HONOLULU ACADEMY OF ARTS** *map page 215, D-2*

Chinese marble horses flank the entrance walkway of this airy, quasi-Spanish building with a central court and five garden patios. In its 33 galleries, the academy presents a solid collection, particularly of Chinese and Japanese art. It houses the James A. Michener Collection of 5,400 Japanese prints, the Kress Collection of Italian Renaissance paintings, the Watumull Collection of Indian Sculpture, and decorative and graphic arts. The eclectic collection runs from Gauguin and van Gogh to Alexander Calder; from Korean celadon bowls to Persian tiles and New Guinea wood carvings. On view are Hawaiian *kapa* cloth; Japanese bronze, and Chinese jade; Delacroix, Homer, Picasso and Flemish tapestry. Contemporary art holds forth at the Clare Booth Luce pavilion. The new Henry R. Luce Wing's second floor is dedicated to Hawaiian art; on its first floor are changing exhibitions by contemporary artists in Hawai'i. In addition, the building houses a library, theater, shop, the Pavillion Cafe, and a fully equipped center for studio art classes.

The museum collection was begun by Anna Rice, descendant of missionaries and Kaua'i plantation owners, who in 1874 married Charles Montague Cooke, also a descendant of the mission. Financial success led to European travel and gave Anna the means and opportunity to begin collecting—at first just a few pieces for her parlor. Back in Honolulu, Anna bought Chinese ceramics, then Japanese art, and the paintings of local artists.

By 1920, when the Cooke home could no longer hold her burgeoning collection, Anna and her family planned a museum, which opened in 1927 on land of the former Cooke home. It was built of materials that are a part of Hawai'i's history. Its Chinese paving blocks originally arrived as ballast in vessels of the sandalwood trade. The tiles in the Chinese court had come to Honolulu 80 years earlier, and the lava rock in walls was quarried from a Honolulu suburb. The slabs of shellrock cut into flagstone that pave the entry and patios came from Moloka'i. *900 South Beretania Street; 808-532-8701.*

In partnership with the Honolulu Academy, the Doris Duke Foundation of Islamic Art holds guided tours of **Shangri La** (808-532-3853), the Hawaiian home of the heiress and philanthropist Doris Duke (1912–93). Built by Duke in the late 1930s, the Islamic-style home at Diamond Head features a rare collection of 3,500 objects from cultures and regions of the Islamic world, many embedded in the home's structure. Here Duke's passion for Islamic art was played out; she collected objects from 1935 until the end of her life.

■ **PUNCHBOWL CRATER** *map page 221, C-2*
Directly above downtown Honolulu, in the foothills of the Koʻolau Mountains, is Punchbowl Crater, which encloses the **National Memorial Cemetery of the Pacific.** The entrance is off Puowaina Drive. From an overlook at the crater rim you can see Honolulu stretching down the slopes to the sea. Diamond Head, Waikiki, and Pearl Harbor curve against the horizon, like a view through the fish-eye lens of a camera. In 2003 more than six million people climbed the road into Punchbowl, making it the most heavily visited attraction in the state.

During World War II, when Punchbowl served as a fire-control post for defense of the harbor, the Territory of Hawaiʻi offered Punchbowl to the federal government for a military cemetery. Many of America's heroes lie here, as well as a memorial to Hawaiʻi's astronaut Ellison Onizuka (who perished aboard the *Challenger* space shuttle). Inside the memorial building are a chapel, mural maps of battles, and marble walls inscribed with the names of 18,000 military personnel missing in action.

■ **CONTEMPORARY MUSEUM** *map page 221, D-1*
Up a quiet, forested mountain slope directly *mauka* (inland) from the crush and din of shopping centers in central Honolulu, is the Contemporary Museum, installed in what was once a home of Anna Rice Cooke. Its many additions combine western, Asian, and island styles of architecture. The museum is set in three acres of secluded Oriental gardens in the Makiki hills, its terraces unfolding like a Japanese scroll.

Exhibits feature international contemporary art of the last four decades as well as the work of twentieth-century Hawaiian artists. A separate pavilion houses David Hockney's environmental installation *L'Enfant et les Sortileges* (The Bewitched Child), based on the sets and costumes conceived for a revival of Maurice Ravel's 1925 opera. Hockney created six new works for an exhibit of his theater designs in Minneapolis in 1983. *L'Enfant* was the largest and most complex. Permanently installed in Honolulu, it is considered the museum's most important acquisition. *2411 Makiki Heights Drive; 808-526-0232.*

■ **BISHOP MUSEUM** *map page 221, A-1*
West of central Honolulu on H-1 off the Houghtailing Street exit, is the Bishop Museum. Set within a compound of buildings that includes a library and planetarium, the museum is a treasure trove of human history and art in the Pacific, with a selection of objects ranging from the maps of Captain Cook to Duke Kahanamoku's surfboard. Its research, exhibitions, and Polynesian collections are exceptional.

The Bishop Museum owes its birth to an affair of the heart. Princess Bernice Pauahi (1831–84), great-granddaughter of Kamehameha the Great and betrothed by royal decree to Prince Lot, fell in love with an American banker, Charles Reed Bishop. As the last direct descendant of the Kamehameha line, the princess inherited massive tracts of royal lands and the collected Hawaiian treasures of the Kamehamehas. The childless Bishops recognized the need to preserve Hawai'i's cultural heritage and agreed that the princess's invaluable personal belongings would become the nucleus of a museum. When the princess died at the age of 53, Charles Bishop fulfilled their plan and built the museum, which was opened in 1892. *1525 Bernice Street; 808-847-3511*

■ **THE PALI HIGHWAY** *map page 221, B/C-1/2*

Straight inland from downtown Honolulu lies the valley of Nu'uanu and **Tenrikyo Mission,** a fine example of a Japanese temple. This serene, red-painted, wood-frame pagoda was moved here from Japan in sections and put up without nails. As the building is off the tourist route, it is rarely crowded. *Take Pali Highway from Beretania Street to 2236 Nu'uanu Pali Highway—about a 10-minute drive.*

A few minutes' drive farther up the valley is **Queen Emma's Summer Palace,** Hanai'akamalama, named for a demi-goddess who was foster child of the moon. This airy, colonnaded, white-frame summer home of Kamehameha IV's queen is surrounded by extensive gardens. Inside are paintings of royalty, a room dedicated to a visit by the Duke of Edinburgh (second son of Victoria) with fine Victorian furniture, and *kahili,* the feather staff symbols of royalty. Probably built in 1847, the house was inherited by Queen Emma, who turned it into a social salon. After her death it was bought by the Hawaiian government (1890) and renovated by the Daughters of Hawai'i. *2913 Pali Highway; 808-595-3167.*

Queen Emma (1836–85) was a blood relative of Kamehameha the Great and a devout Christian, who, with her husband Kamehameha IV, established the Episcopal (Anglican) Church in Hawai'i. She also founded Honolulu's largest hospital, Queen Emma Hospital, usually called Queen's. After the deaths of her husband and son, she took the name Kalele'onalani. In 1874, as Dowager Queen, she ran against High Chief David La'amea Kalakaua in the second election to the Hawaiian throne. The race was close and emotional; Kalakaua won, and the defeated queen never forgave him.

If you continue up the Pali Highway, you'll see a turn off for the **Nu'uanu Pali Overlook.** It's well worth a visit. From the overlook, at an altitude just under 2,000 feet, you can see the windward Ko'olau Mountains stretching northwest in a panorama of sheer, stream-eroded cliffs, or *pali.* Clouds hover over sharp pinnacles and blow away in a spectrum of ever-changing muted colors.

Kuka'ilimoku, a war god, is depicted in wood and feathers at the Bishop Museum.

Honolulu peeks through a clearing between clouds and pali.

It was here, atop the mountain pass, that Kamehameha the Great struck the decisive blow that defeated O'ahu's forces. (See "History" in the Greater O'ahu chapter.) The conclusion of that battle in 1795 assured the king a realm of all the islands except Kaua'i.

■ PEARL HARBOR *map page 255, C/D-3/4*

West of Honolulu on Kamehameha Highway (HI 99) is Pearl Harbor, a splendid natural harbor with a narrow entrance and two expansive inner lochs. Once oysters grew abundantly here, and it was called Wai Momi, or "pearl waters." Its development as a U.S. naval base began at the time of the Spanish-American War in 1898, the same year the U.S. annexed the Republic of Hawai'i.

A legend stalled Pearl Harbor's early development. In 1909 work was under way to build a dry dock over caves believed by Hawaiians to be home to the shark goddess. Hawaiians predicted tragedy. When the dry dock was nearly finished, it collapsed, the seas poured in, and four years of work crumbled. Workmen clearing the debris found the skeleton of a huge shark in the foundation. Hawaiians advised that a *kahuna* (priest) should be asked to placate the angry goddess. After chants

BOMBING PEARL HARBOR

On carrier flight decks readied fighter and attack planes were lined up. The flying crews, also primed for the operation, were gathered in the briefing room. The ships pitched and rolled in the rough sea, kicking up white surf from the pre-dawn blackness of the water. At times wave spray came over the flight deck, and crews clung desperately to their planes to keep them from going into the sea. . . . On a blackboard were written the positions of the ships in Pearl Harbor as of 0600, 7 December. We were 230 miles due north of Oahu. . . .

On the flight deck a green lamp was waved in a circle to signal "Take off!" The engine of the foremost fighter plane began to roar. With the ship still pitching and rolling, the plane started its run, slowly at first but with steadily increasing speed. Men lining the flight deck held their breath as the first plane took off successfully just before the ship took a downward pitch. The next plane was already moving forward. There were loud cheers as each plane rose into the air.

Thus did the first wave of 183 fighters, bombers and torpedo planes take off from the six carriers. Within fifteen minutes they had all been launched and were forming up in the still-dark sky, guided only by the signal lights of the lead planes. After one great circling over the fleet formation, the planes set course due south for Oahu Island and Pearl Harbor. It was 0615.

. . . All of a sudden the clouds broke, and a long white line of coast appeared. We were over Kahuku Point, the northern tip of the island, and now it was time for our deployment.

. . . I saw clouds of black smoke rising from Hickam [Field] and soon thereafter from Ford Island. This bothered me and I wondered what had happened. It was not long before I saw waterspouts rising alongside the battleships, followed by more and more waterspouts. It was time to launch our level bombing attacks so I ordered my pilot to bank sharply, which was the attack signal for the planes following us. All ten of my squadrons then formed in to a single column with intervals of 200 meters. It was indeed a gorgeous formation.

. . . Suddenly a colossal explosion occurred in battleship row. A huge column of dark red smoke rose to 1000 feet and a stiff shock wave reached our plane. I called the pilot's attention to the spectacle, and he observed, "Yes, Commander, the powder magazine must have exploded. Terrible indeed!" The attack was in full swing, and smoke from fires and explosions filled most of the sky over Pearl Harbor.

My group now entered on a bombing course again. Studying battleship row through binoculars, I saw that the big explosion had been on the Arizona. She was still flaming fiercely and her smoke was covering Nevada, the target of my group. Since the heavy smoke would hinder our bomber accuracy, I looked for some other ship to attack. Tennessee, third in the left row was already on fire; but next in row was Maryland, which had not yet been attacked. I gave an order changing our target to this ship, and once again we headed into the anti-aircraft fire. Then came the "ready" signal, and I took a firm grip on the bomb release handle, holding my breath and staring at the bomb of the lead plane.

Pilots, observers, and radio men all shouted, "Release!" on seeing the bomb drop from the lead plane, and all the others let go their bombs. I immediately lay flat on the floor to watch the fall of bombs through a peephole. Four bombs in perfect pattern plummeted like devils of doom. The target was so far away that I wondered for a moment if they would reach it. The bombs grew smaller and smaller until I was holding my breath for fear of losing them. I forgot everything in the thrill of watching them fall toward the target. They became small as poppy seeds and finally disappeared just as tiny white flashes of smoke appeared on and near the ship.

. . . After our bomb run I ordered my pilot to fly over each of the air bases, where our fighters were strafing, before returning over Pearl Harbor to observe the result of our attacks on the warships. Pearl Harbor and vicinity had been turned into complete chaos in a very short time.

Target ship Utah, on the western side of Ford Island, had already capsized. On the other side of the island West Virginia and Oklahoma had received concentrated torpedo attacks as a result of their exposed positions in the outer row. Their sides were almost blasted off, and they listed steeply in a flood of heavy oil. Arizona was in miserable shape, her magazine apparently having blown up; she was listing badly and burning furiously.

Two other battleships, Maryland and Tennessee, were on fire; especially the latter whose smoke emerged in a heavy black column which towered into the sky. Pennsylvania, unscathed in the drydock, seemed to be the only battleship that had not been attacked.

As I observed the damage done by the first attack wave, the effectiveness of the torpedoes seemed remarkable, and I was struck with the shortsightedness of the United States in being so generally unprepared and in not using torpedo nets. I also thought of our long hard training in Kagoshima Bay and the efforts of those who had labored to accomplish a seemingly impossible task. A warm feeling came with the realization that the reward of those efforts was unfolded here before my eyes.

—Captain Mitsuo Fuchida, Imperial Japanese Navy, *I Led the Air Attack on Pearl Harbor,* United States Naval Institute Proceedings, September 1952

The USS Arizona *Memorial is built above the sunken ship.*

and ritual offerings, she apparently relented in her hostility, for no further mishaps befell the dry dock.

In a surprise attack at 7:55 A.M. on December 7, 1941, the forces of Imperial Japan bombed Pearl Harbor. During the next two hours 19 ships were sunk or damaged and 2,300 Americans died. President Roosevelt addressed Congress, declaring December 7th a "date which will live in infamy," concluding his speech with a request to Congress to declare war. It came the following day.

The USS *Arizona,* sunk with 1,102 men entombed in her metal hull, is now the **Arizona Memorial and Visitor Center.** To reach it from Kamehameha Highway (HI 99), follow the signs for the *Arizona;* the entrance is west of the naval base gate. The visitors center is ashore and looks out to the memorial. Brief talks by National Park Service rangers precede documentary films shown in twin theaters and narrated in several languages. Visitors then board the U.S. Navy shuttle boat and disembark at the memorial.

The memorial, an expansive, airy, 184-foot concrete structure, is built above the sunken ship. On a wall of Vermont marble are engraved the names of 1,178 sailors

(above) A small boat rescues men from the USS West Virginia *in Pearl Harbor in 1941.*
(opposite) A monument in Lanaʻi City Park pays tribute to soldiers from this small island who died in World War II and Korea.

and marines killed aboard the battleship. The American flag flies daily from a pole attached to the *Arizona's* severed mainmast.

Pearl Harbor, designated a National Historic Landmark in 1965, is the only U.S. naval base so honored.

On September 2, 1945, the signing of the surrender of the Japanese military took place on the 01 Deck of the USS *Missouri*. In 1998, this memorable battleship embarked on her final voyage, from mothballs in Washington State to museum in Pearl Harbor, where she's moored on Fort Island opposite the *Arizona* Memorial. The two warships represent the beginning and end of World War II in the Pacific. *USS* Arizona, *808-422-0561; USS* Missouri, *808-423-2263.*

MUSIC OF HAWAI'I

The ancient Hawaiians were a poetic people who chanted epic tales of gods and goddesses, genealogy, battles, and escapades of the nobility. The Hawaiian word for poetry, *mele,* also described the ancient poet—the *haku mele,* an arranger of words. Chanters specialized in a single form—perhaps in the unaccompanied *mele oli,* a joyful chant, or the *mele ho'aeae,* passionate poems of love. When dance and the sounds of percussion instruments fashioned from nature accompanied the two or three chanting tones, the chanting form was *mele hula.* While stylized chanting related to religious life and lineage, impromptu chanting was entertainment—sometimes funny and explicit, sometimes bitingly sarcastic. Adept at simile, trained and skillful chanters commanded the respect of Hawaiian chiefs and their retinues.

In the early nineteenth century, when sailing ships began to drop anchor in the islands, their crews sang sea chanties, introducing the concept of melody, as the modern world understands it, to the islands.

By the late 1800s, missionary ardor and imported sounds had thrust aside the old music, and the few practitioners of the old chanting forms passed on their knowledge secretively within their families.

If Hawaiian chants faded into the background, Hawaiians soon were adapting the old to new musical forms. In 1898 Hawai'i became a U.S. territory, and by 1914 half the people on the mainland were singing "On the Beach at Waikiki," popularized by islander Sonny Cunha and composed by Henry Ka'ilimai. Cunha created a new, appealing style with ragtime rhythms and harmonies called *hapa-haole*—a song in English with perhaps a few Hawaiian words.

The heyday of Tin Pan Alley in the 1920s brought about dreadful mainland compositions like "Yacka Hula Hicky Dula," with a chorus of "Aloha Oe" sung backwards. The trend was redeemed by the work of part-Hawaiian musicians such as Johnny Noble ("Aloha Means I Love You" and "Pretty Red Hibiscus"), Johnny K. Almeida ("The Beauty Hula," with Johnny Noble), and Charles E. King ("Kuu Lei Mokihana").

Hawaiian musicians rapidly developed new styles and adapted popular rhythmic trends. They composed the *mele hula ku'i:* a part-western chant and dance style evolved from the early *mele hula.* Falsetto singing gained popularity. American trends filtered into *hapa-haole* music—in the 1930s jazz and blues, and the big band sounds of the 1940s and '50s. In the late 1950s the close triad-harmonies of Tahiti and Samoa were highlights of "Don the Beachcomber" shows, and music of New Zealand's Maori people completed the musical range. If anything defined Hawaiian music, it was the sound of the slack key guitar, which meant strings were tuned down and "slack" compared to those tightened up to match mainland tuning.

In the mid-1970s, Hawaiian music underwent a renaissance that has grown with increasing fervor and includes rediscovery of the *mele* forms of the ancients, even the *mele hula ku'i* chants and songs of nearly one hundred years ago. With the rediscovery of the ancient, there is also a rebounding of the modern, as a newly vital, distinctly Hawaiian, world-class music has emerged.

Among the greatest musicians who spearheaded the Hawaiian musical renaissance were Sonny Chillingworth, Sonny Kamahele, "Atta" Isaacs, and the inimitable Gabby Pahinui, who would finger-pick cascades of notes on his 12-string guitar and sing in a mesmerizing, raspy falsetto. Today three of Gabby's sons, Cyril, Bla, and Martin, carry on his tradition, and have produced some of the finest of modern Hawaiian music.

A favorite in Hawai'i is Don Ho, who in the early 1970s joined the movement with "Tiny Bubbles" and his version of "I Remember You." Although Ho doesn't go outside the islands to perform, he's extremely popular with audiences in Hawai'i, beginning his shows in a slow, genial way and becoming more and more witty and ebullient as his performances progress. One of his gifts is to involve the audience by explaining what the song's words mean.

What is the elusive ingredient of fine Hawaiian music? Perhaps it is a sweetness and a rhythm so connected to nature that it literally pulls on the heart strings of its listeners. Rena Kalehua Nelson, producer and host of a mainland Hawaiian music program, says listeners are constantly calling her to say they find themselves crying when they hear the music on her program—not because it makes them sad, and not because it makes them sentimental, but because it's so gentle and forgiving and that it seems to carry with it *aloha,* the tenderness of life. "Sometimes I worry about it," says Rena Kalehua. "I worry about people driving along the road and then pulling off the road to cry. It's not because of the words. Most people don't understand the words. It's something in the sounds. They're like Hawai'i."

■ TRAVEL BASICS

Honolulu International Airport is the state's travel hub. Budget-minded visitors staying in Honolulu can skip the rental car, take a bus or taxi from the airport to their hotel, and use O'ahu's excellent public transportation system to see the island. **TheBus** is operated by the city and county of Honolulu, which includes the entire island of O'ahu. The fare to any destination is the same, and you can ride all the way around the island for one fare. One-month bus passes can be purchased at any branch of the Bank of Hawai'i (they are sold at the beginning of each month).

Climate: Temperatures in Honolulu vary between 65° F and 85° F. Water temperatures range from 74° F to around 80° F in summer. Winter is the rainy season.

■ VISITOR INFORMATION SERVICES

Hawai'i Visitors and Convention Bureau. Mailing address: 2270 Kalakaua Ave., Suite 801, Honolulu 96815; 808-943-3500, hawaiiconvention.com.
Hawai'i Visitors Bureau. Walk-in office: Royal Hawaiian Shopping Center, 4th Fl., Waikiki; 808-923-1811, gohawaii.com.
O'ahu Visitors Bureau. 877-525-6248.

■ RESTAURANTS

Honolulu and Waikiki diners can visit almost any corner of the globe with all the choices here. There are plenty of establishments with fine dining, impressive views, and top-drawer service, but moderately priced locals' hangouts are to be discovered as well.

$ For restaurant price designations, see page 359.

✕ **Aaron's.** Ala Moana Hotel, 410 Atkinson Dr.; 808-955-4466. The place in town to be seen. Elegant decor atop a hotel with views of Waikiki. Fine Continental menu. Bustling bar has live music and dancing. Dinner only. **$$$**
✕ **Alan Wong's Restaurant.** 1857 S. King St., 5th floor; 808-949-2526. Fish specialities with Asian-style sauces; *furikake* salmon with *ume chiso* rice cream on linguine. Chic dining Pacific style. Right on the street; valet parking. Dinner only. **$$$**
✕ **Asian Express.** 2330 Kalakaua Ave., Waikiki; 808-922-1848. Cambodian and Vietnamese cuisine; also Thai, though you have to request it. Specializes in pho

(Vietnamese noodle soup) in many styles. Try the sweet mochi rice with azuki beans for dessert. **$**

✗ **Assaggio Restaurante Italiano.** Ala Moana Center; 808-942-3446. Assaggio means "to taste," and this restaurant uses top-quality ingredients. Good service; quiet hideaway in a busy shopping center. **$$**

✗ **Auntie Pasto's.** 1099 S. Beretania St.; 808-523-8855. Youthful hangout where diners wait outside for seating. Neighborhood place with generous portions. **$**

✗ **Azteca Mexican Restaurant.** 2617 Koko Head Ave.; 808-735-2492. Good food in residential area; hefty portions. Try the flan. **$**

✗ **Bali by the Sea.** Hilton Hawaiian Village, 2005 Kalia Rd., Waikiki; 808-941-2254. Antiques and etched glass oceanside. French and Continental seafood dishes. **$$$**

✗ **Benihana of Tokyo.** Hilton Hawaiian Village, 2005 Kalia Rd., Waikiki; 808-955-5955. Touristy Japanese decor and menu. *Teppanyaki* (stir-fry at your table) is colorful but a bit uninspired. **$$**

✗ **Big City Diner-Kaimuki.** 3565 Waialae Ave.; 808-738-8855. Large portions of American, local, and Asian comfort foods are served in a friendly local atmosphere. This Hawaiian-style modern diner attracts businesspeople and families. Several TVs blare out ball games; there's an old-style small bar. **$–$$**

✗ **Bubba Gump Shrimp Company.** Ala Moana Center; 808-949-4867. Louisiana food in the atmosphere of the Tom Hank's movie. Really big margaritas; shrimp, BBQ ribs, steaks, chicken, burgers, and a great kids' menu. Open-air section; very casual. **$$**

✗ **Cafe Miro.** 3446 Wai'alae Ave.; 808-734-2737. A prix-fixe three-course menu melding Eastern and Western influences. The humdrum decor belies the wonderful food. The duck is excellent. Bring your own wine. Closed on Mondays. **$–$$**

✗ **Cappuccinos.** Waikiki Joy Hotel, 320 Lewers, Waikiki; 808-923-2300. In this sophisticated dining room, chef Ernesto Mera creates contemporary American cuisine with Asian touches, using the finest produce. **$$$**

✗ **Chef Mavro's.** 1969 S. King St.; 808-944-4714. Take a short taxi ride from Waikiki for a special treat; Chef Mavrothalassitis offers a prix-fixe meal, perfectly paired glass of wine with each menu item, even dessert. Dinner only. **$$$**

✗ **Chez Michel.** Royal Garden Hotel, Waikiki; 808-955-7866. A longtime favorite newly located in a boutique hotel. Amiable bistro with authentic French menu. Good wine list; dinner only. **$$$**

✗ **Chiang Mai Thai Restaurant.** 2239 S. King St.; 808-941-1151. Superb, exotic northern Thai cuisine. Some of the best green curry in town. **$–$$**

✗ **Compadres Mexican Bar & Grill.** Ward Centre, 1200 Ala Moana Blvd.; 808-591-8307. Light and bright with Mexican *objets*. Wide selection menu; huge portions; famous for the brimming pitchers of margaritas. **$–$$**

✗ **Daruma.** Royal Hawaiian Shopping Center, 2201 Kalakaua Ave., Waikiki; 808-926-8878. Simple Japanese decor. Order from photos on the menu. **$**

✗ **Diamond Head Grill.** W Hotel, 2885 Kalakaua Ave., Waikiki; 808-922-3734. Luxury dining among Honolulu's upwardly mobile. Beautifully blended flavors in a regional cuisine with locally grown vegetables and herbs and fresh seafood. Service is highly attentive without being smothering. Local artists' work on display. Food equals the scene. **$$$**

✗ **Don Ho's Island Grill.** 1 Aloha Tower Dr.; 808-528-0807. Beside Honolulu Harbor. Traditional live Hawaiian music; romantic old Hawai'i decor; reliable food and casual ambience. **$$**

✗ **Donato's Restaurant.** Manoa Marketplace; 808-988-2000. Authentic southern Italian and Mediterranean cuisine; a style of cooking quite different from the most common Italian dishes. Fresh local and imported ingredients. Located in Manoa Valley, behind Waikiki; dinner only. **$$$**

✗ **Duc's Bistro.** 1188 Maunakea St.; 808-531-6325. European cuisine with Asian influences and fresh ingredients served with charm on the edge of Chinatown. Good wine selection; live piano played softly; valet parking. **$$–$$$**

✗ **Duke's Canoe Club.** Outrigger Waikiki Hotel; 808-922-2268. Oceanfront dining, island entertainment, and an old Waikiki ambience. **$–$$**

✗ **Eggs 'n' Things.** 1911B Kalakaua Ave., Waikiki; 808-949-0820. Have a hearty breakfast at midnight. Open overnight from 11 P.M. to 2 P.M. **$**

✗ **Fisherman's Wharf.** Ala Moana Blvd. at Kewalo Basin; 808-538-3808. Crammed with decor of the sea. Long-time favorite for fresh fish at cruise-boat harbor. Nice bar and good service. **$$**

✗ **Golden Dragon.** Hilton Hawaiian Village, 2005 Kalia Rd., Waikiki; 808-946-5336. Ornate Chinese decor with dragons, black lacquer, and silk. Overlooking lagoon. Cantonese menu with nouvelle touches; order the specialty Beggar's chicken in advance. Fine service; dinner only. **$$$**

✗ **Goma Ichi Ramen.** 631 Ke'eaumoku St.; 808-951-6666. Honolulu is full of Japanese noodle shops, but this is one of the most attractive. Perfect steaming noodles in broth, served in large bowls and topped with fish or meat and veggies. **$**

✗ **Hackfields.** Macy's, Ala Moana Shopping Center; 808-945-8243. Calm hideaway in busy shopping center. American cuisine with nouvelle touches; wonderful Cobb salad. **$$**

✗ **Hanohano Room.** Sheraton-Waikiki Hotel, 2255 Kalakaua Ave., Waikiki; 808-922-4422. Atop the tallest hotel on the beach. Pleasant room with window views of Waikiki Beach. Fresh fish. Background music in evening. Breakfast and dinner. **$$$**

✗ **Happy Day.** 3553 Waialae Ave., Kaimuki; 808-738-8666 . A seafood restaurant also serving Chinese food, this is about as good as it gets. Hong Kong–style dim sum breakfast, taro basket dishes, noodles. Popular with residents. **$$**

✗ **Hau Tree Lanai.** Otani Kaimana Beach Hotel, 2863 Kalakaua Ave., Waikiki; 808-921-7066. Al fresco dining beside beach in upper Waikiki. Built under enormous *hau* tree. Standard American menu; good value. **$$**

✗ **Hee Hing.** Diamond Head Center, 449 Kapahulu Ave.; 808-735-5544. Chinese dining on the fringe of Waikiki. Extensive menu. **$**

✗ **Hoku's.** Kahala Mandarin Oriental Hotel, 5000 Kahala Ave., Diamond Head; 808-739-8780. Stylish; beach view. Asian influences with fresh, natural foods of the Pacific. **$$–$$$**

✗ **House Without a Key.** Halekulani Hotel, 2199 Kalia Rd., Waikiki; 808-923-2311. A favorite with locals and repeat visitors. One of the best places for a drink beside blue ocean while watching a brilliant sunset and Hawaiian entertainment. Full buffets or appetizers. **$$–$$$**

✗ **Hy's Steak House.** Waikiki Park Heights Hotel, 2440 Kuhio Ave., Waikiki; 808-922-5555. Wood-paneled, hunting theme decor. Superb steak house; fresh fish catch of the day. Excellent service. Entertainment in lounge. **$$$**

✗ **India House.** 2633 S. King St.; 808-955-7552. Small and bright with Indian decor. Excellent North Indian vegetarian and non-vegetarian curries, samosas, tandooris; ask for *saag paneer* (world's tastiest spinach). Near the University. **$$**

✗ **Indigo.** 1121 Nu'uanu Ave.; 808-521-2900. Next to the Hawai'i Theatre downtown. Chinese fusion cuisine such as duck with raspberry hoisin sauce, shrimp stir-fried with risotto, and pleasantly unusual dim sum. Ask for a table in the Thai garden. **$–$$**

✗ **John Dominis.** 43 'Ahui St.; 808-523-0955. One of Honolulu's premier restaurants. Waterside at Point Panic with good views of surfers. Fresh fish and seafood menu. Highly rated and a bit overpriced. Dinner only. **$$$**

✕ **Jose's Mexican Restaurant.** 1134 Koko Head Ave.; 808-732-1833. Good basic Mexican fare; family style. **$**

✕ **Kacho.** Waikiki Parc Hotel, 2233 Helumoa Rd., Waikiki; 808-921-7272. Traditional (if pricey) Japanese food; popular with Japanese businessmen; good service. **$$$**

✕ **Keo's Thai Cuisine.** 2028 Kalakaua Ave., Waikiki; 808-951-9355. Honolulu's trendy Thai-food hot spot. Excellent spicy dishes and great people-watching. **$$$**

✕ **Kincaid's Fish, Chop & Steak House.** Ward Warehouse. 1050 Ala Moana Blvd.; 808-591-2005. Overlooks the sport-fishing boats in Kewalo Basin. Pleasant bar. Award-winning steaks and seafood. **$$**

✕ **Korean BBQ Express.** Ward Warehouse, 1050 Ala Moana Blvd.; 808-596-8023. No elaborate decor, just substantial Korean barbecued ribs and *kim chee.* **$**

✕ **Kyo-Ya.** 2057 Kalakaua Ave., Waikiki; 808-947-3911. Traditional Japanese pagoda; waitresses in kimonos. Authentic fare; you can pre-arrange dinner in the tatami-floored rooms upstairs. **$$**

✕ **La Mer.** Halekulani Hotel, 2199 Kalia Rd., Waikiki; 808-923-2311. Sophisticated Hawaiian decor. Some rate it the top spot in the islands. Beautiful view of Diamond Head. Menu is strictly French; game in season. Flawless service. Jacket/tie required. Dinner only. **$$$**

✕ **Lewers Lounge.** Halekulani Hotel, 2199 Kalia Rd., Waikiki; 808-923-2311. An intimate clublike lounge in the original hotel building, with live contemporary light jazz and standards. Cocktails, appetizers, and desserts served nightly; no cover. On the adjacent terrace, the state's very best English tea is served—with fine teas, the requisite dainty sandwiches, and creamy desserts. **$$**

✕ **The Magic of Polynesia.** Waikiki Beachcomber Hotel, 2300 Kalakaua Ave., 808-922-4646. This lavishly produced dinner show starring John Hirokawa is somewhat of a cross between David Copperfield and Don Ho. The food is good, and the entertainment is great. Make reservations. **$$**

✕ **Maple Garden.** 909 Isenberg St.; 808-941-6641. Good Mandarin Chinese food in a residential neighborhood. **$**

✕ **Mariposa.** Neiman Marcus, Ala Moana Center.; 808-951-3420. Atop the sculpture-filled store, with a spectacular, fishing-harbor view in a casual setting. Hawaiian regional and Southwestern cusine. Extensive wine list; valet parking. **$$–$$$**

✕ **Matteo's.** Marine Surf Hotel, 364 Seaside Ave., Waikiki; 808-922-5551. A *kama'aina* favorite. Dark Italian surroundings with nice booths. Classic fare and game in season. Famed for its wine cellar. Dinner only. **$$$**

✕ **Michel's.** Colony Surf Hotel, 2895 Kalakaua Ave.; 808-923-6552. In the shadow of Diamond Head. Famous dining room with European baroque art works. Overlooks the beach. Sophisticated French Continental cuisine. Dinner only. **$$$**

✕ **Morton's Steakhouse.** Ala Moana Center; 808-949-1300. The Honolulu branch of this famed Chicago restaurant serves fresh seafood and prime aged steaks; legendary hospitality. Take the private elevator on the ocean side of the shopping center. Dinner only. **$$$**

✕ **Murphy's Bar & Grill.** 2 Merchant St.; 808-531-0422. Downtowners gravitate to this lively bar's Celtic atmosphere and occasional entertainment. Hearty Continental food; lunch and dinner. **$–$$**

✕ **Nick's Fishmarket.** Waikiki Gateway Hotel, 2070 Kalakaua Ave., Waikiki; 808-955-6333. Traditional wood paneling and romantic lighting. Fresh fish and seafood menu; Nick's Salad is a favorite with residents. Live music and dancing in the bar. **$$$**

✕ **Oceanarium.** Pacific Beach Hotel, 2490 Kalakaua Ave., Waikiki; 808-921-6111. Family dining amid spectacular views into a 3-story, 280,000-gallon indoor oceanarium alive with darting reef fishes, stingrays, sharks, and frequent divers. Try it for Sunday brunch. **$$–$$$**

✕ **Old Spaghetti Factory.** Ward Warehouse; 808-591-2513. Complete dinners served among Old World antiques. Reasonable and reliable. **$**

✕ **The Olive Tree.** Kahala Mall, 4614 Kilauea Ave.; 808-737-0303. Greek food. Lamb and fish souvlaki, octopus and calamari salad; good baklava. **$**

✕ **Onjin's Cafe.** 401 Kamakee St.; 808-589-1666. Chef Onjin opened her own restaurant, and residents line up for her exotic Hawaiian-Asian dishes. A simple, contempoary café. Reservations a must. **$$**

✕ **Ono Hawaiian Foods.** 726 Kapahulu Ave.; 808-737-2275. A tiny room on the fringe of Waikiki serving only Hawaiian food. Order dishes individually or in combination plates. Closes at 7:30 P.M. **$**

✕ **Orchids.** Halekulani Hotel, 2199 Kalia Rd., Waikiki; 808-923-2311. Open and airy, next to lawns at beachside. Fresh local ingredients with a Continental touch. Game in season. **$$$**

✕ **Outback Steakhouse Waikiki.** 1763 Ala Moana Blvd; 808-961-6274. This resturant is centered on high-quality steaks. Australian "Tucker" includes seafood, ribs, and fresh fish. Great lobster. Dinner only. **$$–$$$**

✕ **Padovani's Bistro & Wine Bar.** Doubletree Alana Waikiki Hotel, 1956 Ala Moana Blvd.; 808-946-3456. Extraordinary world-class cuisine with tasteful Old Hawai'i decor. Freshly baked breads and the island's most extensive wine list. **$$$**

✘ **Paradise Café.** Ala Moana Center; 808-946-0205. Delicious selection of hot and cold sandwiches, salads, fresh-baked goods. In the center's food court; noisy and fun. **$**

✘ **People's Cafe.** 1310 Pali Hwy.; 808-536-5789. Simple atmosphere. Office workers craving a Hawaiian lunch traditionally come here. Order dishes individually or in combination plates. Near downtown. Closes at 7:30 P.M. **$**

✘ **Restaurant Suntory.** Royal Hawaiian Shopping Center, 2233 Kalakaua Ave., Building B., Waikiki; 808-922-5511. Authentic Japanese food, some say the best *teppanyaki* in the city. A favorite with Japanese business executives. **$$$**

✘ **Royal Garden Chinese Restaurant.** Ala Moana Hotel, 3rd floor; 410 Atkinson Dr.; 808-942-7788. Wide-ranging Chinese menu; open until 5 P.M. **$$**

✘ **Roy's Restaurant.** Hawai'i Kai Corporate Plaza, 6600 Kalaniana'ole Hwy., Hawai'i Kai; 808-396-7697. Innovative Pacific Rim cuisine by Roy Yamaguchi, served in a bustling, California-chic dining room overlooking Maunalua Bay. Knowledgeable staff. Perfect for a small dinner party. **$$$**

✘ **Ruth's Chris Steak House.** Restaurant Row, 500 Ala Moana Blvd.; 808-599-3860. The thickest, juciest, tenderest steak you can find; USDA prime beef. Upscale decor; soft music; excellent service. **$$$**

✘ **Ryan's Grill.** Ward Centre, 1200 Ala Moana Blvd.; 808-591-9132. Youngish executives' meeting place; somewhat noisy. Basic American menu. **$**

✘ **Sam Choy's Diamond Head.** 449 Kapahulu Ave.; 808-732-8645. Comfortable and popular with residents. Known for Hawaiian seafood dishes and Asian braised osso buco. Nightly specials. **$$–$$$**

✘ **Sarento's, Top of the Ilikai.** 1777 Ala Moana Blvd.; 808-955-5559. Superb Italian-Mediterranean cuisine with glorious views of Honolulu; intimate seating. **$$–$$$**

✘ **Stuart Anderson's Cattle Co.** Ward Warehouse, 1050 Ala Moana Blvd.; 808-591-9292. Cowboy decor and fine steaks. Music. Family restaurant; crowded. **$$**

✘ **Surf Room.** Royal Hawaiian Hotel, 2259 Kalakaua Ave., Waikiki; 808-923-7311. Covered terrace on the beach. Understated atmosphere with traditional food and service. Outdoor bar. Wonderful Sunday brunch. **$$$**

✘ **3660 On the Rise.** 3660 Waialae Ave.; 808-737-1177. The *ahi katsu* appetizer is a classic, and the Angus New York steak pan-seared with garlic is a favorite. Try the oysters baked with *masago* aioli and accented with shichimi; award-winning desserts. Dinner only. **$$–$$$**

✗ **Trellisses Garden Restaurant.** Radisson Prince Kuhio Hotel, 2500 Kuhio Ave., Waikiki; 808-921-5566. Gardenlike atmosphere; standard menu. **$**

✗ **Verbano.** 3571 Waialae Ave., Kaimuki; 808-735-1777. An Italian restaurant where the pasta is fresh and al dente. Garden-fresh local ingredients, innovative salads. A muted atmosphere in the Kaimuki district *mauka* from Waikiki. **$$**

✗ **Wisteria.** 1206 S. King St.; 808-591-9276. Family favorite serving hearty portions of Japanese and some American dishes. **$**

✗ **Yanagi Sushi.** 762 Kapiʻolani Blvd.; 808-597-1525. Nicely presented, fairly priced sushi in comfortable dining rooms. Private rooms for groups. Near downtown. Service until 2 A.M. **$$**

✗ **Zaffron.** 69 N. King St.; 808-533-6635. Spicy mixed plates combine Chinese with robust Indian curries. No sticky rice here—it's biryani with spices and chicken. Lunch Tues.–Fri.; dinner Thurs.–Sat. **$**

■ LODGING

More than 69,000 hotel and condo units are available in Honolulu. According to state sources, the city takes first rank in occupancy percentages—some 75 percent (the national average is about 65 percent)—and reservations are recommended. Packages are numerous for rooms, family suites, and condos, with and without kitchenettes, pools, and restaurants.

▥ For agencies offering listings and booking services for bed-and-breakfasts, hotels, and condominiums on all islands, see page 359.

$ For room price designations, see page 359.

■ BEACH HOTELS

▥ **Halekulani Hotel.** 2199 Kalia Rd.; 808-923-2311 or 800-367-2343. The premier hotel in the Hawaiian Islands, airy and posh with state-of-the-art computerized services. **$$–$$$**

▥ **Sheraton Moana-Surfrider.** 2365 Kalakaua Ave., Waikiki; 808-922-3111 or 800-325-3535. The first Waikiki hotel, carefully restored in 1991. Open, airy, and light; terrace dining. Wonderful Old Hawaiian style. Breezeway on the 6th floor. **$$–$$$**

▥ **Sheraton Royal Hawaiian.** 2259 Kalakaua Ave., Waikiki; 808-923-7311 or 800-325-3535. The doyenne "Pink Lady of Waikiki." Dignified, with a dining terrace right at the beach and beachside ballroom. The feeling of gracious Hawaiʻi pervades. **$$–$$$**

⊞ **Waikiki Beachcomber Hotel.** 2300 Kalakaua Ave., Waikiki; 808-922-4646 or 800-622-4646. Across the street from beachside, this hotel features Don Ho in an intimate supper club setting. **$$–$$$**

■ **NATIONAL CHAINS**

⊞ **Hilton Hotels.** Waikiki complex: Hilton Hawaiian Village; 800-445-8667.

⊞ **Outrigger Hotels and Ohana Hotels.** 22 hotels in Waikiki. 2375 Kuhio Ave.; 800-688-7444 or 800-462-6262.

⊞ **Sheraton Hotels.** 800-325-3535.

■ **DIAMOND HEAD HOTELS**

⊞ **Kahala Mandarin Oriental.** 5000 Kahala Ave.; 808-739-8888 or 800-367-2525. This luxury resort in a residential area is a golfer's heaven and site of the annual PGA Sony Open in Hawai'i Tournament. Two restaurants feature stunning ocean views. **$$$**.

⊞ **Otani Kaimana Beach Hotel.** 2863 Kalakaua Ave.; 808-923-1555 or 800-356-8264. A cheerful and charming hotel at the quiet end of Waikiki, near Diamond Head. Rooms are smallish but attractive and have full amenities. Dining on the open terrace. **$$–$$$**.

■ **BOUTIQUE HOTELS**

Spacious, elegant rooms and luxurious corporate suites with top amenities, decorative art, and fine restaurants.

⊞ **Doubletree Alana Waikiki.** 1956 Ala Moana Blvd., Waikiki; 808-946-3456 or 800-367-6070. **$$–$$$**

⊞ **Waikiki Joy Hotel.** 320 Lewers St., Waikiki; 808-923-2300 or 800-733-5569. **$$–$$$**

⊞ **Waikiki Royal Suites.** 225 Beach Walk, Waikiki; 808-926-5641 or 800-535-0085. **$$$**

■ **GOLFING IN HONOLULU**

Golf in Hawai'i began more than 100 years ago, when Samuel Mills Damon and the Scotsman Donald MacIntyre laid out the Moanalua Golf Course in 1898. You still can play this course, one of the oldest west of the Mississippi. Resort courses in the Land of Aloha took off in 1962 with the opening of a Robert Trent Jones–designed course on Maui, rapidly followed by courses on all major islands. Unlike those of other golfing locations, all courses in the Aloha State are open to the public.

Ala Wai Municipal Course. 808-733-7387 or 808-7735-6534. Make a tee time well in advance, because this is one of the busiest courses in the world. This 18-hole course offers three sets of tees; par 70. It's a flat layout with flowering trees and palms beside the Ala Wai Canal.

Hawaii Kai Championship and Executive Courses. 808-395-2358. Above Sandy Beach, near the eastern tip of the island, these public courses are popular with visitors from Japan. The 18-hole Championship Course offers three tees and a few surprise lakes; par 72. The 18-hole Executive Course is laid out over hills and valleys; par 73. Both courses are known as forgiving, and are good for beginning and intermediate golfers.

Moanalua Golf Course. 1250 Ala Aolani; 808-839-2411. Play this par-36 nine-hole course twice. The fees are nominal, you can rent a cart, and its early Honolulu charm is appealing. Play is first-come, first-served; no reservations.

■ WAIKIKI SPAS

In Waikiki, two spas feature beauty treatments, massages, saunas, complete salon services, and special packages for bridal couples.

Hawaiian Rainforest Spa. Pacific Beach Hotel, 2490 Kalakaua Ave.; 808-922-1233. This one has an acupressure whirlpool and a wet room with Vichy shower.

Na Ho'ola Spa. Hyatt Regency Waikiki. 2424 Kalakaua Ave.; 808-923-1234.

■ RECOMMENDED TOURS

The bus tours sponsored by **Kapi'olani Community College** in Honolulu are rewarding, informative, and enjoyable experiences. Historian tour guides describe Little Tokyo, plantation history, botany, royalty, and famous cemeteries. *Reservations recommended; 808-734-9234.*

The walking tour **Journey to Old Waikiki** will give you a whiff of the Waikiki that once was a haunt of Kamehameha, kings, revolutionaries, and Robert Louis Stevenson. You can go on a ghost walk and hear descriptions of the Hawaiian fireballs that shoot around at night—if you know how to recognize them—or walk in graveyards to hear stories of gigolos, renegades, and Japanese samurai. *Honolulu Timewalks, 808-943-0371.*

GREATER O'AHU
GATHERING PLACE

From your aircraft, you've had a glimpse of approaching islands. Now, in descent, O'ahu looms up. The southern tail of this manta ray–shaped island is slashed by a half-sunken volcanic crater filled with a lagoon—its waters sparkling in shades of aquamarine and bright sapphire that edge out into the purple-blue of deep ocean. As your aircraft flies along the southeast coast to turn and make its approach for landing, you'll see green residential valleys lined up one after another between forested ridges, each cleft running down to the shoreline where the tall towers of Waikiki and downtown Honolulu face the sea. The two lochs of historic Pearl Harbor come into view as you slip down to the airstrip.

O'ahu, the Gathering Place, is an island that offers an amazing array of life's more bucolic pleasures. Here sunbathers stretch out on golden beaches, and

This house, used to isolate a ship's smallpox sufferers, was on the site of present-day Kapi'olani Park, below Diamond Head. Painting by Paul Emmert, 1853.

swimmers glide through serene waters above gently sloping seabeds. Surfers ride enormous curls of waves that rush ashore in a thunderous roar, and picnickers barbecue and sing to the ukelele on quiet beaches under Pacific stars.

Oʻahu's geography is one of soaring, knife-sharp, volcanic mountains and pristine and residential tropical valleys—all surrounded by more than 50 miles of palmy beach. Driving through rural Oʻahu, one encounters the lifestyle of an earlier Hawaiʻi, and between the small towns hugging white sandy beaches nothing intrudes on nature and her creations.

In addition to *makai* (toward the sea) and *mauka* (toward the mountains), directions on Oʻahu are given by citing landmarks: If you are directed to go *ʻewa*, it means to go west toward the ʻEwa Plain. If you are sent Diamond Head or Koko Head, it means to go in their direction, or east.

■ HISTORY

The dominant political force in the Hawaiian Islands, before the ascendance of Hawaiʻi's Kamehameha the Great, was the tattooed and bloodthirsty Kahekili, scion of Maui's ruling family and probably Kamehameha's real father. In 1782 Kahekili, ruler of Molokaʻi and Lanaʻi, conquered Oʻahu and established a capital at Waikiki. Captain George Vancouver, who had served as a young officer on the Cook voyages, visited Waikiki in 1783 and wrote of Kahekili:

> He came boldly alongside, but entered the ship with a sort of partial
> confidence, accompanied by several chiefs who constantly attended him.
> His age, I suppose, must have exceeded 60. He was greatly debilitated
> and emaciated, and from the color of his skin I judged his feebleness to
> have been brought on by an excessive use of the ava [alcoholic drink].

Kahekili died at Waikiki in July 1794, and was succeeded by his son and heir, Kalanikupule. In January 1795, Kalanikupule commandeered a European brig and tried to sail to the Big Island of Hawaiʻi to attack the upstart warrior Kamehameha. The assault failed, and before the year ended terrible battles were fought. After conquering Maui and Molokaʻi, Kamehameha gathered his fleet of war canoes and, taking with him a few western riflemen, crossed the Kaiwi Channel. He landed at the sheltered bay of Waikiki in the lee of Diamond Head.

When Kalanikupule withdrew inland, leaving Oʻahu's capital undefended, Kamehameha made it his own. Soon Kamehameha's warriors were pushing

A Two-Cent Missionary

Among the rarest and most famous postage stamp issues ever produced are the Hawaiian Missionaries. These stamps were first printed in Hawai'i in 1851, and were primarily used on mail that missionaries sent back home to New England. Very few have survived, one reason being the fragile pelure paper on which they were printed. They came in 2-, 5-, and 13-cent denominations, but the 2-cent issue has become the rarest of all, with only 15 copies known to exist. *Scott's Stamp Catalogue* values a specimen in mint condition at $500,000. Those that are left seem to be imbued with the island's mystique, and stories centered around them are numerous.

One such story dates from Paris in the 1890s and the collection of a well-known philatelist by the name of Gaston Leroux. Leroux was found murdered in his flat, and the detectives assigned to the case couldn't seem to come up with a suspect or a motive. Leroux didn't have any enemies, and the valuables in his apartment had been left untouched. Eventually, one canny French detective noticed Leroux's stamp collection, turned the pages in his album, and saw that a stamp was missing—what else but a 2-cent Hawaiian Missionary.

The detective's suspicions eventually focused on Hector Giroux, another stamp collector, and an acquaintance of the murdered man. Posing as a stamp collector himself, the detective went for a visit, and before long the two men became quite chummy. One day the conversation came around to the subject of the Hawaiian Missionaries, and Giroux proudly brought out the 2-center—the same one missing from the murdered man's collection. After he was arrested and questioned, Giroux finally admitted he'd killed Leroux because he'd refused to part with his 2-cent Missionary.

There are only 15 known copies of this valuable stamp.

Kalanikupule's forces up the funnel of Nu'uanu Valley. Unable to regroup in the narrowing valley, many of Kalanikupule's men at the sides of the phalanx scattered up the mountainsides and melted away into forests. Kalanikupule himself slipped away, but his central forces were trapped. Backed to the rim of the sheer cliff at the top of the valley, they were driven over the mountain's knife-sharp edge and died on the jagged lava rocks below. Kamehameha emerged from this battle the monarch of all the islands except Kaua'i. When Kalanikupule reappeared some months later, Kamehameha sacrificed him to Kuka'ilimoku, his god of war. The **Nu'uanu Pali Lookout** is the site of that bloody battle.

■ SOUTHEAST O'AHU

Southeast O'ahu curves around the bottom of the Ko'olau Mountains to form a coast famous for bodysurfing beaches, just 20 minutes from Waikiki. To the east, HI 1 becomes Kalanianaole Highway (HI 72) and follows the coast around to the windward side of the island. The road winds gently behind Koko Head Crater to Makapu'u, passing inland turnoffs into residential areas crouching in rising valleys. On the ocean side of the road, low volcanic cliffs edge the sea.

■ KOKO HEAD AND HANAUMA BAY *map page 255, F-4*

Nine miles from Waikiki, the Kalanianaole Highway reaches Koko Head and Hanauma Bay. The turquoise lagoon of Hanauma Bay lies in a sunken crater on the east side of Koko Head. The bay is colored in a spectrum of blues, greens, and purples and fronted by a curving swath of sand half a mile long. Hanauma Bay was formed about 6,000 years ago when the sea level rose and a side of Koko Head's crater collapsed, allowing the sea to rush in. On each side of the crater, lava shelves cut by wave action run out to each point. The waters on the right side of the bay are called Witches' Brew, because of their roiling when the surf turns rough. The seas on the left are named Toilet Bowl for the swirling waves, flushing and filling a tidal pool. In the middle of the bay is Keyhole, a deep, sandy-bottomed pool in the reef that from the cliff above looks like an enormous, brilliant aquamarine gemstone.

The Hanauma reef, stretching across the entire bay and separating shallow bay from deep ocean, may offer the calmest snorkeling in all the islands. Inside the placid lagoon, creatures of the sea (including schools of *ulua,* which dart about, their spots or "stars" blinking on their three-foot blue-green bodies) flourish and perform for anyone who puts on a mask and floats in the limpid waters.

Hanauma (Hand Wrestling) Bay was once a place to play *uma,* a sport in which two men hand-wrestle from a kneeling position on the beach. It was also one of the most popular places on O'ahu for launching canoes. Mo'okua O Kane'apua Hill, overlooking the bay on the right, is a fine place to take wind directions, and an artful canoeist could take a "reading," then scoot down to the water, catching the wind and current to wherever he would go.

Hanauma Bay has suffered from too many visitors, some 13,000 a day, as tour buses and diving and snorkeling companies used to bring busloads of people down into the ecologically fragile waters. This overuse has been stopped by the city, and now bus tours only pause for views from above. The city's Department of Parks & Recreation allows individuals to descend to the bay after a short orientation that includes viewing a film. The city also now charges beach and parking fees.

The brightly colored fish at **Hanauma Bay Nature Preserve,** an underwater wildlife preserve, are so tame that instead of bolting away they'll swim right up to you. To visit, walk down the steep road (or take a shuttle ride) from the parking lot at the top of the hill, just off the highway. *808-591-9013.*

■ **KOKO HEAD TO SANDY BEACH** *map opposite, F-4*
As it continues east, Kalanianaole Highway curves past the white-sand beaches and rough lava shores that are part of **Koko Head Regional Park.**

At **Halona (Peering Place) Blowhole,** ocean water, forced through an irregularly shaped chimney in the lava cliff, geysers like a mini Old Faithful and falls onto a lava shelf at the lookout. Be sure to stay behind the rail: accidents happen when unwise visitors climb out on the shelf where the sea can sweep them away. This lookout is a fine spot for whale-watching from December to April, when the humpbacks mate and calve.

Wedged between the Blowhole Lookout and Halona Point, is **Halona Cove,** a tiny patch of white sand sometimes called *From Here To Eternity* Beach, because it was the site of the movie's (not the book's) steamy beach scene. A steep path leads down to the sand from the parking lot. The same waves that spout through the blowhole also surge into the cove, and swimming is safe only when seas are calm.

Unless you are an experienced surfer, you would be wise to spend your time sunbathing on the broad unshaded strand of **Sandy Beach.** Avoided by Hawaiians in early days because of its heavy rip tides and roiled backwash, Sandy Beach was "discovered" by servicemen in World War II, who, ignoring its dangers,

O'AHU

Elevation
in feet

13,796
9,000
7,000
5,000
4,000
3,000
2,000
1,000
Sea Level

0 4 8 Miles
0 4 8 12 Kilometers

Ka'ena Point
Kahuku Point
Kawela Bay
Waialee
Sunset Beach
Sunset Beach
Waimea
Pupukea
Kawailoa Beach
Kawailoa
Haleiwa
Mokule'ia
Waialua
Mahahoe Point
GOAT ISLAND
Malaekahana State Park
La'ie Point
Polynesian Cultural Center
Kahuku
La'ie
Hauula
Punalu'u
Kahana
Kualoa Ranch
Kualoa Point
Ka'a'awa
Ka'a'awa Point
Waikane
Waiahole
Kahalu'u
Heeia
Kane'ohe Bay
Kane'ohe
Mokapu Point
Ulupau Crater
Hawai'i Marine
Corps Base
Kailua Beach
Kailua
Pohakupo
Maunawili
Ahuimanu
Pacific Palisades
Pearl City
'Aiea
Halawa Heights
Waimalu
KO'OLAU RANGE
Pu'u Pauao
2,685 ft
Eleao
2,664 ft
Pu'u Kahuauli
Kualii

Kailua Beach
Wailea Point
Bellows Field Beach Park
Waimanalo
Waimanalo Beach Park
MANANA ISLAND
KAOHIKAIPO ISLAND
MOKULUA ISLAND
Makapu'u Beach
Makapu'u Point
Makapu'u Light
Sea Life Park
Koko Crater Botanical Gardens
Koko Head
Hanauma Bay
Nature Preserve
Halona Cove
Halona Blowhole
Sandy Beach
Koko Head Regional Park
Kawaihoa Point
Pauliolo Point
KOKO HEAD

Pu'u Pauao
Bole Pineapple
Visitor Center
Wahiawa
Walpio Acres
Mililani
Waipahu
Ewa
Village
EWA PLAIN
Makakilo
City
Kapolei
Makaha Beach
Lahilahi Point
Makaha
Waianae
Ma'ili
Ma'ili Point
Ka'ala
4,030 ft
WAIANAE RANGE
Kolekole Pass
Palikea
3,098 ft
Kaukonahua
Hanakuii
Honokai Hale
Barbers Point
Ewa Beach
U.S.
Naval
Reservation
Hickam
A.F.B.
Honolulu
International Airport
U.S.
Naval
Res.
Pearl
Harbor
HONOLULU
Waikiki
Diamond Head Crater
DIAMOND HEAD

Farrington Hwy
Kamehameha Hwy
Kamehameha Hwy
Kamehameha Hwy

see
Greater Honolulu map, page 221
see
Waikiki map, page 203

Kahuku Point

Ko'olau Range

Likelike Hwy
Pali Hwy
Kalanianaole Hwy
NU'UANU VALLEY
KALIHI VALLEY
MANOA VALLEY
Kamananui
3,105 ft

83
83
99
750
76
95
93
83
61
65
65
63
72
92
H1
H1
H2
H3
H3
H3
61

Waimanalo Bay

Kaiwi Channel

Ka'a'awa Point

NORTH
COMPASS

Waimea Bay
Waialua Bay

suffered many accidents. By 1944 the military designated Sandy off-limits. In the 1960s, however, the beach became popular with local surfers. Only experienced bodysurfers can cope with its murderous shore break, and understand the changes in the ocean bottom wrought by pounding waves. There's a popular lunch wagon and beach facilities.

The 60-acre basin of Koko Head Crater provides a hot, dry climate that is ideal for the **Koko Crater Botanical Gardens** xeriscape collections. The two-mile loop trail passes through a swath of colorful plumeria trees, dryland palms, aloes, and a grove of native *wiliwili* trees. *Opposite Sandy Beach. Drive mauka (inland) on Kealahou Street; 808-522-7060.*

■ **MAKAPU'U POINT** *map page 255, F-4*
On the easternmost tip of O'ahu is a craggy palisade rising 420 feet above crashing seas. Its name means "bulging eye"—after a stone image with eight protruding eyes said to have been in a cave at the base of the point. On its summit, facing the perilous Kaiwi Channel, is the **Makapu'u Point Light House,** landfall light for vessels bound from the mainland. Its light is visible from the deck of a ship at a distance of 28 miles, and its reflection has been seen from 45 to 50 miles at sea. The light is turned on a half-hour before sunset and secured a half-hour after sunrise.

Possibly the most famous beach in the islands for bodysurfing (surfboards are not permitted), the wide square of white sand at **Makapu'u Beach** is flanked by a finger of shiny black lava in the water on the left, and the tall lava cliff of Makapu'u Point on the right. As there is no protecting reef, enormous swells roll in slowly before crashing near shore, and surfers have a long ride without fear of hitting coral. These waters are dangerous for the inexperienced; in winter the waves break at the shoreline, and bodysurfers and swimmers can be caught in the pounding break. In summer the waves break offshore and the swimming is good close to the beach. Lifeguards use the flag system here—red for dangerous waters and green for safe.

A few hundred feet down the highway is the entrance to **Sea Life Park,** the marine world home of the hybrid wholphin (whale and dolphin). Great tanks here are filled with marine life. The park also has water exhibitions and research programs.

Kayaking can be blissful along selected stretches of O'ahu's coastlines.

■ WINDWARD O'AHU

The windward shore runs from Makapu'u Point up the eastern side of the island to Kahuku Point. You can drive to the windward side by following the shoreline all the way around from Makapu'u and through Waimanalo town. Or, you can travel there from central Honolulu by taking the tunnels that pierce the Ko'olau Mountains—Nu'uanu Pali Highway (HI 61) or Likelike Highway (HI 63)—a distance of 10 miles. Interstate H-3, another route, passes through uninhabited Halawa Valley. The two main windward towns of Kailua and Kane'ohe are large suburbs beside deep bays. Farther north, villages dot the shoreline.

The **Ko'olau Mountains** drop almost straight down in volcanic folds onto a collar of lush agricultural lands that meet miles and miles of uncrowded beaches, some with wonderful swimming, others filled with coral. The drive along the windward coast is one of the most spectacular in the islands, passing the convolutions of sheer, green-blanketed *pali* looming inland. In the evening light the mountains grow shadowed from green to purple to deepening black.

■ WAIMANALO BAY *map page 255, E/F-4*

The northeast trade winds make windward waters popular with windsurfers and with sailboat and motor-vessel enthusiasts. One of the fine beaches located off Kalanianaole Highway is **Waimanalo Beach Park,** a three-and-one-half-mile stretch of soft white sand accompanied by 38 acres of county park. The beach is at the southeast end of the bay; a coral reef about a mile out breaks up the surf. The recreation area is a mile north in a grove of ironwood trees (residents call it Sherwood Forest), and it has facilities, lawns, camping, and sports grounds. Both areas are excellent for year-round swimming. Board- and bodysurfers find the largest waves in the bay off the recreation area. The view from Waimanalo (Potable Water) takes in two offshore seabird sanctuaries, Kaohikaipo, or Turtle Island, and Manana, usually called Rabbit Island for its crouching profile.

Just north of Waimanalo Beach Park, at Bellows Air Force Station, is **Bellows Field Beach Park.** The long, broad, finely packed sands are backed by a dense grove of ironwood trees. It's an excellent family beach: the swimming is safe and coral-free, and boogie-board surfers can play in the small waves. Most of the beach is open on weekends, and camping by permit is allowed.

■ **KAILUA** *map page 255, E-3*

Kailua Beach at Kailua town is set before ironwood trees and bisected by Kailua Stream. The sands are broad and white, and the seabed slopes gently. Long known to canoe paddlers, Kailua has been discovered by windsurfers and is considered one of the best sites for this sport in the islands. Even if you don't get wet, go on the weekend just for the sight of ballooning sails, patterned with flying fish and rainbows, skimming over turquoise water at an awesome speed.

Seldom visited **Ulupo (Night Inspiration) Heʻiau,** one mile south of central Kailua, is perhaps the best place on Oʻahu to see a sacred temple. (Ironically, it's located behind the YMCA at 1200 Kailua Road.) Legend has it that *menehune,* or elves, built it, and being *menehune* they did it in a single night. The large open platform, 30 feet high and 140 feet long, is well preserved. Archaeologists believe Ulupo arose as a temple consecrated to agriculture, and later evolved into a human sacrificial *heʻiau* dedicated to war.

Early on a weekday morning the freeway into Honolulu is jammed with commuters from the Kailua area.

■ KUALOA RANCH *map page 255, D-2*

Sprawling across 4,000 acres in Ka'a'awa at the foot of the Ko'olau Mountains, Kualoa Ranch runs cattle, grows plants, and maintains fish and aquaculture ponds. Home to one family for the past 150 years, the land was purchased from Kamehameha III to build Hawai'i's first sugar mill. Today the ranch features horseback riding and other outdoor activities, and the land is kept free of commercial development. *808-237-7321.*

■ LA'IE DISTRICT *map page 255, D-1*

One of O'ahu's best kept secrets, **Malaekahana State Park** is a good place to while away a day at a tropical beach park about as far from Waikiki as you can go on O'ahu. The long and narrow sands are backed by acres of coco palms, ironwood, and hala trees. Watching the sun disappearing from the empty, rosy sands at sunset, you might imagine you're in paradise—and you are. This area is seldom crowded; it has good year-round swimming and body-, board-, and windsurfing; and its extensive facilities attract families. Malaekahana also has a fine camping site

(above) Tours at the Polynesian Cultural Center in La`ie district are entertaining and informative. (following spread) The Ko'olau Mountains provide a magnificent backdrop for the Byodo-In, a Buddhist temple not far from Kailua.

(state permit required), or you can rent a tent-camp or one of the five large and rustic cabins. The rentals are handled at a kiosk near the north entrance from the highway. *About 23 miles north of Kane'ohe town; 808-293-1736.*

Offshore from Malaekahana State Park, opposite the curve of white beach, lies Moku'auia, or **Goat Island** (the goats are gone). Small and low-lying, the island is a state bird refuge open to visitors. Swimming, snorkeling, and picnicking are permitted at a small, white-beach cove on its inland side. If you wade out at low tide, beware of spiny sea urchins.

In the district of La'ie stand a gleaming white Mormon temple and visitors center and the Hawai'i campus of Brigham Young University. Nearby, the Mormon church operates the 42-acre **Polynesian Cultural Center,** which has one of the best entertainment tours in the islands. Here Polynesians from throughout the Pacific live and perform. Take some time to examine the migration museum, a *halau waa* (canoe house), murals and tiki figures, and Moai, the stone statues of Rapa Nui (Easter Island). From 6 to 20 feet tall, Moai have mystified scientists for generations. Reservations for this all-day tour can be made at your hotel desk.

■ KAHUKU POINT   *map page 255, C-1*

As it continues north, the road passes open fields and roadside stands selling home-grown fruit. The windward shore ends at the one resort hotel on this coast, the 880-acre Turtle Bay Hilton on Kahuku Point. Surrounded by flowering bougainvillea, bright red flambouyant trees, and tall cocos, the resort's golf course glistens, and 12 miles of trails beckon walkers. It's a peaceful retreat, far away from the city, where only the sounds of the surf fill the night.

■ CENTRAL O'AHU

Branching off H-1 near Pearl Harbor, HI 750, HI 99, and H-2 lead through the saddle between the Ko'olau Mountains on the east and the Waianae Mountains on the west to **Wahiawa.** An old Army town in the middle of the island, Wahiawa has bars, pawn shops, fast-food restaurants, and a lovely old restaurant called Kemo'o Farm. The town is the site of the U.S. Army's **Schofield Barracks,** traditional home of the Twenty-fifth Division. The central Leileihua plain, now studded with modern bedroom towns, has become O'ahu's population center.

H-1, H-2, and H-3 are *interstate* highways, an amusing description for highways that adjoin an ocean. Interstates came to Hawai'i after statehood was achieved in

1959, when Sen. Hiram Fong argued that the large body of water between Hawai'i and California was not the fault of Hawai'i's residents, and that they deserved to receive a fair share of interstate highway funds. Congress agreed. H-3, running from Kane'ohe through pristine Halawa Valley to connect with H-1, opened in 1997 after years of environmental controversy.

Kolekole Pass is the winding gap (1,724 feet high) in the Waianae Mountains that leads to leeward O'ahu. The rocky, volcanic pass is on Army property—and sometimes closed during maneuvers. The splendid view of white beaches along the Waianae Coast is one few visitors experience. Enter at Schofield's Foote Gate off HI 750, and check there for information and directions. It's about a 10-mile trip.

If you continue north beyond Wahiawa, you'll pass through miles of pineapple fields. At the **Dole Pineapple Visitor Center,** on HI 99, you can buy fresh pineapple juice, pineapple ice cream, and fresh fruit packed to carry home. Or you can get yourself purposely lost in Dole's **Pineapple Garden Maze.** Planted in puzzling walls of pink hibiscus and flowering heliconia, the 100,000-square-foot maze is listed in the *Guinness Book of World Records* as the largest in the world. Punch your time-card at all six stations along the 1.7-mile path in good time and you'll receive a prize. Emergency maps can be retrieved for the terminally lost. Families can delight on a ride aboard the ***Pineapple Express,*** a diesel engine train with four coaches. The 20-minute tour carries you through plantation fields where a new variety of extra-sweet pineapples now grows; stunning views of the Waianae Mountains accent this little jaunt. *Dole Plantation, 808-621-8408.*

Farther north, the Leileihua saddle begins to widen. Broad views of blue-green ocean lie ahead.

■ NORTH SHORE

Washed by some of the most celebrated and daunting winter surfing waters in the world, O'ahu's north shore is a 20-mile stretch of piney ironwoods, coconut, and mango trees, their leafy profusion concealing narrow lanes where beach homes face the sea. The north shore seems a piece of Old Hawai'i—many of its buildings weathered and secluded in the tropical green of long-established palms and plantings. North-shore mountain streams gently flow across beaches to the ocean. There's a South Seas ambience, and it is easy to realize you are on an island in the most isolated archipelago in the world.

Dole's Pineapple Garden Maze is a fun place to wander.

If you've heard of surfing, you've heard of the north shore. In winter months, world-class surfers from every nation where the sport is pursued come to challenge some of the most formidable surf in the world. Even if you know little about the art of surfing, it's an extraordinary experience to watch powerful young men and women riding in the maw of towering 30- to 40-foot waves and gliding down nature's most fearsome walls of heaving water.

■ **WAIMEA BAY** *map page 255, C-1*

For years surfers have come to the dazzling cobalt waters of Waimea Bay for international competition classics. Much of the action centers on nearby **Sunset Beach** and **Haleiwa,** where surfing's Triple Crown is held from mid-November to mid-December. In summer, Waimea Bay waters are placid, and swimming is good at its wide cream-colored beach. The valley extending up from Waimea Bay is a wilderness where time has restored the land tenderly, and man has trod it lightly.

■ **PUPUKEA** *map page 255, C-1*

The marine reserve and snorkeler's haven next to Sunset Beach has some of O'ahu's best underwater sights. Look for *ulua,* the blue crevally jackfish that swims close to shore. Opposite the beach several narrow lanes bolt upward through green hills that rise steeply from the road to a high plateau. During World War II, Pacific Army forces trained for jungle warfare here, and a large encampment sprawled before the expansive view. Visitors now drive here to buy fresh tropical fruits sold at the roadside all summer long by islanders who tend small orchards and ranches.

■ **KAHOKUWELOWELO HE'IAU** *map page 255, C-1*

In ancient times the most important *he'iau* on the north shore was Kahokuwelowelo, across from the present Kawailoa Beach Park. Named for a comet, it was here that

North shore surfers and swimmers watch the Banzai Pipeline during winter surf.

the *kahuna-kilokilo* (specialized priests) pondered the stars. Only traces of stonework remain at this oval-shaped scientific temple.

■ **MOKULE'IA** *map page 255, B-2*

The beach here is not crowded, and the swimming is good, but Mokule'ia (Place of Abundance) is known for world-class polo. Teams from Argentina, England, Germany, Italy, and Mexico, as well as the mainland U.S. and neighbor islands, can be seen on ponies pounding down the beachside field. The Hawaii Polo Club (808-637-9022) plays matches every Sunday afternoon from mid-May to mid-October.

If you drive west over the one-lane Haleiwa Bridge to Mokule'ia, the road soon comes to an end. A rugged two-mile track along uninhabited coastline leads through tidepools to **Ka'ena Point.** This sliver of sand and lava rock pierces the ocean under a pointed cliff separating the north shore from the leeward shore. The cliff, shaped like the prow of a huge ship, creates a bow wave in the sea.

■ **LEEWARD O'AHU**

The **Waianae Coast** is the arid, leeward side of O'ahu. At its northern tip the island is untouched by roads. Farrington Highway (HI 93) follows the length of the shoreline from central Honolulu north to the end of the paved road. From the roadhead, if seas are calm, you can walk, wade, and inspect tidal pools for some four miles—all the way to the sharp tapering point of Ka'ena that separates leeward O'ahu from the north shore.

Even though developers have come into the area, leeward O'ahu is still a place apart. Along the coast there are no souvenir shops or tour buses. Leeward residents, living in rural towns, have resisted both development and visitors. Muggings and car thefts have given the area a bad reputation. The Makaha Golf Club lies in Makaha Valley. For some unknown reason, wild peacocks gather each evening at the two adjacent condo towers to preen and screech. Some 3,000 of the birds inhabit the valley, including a number that are all white.

During the summer, swimming is good along the wide, white strands of the Waianae Coast. In winter the seabeds steepen and the breakers become some of the most formidable surfing waves in the islands. Each year at **Makaha Beach** competitions are held. The Buffalo Big Board Surfing Classic in February is the best time for spectators, when old-time surfers use the old-fashioned long boards that can weigh nearly one hundred pounds. (See the Surfing chapter.)

■ TRAVEL BASICS

An easy loop drive of less than 100 miles takes visitors past most of O'ahu's famous beaches and historical sites. You might find it convenient to use **TheBus,** O'ahu's excellent public transportation system. It goes to any destination, or all around the island, for the same fare. If your stay is extended, buy a one-month bus pass at any branch of the Bank of Hawai'i (sold at the beginning of each month).

Climate: O'ahu enjoys a comfortable tropical climate influenced by the northeast-erly trade winds. Temperatures vary between 65° F and 90° F. Water temperatures range from 74° F to around 80° F in summer. Winter is the rainy season.

■ VISITOR INFORMATION SERVICES

Hawai'i Visitors and Convention Bureau. Mailing address: 2270 Kalakaua Ave., Suite 801, Honolulu 96815; 808-943-3500, hawaiiconvention.com.
Hawai'i Visitors Bureau. Royal Hawaiian Shopping Center (walk-in office), 4th Fl., Waikiki; 808-923-1811, gohawaii.com.
O'ahu Visitors Bureau. 877-525-6248.

■ FOOD AND LODGING

⊞ For agencies offering listings and booking services for bed-and-breakfasts, hotels, and condominiums on all islands, see page 359.
$ For room and restaurant price designations, see page 359.

LEEWARD AND NORTH SHORE

✗ **Cafe Hale'iwa.** 66-460 Kamehameha Hwy., Hale'iwa; 808-637-5516. A local breakfast favorite of surfers in an old-fashioned setting with ceiling fans. Local and Mexican dishes, hearty sandwiches, and tasty vegetarian burritos. Closes at 2 P.M. **$**
✗ **Jameson's by the Sea.** 62-540 Kamehameha Hwy., Hale'iwa; 808-637-4336. Elegant dining on the rural north shore. Beautiful view of Hale'iwa Harbor. American menu; fresh fish and seafood. Downstairs terrace serves chowder and burger lunch. **$$**
⊞ **Azul.** Marriott 'Ihilani Resort, 92-1001 Olani St., Kapolei; 808-679-0079 or for reservations, 808-679-3166. Fine dining with Mediterranean cuisine at this posh, secluded resort, up the leeward coast about an hour's drive from Waikiki. **$$$**

⊤ **Makaha Surfside.** 85-175 Farrington Hwy., Makaha; 808-696-6990. Condos with basic amenities and swimming pool in a country, beachside setting. **$**

⊤ **Marriott ʻIhilani Resort and Spa.** 92-1001 Olani St., Kapolei; 808-679-0079 or 800-626-4446. An upscale destination resort on Oʻahuʻs leeward shore beside lagoons and an undulating golf course. Private lanai. **$$$**

Southeast and Windward

✕ **Bueno Nalo.** 41-865A Kalanianaʻole Hwy., Waimanalo; 808-263-1999. Mexican restaurant in Hawaiian rural community. Traditional decor and menu; hefty portions. Bring your own liquor. **$**

✕ **Crouching Lion.** 51-666 Kamehameha Hwy., Kaʻaʻawa; 808-237-8511. On the highway under the mountain configuration of a lion; a haven along this quiet shore. Indoor and outdoor dining. Good American menu and lively bar. **$$**

✕ **Giovanniʻs Aloha Shrimp.** Wagons in Kahuku and Haleʻiwa; 808-293-1839. The graffiti-covered wagons look disastrous; never mind, the shrimp-in-shell is delicious, spicy or grilled, and youʻll sit at picnic tables under awnings. Pick up a smoothie at the adjacent wagon and delve into a messy feast. **$**

✕ **Saengʻs Thai Cuisine.** 315 Hahani St.; Kailua; 808-263-9727. Simple Thai decor and good food with fresh local ingredients.

⊤ **Turtle Bay Hilton.** Kahuku; 808-293-2800 (condos); 808-293-8811 (hotel) or 800-445-8667. The only complete resort on the windward coast. Typical Hilton, with golf, tennis, and horseback riding. Rooms have private lanais; separate cottages lie adjacent to the hotel. **$$–$$$** The hotelʻs restaurant, ✕ **The Cove,** serves an American menu; fresh fish and seafood. Dinner only. **$$**

■ Golfing on Greater Oʻahu

If youʻve wondered which golf course in the United States is rated the most difficult—youʻve found it. The Koolau Course is it. Even though officialdom does not recognize slope ratings above 155, its rating is 162.

Kahuku Golf Course. Kahuku; 808-293-5842. This delightful 9-hole municipal course in rural Oʻahu has one set of tees; par 35. Itʻs good old-fashioned, unpretentious golf. The fairways and greens are a bit bumpy, but the ocean views are tops.

Koolau Golf Course. 45-550 Kioaole Rd., Kaneʻohe; 808-236-4653. Right from the beginning, youʻll know what youʻve encountered. Hole No. 1 requires accuracy, luck, and a drive of 593 yards; par 5. Its bunkers and jungle are formidable and an approach shot could fall into oblivion. The course is nestled directly beneath the steep purple-hued Ko'olau Mountains on the windward side of the island. Hole No. 18 is considered one of the most demanding finishing holes in the state.

Ko Olina Golf Club. West Beach; 808-676-5300. An 18-hole course with three sets of tees; par 72. Laid out over undulating green hills and valleys, this course features a drive-under waterfall and streams crossed by stepping stones.

Makaha Golf Club. 84-626 Makaha Valley Rd.; 808-695-9544. A popular 18-hole public course set between folds of the Waianae Mountains; par 72. Lush with tropical plantings, it begins near the ocean at the valley mouth and wends its way upward; since it is on the island's leeward side, wind blows down the valley. Grain runs with the wind. On this classic course you will use every club in your bag.

Pearl Country Club. 'Aiea; 808-487-3802. An 18-hole course with two sets of tees; par 72. This is a tough course designed for accuracy by Akiro Sato. Set in the hills above Pearl City, the course brims with glorious views of Pearl Harbor and the *Arizona* and *Missouri.*

Turtle Bay Hilton Golf and Tennis Club. Kahuku; 808-293-8574. Two resort courses designed by Arnold Palmer (1992) and George Fazio (1984): the Palmer Course with 18 holes and five sets of tees; and the Fazio Course with 18 holes and three sets of tees. Both courses are par 72. They're situated under the big sky of O'ahu's north shore and backed by lush green mountains.

■ O'AHU SPAS

(See also Waikiki Spas, page 249.)

Marriott 'Ihilani Spa. 92-1001 Olani St., Kapolei; 808-679-0079 or 800-626-4446. Fitness, nutrition, beauty, stress-reduction, and weight-loss programs; hyrdotherapy, aromatherapy, and thalasso treatments; personal trainers, saunas, steam rooms, Roman pool, needle shower, and spa cuisine.

■ OUTDOOR ADVENTURES

■ HIKING

Many who visit Hawai'i want to go out and encounter the majestic mountains and serene vistas of these alluring islands. Ecotourism expeditions on land and water are offered by companies in guided one- to five-day adventures. Hikers, however, tend to take off on their own up lush Hawaiian trails. It's easy to arrange a stay in a hotel with as much comfort as you like, then dash off without preparation expecting to spend your day amid tropical bird-sounds and forest quietude. On Oʻahu, in less than an hour you can leave town and drive to a remote trailhead.

Thousands of trekkers are drawn to Oʻahu's 200 beckoning trails. Often they are thinking, "How can you get lost on an island?" You can. It's a good idea to keep in mind that these islands are mainly wilderness areas. If you get lost on the mainland, the rule is to follow a streambed. In Hawaiʻi, don't do it; a mountain forest stream usually leads to a waterfall, a dead end. The beckoning, purple-hued mountains can be trecherous; muddy trails are slippery, and ancient lava may crumble underfoot. A fall can be steep. Accomplished trekkers have fallen and landed on inaccessible ridges with precipitous drops of 2,000 or more feet. In 1999 the Honolulu Fire Department's rescue unit reported more than 40 searches and 30 incidents of assistance.

To enjoy the remote valleys and rugged mountains where you can ascend to 4,000 feet rather quickly, think Boy Scout and "Be prepared!" Start out early. Wear bright clothing, carry a whistle, first-aid supplies, water, food, and a flashlight. Take along a cellular phone and warm jacket; if you become stranded, the overnight will be misty and cold. Wear boots, not sneakers, and tell someone where you are going. You can call the National Weather Service (808-973-5286) for the day's forecast.

For information about hiking trails and skill level on Oʻahu, check with the **Hawaiʻi State Division of Forestry and Wildlife** (1151 Punchbowl St., Rm. 325, Honolulu 96813; 808-587-0166). For guided adventures, order the ***Directory of the Hawaiʻi Ecotourism Association*** ($5; $7 outside the U.S.; 808-956-2866; hawaiiecotourism.org).

Diamond Head. State Division of Forestry and Wildlife, Honolulu; 808-587-0166. Under a mile long, this is a "must do" in Honolulu. Though short, the hike is hot and dry, but the vistas are stunning. To reach the trailhead from Honolulu, drive south on Kalakaua Avenue, take a right on Diamond Head Road, a left at the sign marked Diamond Head State Park, and go through the tunnel. There is a trail fee, but free hiking maps are available.

Maakua Gulch Trail. State Division of Forestry and Wildlife, Honolulu; 808-587-0166. This lovely three-mile hike (one way) leads you into the narrow, twisting canyon of Maakua Gulch. At first the trail crisscrosses the stream, then the streambed itself becomes the trail. Apples and guavas grow alongside the trail, and at the foot of the waterfall lie irresistible pools. From Honolulu take HI 63 north, turn left on HI 83, left again on Hauula Homestead Road (just past Hauula Beach Park), then right on the dirt Maakua Road, where there's a small dirt lot at the trailhead.

■ WATER ACTIVITIES

Aloha Beach Services. 2365 Kalakaua Ave., Honolulu; 808-922-3111, ext. 2341. Surfboard rentals and lessons.

Atlantis Submarines. 1600 Kapi'olani Blvd., Honolulu; 808-973-9811. Underwater tours in submarines up to 1,000 feet long.

Hawaiian Waters Adventure Park. 400 Farrington Hwy., Kapolei; 808-945-3928. Body-surf in man-made waves and float down a riverlike stream in a tube. There are water slides, children's and adult pools, geysers, and amenities.

Naish Hawai'i. 155A Hamakua Dr., Kailua; 808-261-3539. Beginning windsurfing lessons available. Naish and his family build, sell, and rent boards; "windsurfari" trips available.

South Seas Aquatic. 2155 Kalakaua Ave., Ste. 112, Honolulu; 808-922-0852. Two-tank boat dives; beginning scuba courses available.

Tradewind Charters. 1833 Kalakaua Ave., Honolulu; 808-973-0311. Instruction following American Sailing Association standards. Also sunset sails with food and drink; scuba and snorkeling dives.

■ FESTIVALS AND EVENTS

■ JANUARY

Sony Open in Hawai'i PGA Tournament. Nationally televised premier golf tournament in the islands. Wai'alae Country Club, Honolulu; 808-734-2151.
Windsurfing Regatta. Amateur Windsurfing Association sponsors these events once a month throughout the year. Kailua Bay; call Hawai'i Visitors Bureau, 808-923-1811.
World Bodyboarding Championships. Banzai Pipeline; 808-325-7400.

■ FEBRUARY

Narcissus Festival. Celebrates Chinese New Year; Chinatown Open House with lion dances, firecrackers, food booths, arts and crafts. Honolulu; 808-533-3181.
NFL Pro Bowl. Pro football at Aloha Stadium. Honolulu; 808-486-9555.
ORIX Hawaiian Ladies Open Golf Tournament. Ko Olina Course, Kapolei; 808-671-5050.

■ MARCH

Hawaiian Song Festival and Song Composing Contest Finals. Queen Kapi'olani Park Bandstand, Waikiki; 808-523-4182.
Honolulu Festival. Celebrates Japanese culture with crafts, drummers and dancers,

games, tea ceremony, *mochi* (sweets) pounding, kite flying, and a parade. Honolulu; 808-949-2255.

St. Patrick's Day Parade. From Ft. DeRussy to Queen Kapiʻolani Park, with a post-parade party at the Hawaiian Waikiki Beach Hotel. Waikiki; call Hawaiʻi Visitors Bureau, 808-923-1811.

■ APRIL

Honolulu International Bed Race. In addition to the wacky trundling of wheeled beds, there's an Electric Light parade, a Food Faire, a marching band, and fireworks. Kapiʻolani Park Bandstand, Waikiki; call Hawaiʻi Visitors Bureau, 808-923-1811.

Professional Championship Rodeo. Rodeo, country music, dancers. New Town & Country Stables, Waimanolo; 808-259-9941.

Scottish Festival. Celebrates the Scots of Hawaiʻi with pipe bands, dancers, clan exhibits, food, crafts. Kapiʻolani Park, Waikiki; 808-235-7605.

■ MAY

Hawaiian International Ocean Challenge. Six-person teams of the world's best lifeguards in kayak, surf rescue, swim, paddleboard, and outrigger canoe races. Makapuʻu Beach and Waikiki Beach; 808-521-4322.

Lei Day Celebration. Lei-making competitions and workshops. Crowning of lei queens. Queen Kapiʻolani Park, Waikiki; call Hawaiʻi Visitors Bureau, 808-923-1811.

■ JUNE

Annual King Kamehameha Hula Competition. International competitions in chanting, *Kahiki* (ancient) and *Auana* (modern) hula. Blaisdell Arena, Honolulu; 808-536-6540.

Biennial Transpacific Yacht Race. Odd-numbered years. San Francisco to Waikiki; Waikiki Yacht Club, 808-949-7141.

Fancy Fair. Food, entertainment, and crafts. Mission Houses Museum, Honolulu; 808-531-0481.

Hawaiian Islands State Bodybuilding Championships. Blaisdell Concert Hall, Honolulu; 808-988-7887.

King Kamehameha Celebration Floral Parade. The day after the statue decoration ceremony; women horseback riders in *Paʻu* costume, bands, cultural arts and crafts demonstrations. From King and Richards streets in downtown Honolulu to Waikiki; 808-586-0333.

King Kamehameha Celebration Statue Decoration Ceremony. Every June 11 the revered statue is draped in a 13-foot flower lei; music and hula performances; a great photo opportunity. 808-586-0333.

■ JULY

Annual Tin Man Triathlon. A 10K run, 800-meter swim, 40K bike ride. Ala Moana Beach Park, O'ahu; 808-732-7311.

Annual 'Ukulele Festival. Hundreds of 'ukulele players perform. Queen Kapi'olani Park Bandstand, Waikiki; 808-523-4523 or 808-732-3739.

Bon Odori Festivals. Bon dances held at temples all over the islands. Jodo Mission; 808-949-3995.

Prince Lot Hula Competitions. Ancient and modern hula. Moanalua Gardens, Honolulu; 808-839-5334.

Walter J. MacFarlane Canoeing Regatta. The premier canoe-paddling competition in the islands. Competing canoe clubs from around the state. Finishes at the Outrigger Canoe Club in Waikiki; 808-689-6798 or 808-923-1585.

■ AUGUST

Annual Kolekole Pass Half-Marathon and 6-Mile Walk. Run, walk, or racewalk through the Waianae Mountains on a military road usually closed to the public. The route follows ancient Hawaiian trails. 808-486-8420.

Hawaiian Professional Championship Rodeo. One of the state's biggest outdoor events. Professional cowboys and bullriders. New Town & Country Stables, Waimanalo; 808-259-9941.

Hawai'i State Windsurfing Course Racing Championships. Kailua Bay; call Hawai'i Visitors Bureau, 808-923-1811.

O'ahu Perimeter Ride. 134-mile bike ride or a West O'ahu Perimeter ride of 70 miles. Both start from Kapolei Recreation Park; 808-735-5756.

State Outrigger Canoe Racing Championships. Ke'ehi Lagoon or Kane'ohe Bay; 808-689-6798.

■ SEPTEMBER

Annual Ka Himeni 'Ana. Concert and contest of old-style Hawaiian singing. Songs are Hawaiian and pre-World War II. Orvis Auditorium, University of Hawai'i, Honolulu; 808-842-0421.

Annual Na Wahine O Ke Kai Outrigger Canoe Race. The ultimate challenge in women's outrigger paddling. Canoe clubs world wide participate in this race. From Moloka'i to O'ahu across the rough waters of Kaiwi Channel; 808-337-2323.

Annual Okinawan Festival. Labor Day weekend. Cultural dances, arts and crafts, food. Queen Kapi'olani Park, Waikiki; call the Okinawa Center, 808-676-5400.
Diamond Head Wahini Windsurfing Classic. Professional women windsurfers in slalom and wave-jumping competition. Diamond Head Beach; 808-521-4322.
Portuguese Heritage Festival. Food, entertainment, dances, cultural displays. McCoy Pavilion, Ala Moana Park; 808-845-1616.
Waikiki Rough Water Swim. Labor Day. 2.4-mile swim from Sans Souci Beach to Duke Kahanamoku Beach. 808-228-1350.

■ OCTOBER
Annual Moloka'i Hoe Outrigger Canoe Race. The men's turn at the ultimate canoe challenge. Canoe clubs worldwide participate. Across the channel from Moloka'i to O'ahu; 808-337-2323.
$1 Million Hula Bowl Hole-in-One. Ala Wai Driving Range; 808-732-6426.
Hawai'i International & World Masters Rugby Tournaments. Queen Kapi'olani Park, Waikiki; 808-922-7825.
Talking Island Festival. Storytelling on four stages, followed by three-week tour to other islands with performances in hotels; oral histories, Pacific tales. McCoy Pavilion, Ala Moana Park; 808-523-4182.

■ NOVEMBER
Festival of Trees. Display of one-of-a-kind decorated trees, wreaths, and gifts. Amfac Plaza, Honolulu; 808-547-4397.
Hawai'i International Film Festival. Cross-cultural films by filmmakers from Asia, the Pacific, and U.S. Free, but tickets required. Honolulu; 808-528-3456.
King Kalakaua Regatta. Outrigger canoe sailing and racing, surf-ski, and paddle board competition. Finishes in Honolulu Harbor. 808-337-2323.

■ DECEMBER
Aloha Bowl. College Football played on Christmas Day; televised. Aloha Stadium, Honolulu; 808-486-9555.
Honolulu Marathon. The biggest run of the year; thousands of international participants. Enter by mid-August. 808-737-4340.
Makaha Pro-Am & Open Golf Tournament. Aloha Section PGA.. Sheraton Makaha; 808-695-9544.

K A U A ' I
G A R D E N   I S L A N D

From the unpeopled heartland of Kaua'i, plunging waterfalls, lacy streams, and canyons slash down in every direction, creating habitats for plants and birds that exist nowhere else. Wai'ale'ale, its central misty peak, is the wettest spot in the world, and Kaua'i's seven rivers are luxuriantly lined with tropical growth in more shades of green than you can name. Chartreuse leaves lined with magenta veins adorn plants growing in wild abundance. In contrast, from Kaua'i's largely impenetrable center a rift cuts toward the southwest, creating a deep and arid chasm that rivals the splendor of the Grand Canyon.

Kaua'i is the oldest, most northerly of the main Hawaiian Islands. Its forests are perfumed with the licorice-scented *mokihana* berry found only on the wild terrain of this island. The spindly *mokihana* tree grows to about 20 feet and bears small greenish flowers. Its pastel-green, leathery, and cube-shaped berries are strung to make a lei associated with the king and acclaimed in Kaua'i island chants. Because the intoxicating scent is long-lasting, ancient Hawaiians once dried *mokihana* and placed them among their ceremonial *kapa* garments.

Visitors flying toward Kaua'i catch sight of a green glimmer on the sea, then the central peak of the roughly circular island seems to rise like a coned hat from the water. Below, the island's fields and beaches form a luxuriant flat brim, encircling all but the untamed northwest Na Pali Coast. Fringing the brim are 50 miles of white-sand beaches studded with coco palms falling away toward limpid seas. These soft, white, sandy strands of Kaua'i are the "tropics" of Hollywood movies. Here the director of *South Pacific* found Bali Ha'i, Elvis Presley warbled in *Blue Hawaii,* and Indiana Jones fled for the beach from headhunters in *Raiders of the Lost Ark.* Dinosaurs roamed Kaua'i in both *Jurassic Park* movies.

If you take a helicopter tour of any island, do it here, though be prepared for a strange reaction known as Gasp Syndrome. Even highly experienced travelers speak in superlatives of Kaua'i. The intrepid British traveler Isabella Bird wrote in 1873 that "Kaua'i, though altogether different from Hawai'i, has an extreme beauty altogether its own, which wins one's love."

A family prepares for snorkeling at Ha'ena Beach.

Modern Kaua'i was built on a sugar-based economy. In a world market burdened with falling prices, sugar plantation agriculture, born on Kaua'i and a thriving industry for more than 150 years, is disappearing. This distresses the people of Kaua'i. Sugar has provided a treasured lifestyle, where rural simplicity and stability foster strong family values. Kaua'i tries to maintain that way of life with alternative crops, including seed corn, coffee, and papaya, but tourism is outpacing diversified agriculture. Hotels sprout on the island's eastern shores, from Poipu in the sunny, dry south to Princeville and Hanalei in the north, where dark green beds of taro flourish in the stream-fed valley.

As the economic base of the island shifts to tourism, residents struggle to reconcile Kaua'i's beauty with development. Agritourism, with guests at work on small farms, is becoming popular and could help to sustain the island's agricultural base. Open horizons are preserved by a county law stating that no hotel on Kaua'i can be taller than a coconut tree.

A visit to Kaua'i is like a return to yesterday in Hawai'i. Untouched by large development, the southern town of Lihu'e is Kaua'i's county seat. Fanning out from town, green-gold agricultural fields creep up volcanic ridges separated by valleys slanting into the island's center. Valleys and ridges radiate from the forest reserve's center like slices of green fruit.

■ HISTORY

The first Polynesians arrived on Kaua'i between A.D. 500 and 700. Probably from the Marquesas, they were subdued by later arrivals who came from Tahiti in A.D. 1000. One theory has it that the Tahitian word *manahune,* or "outcast," gave rise to the legends of the *menehune*—Hawai'i's "little people," or elves. Kaua'i, usually considered the home of the *menehune,* is filled with tales of them and their engineering feats in stone. They are credited with building the mysterious irrigation ditches, fish ponds, and temples found on the island.

Menehune worked only at night, always completing a project requiring great strength by dawn—or leaving it eternally undone. They were believed to be jolly, noisy little fellows with big eyes and red faces, who stood about three feet tall. Long ago they supposedly numbered in the thousands, and legend has it that their king, Ola, was worried about *menehune* marrying into the newly arrived Tahitians, an alien race. He ordered his people to go from Kaua'i, decreeing that if a *menehune* was seen on the island, he would be turned to stone. The *menehune* left no

Hokule'a *is a re-creation of a double-hulled canoe such as those sailed by the first Tahitian colonists to Hawai'i. In 1976, it made a round-trip voyage to Tahiti covering 6,000 miles.*

hint of their destination, and the builders of the island's gigantic structures even now are a mystery to archaeologists.

Some islanders believe the *menehune* returned to their legendary home on the fabled lost continent of Mu, now beneath the seas of Polynesia, and that Kaua'i is its crown. Others will tell you that not all the *menehune* left—and that some still lurk in remote valleys, hiding so they won't be seen and turned to stone.

When Captain Cook arrived on Kaua'i in 1778, he found people fishing from canoes on the reefs and farming on the coastal plains and in the valleys of the Na Pali coast. In wintertime, when pounding surf kept canoes ashore, Na Pali villagers hacked trails across the island's jungled center, using coconut-fiber ladders to pass over the steepest ridges.

In 1815 Anton Schaeffer, an ambitious German, showed up on the shores of Kaua'i. Posing as a medical doctor and agent of the Russian-American Trading Company of Alaska, he had in fact been sent to retrieve the cargo of a wrecked Russian ship. An insatiable opportunist, Schaeffer came up with a scheme to take

EARLY KAUA'I

British writer Isabella Bird, an intrepid world traveler, visited Kaua'i in 1873. The following is an excerpt from a letter written to her sister Henrietta back home in Edinburgh.

We took three days for our journey of twenty-three miles from Koloa, the we, consisting of Mrs. ____, the widow of an early missionary teacher, venerable in years and character, a native boy of ten years old, her squire, a second Kaluna, without Kaluna's good qualities, and myself. Mrs. ____ is not a bold horsewoman, and preferred to keep to a foot's pace, which fretted my ambitious animal, whose innocent antics alarmed her in turn. We only rode seven miles the first day, through a park-like region, very like Western Wisconsin, and just like what I expected and failed to find in New Zealand. Grassland much tumbled about, the turf very fine and green, dotted over with clumps and single trees, with picturesque, rocky hills, deeply cleft by water-courses were on our right, and on our left the green slopes blended with the flushed, stony soil near the sea, on which indigo and various compositæ are the chief vegetation. It was hot, but among the hills on our right, cool clouds were coming down in frequent showers, and the white foam of cascades gleamed among the ohias,

In the days of Isabella Bird's visit, it was common to find Hawaiians pounding taro to make poi, *the staple food of Hawai'i.*

whose dark foliage at a distance has almost the look of pine woods.

Our first halting place was one of the prettiest places I ever saw, a buff frame-house, with a deep verandah festooned with passion flowers, two or three guest houses, also bright with trailers, scattered about under the trees near it, a pretty garden, a background of grey, rocky hills cool with woods and ravines, and over all the vicinity, that air of exquisite trimness which is artificially produced in England, but is natural here.

Kaluna the Second soon showed symptoms of being troublesome. The native servants were away, and he was dull, and for that I pitied him. He asked leave to go back to Koloa for a "sleeping tapa," which was refused, and either out of spite or carelessness, instead of fastening the horses into the pasture, he let them go, and the following morning when we were ready for our journey they were lost. Then he borrowed a horse, and late in the afternoon returned with the four animals, all white with foam and dust, and this escapade detained us for another night. Subsequently, after disobeying orders, he lost his horse, which was a borrowed one, deserted his mistress, and absconded!

The slopes over which we travelled were red, hot, and stony, cleft in one place however, by a green, fertile valley, full of rice and kalo patches, and native houses, with a broad river, the Hanapépé, flowing quietly down the middle, which we forded near the sea, where it was half-way up my horse's sides. After plodding all day over stony soil in the changeless sunshine, as the shadows lengthened, we turned directly up towards the mountains and began a two hours' ascent. It was delicious. They were so cool, so green, so varied, their grey pinnacles so splintered, their precipices so abrupt, their ravines so dark and deep, and the lower slopes covered with the greenest and finest grass; then dark ohias rose singly, then in twos and threes, and finally mixed in dense forest masses, with the pea-green of the kukui.

It became yet lovelier as the track wound through deep wooded ravines, or snaked along the narrow tops of spine-like ridges; the air became cooler, damper, and more like elixir, till at a height of 1500 feet we came upon Makaueli, ideally situated upon an unequalled natural plateau, a house of patriarchial size for the islands, with a verandah festooned with roses, fuchsias, the water lemon, and other passion flowers, and with a large guest-house attached. It stands on a natural lawn, with abrupt slopes, sprinkled with orange trees burdened with fruit, ohias, and hibiscus. From the back verandah the forest-covered mountains rise, and in front a deep ravine widens to the grassy slopes below and the lonely Pacific,—as I write, a golden sea, on which the island of Niihau, eighteen miles distant, floats like an amethyst.

—Isabella Bird, *Six Months in the Sandwich Islands,* 1890

advantage of the young king of Kaua'i, Kaumuali'i, and at the same time claim Kaua'i for the czar of Russia. Schaeffer promised Kaumuali'i that the Russians would fight on his side against the increasingly predatory King Kamehameha of the Big Island, if, in return, he'd allow Schaeffer to build a fort at Waimea.

Hoping to keep Kamehameha out of Kaua'i, Kaumuali'i agreed, and Schaeffer built his fort. After mounting it with 38 cannons, he named it Elizabeth after the czarina and flew the flag of Russia over the bay where American whalers and sandalwood trading vessels lay at anchor.

The alarming news of the menacing fort was brought to O'ahu and then to Kamehameha on the Big Island by American traders. In 1816 an expedition ship of imperial Russia called at Honolulu, and its commander, Lieutenant Otto von Kotzubue, told everyone who would listen that the "Russian" Schaeffer was an imposter. Von Kotzubue sailed on to Kailua-Kona and repeated this to Kamehameha. Agitated by reports from the Americans that Schaeffer and the young king might be preparing to invade O'ahu, Kamehameha sent a message to Kaumuali'i on Kaua'i that Schaeffer must be ousted, or the Americans would drive

Villagers enjoy a luau outside a grass house around 1890.

him out. By that time Schaeffer's imperious manner had alienated Kaumualiʻi, who took Kamehameha's message seriously. In May 1817 the young king of Kauaʻi stripped Schaeffer of the lands he had given him, and an irate mob drove the imposter from the island.

In his onslaught to unite the islands years earlier, Kamehameha had attempted to invade Kauaʻi and was thwarted by ferocious channel storms that took a heavy toll on his war canoes. In the end, Kamehameha utilized his formidable political acumen to entice Kaumualiʻi to yield his dominion, while allowing him to retain control of Kauaʻi as its governor. Although the people of Kauaʻi take pride in the fact that they were never defeated in war, it was Kamehameha who realized he could achieve his end without bloodshed—and his diplomatic acuity was equal to the task.

After Kamehameha's death in 1819 he was succeeded by his son Liholiho, who became Kamehameha II. Distrusting Kaumualiʻi, the new king tricked him into taking a cruise on a luxury ship Liholiho had acquired in exchange for sandalwood. The kidnapped Kaumualiʻi was taken to Oʻahu and forced to marry Kaʻahumanu, the great warrior's widow and favorite wife. Through the grand design of royal plotting, Kauaʻi was secured. Kaumualiʻi died on Oʻahu in 1824.

By the mid-nineteenth century, life on Kauaʻi was dominated by the sugar industry. It all began in 1833 when three New Englanders with missionary ties, William Ladd, Peter Allan Brinsmade, and William Hooper, arrived in Honolulu to establish a trading house. They formed Ladd & Company and leased 980 acres at Koloa on Kauaʻi from Kamehameha III at an annual rent of $300.

Local chiefs didn't like what was happening, and placed *kapu* on Hooper's effort to plant sugar. Although he was "well nigh starved into a retreat," in 1835 the stubborn Hooper laid out 12 acres. This planting marked the beginning of the sugar industry in the Hawaiian Islands.

A year later the Ladd & Company plantation was grinding cane for molasses. The company's third mill, built in 1837 on property later known as Koloa Plantation, set the pattern of plantation-style agriculture in the islands, with channel irrigation, mills, churches, schools, and stores. Workers, most of whom were imported, received medical care, housing, a ration of fish and *poi,* and meager wages. Sweet cane became the king of Kauaʻi.

Koloa was placed on the National Register of Historic Places in 1962. It is of major significance, because sugar played the dominant role in Hawaiian economics and politics, and it probably was the key factor in America's annexation of the Hawaiian Islands.

■ SOUTH KAUA'I

A land of sunshine and infrequent coastal rain, southern Kaua'i is contoured by miles of wide, white beaches. Following the coast from the capital of Lihu'e, on the island's east shore, HI 50 (Kaumuali'i Highway) travels in a southwesterly direction. At the gap in the Hoary Head Range, HI 520 veers straight south through Koloa sugar lands to the sunlit beaches and hotels of Poipu. Between Lihu'e and the beaches, visitors can see an old-fashioned sugar plantation, the old sugar mill that marks the birth of the cane industry in the Hawaiian Islands, a fish pond said to be the work of *menehune,* and tropical gardens. If you just zip through, it's easy to backtrack; Poipu is about 30 minutes from the airport.

HI 50 continues across the bottom of the island, ending in the dry southwest at Mana. About halfway between Poipu and the end of HI 50, HI 550 branches up to the mountain parks—Waimea Canyon slashing through an ancient dry rift zone and, higher up, the rain-watered lands of Koke'e State Park.

■ LIHU'E AND VICINITY *map page 285, E-3/4*
In the mid-nineteenth century, thousands of acres of sugar cane were planted in southern Kaua'i. To serve this agricultural area, two transplanted Americans, Boston businessman Henry Pierce and banker Charles Reed Bishop, founded the town of Lihu'e near a natural slash in the eastern coastline at Nawiliwili Bay, where the island begins its southern curve.

Japanese and Filipino immigrant laborers came to work in the fields around Lihu'e, and by 1860 rural villages dotted the area, each dominated by a sugar mill and doused in the scent of molasses. Lihu'e became the center of activity and county seat for Kaua'i and neighboring Ni'ihau.

■ LIHU'E HISTORY TOUR

Kaua'i Museum
This museum is a gem for history buffs. Small and accessible, its collection of Hawaiian artifacts is considerable and includes featherwork pieces, a hand-carved canoe, stone tools, rare native bowls, and a missionary four-poster *koa*-wood bed with Hawaiian quilts. An exhibit called "The Story of Kaua'i" describes the history, geography, and cultural heritage of the island in skillfully conceived displays, including a contour map and diagram of Waimea village as it was in 1778 when

HAWAIIAN QUILTS

When the missionary ladies of New England introduced quilting to the Sandwich Islands more than 170 years ago, a new avenue was opened for Hawaiian creativity.

Hawaiian designs always represent a single emotion—wisdom or love—or a quilt may tell a story. Perhaps the imagery was disclosed in a reverie and celebrates the birth of a child, or it may be a visualization of fish in a bright coral reef, a sun-dappled valley, or even a faithless lover. Hawaiians take their inspiration from the flowers, trees, and fruits of the islands, and from the mysteries of dreams. Contemporary designs tend to flow in bolder, larger patterns with more colors than earlier quilts.

The traditional Hawaiian quilt is made from a single piece of fabric, with two contrasting colors. Patterns are cut from fabric folded into eighths, in the manner of snowflake patches taught by the missionaries, and the stitching is done in the echo or contour style, which suggests an undulating wave as it radiates out to the borders. The rows of Hawaiian stitches are six-eights of an inch apart; mainland American quilting rows are wider—from one to two inches apart.

In the heady days of monarchy, quilts celebrated objects—such as King Kalakaua's crystal—and recorded great events in Hawaiian history. During the 1890s, an anguished time for Hawaiians with the monarchy overthrown and the beloved

Queen Lili'uokalani imprisoned, flag quilts were made in secret and kept disguised. Hawaiians made them as a form of personal allegiance. Turn over a striking flower-design quilt and the flag is revealed. Queen Lili'uokalani stitched a quilt during her imprisonment. A record of her life, it has reappeared after a century of hiding; you can see it now in the very room of 'Iolani Palace where it was stitched. The warmth of *aloha* comes through the quilter's hands, and a Hawaiian quilt is a treasured gift, one passed through generations carrying its *aloha,* the gift of sharing.

A quiltmaker demonstrates his art at the Bishop Museum.

Captain Cook landed his launch here. *Mid-town, across from the government buildings on Rice Street; 808-245-6931.*

Menehune (Alekoko) Fish Pond

At the south end of Lihu'e, drowsy Nawiliwili Stream flows into a bulge where it meets Nawiliwili Bay Harbor. A stone wall more than 900 feet long forms an ancient fishpond, still in use for raising mullet. It predates the arrival of Tahitians, and its origin is unknown. Tradition has it that the wall, now tree-covered, was built in a single night by *menehune.*

Nawiliwili Bay Harbor

Farther up Hulemalu Road, an overlook provides a fine view of the harbor. On December 30, 1941, in a little-known incident, a Japanese submarine surfaced in the bay under a full moon and shelled the shoreline. No one knows why their fire was not returned. Some say the U.S. soldiers stationed at the harbor were manning a new gun and hadn't received their ammo yet; others say the concrete gun base hadn't hardened.

Grove Farm Homestead

Here is an interesting stop for those interested in the sugar industry and its relationship to Hawaiian politics from the monarchy into territorial days. Now a museum, this spacious two-story home is set on a broad lawn edged in gardens. Once the headquarters of an 80-acre complex that flourished from the 1860s into the 1930s, it is Hawai'i's finest example of a plantation period home. Inside are salons once used for entertaining or quilting, two libraries, a music room, upstairs bedrooms, a morning room, a formal dining room, and extensive kitchens.

Quilting was a tradition at the Homestead. The book *The Wilcox Quilts In Hawaii* is a record of generations of family quilting, with pictures of antique quilts and stories about the quilts and their makers and collectors. Also in the book is a recipe for concocting *ko'ele pala'u*—a sweet-potato wine everyone guzzled for a week in celebration of a completed *pu'iki,* or quilt.

When George Norton Wilcox founded the plantation, oxen hauled the cane from field to mill, and the molasses to Nawiliwili Harbor. Later steam-powered sugar trains did the same work, running on narrow-gauge rails. As late as 1957, four locomotives plied Grove Farm fields. *Off Nawiliwili Road; 808-245-3202.*

(following spread) The cove at Poipu Beach Park is one of the safest swimming beaches on Kaua'i.

■ **OLD KOLOA SUGAR MILL** *map page 285, D-4*
About five miles south of Lihu'e, the main road forks at Knudsen Gap in the Ha'upu Range. If you turn *makai* onto HI 520, you'll find arching branches of eucalyptus trees forming an unbroken mile of leafy tunnel on the way to the old sugar town of **Koloa.** At the junction of Maluhia and Koloa roads stands a weathered chimney, a relic from the Old Koloa Sugar Mill, the last mill of Ladd & Company, the first successful sugar plantation in Hawai'i. Built in 1841, the massive square stone foundations of the plantation's third mill lie in ruins at the edge of a cane field bordering Waihohonu Stream. Although the mill has long stopped grinding sugar, the land still sprouts cane.

Close to the ruins is a sculpture honoring ethnic groups who worked on the plantation—Hawaiian, Japanese, Chinese, Korean, Filipino, Portuguese, and Puerto Rican. At one time there was one more figure in the grouping—a Caucasian on horseback representing the foreman. He has disappeared. A number of plaques are placed in the area, with facts about the history of sugar on Kaua'i.

■ **GARDENS OF LAWAI** *map page 285, C/D-4*
Off HI 50, near Lawa'i, Hailima Road leads to two famed gardens that may be seen on a combined walking tour. The well-planned displays are part of the **National Tropical Botanical Gardens,** which include a third garden called Limahuli on the north coast of Kaua'i. The three facilities are devoted to science, nurseries, and education.

Begun by Queen Emma in the 1860s, the gardens near Lawa'i were enlarged by sugar baron Alexander McBryde and perfected by the hand of Robert Allerton, an American businessman who bought the estate in 1938. Allerton and his son John Gregg added new specimens and European statuary.

One of these gardens is Lawa'i Kai, popularly known as the Allerton Gardens and famed for its artful landscaping following Lawa'i Valley. Its manicured trail passes a purple cascade of bougainvillea, a Japanese teahouse, gazebos, and an Italian garden. Anthurium, ficus, tall shower trees of pink or bright yellow, plumeria, and colored gingers gather around waterfalls; night-blooming cereus and cactus turn toward the sun.

Visitors to the Lawa'i gardens must make reservations well in advance; only some nine people at a time are taken through the research gardens and down Lawa'i Kai. Guided tours begin at Spouting Horn, where guests are picked up by a restored 1951 DeSoto woodie. *808-742-2623.*

Reservations are essential at the National Tropical Botanical Gardens.

In 17-acre **Limahuli,** visitors walk amid cultivated taro planted in ancient stone terraces on the north shore of the island, opposite Keʻe Lagoon. *808-826-1053.*

■ **Poipu Beaches** *map page 285, D-4*
Past Koloa town, where old plantation buildings have been transformed into crafts galleries, boutiques, and cafés, the Poipu Road continues three miles to Poipu (Crashing Waves), on the southernmost tip of the island. Here along the southern shore, separated from the wet mountains by lowlands, the climate is dry, though it can cloud over in the afternoon.

As sugar wanes, tourism waxes. Poipu—once a sleepy beach where the Kimball family (of Waikiki's Halekulani Hotel) kept a 50-room leafy hideaway named Waiʻohai—has emerged as the center of tourism on the island. When the Hyatt Regency Kauaʻi announced it would build at Poipu, those who care about preserving Kauaʻi's beauty were understandably nervous. They heaved a sigh of relief when the hotel opened in 1990. With its *koa* wood and lava rock gardens, its cool and restful ambience feels decidedly Hawaiian and is reminiscent of Waiʻohai.

At Poipu, visitors and residents play on three beaches. Between two rocky points a 500-yard-long strip of soft white sand lies before a small bay flashing with the colored sails of windsurfers. Because the waves are predictably steady and for most of the year not too formidable, intermediate and beginning body- and board-surfers migrate here for smooth blue-water rides.

The small adjacent beach, **Wai'ohai,** is the realm of snorkelers. Underwater, golden butterflyfish dart in the reef. The Achilles tang fish (with a big orange spot near the tail glowing like neon on its black body) and shimmering-gold, white-banded surgeonfish peck at the coral for tiny bits of food. Sheltered on each side, the adjoining **Poipu Beach Park** has facilities and a lifeguard tower, and is one of the safest swimming beaches on the island. Because it's a fine place to take children, residents call it Mama's Beach. At the west end the shoreline forms a *tombolo*—a sand bar that connects an island with the mainland or with another island. This *tombolo* joins the park shore with an offshore islet, creating a point of velvety beach called **Nukumo'i.**

West of the hotels and beaches is Poipu's **Spouting Horn.** One of Hawaii's many blowholes, Spouting Horn lava tube builds geysers of ocean spray reaching up 50 feet. Breaking surf rushes into a narrow chimney of lava, forcing a column of whitewater spray and compressed air to leap like a briny fountain from its hole in a noisy blast. If you go late in the afternoon, the spray is colored in rainbows of the setting sun.

Legend says the howl caused by shooting water and air comes from a sorrowful and enraged *mo'o*, or lizard. The *mo'o* swam from Ni'ihau to Kaua'i, sobbing over the loss of two sisters. Unable to see through his tears, he overshot his landing and was carried into the blowhole, to be trapped forever. We hear him moan when the horn spouts.

■ **ROAD TO WAIMEA** *map page 285, B/C-3/4*

Continuing west along the coast, HI 50 passes through small rural towns where wet taro beds flourish and avocado trees shade farmsteads. Chickens scrabble and dogs laze in the sun. **Hanapepe** town, aflower in bouganvillea, is home to the popular Friday Art Night. From 6 to 9 P.M. galleries are open and gourmet appetizers are served in this creative hub of Kaua'i's artistic community.

Where the south coastline curves inward, lies **Waimea.** The name, meaning "red water," refers to waters flowing down over the red earth of the Koke'e Plateau, rising behind the coast.

Captain Cook Monument

The ambience of dusty, sleepy Waimea town does little justice to its history. At a small, palm-fringed park in the middle of downtown stands a lava monument to Captain Cook, who made his first landing in Hawai'i here in 1778. In bronze bas-relief the two ships of Cook's expedition are depicted entering Waimea Bay, as Hawaiians, in profile, turn toward them. Waimea wakes up once a year on the last weekend in February for a Captain Cook carnival with games, rides, and gallons of beer.

Fort Elizabeth

At the mouth of the Waimea River, the stone walls of Fort Elizabeth (named for the czarina of Russia) stand in mute testimony to the attempt by the imposter Anton Schaeffer to take Kaua'i for the Russian crown—which had not authorized any such action. The fort's 10-foot stone walls now blossom with fragile yellow 'ilima flowers. A short footpath leads from the highway parking lot to the site, where you can pick up a self-guided trail map from a box. Markers on the platform tell what used to be there. The fort was acquired by the state in 1969, and 10 years later was designated a National Historic Landmark.

Menehune Ditch

Menehune Ditch Road turns *mauka* from the mouth of the Waimea River up into the valley about a mile to the Swinging Bridge, a footbridge that gives access to the east bank. Near the west side lies Menehune Ditch (Kiki a Ola), a narrow irrigation ditch sliding into a tunnel cut into the base of a bluff. An ancient row of rectangular stones, cut to fit tightly, edges the ditch and is still in use to divert water into taro patches. How this ditch, wall, and tunnel were devised in an engineering style not practiced by Hawaiians confounds archaeologists. Surely the elves of Kaua'i, the industrious, nocturnal *menehune* were here.

■ WAIMEA CANYON *map page 285, B-2/3*

Twenty minutes up into the mountains behind Waimea town an astonishing panorama opens—the Grand Canyon of the Pacific, a spectacular sight even on an island rife with scenic views. On the brink of a great gorge 3,400 feet deep, you may find colors streaming toward you. As though a giant were pouring rainbows in an ever-changing kaleidoscope, clouds billow by and are reflected in orange, red, and purple, the dry hues of the desert. Changing patterns crawl over canyon walls.

Tropical greens and yellows sprinkle the chasm floor below, where a sun-lit thread of water seems too insignificant to have carved such a spectacle. We are reminded that there are times when the placid Waimea River, gorged by waterfalls pouring down from the mountains, transforms into a raging flood carrying off rocks and trees and endlessly altering and sculpting the contours of the canyon.

From the lookout, etched by wind and water, fluted lava strata expose geologic time. Cutting into the heartland of Kaua'i, measuring one mile across and 10 miles long, Waimea Canyon is one of nature's tributes to cloud and shadow, sunlight and water.

From town, Waimea Canyon Drive sweeps up in a winding well-angled road that merges with another from Kekaha. Both are numbered HI 550.

■ KOKE'E STATE PARK   *map page 285, B-2*
Continuing up the Waimea-Koke'e ridge, the road (now called Koke'e) ends in the mountain refuge of Koke'e State Park, 4,345 acres of rain forest. Here, just 40 miles from warm Lihu'e, the air is brisk and sometimes cold. On a tree-fringed open meadow, birds and jungle fowl chatter. If you are lucky, you might see the bright red *i'iwi* bird with its hooked salmon-colored bill.

Here you find a small natural history museum, a basic restaurant, and state-operated rustic cabins and camping facilities. From the Koke'e park center, at 3,600 feet, 45 miles of strenuous hiking trails lead eastward into the wetlands of the **Alaka'i Wilderness Preserve.** These 10 square miles of rainy, chilly swamp-forest extend toward mist-covered Mount Wai'ale'ale. In the depths of the swamp may live the last Kaua'i *'o'o* birds.

Of Alaka'i Swamp, Eric Knudsen, scion of a Kaua'i family, wrote in 1940:

> Alakai means to lead—and if ever you need a guide it is there. The land undulates like the waves of the sea, little lines of stunted lehua trees run hither and thither, long open glades lie between and all are dotted with water holes of all shapes and sizes. Some are supposed to be deep enough to drown a person, and if you fall in and try to climb out the turf breaks like rotten ice and you cannot pull yourself out. All is wet, the turf you walk on is soggy. . . . To step on a seemingly solid piece of earth and sink to your knees instead is a bit

Lucky hikers may see the bright red i'iwi *bird at Koke'e State Park.*

disconcerting. . . . When the fog swirls in and all turns grey it is impossible to tell the points of the compass and every hillock and swale looks exactly alike and it is impossible to see the person ahead and when rain comes as it so often does it is very cold. Many a man has lost his way. . . .

■ **KALALAU LOOKOUT** *map page 285, B-1/2*
Past Koke'e meadow, the road climbs to Kalalau Lookout. From here at its head, the lush green valley plunges to the distant north shore seas of the rugged Na Pali Coast. Towering 4,000-foot cliffs cradle the valley as it slips onto a perfect beach. Birds flutter beneath you. Clouds form and disperse. It is this isolated Eden, nearly inaccessible and bursting with wild fruit, that Jack London chose for his tragic story of the fugitive "Koolau the Leper," who hid here to avoid being shipped off to the Moloka'i leper colony.

The best way to see the canyon, Koke'e, and the lookout is to start at the top. Go straight to the lookout in the morning, before clouds build up in Kalalau.

With annual rainfall averaging 460 inches, Mount Wai'ale'ale is the wettest spot on earth.

Then picnic at Koke'e (or buy a snack) and come down to the canyon overlook. Toward the end of the day, descend from the canyon down the switchbacks and stop often for stunning panoramas of the canyon in ever-changing light, each stratum a different color—from black to tan to red, and finally, to white.

■ MOUNT WAI'ALE'ALE *map page 285, D-2*

Hidden in rain clouds, the central mountain of Wai'ale'ale (Overflowing Water) seldom shows its crown. Rigorous and remote, its soggy hiking trails wind through the Alaka'i wetlands, the world's only highland swamp. On the slopes of this boggy, sunless land, trees grow no higher than your kneecap. A stretch of boardwalk over the boggy terrain makes possible a close look at the rare flora.

Up an oozing trail high on a squashy ridgeline stands a rain gauge. Annual rainfall measurements vary from 426 to 624 inches—more than 50 feet—making this the wettest spot on earth (although Cherrapunji in India's eastern Meghalaya state makes the same claim).

■ WEST KAUA'I

Western Kaua'i curves in a shore of continuous wide, white sands bathed in hot sun. Facing open sea and with no protecting reef, the shore is thrashed by incoming rollers in wintertime, when swimming becomes perilous.

Where the south-shore highway ends at Mana (pronounced ma-*NA*), a secondary road leads northward to the almost desert sands of Polihale. One of the longest, widest beaches in the islands, the **Mana (Arid) shore** runs for 15 miles—from Kekaha in the south to its abrupt end in the northwest at the massive bulk of the Na Pali cliffs.

The **Pacific Missile Range** (PMR) facility stretches around Mana's Nohili Point and reaches across Barking Sands Beach. This civilian-operated U.S. naval facility is crammed with electronics—under the sea, ashore, and up at Koke'e. Its radar can pinpoint the range and bearing of vessels within 1,000 square miles of ocean. From its high-frequency radio station operated by the U.S. Department of Commerce, time signals are received by trans-Pacific ships and aircraft. PMR maintains a close relationship with the community.

At Major's Bay, within the boundaries of the PMR, sand dunes 60 feet tall back the beach at **Barking Sands.** The sands bark—or woof or sing or hoot. Stirring up the sands by rapidly sliding down a dune is said to produce a doglike yelp, or a hoot like an owl's. Old chants speak of "sounding sands," *keone kani*. Even if the sands won't bark for you, you'll find the beach majestic.

At the north end of the Mana shore (the southern extremity of the Na Pali Coast) more than two miles of beach merge into **Polihale State Park.** Where HI 50 ends near the PMR, follow signs five miles west to the beach on well-maintained cane-haul (dirt) roads. Beyond the north end of the beach stands **Polihale He'iau,** a powerful place dedicated to departing spirits.

Polihale Beach is hot and dry, with brilliant white sand—a sunbather's dream of heaven, sprawling over 140 acres. This is a wilderness beach without a lifeguard, although basic facilities are available. If you like tent camping beneath a star-spangled sky with the only sounds those of the falling surf, Polihale is the place to be. (You'll need a state permit.) When you're ready to swim, try Queen's Pond. It's protected by a small reef, about mid-way along the beach, and is popular for swimming and all kinds of surfing. Follow the main park road south to an access road leading up to the dunes above the pond. Watch for deep sand.

■ NA PALI COAST   *map page 285, B/C-1*

Remote, nearly inaccessible, soaring volcanic cliffs and emerald valleys form the coastline of the **Na Pali Coast State Park.** Stretching from Polihale Beach at the south end to Ha'ena Beach at the north, the Na Pali Coast spills into the sea—sheer cliffs slashed by beach-fronted valleys, one after the other, each isolated from the next by a cascade of mountainous lava, each valley lush and fertile with a stream, each razor-sharp barrier blanketed in green. Seen from a helicopter or boat, the raw power of nature, building cathedral-like spires and domes of sharp or rounded lava, fills you with awe.

In summer months a boat can deposit you with a picnic lunch on a valley beach for the entire day. Next to Kalalau—the valley seen from the lookout above Koke'e—lies **Honopu,** which is inaccessible by land. Here, behind wide searing sands, sheer cliffs rise in a solid semicircle. At one side waves have carved a lava archway on the beach. Through it drops a waterfall trickling off into the sea. A perfect place. (Hollywood chose the Valley of Honopu to film for the home of *King Kong.*) Beyond the arch lies a double beach, where the water is whitecapped, brilliant royal blue, and deep.

The raw power of nature inspires awe along the Na Pali Coast.

From the Ha'ena side on the island's north shore, an 11-mile trail snakes into **Kalalau** and down to its beach. The trail takes you past mystical Hanakapi'ai Falls, it's green-cast waters dropping 200 feet over sheer volcanic walls into a pool perfect for chilly swimming. If you go, carry water and plan on a full day trek to go there and back. In ancient times Hawaiians lived in the isolated valleys, leaving a record in temples, burial grounds, and legend. Kalalau was a major community and important in the cultivation of taro. As the new sugar towns developed, many Hawaiians were lured away from Kalalau, and by 1919 the last inhabitants had left. The following year cowboys and cattle were brought in by barge, and grazing continued in Kalalau until the early 1970s, when the state acquired the valley.

Attracted by its remote beauty and mysterious structures (said to be the work of *menehune*), many hippies moved into Kalalau in the late 1960s, and the ecology was seriously disturbed. In 1980 the state stepped in to erect facilities and regulate camping, which is now allowed only at the shoreline and by permit. The intruders are gone, and the tropical growth renewed. Today the valley beckons trekkers in search of the perfect wilderness.

Though placid in the summer months, during the winter season the seas off Na Pali crash ashore in thunderous waves that pound the beaches of each valley and push off the cliffs in powerful back-waves that collide in riptorn currents, dispersing the sandy beaches, only to bring them back in the spring.

■ East Kaua'i

From Lihu'e, beaches and rural towns follow the contour of the island up its east flank. HI 56 runs through cane lands, past hotels that dot beaches of the Wailua area to the north shore. Here is the action on the island; from Lihu'e to Kapa'a you'll encounter boutiques, restaurants, and perhaps an orchid show or a farm fair.

■ Wailua River *map page 285, D/E-3*

Wailua Falls

Just north of Lihu'e, a single-lane paved road leaves the highway and curves up through four miles of sugar fields to Wailua Falls, on the 12-mile-long Wailua River, Hawai'i's only navigable waterway. Dropping 80 feet, the falls are usually seen as two. When waters draining from the island's central core are heavy, Wailua (Two Waters) merges into a solid line of wide falling water. Fish, tossed in the air by its force, often take flying plunges into the cold pool below.

Poliahu He'iau

On a bluff above the river lies the *he'iau* named for the snow goddess Poliahu, a sister of Pele. Ruling chiefs prayed at this large temple that closely resembles a Tahitian *marae* (temple). Once a site where human sacrifice was offered, the area now overlooks a scene of pastoral calm, as cattle graze the riverbanks.

Bell Stone

Directly south of Poliahu a dirt road leads to the Bell Stone, once a means of transmitting news. When struck, the stone sent a ringing peal out over wide distances to announce the birth of a royal child. Some scholars believe the stone might have served as an alarm should an attacking force enter the river. There are two stones; no one is quite sure which was the Bell Stone. You can try ringing one yourself.

Fern Grotto

At the marina near the river mouth at Wailua Bay, visitors board launches that wind up the Wailua River, past dense tropical greenery to the Fern Grotto. From the lava ceiling, tropical ferns hang in canopylike green stalactites. In the natural amphitheater, expect a serenade—or a wedding; it's a favored place to say "I do." If you'd rather skip the touristy trip, the river is open to kayaking and waterskiing. The grotto itself is accessible only by boat.

Wailua Beach

At the mouth of the river, waves breaking on a sand bar at Wailua Beach attract body- and board-surfers. The 100-foot-wide beach is long and unshaded—good for sunbathing. It's wise to remember that caressing trade winds make you feel deceptively cool, and you can easily forget the burning power of the sun. After a heavy rain the sandbar at the river's mouth is eroded away by pouring water, revealing boulders carved with petroglyphs.

Sleeping Giant

North of Wailua Beach, HI 56 passes rural towns and beaches. Just beyond the shops of Waipouli Complex, look west to the mountain formation named the Sleeping Giant. According to legend, a huge and friendly creature slept on the ridge after a great feast. *Menehune* tried to waken him by tossing stones, so he swallowed them and turned into rock. The giant's feet are in Kapa'a, his head in Wailua.

(following spread) At the Fern Grotto, on the Wailua River, tropical ferns hang from the lava ceiling in an umbrella-like canopy of greenery.

■ HOLE IN THE MOUNTAIN *map page 285, E-1/2*

Through fields of sugarcane and just north of the 15-mile marker, another formation emerges. Hole in the Mountain pierces the ridge at the right of the tallest spire of the Anahola Mountains. The legend of this hole is nearly the same as the Tahitian tale of the island of Mo'orea, where a hole was made when a giant hurled his spear through the mountain to release water.

Continuing northward, the road passes through **Kapa'a** town, where eclectic shopping is the norm.

■ NORTH SHORE

Swathed in tropical growth, Kaua'i's north shore seems nearer to paradise than any other place in the islands. The landscape has the effect of inspiring the mind to conjure up visions of *menehune,* and gods appear to rest on misted peaks blanketed in forest green. Rain brings rainbows, and on moon-filled nights you might see a moonbow—moonbeams coloring a misted arc.

Following the island contour, HI 56 turns west along the north shore, through Hanalei and on to the end of the road at Ha'ena. Luscious beaches dapple the shoreline and no tourist development intrudes on this dreamy scene. In 1873 Isabella Bird wrote of Hanalei, "Indeed, for mere loveliness, I think that part of Kaua'i exceeds anything that I have seen."

■ KILAUEA POINT *map page 285, E-1*

The most northerly neck of land in the eight main islands is Kilauea Point, jutting out to sea below the highway. Topped with a picturesque lighthouse, its sea-battered cliff shields a tiny cove. Down at the end of the short, pot-holed Kilauea Road, you'll hear a clamoring din. Here the overlook opens onto a view of fluttering massed sea birds.

Visitors quickly become bird-watchers at the **Kilauea Point National Wildlife Refuge.** Red-footed boobies cling to cliffs; frigate birds, with their forked tails wide to the wind, zoom over pounding surf to steal dinner from other birds with their long hooked beaks; Laysan albatross fly in from the low atolls of the northwest; and wedge-tailed shearwaters spend the summer nesting in burrows that pock the cliff.

In the cove, sea turtles swim and porpoises play, while Hawaiian monk seals sun on rocks below the point. During their annual winter visit to Hawai'i, whales cavort offshore on their way to Lahaina Roads, then back again when spring comes. At the visitors center, housed in a former Coast Guard station, you can borrow binoculars or use the telescope for a closer look. *808-828-1413.*

■ **PRINCEVILLE** *map page 285, D-1*
In the 1850s the Hanalei Plateau was a sugar plantation owned by an Ayrshire Scotsman, Robert Wyllie (1798–1865), who bestowed the name Princeville on the area in honor of Prince Albert Kauikeao'uli, son of Kamehameha IV and Queen Emma. This prince, last child born to Hawaiian monarchs, died at the age of four. Wyllie later became the King's foreign minister. Other plantation owners introduced ranching here, and you still may see cattle grazing on the plateau.

Princeville, the largest development on Kaua'i, was built on the plateau and may be more of everything than the north shore should sustain. Its megaresort complex sprawls over 11,000 acres above Hanalei Bay. There are 10 condo complexes, a shopping center, restaurants, two golf courses, endless upscale homes, tennis courts, and a small airport. The Princeville Hotel, built down a hillside, is light, airy, and open to a broad view of the bay.

■ **HANALEI** *map page 285, D-1*
Past Princeville the road bends and broadens. From this overlook the **Valley of Hanalei** (Wreathed Bay) stretches out in a sweeping patchwork of dark green taro farms edged by the flashing silver waters of the Hanalei River. Nearly all of the *poi* consumed in Hawai'i comes from these taro patches. One of the oldest cultivated foods in the world, taro is crammed with vitamins, minerals, and fiber. All parts of the plant are eaten. In their double-hulled canoes, Hawai'i's first settlers brought taro wrapped in *ti* leaves to plant as their staple crop in the new land. Today the bulbous purple roots are shipped to *poi* factories in Honolulu. Known to visitors as a *lu'au* staple, easily digestible *poi* is a traditional food for babies.

At the back of the valley, blue-green mountains rise into shadow and dissolve in cloud-shrouded peaks. Waterfalls ribbon down cliffs. Much of the upper valley is the 917-acre **Hanalei National Wildlife Refuge,** under the aegis of the U.S. Department of the Interior. The refuge was created to preserve the fields of taro for the rare birds that nest in the taro leaves. Brown-bodied, with a red bill and brow, rare Hawaiian gallinules *('alae 'ula)* live here and never leave. Ancient Hawaiians believed the red markings were made by the gods after a bird snapped off one of their firebrands.

A wooden, single-lane bridge over the river is the entrance to Hanalei Valley. From time to time there have been moves to raze the quaint span, built in 1912, and replace it with something more modern. But that might encourage development, so the bridge, repaired and repainted, stays. No tour buses or heavy equipment can pass.

Except for the utility poles and paving on the road leading through Hanalei Valley toward the bay, the scene before you remains almost as it was generations ago. No buildings rise until you reach slow-paced **Hanalei village,** where you might visit the Old Hanalei Coffee Company for a fragrant cup of locally grown bean, or pick up a healthy snack across the street at Hanalei Natural Foods. Park yourself on one of the sun-bleached wooden benches to eat al fresco. On Tuesdays the Sunshine Market at **Waipa** is the place to buy inexpensive orchids and a rich array of exotic fruit.

Hanalei village is still quiet and a long way from the whirl of Lahaina's art colony, but artists are drawn increasingly to the awesome workings of nature at Hanalei Valley. The laid-back art scene here attracts artists and artisans who work in many media.

■ HANALEI BEACHES *map page 285, D-1*

If you seek a large and perfect crescent beach, you need look no further than Hanalei Bay, where the beaches are considered by some residents to be the best on the island. Trees frame white sands, a silvery river wades into turquoise ocean, and there are two miles of curving beach with facilities and tent camping by permit.

At the eastern end of the bay, where the Hanalei River joins the sea, **Hanalei Beach Park** faces a gentle sloping bottom good for summer swimming. Here the surf breaks on the sand bar, making it a good place for summertime beginning surfers; winter, however, brings pounding waves.

The beach next to Hanalei Pier is called **Black Pot**—named after a cooking pot once kept here to prepare fish feasts. Since the 1940s this has been a traditional gathering place, accommodating all kinds of surfing and paddling. Because a sand bar at the river mouth comes and goes, only shallow-draft hulls can cross at any time. Other boats must wait for high tide. Yachts anchor offshore in the summer.

At about the middle of the bay's shore is **Wai'oli Beach Park,** the site of north shore surfing competitions. The beach is known also as Pinetrees for its backdrop of ironwood trees (they're actually acacias).

A patchwork of taro farms in Hanalei Valley supplies nearly all of the poi *consumed in Hawai'i.*

NI'IHAU—FORBIDDEN ISLAND

In sun or shadow, the island of Ni'ihau rears a brooding face 17 miles across the Kaulakahi Channel from Kaua'i. More than a century ago, New Zealander Elizabeth Sinclair bought Ni'ihau from King Kamehameha V for $10,000. Today the island is off-limits to all but those who live there. There are no guns on Ni'ihau, no modern electricity, no telephones, paved roads, crime, or traffic. Residents ride horses, communication is by shortwave radio, and transportation to neighboring Kaua'i is made in a World War II landing boat or a seven-passenger helicopter. Visitors may take helicopter tours (which originate in Kaua'i) of Ni'ihau and land briefly at bleak points well to the north and south of the main village.

Except for an occasional visit by an official from the Department of Education, Ni'ihau's 230 residents, all of whom are native Hawaiian, live undisturbed in the main village of Pu'uwai. Hawaiian is spoken almost exclusively, although English is taught at the single elementary school. After eighth grade, students move to schools on Kaua'i, or, funded by Robinson scholarships, to the Kamehameha School on O'ahu. Traditionally, Ni'ihau islanders were employed in ranching or making charcoal. The majority of residents now wish to join the U.S. Navy's plans to expand the Pacific Missile Range Facility. They know that without employment of some sort, the living language and cultural resource is doomed.

Ni'ihau found itself briefly involved in World War II when a Japanese pilot who had attacked Pearl Harbor crashed his plane in a Ni'ihau field on December 7, 1941. The island's residents took him prisoner, but because he had no way to leave the island, he was not confined. After forcing a Japanese-American ranch employee, Yoshio Harada, to help him lay hands on a machine gun from the downed plane, the flyer terrorized the islanders for five days. In a splendid display of courage and strength, the islander Hawila Kaleohano disarmed the man and confiscated his papers. The pilot drew a hidden pistol and attacked another islander, Benehakaka Kanahele. Kanahele, with five bullets in his body, grabbed the pilot and smashed his head into a stone wall. Newsmen later dubbed the incident the Battle of Ni'ihau—America's first victory in World War II. Kaleohano and Kanahele were decorated for heroism under fire, and Kanahele received the Congressional Medal of Honor. Harada committed hara-kiri.

Ni'ihau is famed for its lei—six-yard multistrands of tiny, smooth, ivory-white shells called *pupu*. The shells are found only on Ni'ihau and were favored by Hawaiian royalty.

■ WEST OF HANALEI BAY *map page 285, C/D-1*

Lumaha'i Beach

A mile beyond Hanalei, around Makahoa Point, lies Lumaha'i Beach, where Mitzi Gaynor tried to wash that man right out of her hair in *South Pacific*. Wide and smooth, nearly a mile long and backed by cocos, the beach curves around a slight bay. Though it's an ideal setting for paintings and photos, this isn't the place to swim. Exposed to open ocean, Lumaha'i is bashed by waves year round. This is no beach to turn your back on; accidents can happen, and rogue waves have been known to take sunbathers. The green sands near the lava outcroppings are made of water-worn olivine. Walk and photograph Lumaha'i and move on.

Ha'ena Beach

West of Lumaha'i, Ha'ena Beach tags the end of the road at the northern edge of the Na Pali cliffs, just as Mana and Polihale tag the ends of the roads at the cliffs' southwestern edge. About five miles past beaches favored by fishermen, Ha'ena is one of the most popular spots on Kaua'i. Beaches of two adjacent Ha'ena parks face open ocean, a bay, and at its west end, the reef-protected **Ke'e Lagoon,** where visitors and residents come from all over Kaua'i to swim, snorkel, and take underwater photographs of rainbow-colored reef fish. (Don't swim in the fast-running channel.)

Ha'ena (Red Hot) State Park

Largely wilderness, the 230 acres of this state park contain ruins of Hawaiian communities dating from A.D. 1000. On the point above Ke'e, a state-owned house marks a trail leading to Ke Ahu o Laka, a terrace for hula performances, and Kauluapaoa He'iau, a temple dedicated to Laka, goddess of hula.

Waikanaloa and Waikapala'e Wet Caves

Across from the beach park are three broad, deep caves, called "wet caves," where dripping water sinks into a sandy floor. Legend has it that the goddess Pele dug the caves. Public facilities are nearby.

If you've circled Kaua'i, enjoyed its beaches and rare tropical beauty, you've found the island is "a promise kept." And like Isabella Bird, you may find it hard to leave Kaua'i.

■ TRAVEL BASICS

When you arrive at Kaua'i's airport, near Lihu'e, you will probably rent a car. A single highway follows the flat coast around three-quarters of the island, linking Lihu'e in the southeast with 11 country towns along the coastline. The highway travels up the island's eastern flank to Princeville and the north shore, coming to a dead halt at Ha'ena and the Na Pali cliffs of the northwest. From Lihu'e, the road loops southward to Poipu and around southern shores, to end at the southern base of the Na Pali coast. Another highway climbs from Waimea in the south and ends in mountain parks.

Those who want to try to see Kaua'i without a car can try the Kaua'i Bus. It runs at peak hours from Lihu'e to Hanalei in the north, and to Kekaha in the west. Call 808-241-6410 for schedules and fares.

Climate: Kaua'i, like all the Hawaiian Islands, enjoys a comfortable tropical climate influenced for most of the year by the northeasterly trade winds. Temperatures vary between 65° F and 85° F. Water temperatures range from 74° F to around 80° F in summer. Winter is the rainy season, but variation can be affected more by location than by season.

■ VISITOR INFORMATION SERVICES

Chamber of Commerce. P.O. Box 1969, Lihu'e 96766; 808-245-7363.
Kaua'i Visitors Bureau. 3016 Umi St., Lihu'e 96766; 808-245-3971 or 800-262-1400.

■ FOOD AND LODGING

☒ For agencies offering listings and booking services for bed-and-breakfasts, hotels, and condominiums on all islands, see page 359.
$ For room and restaurant price designations, see page 359.

■ KAPA'A AND WAILUA *map page 285, E-3*

✕ **Flying Lobster.** Kaua'i Coconut Beach Resort, Kapa'a; 808-822-3455. Delicious fresh seafood, especially lobster, at reasonable prices. **$$**

✕ **Kapaʻa Fish & Chowder House.** 4-1639 Kuhio Hwy., Kapaʻa; 808-822-7488. Just as the name implies: seafood in a casual setting; dinner only. **$$**

✕ **A Pacific Cafe.** Kauaʻi Village, Kapaʻa; 808-822-0013. Pacific Rim and Mediterranean cuisine; dinner only. Excellent fresh fish. Highly popular: make reservations or be ready to wait. **$$**

✕ **Smith's Tropical Paradise.** Wailua Marina State Park; 808-821-6895 or 808-821-6892. Polynesian decor; American fare; fresh fish. Operated by same family that runs boats up Wailua River. Dinner luau. **$$–$$$**

✕ **Wailua Marina Restaurant.** Wailua State Park, 5971 Kuhio Hwy.; 808-822-4311. Simple, family style with local American-Asian menu. Nice river view. **$**

🛏 **Kauaʻi Coast Resort.** 4-484 Kuhio Hwy., Kapaʻa; 808-822-3441 or 800-922-7866. Four 3-story buildings between the Coconut Palms Marketplace and Waipouli Beach. Air-conditioning, lanais, pool, outdoor Jacuzzi. **$$**

🛏 **Kauaʻi Coconut Beach Resort.** Kapaʻa; 808-822-3455. Sandwiched between a large coconut grove and the sparkling blue sea. Attractively appointed rooms; great pool; luau. **$$–$$$**

🛏 **Kauaʻi Sand & Seaside Hotels.** 420 Papaloa Rd., Kapaʻa; 808-822-4951 or 800-367-7000. A good choice for the budget traveler. Carpeted, air-conditioned rooms surround a pool. Steps away from beach. **$**

🛏 **Wailua Bay Resort.** 3-5920 Kuhio Hwy., Wailua; 808-245-3931 or 800-367-5004. Beautifully maintained property surrounds this 242-room hotel; exotic flowers inside and out. Nightclub entertainment; pool, shops, restaurant. **$$–$$$**

■ LIHUʻE *map page 285, E-3*

✕ **Cafe Portofino.** Pacific Ocean Plaza, Nawiliwili; 808-245-2121. Italian cuisine and coffees. The osso bucco is highly recommended. **$$**

✕ **Gaylord's.** Kilohana Sq. in Puhi, 3-2087 Kaumualiʻi Hwy.; 808-245-9593. Al fresco dining in courtyard of restored plantation manager's home. American menu; game in season served amid tropical greenery. **$$**

✕ **Kiibo Restaurant.** 2991 Umi St.; 808-245-2650. Japanese country decor. Simple, local Japanese food; tasty green-tea ice cream. **$**

✕ **Tip Top Cafe & Bakery.** 3173 Akahi St.; 808-245-2333. Coffee shop where macadamia-nut cookies were invented; known for traditional oxtail soup. Local hangout. **$**

⌂ **Kaua'i Marriott Resort & Beach Club.** 3610 Rice St.; 808-245-5050 or 800-228-9290. On beautiful Kalapaki Bay, this is the largest hotel resort on the island, with Polynesian decor and tropical setting. This high-rise led to the law limiting the height of Kaua'i's buildings to "no taller than a coconut tree." **$$$** The hotel's popular restaurant and bar, ✕ **Duke's Kaua'i,** is named for surfing legend Duke Kahanamoku. Salad bar, fresh fish, and live entertainment. 808-246-9599. **$$**

⌂ **Tip Top Motel.** 3173 Akahi St.; 808-245-2333. Motel lodging in town. Locals frequent the restaurant, which is famous for its macadamia-nut cookies. **$**

■ NORTH COAST *map page 285, D-1*

✕ **Cafe Hanalei and Terrace.** Princeville Resort, 5520 Kahaku Rd., Princeville; 808-826-9644. American coffee shop. **$–$$**

✕ **Hanalei Dolphin.** Kuhio Hwy., Hanalei; 808-826-6113. Fresh fish served in rural atmosphere beside the river; dinner only. **$$**

✕ **Hanalei Gourmet.** 5-5161 Kuhio Hwy., #5, Hanalei; 808-826-2524. Order from the deli counter; a very good place for fresh gourmet picnic foods. **$$**

✕ **La Cascata.** Princeville Resort, 5520 Kahaku Rd., Princeville; 808-826-2761. Latin American food and decor; the kitchen is acclaimed for borrowing flavorful accents from Mediterranean cuisines; dinner only. **$$–$$$**

✕ **Tahiti Nui.** Hanalei Village, Hanalei; 808-826-6277. This longtime favorite specializes in Polynesian and American food, and hosts Tahitian dance performances. **$–$$**

⌂ **Bed, Breakfast and Beach.** Hanalei; 808-826-6111. Four charming rooms and a private cottage with 360-degree view; antique furniture. Close to beach. Good location for walking to local restaurants and the village. **$$**

⚏ **Hanalei Bay Resort.** 5380 Honoiki Rd., Princeville; 808-826-6522 or 800-222-5541. Set on 22 acres of north shore hillside, close to the beach. Condos with fine views; 2 pools. **$$–$$$**

⚏ **Princeville Resort.** 5520 Kahaku Rd., Princeville; 808-826-9644 or 800-826-4400. Spacious, open lobbies with marble decor, European antiques, and scenic views of Hanalei Bay and mountains. Two superb suites. A golfer's paradise. **$$$**

■ **POIPU AND KOLOA** *map page 285, D-4*

✕ **The Beach House Restaurant.** 5022 Lawa'i Rd.; 808-742-1424. Romantic oceanfront setting, serving Hawai'i regional cuisine. **$$$**

✕ **Brennecke's Beach Broiler.** Across road from Poipu Beach Park, 2100 Ho'one Rd.; 808-742-7588. Upstairs dining room has an excellent ocean view. Good food at the beach; seafood appetizers and steak burgers. **$**

✕ **Dondero's.** Hyatt Regency Kaua'i, 1571 Poipu Rd., Koloa; 808-742-1234. Pleasant setting, international cuisine. Dinner only. **$$$**

✕ **Tide Pools.** Hyatt Regency Kaua'i, 1571 Poipu Rd., Koloa; 808-742-1234. Casual elegance; American menu with fresh ingredients. Dinner only. **$$**

⚏ **Garden Isle Cottages.** 2666 Pu'uholo Rd., Koloa; 808-742-6717 or 800-742-6711. Above Koloa Landing; seven cottages and 2 houses, 1 with lap pool. Paintings by owner. Studios with refrigerator; 1- and 2-bedroom with kitchens. **$$**

⚏ **Hyatt Regency Kaua'i.** 1571 Poipu Rd., Koloa; 808-742-1234 or 800-233-1234. Comfortable resort and spa. Dining in huts over lagoon. Paddling in lagoon. Fresh- and saltwater pools, golf, tennis, riding. **$$$**

⚏ **Kiahuna Plantation.** 2253 Poipu Rd., Koloa; 808-742-6411 or 800-688-7444. The island's largest condo resort, with plantation-style condos on the beach. Hawaiian ambience and native plants. **$$**

⚏ **Sheraton Kaua'i Resort.** Poipu; 808-742-1661 or 800-782-9488. The 413-room hotel is beautifully appointed—set amid tropical gardens and facing Poipu Beach. Two ocean-front wings, five restaurants, full resort facilities. **$$$**

■ **WAIMEA** *map page 285, B-3/4*

⌕ **Waimea Plantation Cottages.** 9400 Kaumuali'i Hwy, Waimea; 800-992-4632. Set on a former sugarcane plantation, these old plantation managers' cottages were moved from neighboring cane fields and beautifully restored with polished wood floors, tin roofs, and private lanais. They have kitchens, all the amenities, and a charming old-island atmosphere. **$$**

■ **GOLFING ON KAUA'I**

Three courses on the island are on the pros' list of Hawai'i's ten best: Kaua'i Lagoons Kiele, Poipu Bay Resort, and Princeville's Prince. You can buy a package and play all three.

Kaua'i Lagoons Resort Kiele Golf Course. 3351 Hoolaulea Way, Lihu'e; 808-241-6000. Designed by Jack Nicklaus, and one of *Golf Digest's* America's top 100. The Kiele (Gardenia) course favors long hitters who can clear ravines, creeks, and lagoons. Each hole is named for an animal depicted in a statue at the tee. A challenging, Scottish-style links course with open fairways, little water, and undulating greens. Hole No. 13 is a spectacular downhill drive over crashing surf to a diagonal green.

Poipu Bay Resort Golf Course. 3250 Ainako St., Koloa; 808-742-8711. Site of the PGA's Grand Slam each November. The pros advise playing this Robert Trent Jones, Jr. course below the wind. Historical sites are preserved on the course, including an ancient fishing temple; if your ball lands atop the temple platform, leave it—this is a *kapu* place, and trespassing brings bad luck. Endangered *koloa* (duck) and nene geese reside in ponds in the back nine. On the beach below hole No. 16 you can see sunbathing monk seals. Some players consider holes 15 through 18 the best four finishing holes in the state.

Princeville Resort Prince Course. 5520 Ka Haku Rd., Princeville; 808-826-5000. On Kaua'i's majestic north shore, this Robert Trent Jones, Jr. course is rated the number-one layout in the state, and Hawai'i's second most difficult course. Jones's trademark bunkers are in a golfer's heaven with soaring ocean views and a sweep from Mount Wai'ale'ale to Hanalei Bay. Behind the green of hole No. 13 a waterfall gushes from a lava tube right in the middle of a green-carpeted cliff. The clubhouse is three stories of glass, brass, and black marble with every amenity, including a lap pool.

Wailua Municipal Golf Course. 3-5350 Kuhio Hwy., Lihu'e; 808-241-6666. Just two miles from the airport, this 18-hole oceanside course is considered by locals one of the best municipal courses in the state, mainly because of good maintenance and a glorious setting among lush plantings. With quite a number of water hazards, it's not an easy course. You can call Wailua a beautiful bargain.

■ KAUA'I SPAS

Anara Spa. Hyatt Regency Kaua'i Resort & Spa, 1571 Poipu Rd., Koloa; 808-742-1234. With a focus on Hawaiian healing, this 25,000-square-foot facility includes 16 treatment rooms opening onto gardens, fitness classes in yoga and tai chi, a heated lap pool, open-air lava-rock showers, Finnish sauna, botanical soaking tubs, and Turkish steam rooms. The Kupono Cafe serves spa cuisine. A peaceful, meditative atmosphere pervades here.

Princeville Health Club & Spa. Princeville Golf Course clubhouse, Princeville Resort Kaua'i; 808-826-5030. Treatments here last a full hour. Glorious views out the glass walls. The 1,500-square-foot spa offers a heated lap pool, sauna, outdoor whirlpool, steam room, weight and cardio rooms, and massage cabanas pool-side at the hotel.

■ OUTDOOR ADVENTURES

■ BACKROADS

Aloha Kaua'i Tours. P.O. Box 3039, Lihu'e 96766; 800-452-1113. The only firm licensed by the state to tour Koke'e State Park and the Pali-Kona Forest Preserve. New off-the-beaten-path adventures for photo and native plant buffs; four-wheel-drive vans travel old cane-haul roads. Also snorkeling tours.

■ HIKING

Awaawapuhi Trail. Division of State Parks; 808-274-3444. This 3.2-mile trail starts just north of HI 55 (also known as HI 550), about halfway between the museum at Koke'e State Park and the Kalalau Lookout. It climbs 2,500 feet above the sea and offers some of the most unbelievable vistas of the Na Pali Coast.

Kalalau Trail. Division of State Parks; 808-274-3444. This is arguably the best—and subsequently the most popular—backpacking trip in the islands. The 11-mile trail winds through the lush Hanakoa Valley down to the stunning Na Pali Coast. It is accessible only on foot or by boat. Permits are required and limited; reserve them months in advance.

■ HORSEBACK RIDING

Po'oku Stables. Princeville; 808-826-6777. Guided horseback tours to the top of Kalihiwai Falls and Hanalei Valley.

■ WATER ACTIVITIES

Dive Kaua'i. 4-976 Kuhio Hwy., Kapa'a; 808-822-0452. Scuba trips; diving lessons.

Kayak Kaua'i. 808-826-9844. Kayaking tours along the Na Pali Coast with snorkeling in Hanalei Bay.

Mountain Tubing Adventure. Hanama'ulu; 808-639-7383. Operated by Kaua'i Backcountry; float in big blue tubes for 3 hours down a network of former irrigation ditches. Not rigorous, the ride is about drifting, sightseeing, and chatting with fellow tubers. Picnic lunch follows the ride.

NaPali Eco Adventures. 808-826-6804. Coastal excursions, including sea caves; expect to see turtles, flying fish, dolphins, and in-season, humpback whales.

■ FESTIVALS AND EVENTS

■ FEBRUARY
Waimea Town Celebration. Food booths, games, parade, and entertainment. 5K and 10K races. 808-337-1005.

■ MARCH
Prince Kuhio Festival. Songs and dances from the Prince Kuhio era; canoe races, *holoku* (gowns) pageant, and a royal ball. Prince Kuhio Park, Lihu'e; 808-822-5521.

■ **April**

Annual Bonsai Exhibition and Demonstration. Rock planting and miniature landscaping. Borders Books, Lihu'e; 808-546-0862.

■ **May**

Lei Day Celebration. Exhibits, lei-making, entertainment, and crowning of lei queens. Kaua'i Museum, Lihu'e; 808-245-6931.

Prince Albert Music Festival. Four-day festival of Hawaiian and classical music and cultural arts. Princeville Resort; 808-826-6439.

■ **July**

Na Hula O Ka'ohikukapulani. Annual hula exhibition by children. Kaua'i War Memorial Hall, Lihu'e; 808-335-5765 or 808-335-6466.

■ **November**

Kaua'i Open Golf Tournament. Winners of the four major golf championships compete. Poipu Bay Golf Course; 800-742-8711, or Aloha section PGA, 808-593-2230.

FLORA AND FAUNA

> There was then, as there is now, no place known on earth that even
> began to compete with these islands in their capacity to encourage
> natural life to develop freely and radically up to its own best poten-
> tial. More than nine out of ten things that grew here grew nowhere
> else on earth.
>
> —James Michener, *Hawaii*

The astounding assemblage of native plants and birds marks the Hawaiian archipelago as a place apart, and an example of the works and vulnerability of nature.
Hawai'i's flora once consisted of some 1,800 species, 96 percent unique to the
islands. Over the past 200 years, more Hawaiian plant and animal species have
fallen into extinction than on the entire land mass of North America.

The few unique island species that have survived development and the competition of imported plants, animals, and microbes exist in remote Hawaiian valleys
and mountains. One example are the tree lobelias, which are a source of nectar to
birds whose beaks are adapted to the curve of their flowers. Some of Hawai'i's
endangered species are well known, such as the silversword growing on Maui's
Haleakala. Most are virtually unknown—such as the *kaneoha* mint, found only in
the Wai'anae mountains of O'ahu.

When the first Polynesians beached their canoes in Hawai'i around A.D. 700,
they burned lowland forests to clear the land for cultivation of crops native to
Tahiti. Soon they were growing the taro, breadfruit, sweet potatoes, coconuts, and
bananas they had brought with them as seedlings from Tahiti. They nurtured
groves of *wauke*, the paper mulberry, for its bark—which was peeled and beaten
into *kapa* cloth. *'Olona* and *hau* provided fibers for canoe lashings and fishnets;
coco husks provided for sennit (braided cords); and plant materials were harvested
for building homes and for medicines, dyes, and canoes.

Centuries later, a new wave of foreigners began importing another wave of
plants—making for a total of some 2,000 non-native species. The new plants ran
rampant over the landscape and in the process destroyed an enormous percentage

The red lobster claw, heliconia humilis, *is plentiful in Hawai'i.*

(top) The Bird of Paradise is one of the many flower species introduced from other parts of the world. (above) Protea thrive on the leeward slopes of Haleakala on Maui between 2,000 and 4,000 feet.

of the indigenous species. Introduced guavas and Java plum, lantana, bamboos, and gingers escaped into the wild and pushed aside native flora. Today close to 1,000 Hawaiian plant species have become so rare they are considered nearly extinct.

If the European incursion began the destruction of much of Hawai'i's natural world, it was also the beginning of the scientific study of its flora and fauna. Aboard Captain James Cook's ships *Resolution* and *Discovery,* naturalists collected samples and made notes of species never before seen by Europeans. By the 1990s an enormous body of biological information about Hawaiian species lay in museums, books and tracts, manuscripts, journals, and files. That body of knowledge, wrapped in the findings of a report released in 1991, contributed to the documentation of an extinction rate that has been called phenomenal. (See "Hawai'i's Extinction Crisis," prepared by the U.S. Fish & Wildlife Service, the State Department of Land and Natural Resources, and the Nature Conservancy of Hawai'i.) The report, fortunately, has had an impact, and long-term protection programs are encouraging. The goal is set to halt the accelerating descent into extinction of Hawai'i's unique living laboratory.

■ FLORA

Following is a selective list of Hawaiian plants.

'Ahinahina, Silversword *(Argyroxiphium sandwicense)*
Maui's famed indigenous plant is the Hawaiian silversword, known the world round for its single spike thrusting straight up from the volcanic slopes of Haleakala. A rosette of leaves covered in silvery-white hair hugs its base. The swordlike flowering stalk bears up to 500 nodding light yellow flower heads and grows to a height of about 7 feet.

There was a time when silverswords were so profuse that it was a popular sport to uproot and roll them down the mountain, and they were cut and shipped as decorative pieces to China. Further depredation was caused by feral goats and introduced insects. At one time the silversword was reduced to fewer than 100 plants in the crater. The National Park Service has followed conservation procedures since 1927. It is illegal to cut down a silversword.

'Ena'ena, Hawaiian Cudweed *(Gnaphalium sandwicensium, var. Molokaiense)*
Found only in western Moloka'i, 'ena'ena grows on the hot coastal sand dunes behind the beach. These hairy little plants grow about a foot high and bear tight

clusters of muted yellow flowers. The Moloka'i variety differs from other cudweeds in its thick covering of delicate hair that tints the leaves a silvery blue color. *'Ena'ena* means "hot" in Hawaiian and may refer to the arid environment in which it grows.

Kauna'oa, Dodder *(Cuscuta sandwichiana)*

In ancient songs the island of Lana'i was noted for its *kauna'oa,* a strange, ground-running plant that thrives on leeward beaches and whose smooth bare tendrils are a soft peachy color. A parasite rooted in the sand above the highwater mark, *kauna'oa* attaches itself to the stems of host plants, then extends its network of threadlike stems on top of the sand. The tendrils, gathered in handfuls, are twisted or braided to make a thick lei with small pieces of contrasting greenery. The lei requires no tie; after a few hours the tendrils bind themselves together.

Loulu Palm *(Prichardia kaalae)*

Discovered in the forests at the foot of Mount Ka'ala, O'ahu's tallest mountain, the *loulu* is indigenous to that island. A graceful, medium-tall palm, its fringed fronds branch out in a symmetrical pattern around its trunk. Still rare in nature, these palms are propagated for decorative planting. The first cultivated O'ahu *loulu* grows to the right of the main terrace in Honolulu's Foster Botanical Garden.

Mokihana *(Pelea anisata)*

The perfume of the *mokihana* berry scents forests only on the island of Kaua'i. A spindly tree that grows to about 20 feet, it bears small greenish flowers and pastel green berries, or seed capsules. Leathery, cube-shaped, and anise-scented, the berries are strung to make a lei that is associated with Kaua'i island chants. Hawaiians once placed dried *mokihana* among their ceremonial *kapa* garments.

Naupaka *(Scaevola taccada)*

Naupaka is a love story: According to legend, the fire goddess Pele became smitten with a handsome young man, and appearing as a beautiful stranger attempted to entice him. He spurned Pele in favor of his girlfriend. The furious Pele hurled lava and chased him into the mountains. Taking pity on him, one of Pele's sisters transformed him into the white mountain *naupaka* half-flower. Pele then chased his girlfriend to the sea. Again, Pele's sister intervened, turning the girlfriend into a white half-flower as well. And so the lovers exist today, each blooming as a half-flower, never to be reunited. Sea *naupaka* is a hardy, sprawling native shrub growing a few feet high along coastlines and over hot beach lava. Densely branched, it thrives in salty sea water; the succulent leaves wilt in fresh water.

'Ohi'alehua *(Metrosideros collina)*

The *lehua* blossom of the *'ohi'a* tree may be the most sacred flower of the islands, for it belongs to the fire goddess Pele, who now makes her home on the Big Island. Its flaming red pompoms are worn in hula dedicated to the goddess. *Lehua* are gathered only on the way down a mountain, never going up, because Pele surely would cause a heavy mist to descend.

An abundant Hawaiian tree and one of the first growths on new lava, *'ohi'a* is found in all sizes and shapes—from small bonsailike gnarled forms in arid lands to slender giants 80 feet tall in fertile forests. *'Ohi'alehua* creates micro-habitats for herbs and mosses, and Hawaiians once steeped its young reddish leaves *(liko lehua)* for a tonic. Canoe hulls and temple idols were carved from its trunk, and when missionaries learned of the dark sturdy *'ohi'a* wood, they sent great teams of men up into the mountains to cut and haul down logs for new churches.

One of many legends about this tree tells of 'Ohi'a and his lover, Lehua. Pele, attracted to the handsome 'Ohi'a, was rebuffed. Enraged, she slew both lovers. Regretting her outburst, Pele eternally joined the lovers by making the young man's body into a tree capped with the delicate, feminine *lehua* flower.

Flaming red 'ohi'alehua *blossoms are worn in hula dedicated to the fire goddess, Pele.*

A LEI FOR EVERY ISLAND

Flower lei are worn like necklaces and may be wide and flat, thick and round, a single circlet, many strands tied together, or U-shaped. Their message is love, and they are bought for occasions great and small, or for no reason at all.

Traditionally, lei makers relied on inventive use of greenery and natural fibers, seeds, pods, nuts, and the tip or base parts of a flower. When missionary women introduced roses to the islands along with carnations, marigolds, violets, and pansies, the new materials were adapted rapidly by creative Hawaiian lei makers

Learning about lei is learning more about Hawai'i's stories and traditions. For instance, hula dancers believe they gain inspiration from Laka, goddess of the hula, and long ago they placed lei of the shiny, scented, green *maile* leaves on her altars.

Jasmine flowers, or *pikake* (peacock), are traditionally used in courtship and marriage. (They were given the name "peacock" because Princess Ka'iulani had jasmine bushes and peacocks in her garden.) The *pua kika*, or cigar lei, also associated with marriage, is presented to bridegrooms and is made from hundreds of tubular, red-orange, and white cigar flowers strung in a slender round of geometric patterns.

Traditional *haku-lei* styles, which take enormous skill to create, have recently returned to popularity. *Haku* means to set or mount flowers on a backing of banana or other natural fiber, positioning them face-up in greenery, much as jewels are placed into a setting.

The most cherished and elegant of Hawaiian lei is made of the *'ilima* flower. Although it ranges in color from yellow to deep gold to rusty orange, bright orange is preferred. This slender, velvety lei requires 2,000 tiny and easily bruised flowers, which must be picked unopened before dawn, then strung before they blossom in late morning. This fragile lei is associated with, though not restricted to, royalty, and tradition has it that *'ilima* strands many feet long were presented early each morning to Hawaiian monarchs.

Each island has its treasured lei, as described below.

Hawai'i   Red *'ohi'alehua*, delicate and feathery; sacred to Pele, goddess of volcanoes.

Kaua'i   *Mokihana*, a fruit; tiny berries that grow only on Kaua'i, are anise-scented and long-lasting.

Lana'i   Light orange *kauna'oa,* threadlike bare strands gathered in handfuls and twisted into a thick rope; a parasite, it binds itself together.

Maui   Pink *lokelani,* the sweet-scented rosebud of heaven.

Moloka'i   Silver-green *kukui* (candlenut) tree leaves.

Ni'ihau   White *pupu* shells; smooth small shells that are found along the rocky shoreline of this private island.

O'ahu   Orange *'ilima,* velvety and delicate.

A great assortment of lei is found throughout Hawai'i.

Another legend tells that Pele believed her younger sister Hi'iaka, guardian of the 'ohi'alehua forests, betrayed her by seducing Pele's lover, Lohi'au. In her fury, Pele erupted, spewing fire and lava to engulf Hi'iaka's trees. Only then did Hi'iaka act, taking revenge by embracing the young chief. To this day Pele's eruptions pour down lava that consumes 'ohi'alehua trees.

Pua aloalo, Hibiscus *(Hibiscus tiliaceus)*
Pua aloalo, the hibiscus, sports large, showy, cup-shaped flowers with five petals surrounding a yellow stamen. While it is a favored flower to tuck behind the ear (snip off the powdery stamen first), the hibiscus shrivels quickly, making it unfit for a lei. In the early days of tourism it was said a flower behind the left ear meant a lady was committed—the left side belonging with the heart. Behind the right ear—well, maybe. The yellow hibiscus has been Hawai'i's official flower since its designation by the Territorial Legislature in 1923.

Five thousand types of hibiscus are bred today in a range of reddish colors or brilliant yellow, sometimes double-petaled. The blossom of a lowland tree known as *hau,* the hibiscus at one time was crushed and mixed with sap for medicine. The sturdy light wood of the *hau* was used for outriggers on canoes.

■ BIRDS

Blown off course or clutching onto driftwood, a few land birds—15 original species from 11 bird families—long ago found their way across the seas to the isolated islands of Hawai'i. Encountering no predators and no competition, they evolved into some 70 different kinds of birds unique to the Hawaiian chain. More than half are extinct; the others are rare and endangered.

Some of nature's weirdest mutant changes and diversification of a species from a single ancestor are found here. Hawai'i is known to the world's ornithologists for an entire family found only in the Hawaiian Islands—the honeycreepers. They illustrate the process of evolution to a greater degree than any other bird family in the world. From a single ancestral species, 22 species developed on various islands. Some honeycreepers were endemic to a single island—the extinct *aki'apola'au* and *mamo* to Hawai'i, and the *ani'ani'au* to Kaua'i.

Since the first pigeons were released in 1796, more than 156 species of non-indigenous birds have been introduced in the islands. The most familiar species are the common mynah, white-eye and red-crested cardinals, common sparrow, and barred dove.

'Alala, Hawaiian Crow *(Corvus tropicus)*
Once common on the Big Island, the *'alala* is one of the world's rarest birds and is now down to a wild population of only a few. About 18 inches long with a dull black body and brown-tipped wings, it was trapped by early Hawaiians, who used its feathers for *kahili,* the royal standards and symbols of royalty. *'Alala* roamed the island, eating red *'ie'ie* and *'ohelo* berries—sacred to Pele. The bird's adaptability was its downfall: at home on ranches in the 1800s, *'alala* were shot as pests feeding on dead stock.

The most endangered bird species in America, the *'alala* is found in the wild only on a protected private ranch in Kona, where a program in conjunction with the San Diego Zoo is having some success in re-establishing the bird. A federal and state *'alala*-breeding program on Maui, however, has met with small success.

'A'o, Shearwater *(Puffinus auricularis)*
The *'a'o* once nested on all the islands, and today lives only on Kaua'i. Black with a white front and one foot in body length, the *'a'o* has a wingspan of 35 inches. Also known as the Townsend's or Newell's shearwater, the *'a'o* nests in mountain burrows. Traveling in large flocks, its young fly away to sea one evening and do not return for two years. Often on the first flight they are confused by city lights, crash into street lamps, and flounder on the ground. To protect them from cats and cars, Kaua'i residents collect the stricken fledglings, patch them up, and send them off. It is estimated that some 10,000 shearwaters have been saved to fly again.

'Apapane, Honeycreeper *(Himatione sanguinea)*
Because the red-feathered *'apapane* feeds on the red flowers of the *'ohi'alehua,* it is difficult to spot, blending naturally with the flower. Most common of the surviving honeycreepers, it lives in forest treetops and is found on all the main islands.

'Elepaio, Flycatcher *(Chasiempis sandwichensis)*
Less than six inches in length, the endangered brown and white *'elepaio* lives in the forests of Kaua'i, O'ahu, and Hawai'i. An Old World flycatcher, its name comes from its song—e-le-pa-i-o. The bird was the goddess of canoemakers. In early times, Hawaiian canoemakers looking for a good tree trunk learned to avoid those the *'elepaio* were pecking. It meant the trunk was infested with insects and unsuitable for a canoe. Due to predation by introduced animals, O'ahu's little brown and white *'elepaio* is on the federal endangered species list.

'I'iwi *(Vestiaria coccinea)*

Found on all the islands at the turn of the century, the brilliant orange-red *'i'iwi* now lives on Hawai'i, Maui, and Kaua'i. Its long tail and wings are black. *'I'iwi* feathers were used extensively in featherwork capes and helmets. The beak is curved to feed on the flowers of endemic lobelias.

'Io, Hawaiian Hawk *(Buteo solitarius)*

The broad-winged *'io* lives in the forests of Hawai'i, utilizing its sharp talons to prey on rats and spiders. Adults grow to 18 inches and build nests more than a foot deep. The female is large and has dark and light brown color phases. The *'io* is esteemed by some as an *'aumakua,* or ancestor spirit. The endangered bird's lofty circling flight is a symbol of royalty; its name is honored in the name of 'Iolani Palace.

Laysan albatross *(Diomedea immutabilis)*

The Laysan albatros is often known as the gooney bird for its awkward and comical way of landing and moving on the ground. Midway Atoll—in the northern islands of the Hawaiian archipeligo, 1,200 miles west-northwest of Honolulu—hosts the world's largest colony. More than a million of the huge birds, plus major populations of fairy terns, noddies, and tropicbirds, add up to more than 2 million seabirds at the Midway Islands National Wildlife Refuge. Interpretive tours are offered by the U.S. Department of Fish and Wildlife Service. Laysan literally rule the roost on the atoll. You'll be ignored as you bicycle among courting and chick-rearing albatross, or listen to them crooning and giggling in the night.

Nene, Hawaiian Goose *(Branta sandwichensis)*

Hawai'i's official state bird, the nene is a Hawaiian success story. Roaming free today on the slopes of Haleakala on Maui, on Mauna Loa and Kilauea on the Big Island, in bird parks, on a private estate on Hawai'i, and at the Honolulu Zoo, the nene has been saved from extinction by human intervention. A big, bright, multi-colored goose that grows to weigh five pounds and measure 28 inches in length, the nene originally thrived on rugged lava flows, away from ponds or running water. Nesting at elevations between 4,000 and 8,000 feet on Mauna Loa, its food and water sources were native Hawaiian grasses and *'ohelo* berries. Far from water for generations, the webbing on the nene's feet decreased.

At the time of Captain Cook's arrival in 1778, it is believed the nene population was close to 25,000 birds on Hawai'i (and possibly Maui). The near-demise of the

Hawai'i's native nene goose.

nene began with sandalwood logging in nesting areas. As the native habitat was hacked away, the nene fell victim to attacks by introduced mongooses, wild pigs, dogs, and cats. By the early 1950s, only 30 birds remained. Alarmed, the state declared the nene protected and the Division of Fish and Game began a breeding program at Pohakuloa on Hawai'i. By the 1960s, more than 800 nene were hatched.

Today hundreds of nene released on Hawai'i and Maui romp in the rough lava. Still, problems continue to confront the nene. Although the goose will hatch in pens, it must overcome the causes of its near-extinction—changes in habitat and animal attacks when it tries to breed in the wild. Nene means "to sit together and talk." Watch them, but please don't feed them. The nene seem quite sociable.

'O'o *(Moho nobilis)*

Once known as the king of Hawaiian plumage birds, the *'o'o,* a honey eater, was first collected during Captain Cook's expedition of 1779. More than a foot long, its yellow feather tufts under each wing were highly valued for feather capes and helmets. It is believed that yellow feathers from some 80,000 *'o'o* went into the feather cloak of Kamehameha the Great.

Once common, it virtually disappeared around the turn of the twentieth century. Possibly, the endangered Kaua'i *'o'o* still exists, living in the Alaka'i wetlands, but it has not been sighted there recently and may be extinct.

Palila *(Psittirostra bailleui)*

On the cold high slopes of Mauna Kea on Hawai'i, the *palila* survives in an ecological niche with the *na'io* and *mamane* trees. It eats the flowers of the *mamane* and feeds its young on caterpillars snatched off the leaves. The *palila* is six inches

Pueo owl.

long, has a large head and short dark bill, and is yellow, the color of the *mamane* flower. It nests in both *na'io* and *mamane* trees and was once found throughout Hawai'i. Destruction of its habitat, disease, and competition from introduced birds have reduced its population. *Palila* now live above the 7,000-foot level, amid protected stands of trees. Feral sheep that once fed on leaves and seedlings have been removed.

Pueo *(Asio flammeus sandwichensis)*
One of the few owls to hunt in daylight, the short-eared *pueo* soars above the fields, hovering before making a straight dive on its prey—usually a small rat or mouse that it swallows whole. The *pueo* grows to some 18 inches in length, has yellow eyes and white-streaked brown feathers, and lives on all the islands, from sea level to mountain top. Many consider the *pueo* an ancestor spirit, and it is worshipped in some Hawaiian homes.

■ MAMMALS

When the great Polynesian ocean migrations found Hawai'i's shores 1,500 years ago, ancient whale and dolphin species may have roamed island waters. Only seals and tiny bats frolicked on the land. The sea-going canoes carried pigs and dogs—and the Polynesian rat.

Hawaiian Monk Seal *(Monachus schauinslandi)*
Found no other place on earth, the monk seal was separated from relatives in the Caribbean and Atlantic when the Isthmus of Panama appeared some 200,000 years ago. Perhaps the seal was the first mammal ashore on Hawai'i. Hunting the monk seal, explorers and seamen nearly annihilated the species by 1900, yet scientists had

no clue it existed. Not until 1905 was the seal "discovered." Now protected, more than 1,000 monk seals populate the Hawaiian Islands National Wildlife Refuge at the northern end of the island chain—around French Frigate Shoals and Kure Atoll. Joining humans in its love of sandy beaches and nearby shallows, the sweet-faced creature has reappeared on Kaua'i.

Ilio, Dog *(Canis familiaris)*

Dogs, to the early Polynesian voyagers, were everything—except man's best friend. Apparently small and unresponsive dumbbells, dogs were used for barter and in religious rites, the flesh eaten and the bones carved. Cultivated in pens on a vegetarian diet, dogs were a food staple; hundreds might be served at a feast. In 1889 Robert Louis Stevenson was the guest of honor at a luau given by King Kalakaua. Of that day, Arthur Johnstone writes, "It is here that the novelist is said to have tasted his first dish of Hawaiian baked dog, which he did with the best grace at his command, and, after the first bite, with more or less gusto." One of three rabies-free areas in the world (the other two are Australia and Great Britain), Hawai'i maintains a stiff state quarantine.

Iole, Polynesian Rat *(Rattus exulans)*

Rats infested Polynesia, and the Maori of New Zealand ate them. Scientists suppose the Polynesian rat arrived in Hawai'i by stowing away in voyaging canoes. Once in Hawai'i, it evolved into a distinctly Hawaiian rat. The Hawaiians didn't eat rats, but they played with them, placing them in a contest arena where the rats were done in with spears. To counteract the rat's havoc in the cane fields, sugar planters developed tough strains of sugar. Today the Polynesian rat is an intractable pest that eats rare birds and is the bane of wildlife conservationists.

Kohola, Humpback Whale *(Megaptera novaeangliae)*

Although *kohola* is technically the Hawaiian word for "humpback whale," which is the type of whale seen in Hawaiian waters, the word is often used as a generic term for any whale. Whales belong to the order cetacea, which are believed to have evolved from cows, camels, and sheep some 45 million years ago. Over time, cetaceans have completely transformed into aquatic mammals, turning forelimbs into flippers, losing their hind limbs, broadening their tails, replacing hair with a thick layer of fat (blubber), and shifting their nostrils to the top of their heads. Hawaiian royalty wore whale jewelry as a status symbol. The most coveted ornament was a carved tooth of the sperm whale, known as a *lei niho palaoa*. A prize

The Hawaiian monk seal, an endangered species, is now protected in the Hawaiian Islands National Wildlife Refuge and has reappeared on Kaua‘i.

specimen was up to 12 inches long and weighed more than two pounds. Humpback whales cavort and calve in Hawaiian waters during the winter months.

Ope‘ape‘a, Hoary Bat *(Lasiurus cinereus)*

Somehow, thousands of years ago, the little reddish-colored hoary bat flew to the islands under its own steam. Probably descended from the hairy brown bats of the Americas, its original relatives were migratory. Hawai‘i's bat hasn't quite lost that instinct—while other hoary bats store a summer layer of fat before a long flight, Hawai‘i's bats lay on the fat and fly nowhere. Breeding mainly on the islands of Hawai‘i and Kaua‘i, they have been spotted on O‘ahu and Maui.

Pua‘a, Pig *(Sus scrofa)*

In need of meat for his crew, Captain Cook found in 1779 that the largest pigs he could barter for weighed 50 to 60 pounds. Probably the early pigs lived much as they do today, and their population was limited. The native pig of Cook's time interbred with pigs (from imported breeds) that escaped into the wild, and together they evolved into a fearsome beast akin to an enormous European wild boar. Today they rummage in the lush forests, digging muddy wallows that disturb

Green sea turtles, or honu, *are seen frequently feeding on marine plants in Hawai'i's coastal waters. They migrate once every two to five years to breed at French Frigate Shoals in the northwest islands of the Hawaiian archipelago. In their juvenile stage, when the turtles are about the size of a dinner plate, they begin to appear around all the main islands. They mature slowly, taking more than 20 years to reach an adult breeding size of some 200 pounds, but they can live up to 100 years, reaching a weight of 400 pounds.*

the native flora and spreading introduced plants. A boar's head still is a respected hunting trophy. With luck, on Kilauea Volcano you might see a toothy boar's head brought in the night before as offering to Pele.

Other Feral Mammals

Mammals brought to the islands since the arrival of Captain Cook in 1778 include horses, donkeys, cats, dogs, cattle, goats, and rabbits. Some members of every species escaped into the wild and developed feral populations. Wild mammals introduced for sports hunting include axis and mule deer, pronghorn antelope, and mouflon sheep. Some wallabies live in Oahu's Nu'uanu Valley. All now endanger the islands' environment, as does the Indian mongoose, which was introduced for rat control.

REEF FISH

Reef fish are those the snorkeler most likely will see. There are many varieties in Hawai'i. Listed below are a few of the multicolored darting fish to be seen among the coral:

Butterflyfish

Usually up to about six inches in length, brightly colored, and dainty, the body of the butterflyfish is short and narrow. Many of these fish pair off while still small and stay together for life, always swimming one behind the other, darting in and out of reefs.

The long-nose butterfly *(lau wiliwili nukunuku 'oi'oi)* has a bright gold body topped with 12 dorsal spines, a long nose on a black head, and a black tail with *teardrop butterflyfish* black circle beneath. The bluestripe butterfly *(lauhau)* has horizontal blue stripes on a gold body, and is one of the few butterflyfish in Hawai'i that has no vertical black bar through its eye.

long-nose butterflyfish

Triggerfish

The painted triggerfish *(humuhumu nukunuku apua'a)* was made famous by the song "My Little Grass Shack." Hawai'i's small fish with the big name still "goes swimming by." Although it now holds the rank of official state fish, the *humuhumu nukunuku apua'a* did not overly impress early Hawaiians, who considered it an insignificant inshore fish for food. Often, it was used like a twig to cook more tasty morsels from the reef. *Humuhumu*, meaning "to fit pieces together," may refer to the nest it builds, and *nukunuku apua'a* means "nose like a pig." With black painted stripes, brown wedge to the rear, and eyes in the center of its nine-inch body, the fish looks ridiculous. Rows of black spines near the tail allow the *humuhumu* to sideswipe its enemies.

triggerfish

One of the few fish that can attack spiny sea urchins, the *humuhumu* bites off the urchin's spines with sharp teeth and feasts on its soft under-flesh. When frightened or set upon, the fish dives into its nest and raises a large first dorsal fin, which then is locked in place by the sliding second dorsal spine, or "trigger." Once wedged there in its hard-scale covering, no predator can pull the fish.

Moorish Idol

Closely related to surgeonfish, the Moorish idol *(kihi kihi)* is one of the most colorful fishes in Hawai'i. The body is vertically striped with bands of black, yellow, and white, the tail with bands of blue, and the snout is marked with red. The fish can reach a length of eight or nine inches, but its dorsal fins, which are normally long and flowing, shorten as the fish ages. Like butterflyfish, Moorish idols keep the same mate for life; they can be seen from Hawai'i to Australia.

Eels

The long, slick, muscular bodies of eels *(puhi)* make them easily identifiable. Morays are the eels that snorkelers are most likely to see. They are found throughout reefs and are generally not dangerous, unless provoked. The snowflake moray eel averages 17 inches in length and is quite harmless. It's often seen in shallow coral reefs and rocky shorelines, half hidden in crevices, waiting to snatch small, hardshelled prey.

snowflake moray

Pufferfish

This distinctive-looking fish is able to inflate itself with air or water, making it difficult for potential predators to swallow it or dislodge it from crevices. Puffers also have toxic body parts and hard, strong jaws. The whitespotted puffer is covered with small prickles and looks fuzzy when inflated.

whitespotted puffer

Parrotfish

Growing to two feet in length, adult male parrotfish are vibrantly colored; the females are generally red, gray, and brown. Parrotfish *(uhu)* are named for their beaks, which they use to bite off coral for its algae, crushing the coral with teeth at the back of the throat. The rubble passes through the digestive tract and is ejected; in this way they recycle coral into sand. Parrots graze the reefs and are not bothered by peering snorkelers.

The blue-mottled parrotfish adult male has yellow scales with light-blue edges, and pink and blue dorsal fins and tails. The red-lipped adult male parrotfish has a chartreuse green head, back, and dorsal fin, and a light-blue underside.

regal parrotfish

Goatfish

Attaining a length of up to about 16 inches, goatfish are gaudy and plentiful and have double whiskers under the mouth. Once used in ceremonial rites of launching new canoes or entering a *hula halau* (hula school), goatfish are now valued for food and can be found at good fish markets.

Whitespot goatfish *(kumu)* are orange-colored with a white tail and a black horizontal stripe through the eye. They are seen hugging reefs scattered throughout groups of damselfish and carnivorous wrasses. A delicious fish, they often are caught by spear. The red or yellowstripe goatfish *(weke)* has a bright pink body with a horizontal yellow stripe, and a blue back. *Weke* swim in schools in large circles near reefs, and are good eating. White goatfish *(weke'a'a)* are pure white. Don't eat this one during the summer months, when it is said to produce a temporary delirium or "nightmare."

manbar goatfish

All illustrations courtesy of John W. Perry.

WHERE TO SEE REEF FISH

■ HAWAI'I: BIG ISLAND

Aquarium. Kealakekua Bay. State underwater park filled with a variety of colorful reef fish. Depths: 15 to 110 feet.

Pine Trees. North Kona. Underwater lava formations including Golden Arches and Pyramid Pinnacles. Large schools of butterflyfish. Depths: 10 to 50 feet.

■ KAUA'I

General Store. Kukui'ula Bay. Nineteenth-century shipwreck site, with large anchors and chains. Moray eels, lemon butterflyfish, black coral. Depths: 65 to 80 feet.

Sheraton Caverns. Off Poipu. Three huge lava tubes, with lobster and sea turtle nests; a few white tip sharks swim here. Depths: 35 to 60 feet.

■ LANA'I

Cathedrals. South shore. Pinnacles rising from 60 feet below to the surface, creating caverns that are home to lobsters and moray eels. Variable depths.

■ MAUI

Honolua Bay. West Maui. A marine preserve with an array of coral and tropical fish, including manta rays and barracuda. Depths: 20 to 50 feet.

Molokini Crater. 'Alalakeiki Channel. The top of a volcanic crater forms a crescent-shaped marine preserve filled with tame fish. Depths: 10 to 80 feet.

■ MOLOKA'I

Moku Ho'oniki Rock. East end. Former military target now filled with WWII artifacts and home to reef sharks, barracuda, and black coral. Depths: 30 to 100 feet.

■ O'AHU

Hanauma Bay. East of Koko Head. Underwater state park with an array of colorful reef fish and sea turtles. Depths: 10 to 70 feet.

Maunalua Bay. East of Diamond Head. Lava ridges and canyons filled with sea turtles; sunken barge and reefs teeming with barracuda and moray eels. Variable depths.

Pupukea Beach Park. North shore. A marine reserve next to Sunset Beach, featuring a large tidepool, perfect for first-time snorkelers. Nearby "Three Tables" features underwater caverns and ledges. Diveable only in the summer; access is easy from shore. Variable depths.

PLAY OF DOLPHINS

Back to the surface for air, up through the quicksilver interface, having overcome the quite palpable tug from below, and . . . there's life. Dorsal fins approaching: as if to confuse things further, the play of dolphins, the endless circling wheel of their surfacing and diving. And here they are, more or less: squadrons, armadas, flotillas, echelons, convoys, holding just below formation, in a display of skill, the Blue Angels of the deep blue. "Check this out," they seem to be saying, exhibitionists of this liquid Sahara. Forget the spinning, individual dolphins over and again surging up through the surface as if for a toke of gravity, try these group routines to make you *ooo* and *ahh* like the dancing of the Rockettes at Rockefeller Center. So you look: there they are, perhaps 13 of them, one/four/two/four/two, front to back. But even as your eye sees this, the formation alters both depth and angle, though without visible movement, so that as the image is perceived it is already in jeopardy or is in fact lost. Another image taking its place at a different distance, or perhaps now the formation has also changed, is now one lead dolphin and a football-shaped cluster behind. Student body left. Even the MTV-trained eye now beginning to rebel against such transitions. At which point, click, a small pod is within touching distance, dolphins angling, right eyes staring, one's own eye now staring at the cookie cutter shark bites, which seem enormous even as one reminds oneself: *water magnifies*. Further confusing the eye/mind dialogue. The dolphins then not suddenly but suddenly, that is, without apparent use of any force, both simultaneously alongside and heading away, spiraling down in one of those primary patterns, the formula governing growth of the chambered nautilus/proportions of the human body/patterns of leaf growth/ efficiency of projectiles in air.

—Thomas Farber, *On Water*, 1994

Spinner dolphins frolic in the Pacific waters surrounding Hawai'i.

S U R F I N G

When you see ocean rising in a wall of shimmering blue and curling over hollow space with its edge tipped in foam, you can feel the excitement. Riding a wave—pulsing across its face atop the plank of a surfboard—is one of the most exhilarating, invigorating, make-you-whoop-out-loud experiences known to man.

The secret of surfing isn't about conquering the ocean, it's about flowing *with* the ocean. It takes discipline and training, excellent physical condition, grace, and bravery. But don't let that discourage you. With the right waves, board, and attitude—and maybe a quick lesson—anyone with a little coordination can enjoy surfing.

Hawaiians have loved the sport for more than a thousand years. In petroglyphs you can see today on the Big Island there are board-riding stick figures carved by the early Tahitian colonists. Originally known as *he'enalu*, or "sliding on a wave," surfing was a sport everyone enjoyed, from *tutu* (grandmother) to *keiki* (child).

In Kona a *he'iau* dedicated to surfing once stood at Kahalu'u Bay, its terraced rock facing the sea and possibly used as bleachers. The *he'iau kahuna*, or temple

In 1930 young people learned to surf at Waikiki as they do today.

priest, picked vines, handing some to the surfers, and they all beat the water and chanted prayers to the god of the ocean for large waves. In those early times surfing waters favored by the *ali'i*, or royalty, were *kapu* to commoners and the penalty was death. Occasionally a commoner with fine surfing skills could earn the privilege of riding royal surf.

Wintertime, beginning in November, was the favorite time to surf, when stormy winds roiled the ocean and huge waves came pounding ashore on island beaches. Competitions were held, and the people wagered pigs, dogs, canoes, and fishing nets on the surfers. The winners and losers were celebrated in *mele*, or chants.

The acknowledged "father of modern surfing" was the Olympic swimmer Duke Pa'oa Kahanamoku (1890–1968). In the early 1900s, on a long 114-pound *koa*-wood board, he perfected new maneuvers on the waves at Waikiki—riding backward, performing headstands, and surfing at an angle to slide left or right along the face of a wave. Sometimes he surfed with a dog sitting on the front of his board. Duke was the first Hawaiian to take women along to ride tandem on the board; in ancient times tandem surfing was *kapu*.

Duke introduced the sport to Australia in 1915, and after winning Olympic golds in swimming in the 1920s he introduced surfing to the United States, performing in waters off California, New York, and New Jersey.

The heyday of the old-time Hawaiian beach boys, all consummate surfers, began in the 1930s and still exists to some extent. Movie stars, writers, and wealthy tourists came by ship and ensconced themselves at the Moana, Royal Hawaiian, and Halekulani hotels in Waikiki. They made friends with the beach boys who spent their days tending to the visitors, taking the rich and famous out in outrigger canoes and teaching them to ride surfboards. The Hawaiian surfers played music and sang on the beach, drank with the moneyed, enjoyed the rubbed-off glamour, and earned enormous tips.

As surfing became a lifestyle in the 1960s, in Hawai'i and on the mainland surfers began cultivating a tattooed, long-haired, bad-boy image. While nonsurfers wondered what their passion was about, the "surf bums," as they were called then, simply went on pursuing the next wave. As time passed surfing gained recognition as a sport of intense athleticism. Professional surfers are now as well regarded in their watery arena as most-valuable players are on a dry-land football field.

The passion of surfers is the challenge of joining with the wave and flowing with its high-powered energy. The greater the wave the greater the challenge and thrill. In monstrous surf, waves can tower up to 10 times higher than the surfer.

Winter is still the best time to surf, and at international competitions on O'ahu's north shore beaches winter waves may tower more than 30 feet. Although pigs and fishing nets aren't wagered now, there is big prize money from corporate sponsorship. Surfers come from all over—California, Texas, Australia, South America, South Africa, and Singapore—to compete on these enormous waves. In 2004 at the Billabong XXL Big Wave Awards, surfer Pete Cabrinha received substantial prize money for conquering a 70-foot wave at Maui's Pe'ahi surfbreak.

At one time the Hawaiian wave scale was used for competitions. This method arose from the practice of O'ahu's north shore surfers underreporting wave size by measuring the back of the wave. Waves said to be 10 feet actually had a 20-foot drop on the face. Wave heights were measured differently by surfers in other parts of the world. The National Weather Service has tried to standardize wave-height reporting. Today virtually everyone measures the wave face, from trough to peak.

Every surfer needs a board, and these have come a long way since the days of Duke's heavy redwood and *koa* boards. Since the hollow board was invented, surfboards have undergone many additional changes, and board-making spawned an industry. For years "shapers" used a classic method of hand-shaping light-weight polyurethane foam into boards with a thin strip of wood sandwiched in the center. The new era has brought Styrofoam epoxy boards designed digitally; using a program written by a shaper, the basic contours, concavities, and rails are predetermined. Waterflow and resistance reactions can be seen on-screen. The new technology means a new "stick" (surfboard), lighter and stronger, can be re-created again and again. Today's popular surfboards are called longboards, guns, twin fins, and tri-fins. Under 18 inches wide, they are narrower, longer, thicker in the middle, and carry more tail than earlier designs.

One surfing legend of note was Hawaiian Eddie Aikau, who spoke little and surfed from morning to night. In 1977, he was ranked 24th in a field of master surfers at the Duke Kahanamoku Classic competition. With scores rated by length of ride, maneuvers, performance style, and judgment of wave selection, Eddie surfed flawlessly, and won that day at O'ahu's Sunset Beach.

A few months later he sailed aboard the *Hokule'a,* a re-creation of a double-hulled Polynesian voyaging canoe. It was on its second 3,000-mile trip from Hawai'i to Tahiti, and being navigated in the ancient way, when, near midnight on

One section of Maui's Makena Beach offers gently breaking waves for surfers.

March 16, 1978, five hours out of Honolulu, the craft was hit by a rogue swell in the Moloka'i Channel and capsized.

As a storm formed, the crew clung to the craft, hoping to be spotted by commuter aircraft. By morning currents were pulling the vessel out to sea. Against heavy odds, Eddie chose to go for help on his surfboard, though the channel was seething with 20-foot whitecaps that would hit a surfboard broadside from all angles. Wearing a life vest and rain slicker and carrying a knife and light, he set off for Lana'i, about 12 miles distant. Later in the night the other crew members were rescued. Eddie was never seen again.

The big-wave riders of O'ahu's north shore feel that Eddie's spirit hovers at Waimea Bay. On January 21, 1990, the Eddie Aikau Contest was surfed at Waimea, and the day is remembered for perfect 18- to 25-foot waves. Surfers and spectators still talk about that day of positive energy, when the sound of a Hawaiian drumbeat carried over the beach and the wind came out of the valley (a rare occurrence), and surfers rode spectacular waves in memory of Eddie Aikau.

■ Surfing on O'ahu

O'ahu is considered *the* surfing island. Here year-round surfing is the hottest in the Hawaiian Islands, and the international competitions are held annually in this island's big winter surf.

■ South Shore Beaches

Surfers find spots to launch their boards all along the south shore of O'ahu, but there are numerous places find a wave right in Waikiki.

The surfing breaks of Waikiki are out beyond the swimming areas, and while traffic with outriggers, catamarans, and long-distance swimmers can be frustrating, the waves are reliable year-round. Facing the beaches of Waikiki from Diamond Head to the Hawaiian Village Hotel, the long-ride breaks are: **Diamond Head, Tongg's, Old Man's, Publics, Castle, Cunha's, Blowhole, Queens, Canoes, First Break, Cornucopia** (Moana Hotel), and **Popular.** Behind First Break, a long way out to sea, is **Zero Break.**

In the sixties surfers discovered **Point Panic,** at the foot of 'Ahui Street between Waikiki and downtown. North of the small breaks beyond the reef outside of Ala Moana Beach Park is Kewalo Basin, where commercial fishing and cruise boats tie up. At the north end of Kewalo lies rocky Point Panic. There is no sand beach. Here the surf zooms into a sea wall at the University of Hawai'i's Pacific Biomedical Research Center, and board surfers must know how and when to cut off rides, a situation that gives rise to this spot's apt name.

■ LEEWARD BEACHES

Makaha is the most famous surfing beach on the northwest coast. Surfers rode the big winter waves at Makaha well before they attempted the north shore breaks. The first surfers came here with their old-style heavy wooden boards in the 1930s, and in 1952 the first Makaha international surfing championships were held. Contests are held each winter when the north swells run and the waves tower up into walls of moving energy. The name *makaha,* meaning "savage," refers to robbers who once congregated here. Makaha is a place with two personalities—the one, turned inward, friendly, and Hawaiian. The outward face is somewhat hostile, and the casual surfer elicits a frigid greeting from locals, who consider the Makaha surf one of their last few possessions. *84-369 Farrington Highway.*

■ NORTH SHORE BEACHES

From November through mid-May, the big winter surf on the north shore draws experienced board-surfers from around the world. First surfed in the 1940s by Waikiki surfers on heavy redwood boards, the north shore became popular with surfers using modern boards in the early fifties.

Technically, **Sunset Beach** is a two-mile stretch of wide sands where many sections have acquired specific names to indicate surfing sites. Today Sunset refers only to one surfing spot. Public rights-of-way lead to all beaches. Hot spots are east of Hale'iwa town. Moving east up the shoreline, they are:

Laniakea Beach is named for a freshwater spring, and the actual surfing site is off a rocky point to the left. In high winter waters the fast current in the wide channel on the town side can sweep unwary surfers seaward, and rescues are many. *Between Papa'iloa and Pohaku Loa Way.*

Chun's Reef Beach is named for a family of surfers; the wave break is on the right side of a mound in the shoreline Pu'u Nenue. One of the most popular north shore surfing sites, the reef is close to shore and meets the beach. In uncommon fashion, a wind called Hukamakani (wind whistles) blows here from the mountains instead of the sea. *On the eastern side of Pohaku Loa Way.*

JACK LONDON LEARNS TO SURF

When Jack London sailed into Honolulu in May 1907 aboard his barely seaworthy ketch the Snark, *he was already a celebrated writer. He and his wife, Charmian, settled into a Waikiki cottage at the Seaside Hotel and were at once introduced into the life of Honolulu. Together they met the dethroned Queen Lili'uokalani; Prince Jonah Kuhio Kalanianaole, Hawai'i's delegate (nonvoting) to Congress; A. S. Cleghorn, father of the late Princess Ka'iulani; and Sanford B. Dole, politician and pineapple baron. It was after this trip that London wrote* The Cruise of the Snark, *in which, among other things, he describes learning to surf.*

I deserted the cool shade, put on a swimming suit, and got hold of a surfboard. It was too small a board. But I didn't know, and nobody told me. I joined some little Kanaka [Hawaiian] boys in shallow water, where the breakers were well spent and small—a regular kindergarten school....When a likely-looking breaker came along, they flopped upon their stomachs on their boards, kicked like mad with their feet, and rode the breaker in to the beach. I tried to emulate them. I watched them, tried to do everything that they did, and failed utterly. The breaker swept past, and I was not on it. I tried again and again. I kicked twice as madly as they did, and failed. Half a dozen would be around. We would all leap on our boards in front of a good breaker. Away our feet would churn like the stern-wheels of river steamboats, and way the little rascals would scoot while I remained in disgrace behind.

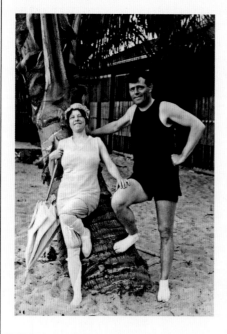

Jack and Charmian London, Waikiki, 1915.

I tried for a solid hour, and not one wave could I persuade to boost me shoreward. And then arrived a friend. . . .

"Get off that board," he said. "Chuck it away at once. Look at the way you're trying to ride it. If ever the nose of that board hits bottom, you'll be disemboweled. Here, take my board. It's a man's size."

. . . He showed me how to properly mount his board. Then he waited for a good breaker, gave me a shove at the right moment, and started me in. Ah, delicious moment when I felt that breaker grip and fling me! On I dashed, a hundred and fifty feet, and subsided with the breaker on the sand. From that moment I was lost.

. . . So it was, next morning, when Ford came along, that I plunged into the wonderful water for a swim of indeterminate length. Astride of our surfboards, or rather, flat down upon them on our stomachs, we paddled out through the kindergarten where the little Kanaka boys were at play. Soon we were out in deep water where the big smokers came roaring in. The mere struggle with them, facing them and paddling seaward over them and through them, was sport enough in itself. One had to have his wits about him, for it was a battle in which mighty blows were struck, on one side, and in which cunning was used on the other side—a struggle between insensate force and intelligence. I soon learned a bit. When a breaker curled over my head, for a swift instant I could see the light of day through its emerald body; then down would go my head, and I would clutch the board with all my strength. Then would come the blow, and to the onlooker on shore I would be blotted out. In reality the board and I have passed through the crest and emerged in the respite of the other side. . . .

The whole method of surf-riding and surf-fighting, I have learned, is one of nonresistance.

—Jack London, *The Cruise of the Snark,* 1908

The Londons returned to Hawai'i a second time in 1915, settling into a cottage on Beach Walk in Waikiki, and later into a cottage near the Halekulani Hotel. London wrote several stories during this time, including Shin Bones, *its theme centering on Hawaiian burial ritual;* The Kanaka Surf, *a surfing tale of a love triangle; and* The Water Baby, *the story of a Hawaiian boy who hoodwinks sharks.*

Internationally famous **Waimea Bay Beach,** with the tallest rideable surf in the world, is the ultimate goal of all big-surf riders. The name Waimea refers to the runoff of red soil from Waimea Valley after a heavy rain. Enormous waves, perilous and exciting in the wide, deep bay, challenge surfers and thrill spectators. When the high surf runs and international competitions are held, huge crowds gather on the beach and on the highway above the bay. In summer Waimea is a flat, calm pool with wonderful waters for swimmers. *61-031 Kamehameha Highway, Waimea.*

The **Banzai Pipeline** takes its name from the Japanese word for "ten thousand years," an equivalent to "Hurrah!" Here the winter swell travels through offshore deep water and builds rapidly as it approaches the seabed shelf. The waves are steep, tossing the crests forward to form tubes, or "pipelines." The waves crash onto a shallow reef and many accidents have occurred. The beach park is the best place to watch surfers at Banzai Pipeline. *Between Banzai Beach and 'Ehukai Beach, 59-337 Ke Nui Road, Pupukea.*

At **Sunset Beach** powerful and perilous waves climb to 20 feet and break on a dangerous shallow reef. This break is the site of several annual competitions. *Shoreline off the 59-100 section of Kamehameha Highway.*

■ SURFING ON MAUI

There are many surfing beaches outside reefs with adequate year-round surf along the western shores of Maui. On the north shore, at the top of the head-shaped knob of west Maui, furious waves make surfing dangerous. Exposed to open ocean and never safe, the boulder-strewn beaches are pounded constantly by heavy surf. Yet some board riders go out in the winter surf that seethes through Honokohau Bay. The road here is a series of switchbacks through gulches and valleys behind the sea cliffs. The best surfing spots are generally hard to reach.

La Perouse Bay, situated on the south coast, is one of the hottest surf spots on Maui. Here the swells and wind are reliable for most of the year, and there are always at least a few surfers. *Past Makena and beyond the end of the paved road.*

The **Lahaina Breakwater** is a good bet to be pumping out good surf even when Maui's other spots are lagoon-flat. Some of Maui's top surfers come here to pull off highly acrobatic maneuvers, making this as good a spot to spectate as to participate. *Just outside of the Lahaina harbor.*

Maui is arguably one of the best windsurfing spots in the world. Here surfers ride the waves at Hoʻokipa.

Honolua Bay is one of Maui's classic spots. This long, fast, powerful break is one of the most coveted in the islands, and you had better know what you're doing if you paddle out. It's best between September and April, with big winter swells often topping 20 feet. The view of the bay from the pineapple fields atop the cliff is awe-inspiring.

On the northeast Maui coast, jagged cliffs, steep, inaccessible valleys, and a constant, howling onshore wind conspire against surfing. But the waves in sparkling **Honomanu Bay** are sheltered by the valley's walls, and it generates 3- to 10-foot surf year-round. *Off Hana Highway, between the town of Keanae and Kaumahina State Park.*

Honokohau is perhaps Maui's best place for the beginner or intermediate surfer to enjoy the fun of surfing without the pressure of hordes of surfers jockeying for the prime waves. *North of Honolua Bay, along Honoapiilani Highway.*

■ SURFING ON KAUA'I

From mellow waves for beginners to intense, double-overhead reef breaks for experts only, surfing on the isle of Kaua'i offers something for everyone.

The three breaks situated in front of the Beach House restaurant in Poipu are some of Kaua'i's most hardcore. **Acid Drop** is an intense, pitching tube that breaks in only a few feet of water above a razor-sharp coral reef; **Longhouse** offers up one of the best lefts in the entire state, streaking fast and long above the reef. Named for its location between the other two spots, **Centers** has much of the same, only it is a bit less punishing to wipe out here due to the relative depth of the water.

The perfect peaks at **Hanalei Point** are arguably the state's best right, and when the swell isn't too large it is a great break for beginners. When the waves do pick up, it's a rollicking ride in perfectly formed barrels. *East side of Hanalei Bay in Black Pot Beach Park, off the Kuhio Highway.*

■ SURFING THE BIG ISLAND

At **Kahalu'u Beach Park,** Hawaiians once beat the water with vines and prayed for big surf. At the seaward side of the reef outside Kahalu'u Bay, experienced surfers can count on superior waves during periods of high surf. These waves create a rip current that moves north along the rocky shore before dispersing in deeper waters. Surfers caught in this seaward rip must flow with it, then, beyond the surf line, paddle south around it and ride in. *North of Keauhou Bay, off Ali'i Drive, South Kona.*

At **Ke'ei Beach** a 300-yard reef fronts the beach, creating the biggest waves and some of the longest rides in the stretch between Napo'opo'o and Honaunau. In 1866 Mark Twain paused here to watch whole families of Hawaiians surfing together. *Palemano Point, south of Kealakekua Bay, South Kona.*

When high winter surf builds up off Kona, the pocket of sand at **White Sands Beach Park** is one of the hottest spots in the Hawaiian Islands for experienced bodysurfers. The break is located outside the point opposite the rest rooms building. *North of Kahalu'u, off Ali'i Drive, South Kona.*

■ BIG WAVE COMPETITIONS

The dates of surfing competitions depend on the size of waves during a scheduled period of time. When the wave measurements indicate big waves, the exact days of the one- to three-day competitions are determined. All surfing events are free. The telephone numbers listed give up-to-the-minute information.

■ OCTOBER TO NOVEMBER
X-Cel Pro International. North Shore, O'ahu; 808-637-6239.

■ NOVEMBER TO DECEMBER
Triple Crown of Surfing. North Shore, O'ahu; Surf News Network, 808-596-7873. The Triple Crown includes Men's and Women's Hawaiian Pro events, Ali'i Beach Park, Hale'iwa; Men's World Cup of Surfing, Sunset Beach; Women's Masters, Sunset Beach; and Annual Pipe Masters (Men's), Ehukai Beach Park. The Masters competitions signal the conclusion of the Association of Surfing Professionals world tour, and are followed by the naming of the men's and women's world champions, and a Triple Crown Champion.

■ DECEMBER TO FEBRUARY
Annual Buffalo's Big Board Surfing Classic. Makaha Beach, Leeward O'ahu; Russ-K Shop, 808-951-7877. Two-day event where old-timers surf on old-style huge and heavy wooden surfboards. Rides are fast.

■ FEBRUARY
Makaha World Surfing Championships. Makaha Beach, O'ahu; 808-325-7400. Features spectacular longboard tandem surfing and canoe surfing, as well as individual surfing and teams of surfers. This is also a Hawaiian cultural event: there's music, entertainment, arts, crafts, and a parade.

TALKING SURF

Surfers like to regale listeners with tales of the wild waves they've surfed. They use English in a style all their own. Here are a few terms to help you decipher their stories.

Aerial	To leave the surface of, and land back on, a wave.
Backwash	The back-flow of a wave after breaking on the beach.
Bailing out	Jumping off a surfboard, usually to avoid harm.
Close out	A wave breaking all at once along its length; unrideable.
Cloud breaks	Places where big waves break on outside reefs, as if in the clouds.
Curl	The curve of the wave's breaking water.
Covered, tucked away, or tubed	To be inside a wave's curl where the water curves above a surfer's head.
Down the line	A long ride.
Drop in on someone	To take off on a wave another surfer is already riding; bad etiquette.
Elephant gun	A giant surfboard used to ride giant waves.
Face	The unbroken front of a wave.
Fin or skeg	The rudder beneath the back end of a surfboard.
Free fall	When the surfer drops straight down the curl of the wave and for a moment surfer and board hang in the air.
Hang ten	All 10 toes hanging over the front (or nose) of the surfboard.
Inside	The water between the wave break and the beach.
Island pull out	Leaving a wave by pushing the surfboard through its back.
Kick out	Leaving a wave by moving your weight to the back (tail) of the board.
Leash	The cord on the rider's ankle attached to the rear of the surfboard.
Locked in	Standing on the surfboard, inside the curl; the ideal place to be on a wave.

Monolith or monster	An enormous wave.
Off the lip or hipshot	Turn by backing off the breaking lip.
Over the falls	To be pulled over the crest of a wave and down into roiling whitewash water.
Pearling	Inadvertently allowing the front of the surfboard to plunge beneath the surface, causing the rider to deep-dive before a wave; derived from pearl diving, which implies a mistake, not a deliberate exit.
Quiver	A set of surfboards for differing wave states.
Rails	The edges of the surfboard.
Ripe	Ideal for surfing, as in a wave.
Ripping	Surfing very well.
Roller coaster	The movement of a surfer up and down the wave face.
Shore break	Waves that break close to shore.
Sliding	Slanting to left or right down a wave.
Smokin' a pipe	Tearing down the face of a wave in the tube.
Snake or shoulder hopper	Another surfer who cuts in on a rider's right of way. One who "drops in" on someone else.
Soup	Whitewash breaking water.
Spinner or 360	A turn full-circle.
Stall	Slowing a surfboard until the wave closes in.
Stoked	Excited, especially after a supreme ride on a supreme wave.
Trough	Bottom slope between two waves.
Tube, pipe, glasshouse, barrel, bowl, or shacks	The tunnel-shaped inside curve of a wave.
Waiting room or line up	The area of ocean swells beyond the breakers where surfers wait to catch waves.
Walking the dog	Walking forward and back on a surfboard to change speed.
Walking the nose	Walking on the front (nose) of the surfboard.
Wall	Large or long wave just before it breaks.
Wipe out	Falling off the surfboard during a ride.
Zigzag	Changing rails, shifting weight, while speeding down a wave face.

GENERAL INFORMATION

■ AREA CODE

The area code for all islands is **808.** Dial 1-808 + number for inter-island calls.

■ GETTING THERE

By Air: Honolulu International Airport is the focal point of Pacific travel. Honolulu, the nation's eleventh largest city, is serviced with multiple daily flights by the major domestic carriers and many charters. Neighboring islands are serviced with direct daily flights, and via Honolulu, from U.S. mainland cities.

A dozen foreign airlines service Hawai'i, connecting Honolulu with the mainland, Asia, Australia, and New Zealand. Direct charter flights from Europe are increasing. Service to islands in the South Pacific runs out of Honolulu on U.S.-owned carriers with frequent flights to Samoa, Tahiti, Rarotonga, and Guam.

By Sea: Luxury cruise ships voyaging in the Pacific regularly stop at Hawaiian ports: Hilo and Kona on the Big Island of Hawai'i; Kahului, Maui; Honolulu, O'ahu; and Nawiliwili, Kaua'i.

■ INTER-ISLAND TRAVEL

By Air: Locals treat island air hops like taking a bus ride, and you can, too. The five major airports of the Hawaiian Islands are Honolulu, O'ahu; Kahului, Maui; Kona and Hilo airports on the Big Island; and Lihu'e, Kaua'i. Two Honolulu-based companies equipped with wide-bodied jet aircraft, **Aloha Airlines** and **Hawaiian Airlines,** service these five airports with some 200 daily flights each, from 6 A.M. to about 9 P.M. (There are no late-night flights between islands.)

Small piston aircraft also service the islands with multiple daily commuter flights out of Honolulu. They service major airports as well as small ones, the latter including Kamuela on the Big Island; Kapalua and Hana, Maui; Kalaupapa, Moloka'i; Lana'i City, Lana'i; and Princeville, Kaua'i. IslandAir is the largest commuter airline. Small-plane flights are wonderful for close-up aerial views.

By Sea: Regular inter-island passenger ferries have never operated on a large scale in the Hawaiian Islands. The open-ocean seas are too rough. However, there are a couple of opportunities to go from one island to another by boat: between

Lahaina, Maui, and Manele, Lanaʻi, a small 24-passenger boat runs five times a day. One way takes one hour. *Call Expeditions in Lahaina, Maui, 808-661-3756.*

In 2004 Norwegian Cruise Lines began inter-island voyages out of Honolulu on a re-flagged ship under the U.S. flag. Sailing under American regulations with American crews, NCL-Americaʼs 2,000-passenger *Pride of Aloha* sails exclusively in Hawaiian waters. NCL-America also offers a cruise on the 1,748-passenger *Norwegian Wind* out of Honolulu, sailing to Fanning Island as well as inter-island. *NCL-Hawaii, 888-625-4292.*

■ INTRA-ISLAND TRAVEL

By Car: The best way to see the islands and travel at your own pace is to rent a car. The state requires a valid drivers license from any signatory to the United Nations Conference on Road and Motor Transport, which very nearly covers the world. Rental agencies require either an English-language license or an international drivers license. By state law, seat belts must be used. Safety seats (which can be rented) are required for children under three.

The major domestic car-rental agencies are on all islands. Advance reservations are recommended; most have a toll-free telephone number. Prices vary and you may want to shop around. Mileage usually is free. Thereʼs a drop-off charge for cars returned to a location different from your pick-up point.

By Public Transportation: There is excellent bus service on Oʻahu and on the Big Island, and limited private bus service on Maui and Kauaʻi. *See individual chapters for details.*

By Moped or Bicycle: Moped agencies abound in Waikiki. Rental offices are found on most of the side streets; most are small companies. The only major company renting mopeds is **Budget,** and their fees are high. Itʼs best to shop around.

Bicycles are popular. Most cycle shops rent all-speed bikes and some specialize in biking tours. Bike races are sometimes held, and information is available from any bike shop in Honolulu, Kona, or Lahaina. Coasting down Haleakala Volcano on Maui is a popular bike tour. Companies in Lahaina take bus tour groups up to the summit for the 38-mile ride coasting down from 10,000 feet to sea level. Call **Cruiser Bob** (808-579-8444), the original company, or **Maui Downhill** (808-877-8787), an equally experienced company. On the Big Island, Kona cycle shops rent two-wheelers and offer escorted tours, including cycle-camping tours.

By Taxi: All islands offer taxi services. Fares are based on mileage, and there's no charge for additional passengers.

■ CLIMATE

All of the main Hawaiian islands are in the tropics. Northeasterly trade winds prevail most of the year, and the climate is generally comfortable. Visitors should beware of taking too much sun; the cooling trades tend to lead you to forget its burning powers. From summer to winter, average temperatures vary slightly. Coastal areas average between 65° F and 85° F. The average year-round temperature of ocean swimming areas is 74° F, and in summer the waters are around 80° F.

The heavy rains come between December and March. These winter rains may last all day for several days or occur only at night. Rainfall varies more by location than with the season. It's an old story in Hawai'i that you can cross to the other side of the street to avoid a shower. In the verdant valleys afternoon showers occur daily.

On every island the windward shores receive more rain than leeward coasts. Volcanic peaks seize the trade winds and block rain clouds from pouring down on the leeward sides. The abundant rain falls on the peaks and on the windward sides. In Hilo, on the windward side of the Big Island, the average annual rainfall is 130 inches, making it the rainiest city in the United States. Conversely, in Kona, on the leeward shore of the same island, you can sunbathe nearly all year long and watch rain clouds drench the slopes just two miles away. Because the volcanic peaks capture the rain, the leeward sides also are the sunniest and driest, with placid ocean waters and an average annual rainfall of 10 to 25 inches.

The trade winds move infrequently from the northeast to the south, when *kona weather* (south wind) comes up. Then, without the cooling trades, you're in for a day or two of sticky weather or a sudden Kona storm.

On the Big Island in winter, the summits of Mauna Kea and Mauna Loa are capped with snow, and atop Haleakala on Maui the mercury also drops below freezing. Mauna Kea, the tallest mountain, is the coldest spot in the islands. A record low of 12° F has been recorded at the summit observatories, and the highest record there is 66° F.

A location near the summit of Kaua'i's Mount Wai'ale'ale, at an elevation of 5,148 feet, holds the world record for the highest annual average rainfall with an amazing 450 inches. Only 15 miles to the southwest, just leeward of the peaks, lies an arid zone with only 20 inches average annual rainfall.

■ DISABLED VISITOR INFORMATION

The Hawaii State Disability & Communication Access Board (DCAB) Web site gives information on wheelchair access, shopping complexes, beaches, and parks. Medical equipment, nursing, and transportation services are also listed. *919 Ala Moana Blvd., Suite 101, Honolulu; 808-586-8121; www.state.hi.us/health/dcab.*

■ EATING HAWAIIAN STYLE

Elegant, romantic dining is widely available on all islands, and in Waikiki you can eat in almost any language. Or choose from other categories throughout the islands—family-type ethnic restaurants, diners, fast food emporia, glitzy discos, and nouvelle cuisine establishments. In the tradition of fine restaurant dining, impressive views and gracious service enhance cuisine made with fresh home-grown and imported ingredients.

The most interesting eating is "local food," a catch-all description for a blend of ethnic tastes. Dishes such as Hawaiian-style chopped steak, saimin (Japanese; broth with noodles, scallions, and fishcake) or chicken adobo (Filipino style), are favored by the general populace, and by suit-and-tie attorneys and legislators, business executives, and beach buffs. The Hawaiian "plate lunch" is the way to explore this unique culinary experience. Begun in World War II when fleets of lunch wagons offered meals to wartime workers who toiled around the clock, plate lunches are modeled after the Japanese bento (cold box lunch), but with one big difference—hot, home-cooked meals.

The most typical Hawaiian plate lunch is beef stew and rice. You might prefer a microcosm of Hawai'i's people in a "mixed plate" of, for example, sweet and sour spareribs (Chinese), chicken katsu (Japanese), Kalua pig (Hawaiian), and a side order of kim chee (Korean). Choose any combination you'd like from an enormous selection that includes pork or chicken teriyaki, kalbi (Korean) shortribs, oyster-sauce chicken (Chinese), chili and rice, mahimahi fish with two wedges of lemon and tartar sauce, manapua (Chinese steamed bun with sweet pork filling), jumbo shrimp, American roast turkey, stuffed cabbage, or a tuna sandwich. Whatever you select for your plate lunch, it will come heaped on a paper plate together with two constants: two scoops of rice and a scoop of macaroni salad.

Entire families are responsible for producing plate lunches, which are dispensed from painted wagons at busy locations. The food is prepared at 4 in the morning at the family's home (kitchens are inspected and licensed by the health department),

HAWAIIAN FISH FOUND ON MENUS

Restaurant diners and game fishing enthusiasts usually encounter the Hawaiian names for local fish. The most popular menu entrée is mahimahi, or dolphinfish (dorado), not to be confused with dolphin mammals. Others are:

Ahi	Yellowfin tuna	*Kawakawa*	Bonito (little
Aku	Skipjack tuna		tuna)
Akule	Mackerel	*Mano*	Shark
'Ama'ama	Gray mullet	*Onaga*	Red snapper
A'u	Pacific marlin	*Ono*	Wahoo
	(swordfish)	*Opakapaka*	Pink snapper
Awa	Milkfish	*Uhu*	Parrotfish
Kahala	Amberjack,	*Uku*	Gray snapper
	yellowtail	*Ulua* or *Papio*	Jack fish

and by 9 A.M. the family is ready for business. In a set-up that takes only 20 minutes, a generator is hooked up, an awning extended, and relishes placed on the counter. Dozens of entrées shelved in every nook and cranny of the wagon are stacked above sodas and "shave ice."

The late 1970s brought high-powered competition to the wagons when mainland fast-food franchises erupted all over the islands. While the new arrivals eventually leveled off, the Hawaiian plate lunch goes on. Local franchisers have adapted in curious ways: at the Zippy's on Vineyard Boulevard in Honolulu—where the decor is trendy and instead of a wagon's cardboard display sign there's colored neon—valet parking is offered to the busy Hawaiian plate-lunch trade.

In the Hawaiian Islands, American, Polynesian, Asian, and European foods reflect the ethnic population mix. Local food is a traditional gift; don't be surprised if your seatmate on an inter-island flight is carrying taro chips from the Big Island, Tip Top cookies from Kaua'i, potato chips from Maui, honey from Moloka'i, or a cake from Dee Lite Bakery on O'ahu. On mainland flights they may be hauling a shopping bag crammed with bags of *poi* and crack seed, chocolate–macadamia nut coffee, and a box of mochi crunch.

Throughout the islands, the dress code at restaurants is almost always casual. Very few luxury restaurants require jacket and tie. Reservations are recommended at fine dining establishments.

Recommended restaurants for each island are listed by town at the end of each island chapter. Price designations for these listings are as follows:

> **RESTAURANT PRICES**
>
> Per person, not including drinks, tax, and tips:
>
> **$** = under $20   **$$** = $20–$30   **$$$** = over $30

■ ACCOMMODATIONS IN HAWAI'I

Hawai'i offers a wide range of lodging facilities across a spectrum of prices and amenities. The travel experience you plan will determine the type of accommodation you will need. You must decide whether to stay at simple lodgings while making day trips, a luxury resort with its own activities, or a combination of the two. Every island except the Big Island is compact, so you can return to home base from any day trip.

At the end of each island chapter you will find a selective list of accommodations. Price designations for these listings are as follows:

> **ROOM RATES**
>
> Per night, per room, double occupancy:
>
> **$** = $70 and under   **$$** = $70–$175   **$$$** = over $175

■ CONDOMINIUMS AND VACATION PACKAGES

Many visitors book their Hawaiian vacation well in advance, taking advantage of the many vacation packages that are available on all of the islands. Package options are numerous, and can range from simple hotel rooms to family suites, to cabins, to condos. You can ask for standard amenities, pools, restaurants, kitchenettes, and rental cars as part of your package. For more information, try the following sources: **Aston Hotels & Resorts.** 800-321-2558. **Hilton Hotels.** 800-445-8667. **Outrigger Hotels.** 800-688-7444. **Sheraton Hotels.** 888-488-3535.

■ BED AND BREAKFAST SERVICES

Two services book B&Bs on *all* islands, with extensive listings in all price ranges: **Bed & Breakfast Hawai'i.** P.O. Box 449, Kapa'a, Kaua'i 96746; 808-822-7711 or 800-733-1632. **Bed & Breakfast Honolulu.** 3242 Kaohinani Dr., Honolulu 96817; 808-595-7533.

RECOMMENDED READING

There may be more books and publications written about Hawai'i than any other island group in the Pacific. Bookshops on the four main islands offer extensive selections on a wide range of subjects. A recommended list:

■ CREATIVE NONFICTION

Farber, Thomas. *On Water.* Hopewell, N.J.: Ecco Press, 1994. An intellectual voyage into the medium of water by a well-known novelist and short-story writer.

■ HAWAIIAN MYTHS AND LEGENDS

Beckwith, Martha Warren. *The Kumulipo.* Chicago: University of Chicago Press, 1951. Honolulu: The University Press of Hawaii, 1972. The Beckwith translation of *The Hawaiian Creation Chant* is widely accepted. Extensive commentary brings insight into traditional hidden meanings in the Hawaiian language that are so evident in this cosmogonic and genealogical chant.

Cox, J. Halley with E. Stasack. *Hawaiian Petroglyphs.* Honolulu: Bishop Museum Press, 1970. Drawings. Discussion of imagery and symbolism at petroglyph sites island-wide.

Kane, Herb Kawainui. *Pele.* Captain Cook, Hawai'i: Kawainui Press, 1987. Color photos of paintings. Stories of Pele, fire goddess of volcanoes.

McBride, L. R. *The Kahuna.* Hilo, Hawai'i: Petroglyph Press, 1983. Black-and-white drawings. During a long association with the National Park Service, McBride specialized in Hawaiiana, gathering stories and information on the ancient Hawaiian education system.

■ HISTORICAL NOVELS AND SHORT STORIES

Chock, Eric and Darrell H. Y. Lum, eds. *The Best of Bamboo Ridge, Hawaii Writers' Quarterly.* Honolulu: Bamboo Ridge Press, 1986. Diverse collection of local literature compiled by one of the best Hawaiian small presses.

Jones, James. *From Here to Eternity.* New York: Avon Books, 1951. Army personnel, conflicts, and love affairs, while stationed in Honolulu during WW II.

London, Jack. *Tales of Hawaii.* Kailua, Hawaiʻi: Press Pacifica, 1984. A trilogy on the plight of the leper in the islands and the machinations of a Chinese patriarch to marry off his children.

Michener, James. *Hawaii.* New York: Random House, 1959. Michener's first sweeping saga. Begins with geologic origins; touches all historical eras up to statehood, and Hawaiʻi's modern population.

Tregaskis, Richard. *The Warrior King.* New York: Macmillan Publishing Co., 1973. Honolulu: Falmouth Press, 1984. Black-and-white photos; genealogy charts. The definitive biography of Kamehameha the Great told by a master writer of men in war. Describes wars to unite islands and the king's voluptuous love life.

■ HISTORY AND REFERENCE

Atlas of Hawaii. Honolulu: University of Hawaiʻi Press, Dept. of Geography, 1983. The most extensive all-around reference on Hawaiʻi.

Beaglehole, J. C. and R. A. Skelton, eds. *The Journals of Captain James Cook on His Voyages of Discovery, Vol. III.* London: Hakluyt Society, 1955–1969. Beaglehole's editorial masterpiece of Cook's logs from the third voyage.

Feher, Joseph. *Hawaii, A Pictorial History.* Honolulu: Bishop Museum Press, 1969. Fine collection of turn-of-the-century photos with commentary.

Forbes, David W. *Encounters With Paradise.* Honolulu: Honolulu Academy of Arts, 1992. Color plates. History and commentary of a once-in-a-lifetime exhibit; international collection of drawings and paintings covering period from Cook's 1778 voyage to 1941.

Fornander, Abraham. *An Account of the Polynesian Race.* New York: Trubner & Co., 1878. The definitive reference text on early Hawaiians and the Hawaiian ethos.

Ii, John Papa. *Fragments of Hawaiian History.* Honolulu: Bishop Museum Press, 1959. Eyewitness account of life under the *kapu* system by a man who lived in Kona during the time of Kamehameha I.

Kaeppler, Adrienne L. *The Fabrics of Hawaii (Bark Cloth).* Leigh-on-Sea, England: F. Lewis Publishers, 1975. Scholarly work on the manufacture of *kapa.* Also by Kaeppler, *Feather Cloaks, Ship Captains, and Lords.* Honolulu: Occasional Papers, Bishop Museum, Vol. XXIV, No. 6, 1970. Stories of two cloaks taken to Scotland and returned to Hawaiʻi.

Kamakau, Samuel M. *Ruling Chiefs of Hawaii.* Honolulu: Kamehameha Schools Press, 1961. The accepted reference text on Hawaiian rulers from the time of Umi, eight generations before Kamehameha I, to the death of Kamehameha III.

Macdonald, Gordon A. and Douglass H. Hubbard. *Volcanoes of the National Parks in Hawaii.* Hawaii Volcanoes National Park, Hawai'i: Hawai'i Natural History Assoc., 1989. Color photos. Descriptions of Mauna Loa and Kilauea volcanoes and the observatory on the Big Island, as well as of Haleakala on Maui. Volcanic activity from 1924–1989.

McGaw, Martha Mary, C.S.J. *Stevenson in Hawaii.* Honolulu: University of Hawai'i Press, 1950. Fine detailed account of Robert Louis Stevenson in Hawai'i.

Pukui, Mary Kawena and Samuel H. Elbert. *Hawaiian Dictionary.* Honolulu: University of Hawai'i Press, 1986. Hawaiian-English and English-Hawaiian. Authoritative collection; 30,000 entries.

Te Rangi Hiroa (Sir Peter Buck). *Arts and Crafts of Hawaii.* Honolulu: Bishop Museum Press, 1957/1988–1990. Series of 14 scholarly tracts on Hawaiian food, fishing, games, musical instruments, weapons, religion, ornaments, and more.

■ NATIONAL PARKS PUBLICATIONS

At park headquarters of Haleakala National Park on Maui and Hawai'i Volcanoes National Park on the Big Island, many special interest and children's books are sold. Subjects include geology and volcanic eruptions, petroglyphs, flora and fauna, hiking guides, and the fire goddess Pele. Publications also available at Volcanoes National Park cover: Pu'uhonua O Honaunau National Historical Park, Hawai'i; Pu'ukohola He'iau National Historic Site, Hawai'i; and Kalaupapa National Historical Park, Moloka'i. *Haleakala National Park Hqs., Maui, HI 96732; 808-572-4400. Hawaii Volcanoes National Park Hqs., Volcano, HI 96785; 808-985-6000.*

At the USS *Arizona* Memorial, books are available concerning the attack on Pearl Harbor in 1941; the building of the memorial; and the War-in-the-Pacific National Historical Park on Guam, 3,300 miles west of Hawai'i. *National Park Service, USS* Arizona *Memorial, Pearl Harbor, HI 96782; 808-422-2771.*

■ NATURAL SCIENCES

Kimura, Bert Y. and Kenneth M. Nagata. *Hawaii's Vanishing Flora*. Honolulu: Oriental Publishing Co., 1980. Color photos. Rare and endangered Hawaiian plants discussed for "semi-serious botanists."

Merlin, Mark David. *Hawaiian Forest Plants*. Honolulu: Oriental Publishing Co., 1980. Color photos. Description and usage of plants found in Hawaiian forests.

Miller, Carey D., et al. *Fruits of Hawaii*. Honolulu: University of Hawai'i Press, 1945/1989. Black-and-white photos. Description, nutritive value, and recipes.

TenBruggencate, Jan. *Wildlife of Hawaii*. (Booklet). Honolulu: *The Honolulu Advertiser*, 1986. Drawings. Descriptions of fish, bird, insect, turtle, toad, and plant life.

Witte, A. and Mahaney, C. *Hawaiian Reef Fish*. Honolulu: Island Heritage Publishing, 1999. Good color photographs and descriptions in a spiral binder.

■ REMINISCENCES

Johnstone, Arthur. *Recollections of Robert Louis Stevenson in the Pacific*. London: Chatto and Windus, 1905. The editor of the *Pacific Commerical Advertiser*, friend of Robert Louis Stevenson, published the poem "The High Winds of Nu'uanu" here for the first time.

The Kauai Papers. Lihu'e, Kaua'i: Kaua'i Historical Society, 1991. First-person stories and written oral histories from the turn of the century.

Lili'uokalani (Lydia Kamaka'eha). *Hawaii's Story*. Rutland, Vermont: Charles E. Tuttle Co., 1964/1990. Hawai'i's last monarch tells her story of historic events, from the time of her childhood to the overthrow of the monarchy: sorrow, prison, parole, and a time to renew.

■ SURFING, DIVING, PADDLING, AND GOLF

Cabral, Ceasar. *Instructional Guide to Surfing, Quick Tips*. Honolulu: Island Heritage Publishing, 2000. A fast course for beginners; black-and-white drawings and descriptions.

Fuller, George. *Hawai'i's Best Golf*. Honolulu: Island Heritage Publishing, 1999. The popular and championship tournament courses on all islands are described by the dean of Hawai'i golf writers. Large photos bound up in school-notebook size.

Jenkins, Bruce. *North Shore Chronicles.* Berkeley: North Atlantic Books, 1990. The *San Francisco Chronicle*'s ace sports columnist and avid surfer goes to the heart of big-wave surfing on the north shore of O'ahu.

Sutherland, Audrey. *Paddling Hawai'i.* Seattle: The Mountaineers, 1988. Black-and-white photos and maps. When it comes to kayaking, Sutherland is the master. Explores secluded coves and wild coasts, many reachable only by water, at six islands; offers wealth of practical information for remote sites.

Thorne, C. and L. Zitnik. *The Divers' Guide to Hawaii.* Kahului, Maui: Hawaii Divers Guide (Maui), 1984. Shore diving off the six major islands, with maps, hazards, and directions to sites.

Wallin, Doug. *Diving and Snorkeling Guide to the Hawaiian Islands.* Kahului, Maui: Pisces Books, 1984. Color photos. Diving and snorkeling off the four main islands.

Wardlaw, Lee. *Cowabunga!* New York: Avon Books, 1991. Surfing history, gear, and etiquette. Where to catch waves; how boards are made.

■ TRAVEL, HISTORIC ESSAYS

Bird, Isabella L. *Six Months in the Sandwich Islands.* London: John Murray, 1890. Rutland, Vermont: Charles E. Tuttle Co., 1974. This intrepid lady climbed on mules and trekked into remote villages and nearly impenetrable forests. Detailed prose in letters written home to Edinburgh in 1873.

Day, A. Grove, ed. *Mark Twain's Letters from Hawaii.* Honolulu: University of Hawai'i Press, 1975. The humor and heart of Twain became famous after these articles were written in Hawai'i for the *Sacramento Union* in 1866. The letters mark his lifelong love affair with the islands.

Day, A. Grove, ed. *Robert Louis Stevenson, Travels in Hawaii.* Honolulu: University of Hawai'i Press, 1973. The frail Robert Louis Stevenson produced some of his finest stories in Hawai'i. Collection of his writings about, in, and from Hawai'i, mainly 1889 to 1893.

Maugham, W. Somerset. *Trembling of a Leaf.* New York: Doubleday & Co., 1921. "Honolulu" essay about a *haole* man in love with a Hawaiian girl.

Stevenson, Robert Louis. *The South Seas.* London: Chatto & Windus, 1912. Contains essays about Hawai'i often not included in subsequent editions.

Stoddard, Charles Warren. *South Sea Idyls.* New York: James R. Osgood & Co., 1873. Diary kept during second visit to Molokaʻi, 1884. Contains the earliest and perhaps best description of Father Damien, the priest who cared for the lepers on Molokaʻi.

■ TRAVEL, MODERN GUIDES

Clark, John R. K. *The Beaches of the Big Island* (1985); *The Beaches of Kauai* (1990); *The Beaches of Maui County* (1989); *The Beaches of Oahu* (1977); *Hawaiʻi's Best Beaches* (1999). Honolulu: University of Hawaiʻi Press. If you plan to explore beaches, you'll want these detailed accounts of the history and geology of every beach. Includes water conditions.

Riegert, Ray. *Hidden Hawaii.* Berkeley: Ulysses Press. Describes little-known sites and remote regions island-wide. Great for hikers.

■ MISCELLANY

Blanding, Don. *Leaves From a Grass House.* Hilo, Hawaiʻi: Petroglyph Press, 1972. Poetry written in Hawaiʻi in the early twenties.

ʻIolani Palace. Honolulu: Friends of ʻIolani Palace, 1988. Color photos. History, description, and restoration of the ʻIolani Palace, residence of the last two reigning monarchs.

McDonald, Marie A. *Ka Lei.* Kailua, Hawaiʻi: Press Pacifica, 1980. Color plates. Everything you always wanted to know about the lei.

Schleck, Robert J. *The Wilcox Quilts in Hawaii.* Kauaʻi: Grove Farm Homestead, 1986. Color photos. Documents acquisition of quilts by the family; offers a glimpse into the lives of early quiltmakers.

(following spread) Waterfalls cascade down the volcanic cliffs of the Big Island's Kohala Coast.

L A N G U A G E

■ BASIC HAWAIIAN

Although the Hawaiian spoken today is vastly different from Old Hawaiian, the roots of the language can be traced back to the early Polynesian colonists and later Tahitian influences. The language was further modified by the development of a local dialect known as pidgin. Originated by landowners who wanted to communicate with their Chinese, Japanese, and Portuguese migrant workers, pidgin has become a strong current in the island's subculture—a language of the people—which is still evolving today.

■ PRONUNCIATION

Syllables in Hawaiian words do not end in consonants. When referring to the capital city, say "Hoe-no-*loo*-loo," not "Hah-na-*loo*-loo"—an immediate sign of an outsider. On the Big Island, the volcano "Kee-lau-*e*-uh" commonly is mispronounced "Kill-*ow*-e-uh."

When Protestant missionaries arrived in 1920, they began the task of transcribing Hawaiian into written form, assembling an alphabet of 12 letters—H, K, L, M, N, P, and W to represent the consonants. The five vowels were to be pronounced identically to the Latin-based Spanish or Italian.

Over time, enhancements were added. A hamza marked the glottal stop—a pause in a word's enunciation. The hamza is often written today with an apostrophe, but be aware that they are used inconsistently and may not always appear on Hawaiian street signs, maps, institutional names, or other literature about Hawai'i.

You may also see a macron used. This appears as a line above a vowel indicating a long sound. All vowels with macrons are sounded, and in short words, the stress is on the next-to-last syllable as in: *wahine* "wa-*hee*-nay" (woman), or *kama'aina* "kah-mah-*eye*-nah" (native-born or old-timer). Long, multivoweled words are composed of groups of syllables and each has a stress.

Hawaiian is robust and eloquent, especially in the grouped syllables:

"Mo-*ah*-nee lay-*hoo*-uh" is the breeze *(moani)* that wafts the fragrance of *lehua* blossoms.

■ How to Interpret Hawaiian Directions

The old Hawaiian way of locating a place is still practiced. *Makai* is toward the ocean, and *mauka* is toward the mountains. (*Ma* means "to"; *ma-kai* "to the ocean"; *ma-uka* "to the uplands.")

Directions are given from the point where one is located when asking the way. For example, if you are in Waikiki and ask for directions to the university, you'll be told to go *mauka* (toward the mountains). Or if you ask how to get downtown from the National Cemetery in Punchbowl, you will be directed to head *makai* (toward the ocean). Because these two words are so wonderfully efficient, new residents quickly adopt the Hawaiian way.

Similarly, there are directions specific to every island, where actual sites are used to guide you to your destination. On Oʻahu, *ʻewa* is to the west, a direction taking its name from a sugar plantation area on western Oʻahu. Diamond Head, Waikiki, and Koko Head are to the east. If, for instance, you are at the Ala Moana Shopping Center and ask the way to ʻIolani Palace, you will be told to go *ʻewa* (west). Or if you're at the Prince Hotel and are looking for the Royal Hawaiian, you will be directed to go Diamond Head, or Waikiki (east). If you are not standing within the boundaries of these sites, the directions are adaptable. If, for example, you are at the Kahala Mandarin, a location beyond (or east of) Diamond Head, and want to visit Hanauma Bay, you will be directed to head Koko Head (farther east).

■ Glossary

ʻAʻa	Jagged, rough, broken lava
Ae	Yes
Ahupuaʻa	Land division, often a pie-slice shape extending from the mountains to the sea
ʻAina	Land, earth
Akua	God, goddess, spirit, or ghost
ʻAumakua	Personal or family gods; deified ancestors who may take other forms; they warn and scold in dreams
ʻAwa	Narcotic drink made from root of the *kava* shrub
Bento	Japanese box lunch
Haole	Any foreigner, usually Caucasian
Hau	Type of hibiscus; the wood once used for canoe outriggers; the bast for rope; the sap and flowers for tonics

Hau'oli	Happy
He'iau	High place of worship
Hilo	First night of the new moon
Hocomalimali	Flatter, use soft words
Hukilau	Group fishing with a *seine,* or net
Hula	Native Hawaiian dance
Hula halau	Hula school or troupe
'Iako	Outrigger boom
Imu	Underground oven
Itai! itai!	Ouch! ouch! (Japanese)
Kahuna	Skilled and wise in any profession; usually a priest, or healer
Kalo	Taro (*Colocasia esculenta*)
Kama'aina	Native-born; literally, "land child"
Kane	Man, male
Kapa	(also called *tapa*) cloth made from the bark of the paper mulberry tree
Kapu	Forbidden
Keiki	Child; *keiki o ka 'aina:* child born on the land
Ki	Commonly known as *ti;* leaves used extensively by ancient Hawaiians for food wrapping, hula skirts, sandals
Kiawe	Algaroba tree (has sharp thorns); introduced in 1828
Kipuka	Calm place in a high sea; has come to mean a bit of land left isolated by flowing lava
Koa	Largest of native forest trees (*Acacia koa*)
Kohola	Coral reef flats; also, humpback whale
Kokua	Help, assistance
Komo	To enter
Komo mai	Come in
Konane	Ancient game similar to checkers played with pebbles in even lines on board; also, bright moonlight
Kumu	Teacher, tutor, model
Kupuna	Grandparent, relative, or close friend; ancestor
Lanai	Veranda, porch
Lana'i	Lana'i island; literally, "day of conquest"

Laulau	Wrapped package; food wrapped in leaves and baked in underground oven
Lei	Necklace of flowers
Lomi	To press or crush; raw lomi salmon, worked with fingers, mixed with onions, and seasoned
Lu'au	Hawaiian feast; also *kalo* (taro) tops baked with coconut cream and chicken
Mahalo	Thank you
Maka'ainana	Commoner, populace
Makahiki	Ancient festival beginning about mid-October and lasting about 4 months, with sports and religious festivities and *kapu* on war
Makai	Toward the sea
Mauka	Toward the mountains or inland
Mele Kalikimaka	Merry Christmas
Menehune	Legendary race of elves on the islands preceding the first Hawaiians
Moana	Open, deep ocean; *'aumoana:* to travel on the open sea
Mo'o	Legendary water spirit, dragon, or lizard
Mu'umu'u	Loose gown
'Ohana	Family, extended family; clan
Okole maluna	Cheers!
Pahoehoe	Unbroken lava that flows rapidly in smooth folds
Pali	Cliffs
Pilikia	Trouble
Poi	Hawaiian staff of life made from *kalo* (taro)
Pupu	Appetizer; also shells
Pu'u	Protuberance; cinder-cone hill
Saimin	Japanese noodle soup
'Ukulele	Instrument brought by Portugese in 1879; literally, "leaping flea"
Wahine	Woman, female
Wiki	To hurry; *hele wiki:* walk quickly

INDEX

Each place name is followed by an abbreviation for the island on which it is found: (H)=Hawai'i; (K)=Kaua'i; (L)=Lana'i; (Ma)=Maui; (Mo)=Moloka'i; (O)=O'ahu.

Abascal, Mañuel 112–113
accommodations. See food and lodging
Aikau, Eddie 342, 344
air travel 354
Akaka, Abraham K. 17
Ala Wai Canal (O) 41, 201
Ala Wai Yacht Harbor (O) 200, 201
Alaka'i Wilderness Preserve (K) 295–296
Alanui (O) 223
Alexander, Samuel 116–117
Alexander & Baldwin Sugar Museum (Ma) 116–117
ali'i 24
Allerton, John 290
Allerton Gardens (K) 290
aloha 17, 25, 220, 286
Aloha Festival 225
Aloha Tower (O) 227
American Factors 124
Anaehoomalu Bay (H) 85
annexation 36–37, 283
area code 354
Arizona Memorial and Visitor Center (O) 235–237
Armstrong, Louis 56
axis deer 177

Bailey, Edward & Caroline 117
Bailey House Museum (Ma) 117
Baldwin, Dwight 121, 123
Baldwin, Henry 116–117
Baldwin House Museum (Ma) 121, 123
banyan tree 123
Barking Sands (K) 297–298
Battery Randolph (O) 211
Battle of Moku'ahai 74
Battle of Ni'ihau 308

Battle of the Red-Mouthed Gun 48
Beissel, James 137
Bell Stone (K) 301
Bellows Field Beach Park (O) 258
Best of the Bamboo Ridge, The 160–161, 164, 360
Big Beach (Ma) 127
Big Island. See Hawai'i
Biggers, Earl Derr 208
bike rentals 355
biking 103, 151
Bingham, Hiram 214, 220
Bird, Isabella 60, 92, 276, 280–281, 304, 364
birds 326–330
Bishop, Charles Reed 230, 284
Bishop Museum (O) 230, 231, 286
Black Pot (K) 307
Bligh, William 29
Blue Ginger Gallery 77
Born in Paradise (von Tempski) 135–136
Bounty 29
Buddha 122, 123
buses 355
Byodo-In 262–263

Cabrinha, Pete 342
Captain Cook Monument (H) 70, 71, 73
Captain Cook Monument (K) 293
Captain Cook town (H) 70, 74, 95
Castle & Cooke 156–157
Chain of Craters Road (H) 64
Chinatown (O) 214
Chock, Eric 90–91, 360
Choris, Louis 25, 32, 33
Church of the Holy Ghost (Ma) 137
Church Row (Mo) 183
Cleghorn, Archibald 202, 226, 346
Clerke, James 29
Cleveland, Grover 37
climate 13, 18, 356; Hawai'i 94; Honolulu and Waikiki 240; Kaua'i 310; Lana'i 171; Maui 144; O'ahu 268

coffee 74, 191
Contemporary Museum (O) 229
Cook, Captain James 26–29, 32, 36, 48, 70, 71, 72–73, 86, 130, 143, 279, 293, 321
Cooke, Anna Rice 228, 229
Cruise of the Snark, The (London) 346–347
cruise ships 354
Cunha, Sonny 238

D. T. Fleming Beach Park (Ma) 125
Damien, Father Joseph de Veuster 176, 177–180, 184–185, 189, 225
Del Monte 180
Desert Strip (Mo) 194
Devastation Trail (H) 58, 60
Diamond Head (O) 198, 211, 212, 213, 271
Dickey, Charles W. 55
disabled visitors 357
Discovery 26, 27–28, 29, 321
Dixon, George 176
Doctor's Pit (H) 93
Dole, James 156–157, 159, 163
Dole, Sanford 37, 346
Dole Food Company 154, 156–158, 180
Dole Pineapple Visitor Center 264
dolphins 338, 339
Douglas, David 93
Duke, Doris 229
Duke Kahanamoku Beach (O) 211

Earhart, Amelia 56
Eight Islands, The (Stevenson) 69, 184
Ellison S. Onizuka Space Center 80
Emma, Queen 230–231, 290, 305
Emmert, Paul 250

***Falls of Clyde* (O) 227**
Farber, Thomas 210, 339, 360
fauna 318–321, 326–339
Fern Grotto (K) 301, 302–303
ferries 354–355
festivals and events: Hawai'i 104–105; Kaua'i 316–317; Maui 152–153; Moloka'i 197; O'ahu 272–275
fish 334–337, 356
Floating Islands and the Return of Lono, The (Kamakau) 72–73

flora 318–326
Fong, Hiram 264
food and lodging 357–359: Hawai'i 95–100; Honolulu and Waikiki 240–248; Kaua'i 310–314; Lana'i 172–173; Maui 144–149; Moloka'i 195–196; O'ahu 268–269
Fort DeRussy Beach (O) 210–211
Fort Elizabeth (K) 282, 293
Fort Riger (O) 211, 213
Fort Street Mall (O) 214, 217
Fosberg, Raymond 159
From Here to Eternity 254
Fuchida, Mitsuo 233–234

Garden of the Gods (L) 162
geography 20
geology 20–23
Gibson, Walter Murray 155–156
Giroux, Hector 252
glottal stops 19
Goat Island (O) 261
Gold Coast (O) 47
golf 46; Hawai'i 100–102; Honolulu 248–249; Kaua'i 314–315; Lana'i 173; Maui 149–150; Moloka'i 196; O'ahu 269–270
Gould, Thomas R. 86
Gray's Beach (O) 208–210
Great Mahele 35–36, 177
Green Sand Beach (H) 66
Grove Farm Homestead (K) 287

Ha'ena Beach (K) 277, 309
Ha'ena State Park (K) 309
Halawa Bay (Mo) 190–191
Halawa Beach (Mo) 191
Hale Koa Hotel (O) 210
Hale O Keawe (H) 16, 68, 69
Hale O Lono Beach (Mo) 192
Hale Piula (Ma) 123
Haleakala Crater (Ma) 23
Haleakala National Park (Ma) 140–143, 151
Haleakala Rain Forest 134
Haleakala Volcano 107, 108, 126, 143
Haleiwa (O) 265
Halekulani Hotel (O) 208
Halema'uma'u 49, 60

Halona Blowhole (O) 254
Halona Cove (O) 254
Halulu He'iau (L) 170
Hamakua Coast (H) 50–51, 89–92
Hamanawa 217
Hana (Ma) 131–133, 145
Hana Bay (Ma) 133
Hana Beach Park (Ma) 132
Hana Cultural Center and Museum (Ma) 132
Hana Highway (Ma) 130, 132
Hana-Maui Hotel (Ma) 131
Hanakapi'ai Falls (K) 300
Hanalei (K) 304, 305–307 Hanalei Beach Park (K) 307
Hanalei National Wildlife Refuge (K) 305
Hanapepe (K) 292
Hanauma Bay (O) 253–254
Hanauma Bay Nature Preserve (O) 254
Hapuna Beach State Recreation Area (H) 81, 82
Ha'uola Gulch (L) 158
Hauola Stone (Ma) 123
Hawaii (Michener) 44, 318, 361
Hawai'i (Big Island) 47–105; climate 94; festivals and events 104–105; food and lodging 95–100; golf 100–102; history 48–53, 66; map 57; outdoors 103–104; spas 102; surfing 350; travel basics 94; visitor information 95
Hawai'i Convention Center (O) 213
Hawai'i facts 12–13
Hawai'i Maritime Center (O) 227
Hawai'i State Art Museum (O) 227
Hawai'i State Capitol (O) 224–225
Hawai'i statehood 17, 40–41
Hawai'i Volcanoes National Park (H) 21, 22, 42–43, 59–65
Hawaiian Homestead Act 180
Hawaiian International Billfish Tournament and Pro-Am 75, 105
Hawaiian Islands Humpback Whale National Marine Sanctuary 119
Hawaiian Missionaries (stamps) 252
Hiki'au He'iau (H) 73
hiking 103, 151, 270–271, 315–316

Hilo (H) 52, 53–56, 95–96
Hilton Hawaiian Village Hotel (O) 211
Hina 56, 174
Hindley, Norman 164
history and culture 20–45, 318, 321; Hawai'i 48–53, 66; Honolulu and Waikiki 198–249; Kaua'i 278–283; Lana'i 154–158; Maui 108–115; Moloka'i 174–180; O'ahu 251–253
HMS Blonde 214
Ho, Don 239
Hoapili, Chief 114
Hockney, David 230
Hokule'a 279, 342, 344
Hole in the Mountain (K) 304
Holualoa (H) 80, 96 Honoka'a 96
Honolulu (O) 198, 213–230; climate 240; golf 248–249; history 198–201; lodging 247–248; maps 215, 221; restaurants 240–247; tours 249; travel basics 240; visitor information 240
Honolulu Academy of Arts (O) 228–229
Honolulu Fish Auction (O) 227
Honolulu Harbor (O) 227
Honolulu Marathon (O) 206
Honopu (K) 298
Ho'okena Beach (H) 66–67
horseback riding 103, 151, 316
Hotel Hana-Maui 138–139
Hotel Lana'i 154
House Without a Key, The (Biggers) 208
Hualalai volcano (H) 23
hula 25, 35, 36, 42–43, 44–45, 53, 176, 208, 219, 309, 324
Hulihe'e Palace (H) 77
Hulopo'e Beach (L) 165, 166–167
Hyatt Regency Kaua'i (K) 291
Hyde, C. M. 178–179

I Led the Air Attack on Pearl Harbor (Fuchida) 233–234
'Iao Needle (Ma) 118
'Iao Valley State Park (Ma) 117–118
Ili'ili'opae He'iau (Mo) 190
immigration 36, 37, 44, 160–161
interstate highways 261, 264

'Iolani Palace (O) 198, 216, 217, 220, 225, 286
Ironman Triathlon World Championship 75–76, 105

Jelsma, Clara Mitsuko 160–161
Johnstone, Arthur 331, 363
Jones, James 19
Journals of Captain Cook 27–28

Ka Lae Point (H) 66
Ka'ahumanu, Queen 31, 32–33, 53, 114, 133, 176, 283
Ka'anapali (Ma) 124, 145–147
Ka'anapali Bay (Ma) 125
Ka'ena Point (L) 162
Ka'ena Point (O) 267
Kahakuloa Coast 126
Kahakuloa village 126
Kahanamoku, Duke Paoa 38, 206, 207, 211, 341
Kahanu Garden(Ma) 131
Kahekili 48, 84, 113–114, 118, 251
Kahekili's Leap (L) 170
kahiko 45
Kahokuwelowelo He'iau (O) 266–267
Kaho'olawe 168–169
Kahuku Point (O) 261
Kahului (Ma) 115–117, 147
Kahului Airport 115
kahuna 23–24, 28, 54, 60, 140, 174, 176, 190, 232, 266–267
Ka'ilimai, Henry 238
Kailua (M) 53
Kailua (O) 259
Kailua-Kona (H) 75–80, 96–97 Kaiser, Henry J. 211
Ka'iulani, Princess Victoria 199, 202, 226, 324
Kalakaua, King David 36, 37, 45, 77, 85, 168, 198, 217, 220, 223, 226, 227, 231
Kalalau (K) 300
Kalalau Lookout (K) 296–297
Kalaniana'ole, Prince Jonah Kuhio 202, 346
Kalanikupule 118, 251–253
Kalaniopu'u, King 29, 48, 74

Kalaupapa Leper Colony (Mo) 176, 180, 183–188
Kalaupapa Lookout (Mo) 183
Kalawao (Mo) 177
Kaloko-Honokohau National Historic Park (H) 80
Kalu'u O Ka O'o (Mo) 140
Kamakahonu (Turtle Eye) Beach (H) 77, 80
Kamakau, S. M. 72–73
Kamakou Preserve (Mo) 189
Kamalo village (Mo) 189
Kamamalu, Princess Victoria 214
Kamamalu, Queen 214
Kamehameha I (the Great) 24, 29, 31–34, 48–49, 53, 54, 56, 70, 74, 76, 80, 82–83, 84, 87, 89, 113–114, 118, 123, 133, 155, 170, 176–177, 189, 208, 213, 214, 230, 231, 232, 251–253, 282–283; statues 30, 56, 85–86, 224
Kamehameha II (Liholiho) 31, 33–34, 208, 214, 283
Kamehameha III 35, 114–115, 117, 208, 220, 260, 283
Kamehameha IV (Liholiho, Alexander) 214, 230–231, 305
Kamehameha V (Prince Lot, Kapua'iwa) 170, 177, 183, 199, 217, 222–223, 230, 308
Kamehameha Day 224
Kamuela (H) 87
Kanaha Beach Park (Ma) 115–116
Kanaha Pond Wildlife Refuge (Ma) 116
Kana'ina, Charles 223
Kanaloa 24, 168–169
Kane 24
Kane'apua Rock (L) 170
Kanepu'u Preserve (L) 159
Kapa'a (K) 304, 310–311
Kapalua (Ma) 148
Kapalua Bay (Ma) 125
Kapalua Bay Hotel & Ocean Villas (Ma) 125, 149–150
Kapana'ia (H) 84
Kapi'olani, Queen 198
Kapi'olani Beach Park (O) 206
kapu 24, 25, 31, 45, 48, 53, 54, 68, 76, 87, 108, 114, 155, 174, 283, 341

Kaua'i 22, 31, 276–317; climate 310; East 300–304; festivals and events 316–317; food and lodging 310–314; golf 314–315; history 278–283; map 285; North Shore 304–309, 312–313; outdoors 315–316; South 284–293; spas 315; surfing 350; travel basics 310; visitor information 310; West 297–298
Kaua'i Museum (K) 284, 287
Kauikeao'uli, Prince Albert 305
Ka'uiki Head (Ma) 133
Kauluapaoa He'iau (K) 309
Kaulula'au 154–155
Kaumauali'i 31
Kaumuali'i, King 282–283
Kaunakakai (Mo) 182–183, 195
Kaunolu Bay Village (L) 170
Kaupoa Beach Village (Mo) 191–192
Kawaiahao Church (O) 77, 93, 220–223
Kawawanakoa, Princess 216
Kealakekua Bay (H) 26, 28, 48, 70–74
Keawe, Chief 68, 69
Keck Observatory 92, 93
Ke'e Lagoon (K) 309
Ke'ei Beach (H) 73–74
Kekaha Kai State Park (H) 80
Kekauleai'ohi 222–223
Kekui'apo'iwa 84
Keopuolani, Queen 31, 35, 176–177, 208
Keoua 48–49, 82–83, 89
Kepaniwai Heritage Gardens (Ma) 118
Kepuhi Beach (Mo) 192, 193
Kihe'i (Ma) 126–130, 149
Kilauea Point (K) 304–305
Kilauea Point National Wildlife Refuge (K) 304–305
Kilauea Volcano (H) 23, 47, 56, 59–65
Kimball, Clifford 208
Kiowea Park (Mo) 183
Kipahulu (Ma) 134
kite-boarding 115–116
Kiwala'o 48, 74
Knudsen, Eric 295–296
Kohala (H) 83–86, 98–99
Kohala District Courthouse (H) 85–86
Kohala Mountain Road (H) 86
Koke'e State Park (K) 294, 295–296

Koko Crater Botanical Gardens (O) 257
Koko Head (O) 253–254
Koko Head Regional Park (O) 254
Kolekole Pass (O) 264
Koloa (K) 283, 290, 313
Kona Coast (H) North 75–83; South 66–74
Kona Pacific Farmers Cooperative and Museum (H) 74
Ko'olau Mountains (O) 258, 262–263
Ku 24
Kuakini, John Adams 76–77
Kualoa Ranch (O) 260
Kuhio, Prince 206
Kuhio Beach Park (O) 206–207
Kuka'ilimoku 24, 48, 133, 231
Kula Botanical Garden (H) 136
Kumulipo, The 141

La Perouse, Comte de 127, 130
Ladd & Company 283, 290
Lahaina (Ma) 114, 115, 120–123, 145–147
Lahaina Heritage Museum (Ma) 123
La'ie District (O) 260–261
Laka 25, 45, 324
Lana'i 154–173; climate 171; food and lodging 172–173; golf 173; history 154–158; map 159; travel basics 171; visitor information 172
Lana'i City (L) 158
Lana'i City Park (L) 236
land ownership 35–36, 177
language 19, 368–371
Lapakahi State Historical Park (H) 83
Larkin, Philip 210
Lawa'i gardens (K) 290–291
Lawa'i Kai (K) 290
leis 44, 170, 308, 324–325
L'Enfant et les Sortileges (Hockney) 230
leprosy 176, 177–180, 183–188
Leroux, Gaston 252
Lewers, Robert 208
Lihu'e (K) 284–287, 311–312
Lili'uokalani, Queen (Lydia Kamaka'eha) 36, 199, 207, 217, 226, 286, 346; statue 225
Lili'uokalani Gardens (H) 56
Limahuli (K) 291

Lindbergh, Charles A. 134, 189
Little Beach (Ma) 127
Lodge at Koʻele (L) 157, 172
lodging. See food and lodging
London, Jack 19, 200–201, 202, 296, 346–347, 361
Lono 24, 26, 70, 208
Luahinewai Beach (H) 78–79
Luahiwa (L) 165
Lumahaʻi Beach (K) 309
Lunalilo, King 168
Lunalilo, Prince William Charles 222–223
Lyman, David & Sarah 54
Lyman House Museum (H) 54

Maʻalaea (Ma) 118–120, 148
Maʻalaea Harbor (Ma) 120
Mahukona Beach Park (H) 83–84
Makaha Beach (O) 267
Makahiki 28, 208
Makalawena Beach (H) 80
Makapuʻu Beach (O) 257
Makapuʻu Point and Lighthouse (O) 257
Makawao (Ma) 136
Makena (Ma) 149
Makena Beach State Park 127, 343
Malaekahana State Park (O) 260–261
Malama 183
mammals 330–333, 339
Mana Shore (K) 297
Manele Bay (L) 157
Manele Bay Harbor (L) 165
Manele Bay Hotel (L) 157, 163
"Mango Tree, The" (Chock) 90–91
Mark Twain Monkeypod Tree 65–66
Marks, Richard 185, 197
Masters' and Mates' Reading Room 123
Matson Shipping Company 38–39
Maui 107–153; Central 115–118; climate 144; East 126–134; festivals and events 152–153; food and lodging 144–149; golf 149–150; history 108–115; map 109; outdoors 151–152; spas 150–151; surfing 348–349; travel basics 144; Upcountry 134–137, 148; visitor information 144; West 118–126
Maui (demigod) 108, 133, 141

Maui Arts & Cultural Center (Ma) 115
Maui Ocean Center (Ma) 119
Mauna Kea Beach Hotel (H) 81
Mauna Kea volcano (H) 23, 92, 93
Mauna Lani Resort (H) 46
Mauna Loa Volcano (H) 23, 59, 65
Maunaloa 192
McBryde, Alexander 290
Melville, Herman 214
menehune 133, 259, 278–279, 287, 293, 300, 301 Menehune Ditch (K) 293
Menehune Fish Pond (K) 287
Michener, James 19, 44, 318, 361
Mission Houses Museum (O) 223–224
missionaries 35, 53, 76–77, 114–115, 162, 177, 214, 217, 223–224, 252, 286
Moana Hotel (O) 198, 200
Moana-Royal Hawaiian Beach (O) 207–208
Mokuaikaua Church (H) 77
Mokuleʻia (O) 267
Mokupapapa Discovery Center of Hawaiʻi (H) 55
Molokaʻi 174–197; festivals and events 197; food and lodging 195–196; golf 196; history 174–180; map 181; outdoors 196–197; tours 197; travel basics 195; visitor information 195
Molokaʻi Forest Reserve (Mo) 189
Molokaʻi Light Station (Mo) 188
Molokaʻi Ranch (Mo) 177, 191–192
Monsarrat, Charles 214
Moʻokini Heʻiau (H) 84
Moʻomomi Beach (Mo) 194
mopeds 355
Morgunova, Lyubov 206
Mormons 155–156, 261
Mount Lanaʻihale (L) 158
Mount Waiʻaleʻale (K) 296, 297
movies 254, 276, 298, 309
Muindi, Jimmy 206
Munro, George C. 158, 159
Munro Trail (L) 158, 171
music 238–239

Na Pali Coast (K) 298, 299, 300
Na Pali Coast State Park (K) 298
Naʻalehu 65, 99

Naha Stone (H) 54
Nahi'ena'ena, Princess 114–115
Nahinu, D. H. 67
Nani Mau Gardens (H) 53
Nanue Falls (H) 88
Napili 148
Napili Bay (Ma) 124–125
Napo'opo'o Beach Park (H) 73
National Labor Relations Act 40
National Memorial Cemetery of the Pacific (O) 229
National Tropical Botanical Gardens (K) 290, 291
Nawiliwili Bay Harbor (K) 287
Nelson, Rena Kalehua 239
nene goose 143, 189, 328–329 Nene O
   Moloka'i sanctuary (Mo) 189
New Otani Kaimana Beach Hotel (Mo) 202, 213
Newby-Fraser, Paula 76
Ni'ihau 308
Norfolk pines 157, 158
North Kohala Peninsula (H) 83–86
Nukumo'i (K) 292
Nu'uanu Pali Lookout (O) 253
Nu'uanu Pali Overlook (O) 231–232
Nu'uanu Valley (O) 31

O'ahu 250–275; climate 268; festivals
   and events 272–275; food and lodging
   268–269; golf 269–270; history 251–253;
   Honolulu and Waikiki 198–249; map 255;
   outdoors 270–272; spas 270; surfing 265,
   267, 344–348; travel basics 268; visitor
   information 268
Old Koloa Sugar Mill (K) 290
Olowalu 148
On Water (Farber) 210, 339, 360
Oneloa Beach (Ma) 125
Onizuka, Ellison S. 80, 229
Onizuka Center for International Astronomy 93
outdoor activities: Hawai'i 103–104; Kaua'i
   315–316; Maui 151–152; Moloka'i
   196–197; O'ahu 270–272
Outrigger Canoe Club (O) 201
outrigger canoe race (Mo) 192

Pa'ao 23–24
Pacific Missile Range Facility (K) 297
Pacific Tsunami Museum 55
Pahinui, Gabby 239
Painted Church (H) 59
Pakuhiwa (Mo) 189
Palaoa Point (L) 170
Palapala Ho'omau Congregational Church (Ma) 134
Pali Highway (O) 230–232
Pali Kaholo (L) 170
Pan American Airlines 39–40
Papohaku Beach (Mo) 194
paragliding 151
Parker, John 86–87
Parker Ranch (H) 86–88
Pauahi, Princess Bernice 230
Pearl Harbor (O) 37, 39, 168, 232–237, 308
Pele 24, 25, 45, 47, 49, 56, 59, 60, 64, 65,
   140, 301, 309, 322, 323, 326
petroglyphs 22, 60, 69, 81, 165, 170, 301, 340
Phallic Rock (Mo) 182, 183
Pierce, Henry 284
Pi'ilanihale He'iau (Ma) 108, 131
Pina'o stone (H) 54
Pineapple Express (O) 264
Pineapple Garden Maze (O) 264, 265
pineapples 37, 40, 156–158, 180, 191, 264
Pioneer Inn (Ma) 123
plants 318–326
Pohakupule Beach (Ma) 126
poi 218–219, 280, 305, 306
Poipu (K) 291–292, 313
Poipu Beach Park (K) 288–289, 292
Poliahu He'iau (K) 301
Polihale He'iau (K) 298
Polihale State Park (K) 298
Polihua (Egg Nest) Beach (L) 155, 163
polo 267
Pololu Beach (H) 85
Pololu Valley (H) 84–85
Polynesian Cultural Center 260, 261
Polynesians 23, 48, 143, 278, 318
Pools of 'Ohe'o (Ma) 133–134
population 13, 44
Princeville (K) 305 Puna (H) 24, 56, 59
Punalu'u 99

Punchbowl Crater (O) 229
Pupukea (O) 266
Pu'u Keka'a (Ma) 124
Pu'uhonua O Honaunau (H) 68–69
Pu'ukohola He'iau (H) 48–49
Pu'ukohola He'iau National Historic Site (H) 82–83
Pu'uopelu Heritage Area (H) 87

Queen Emma's Summer Palace (O) 230–231
Queen's Surf Beach (O) 206
quilts 286, 287

Ranch Lodge (Mo) 191–192
ranches 86–88, 135–136, 137, 177, 191–192, 260, 300, 305
Red Sand Beach (Ma) 133
reef fish 334–337
Republic of Hawai'i 36–37
Resolution 26, 27–28, 321
restaurants. See food and lodging
Rockefeller, Laurence 81
Roosevelt, Franklin D. 235
Roosevelt, Teddy 37
Roughing It (Twain) 63, 218–219
Royal Hawaiian Hotel (O) 39, 208
Royal Kona Coffee Company (H) 74
Royal Lahaina Resort (Ma) 124, 125
Ruth, Babe 56

Sacramento Union **218**
St. Joseph's chapel (Mo) 189
Sandalwood Boat (Mo) 189
Sandy Beach (O) 254, 257
Sans Souci Beach (O) 202
Sawkins, James G. 55
Schaeffer, Anton 279, 282–283, 293
Schofield Barracks (O) 261
Sea Life Park (O) 257
Shangri La (O) 229
Shipwreck Beach (L) 162, 163
silversword plant 142, 143, 321
Sinclair, Elizabeth 308
Six Months in the Sandwich Islands (Bird) 280–281, 364
skiing 103
Sleeping Giant (K) 301

Smith & Bronte Landing (Mo) 189
Socher, Jonathan 192
Spanish-American War 37
spas 102, 150–151, 249, 270, 315
Spouting Horn (K) 292
Spreckels, Claus 116–117
stamps 252
Stevenson, Robert Louis 19, 66–67, 69, 178–179, 184, 202, 226, 227, 331
Stoddard, Charles Warren 121
Stones of Kapaemahu (O) 207
Stuck in Irons House (Ma) 121
Studio 7 Gallery 80
sugar industry 35–36, 37, 40, 50–51, 83, 89, 112–113, 115, 116–117, 124, 155–156, 260, 278, 283, 284, 287, 290, 300, 305
Suisan Fish Market (H) 56
Sunset Beach (O) 265
surfing 38, 340–353; competitions 351; glossary 352–353; Hawai'i 350; Kaua'i 350; Maui 348–349; O'ahu 265, 267, 344–348; Waikiki 207, 209–210

taro 191, 218–219, 280, 300, 305, 306
taxis 356
"Teapot Tales" (Jelsma) 160–161
Tedeschi Vineyard (Ma) 137
Tenrikyo Mission (O) 230
Thurston Lava Tube (H) 22, 60
tourism 38–41, 156–158, 180
tours 197, 249, 315
transportation 354–356
travel basics Hawai'i 94; Honolulu and Waikiki 240; Kaua'i 310; Lana'i 171; Maui 144; Moloka'i 195; O'ahu 268
Travels in Hawaii (Stevenson) 67
Tregaskis, Richard 19, 31
tsunami 55, 188, 191
Turtle Bay Hilton (O) 261
Twain, Mark 19, 60, 63, 65–66, 74, 141, 174, 218–219

'Ualapu'e Fish Pond (Mo) 189
Ulupo He'iau (O) 259
U.S. Army Museum 210–211
'Upolu Point (H) 84
USS Arizona (O) 233–237

USS Missouri 237
USS West Virginia 237

Valley of Hanalei (K) 305
Van Liere, Luc 76
Vancouver, George 29, 87, 143, 177, 251
Veterans Act 40
visitor information: Hawai'i 95; Honolulu and
Waikiki 240; Kaua'i 310; Lana'i 172; Maui
144; Moloka'i 195; O'ahu 268
Volcano House Inn (H) 60
Volcano village (H) 59, 99–100
volcanoes 20–23
von Kotzebue, Otto 32–34, 282
von Tempski, Armine 135–136
Voyage of Discovery into the South Sea and
Behring's Strait, A (von Kotzebue) 32–34

Waha'ula He'iau (H) 24
Wahiawa (O) 261
Wai'akea Peninsula (H) 56
Waialua 196
Waianae Coast (O) 267
Wai'anapanapa State Park (Ma) 128–129,
130–131
Wai'anuenue Falls (H) 56
Waikamoi Preserve (Ma) 134
Waikanaloa (K) 309
Waikapala'e 309
Waikiki (O) 38–39, 41, 198, 201–211;
climate 240; history 198–201; lodging
247–248; map 203; restaurants 240–247;
spas 249; surfing 207, 209–210; tours 249;
travel basics 240; visitor information 240

Waikiki Aquarium (O) 202–203
Waikiki Historic Trail 207
Waikoloa complex (H) 81
Wailea (Ma) 126–130, 149
Wailua Beach (K) 301, 310–311
Wailua Falls (K) 110–111, 300
Wailua River (K) 300–301
Wailuku (Ma) 117, 147
Waimanalo Bay (O) 258
Waimanalo Beach Park (O) 258
Waimea (H) 86–88, 100
Waimea (K) 292–293, 314
Waimea Bay (O) 26, 265
Waimea Canyon (K) 293–297
Wai'ohai (K) 292
Wai'oli Beach Park (K) 307
Waipa (K) 307
Waipi'o (H) 48
Waipi'o Valley (H) 89–92
Warnecke, Carl 224
water activities, 103–104, 151–152, 272, 316
"Water Born" (Hindley) 164
Webber, John 28, 29
wet caves (K) 309
whales 118–119, 121, 127, 254, 304–305,
331–332
whaling 35, 114, 115, 120, 136
Wilcox, George Norton 287
Wilcox Quilts In Hawaii, The 287, 365
Wood Valley Temple (H) 65
World War II 39, 40, 115, 163, 168, 211,
213, 229, 232–237, 254, 257, 266, 287,
308
Wyllie, Robert 305

COMPASS AMERICAN GUIDES

Alaska	Las Vegas	Pacific Northwest
American Southwest	Maine	Pennsylvania
Arizona	Manhattan	San Francisco
Boston	Massachusetts	Santa Fe
California Wine Country	Michigan	South Carolina
Cape Cod	Minnesota	South Dakota
Chicago	Montana	Tennessee
Coastal California	Montréal	Texas
Colorado	Nevada	Utah
Connecticut & Rhode Island	New Hampshire	Vermont
Florida	New Mexico	Virginia
Georgia	New Orleans	Washington Wine Country
Gulf South	North Carolina	Wisconsin
Hawaii	Ohio	Wyoming
Idaho	Oregon	
Kentucky	Oregon Wine Country	

ACKNOWLEDGMENTS

■ FROM THE AUTHOR

Mahalo Nui to former series editor Kit Duane, whose friendly advice and piercing questions kept me on a straight course and eager to have her comments. She knows the gift of *aloha*.

I am grateful for the invaluable assistance of David Forbes, curator of "Encounters with Paradise" at the Honolulu Academy of Arts and good friend, and for the *kokua* of the academy's Carol Khewhok. Grateful recognition for technical advice goes to my late husband Capt. Tom McGlaughlin for his knowledge of the sea, to my friend Dr. Yvonne Bickerton for reference to her study on *awa*, and to Dr. Scott Medbury, botanist at Foster Botanic Gardens. I am indebted to many National Park Service rangers at Volcanoes National Park and to geologists at the U.S. Geologic Survey on the Big Island for their invaluable discussions.

Institutions providing help through publications are the Bishop Museum Press, Friends of 'Iolani Palace, Kaua'i Historical Society, Lahaina Restoration Foundation, Mission Houses Museum, and the University of Hawai'i Press. I appreciate the treasure-houses of information at the Archives of the State of Hawai'i and the Hawaiian Historical Society.

With much *aloha* I acknowledge the steadfast support and literary experience of Lt. General Victor H. Krulak, U.S.M.C. (ret), and James L. Greenfield at the editorial board of the *New York Times*.

■ FROM THE PUBLISHER

For their generous contributions to this book, we thank Rena Kalehua Nelson, producer and host of "Na Mele 'O Ka Oina," KPFA radio, Berkeley, for her invaluable assistance in understanding Hawaiian music; Thomas Farber for excerpts from *On Water*, © Thomas Farber; Manuel Abascal for his essay "Cane Cutter's Journey"; Bamboo Ridge Press of Honolulu for assistance in finding modern Hawaiian writers of merit and for these selections from *The Best of Bamboo Ridge* published in 1986: *The Mango Tree*, © Eric Chock; *Teapot Tales*, excerpts from the biography of a Japanese homesteader, © Clara Mitsuko Jelsma; and "Water Born," © Norman Hindley.

Compass American Guides would also like to thank the following individuals or institutions for the use of their illustrations or photographs. All photographs in this book are by Greg Vaughn unless noted below.

Page 3, Paul Chesley

HISTORY & CULTURE
Page 25, Bancroft Library, University of California, Berkeley ▪ Page 26, Hawaii State Archives ▪ Page 29, Beinecke Rare Book and Manuscript Library, Yale University ▪ Page 32, Bancroft Library, University of California, Berkeley ▪ Page 33, Bancroft Library, University of California, Berkeley ▪ Page 37, Oakland Museum of California ▪ Page 38, Hawaii Visitors and Convention Bureau ▪ Page 41, Paul Chesley ▪ Page 44, Hawaii Visitors and Convention Bureau

HAWAII: THE BIG ISLAND
Page 49, Wayne Levin ▪ Page 55, Honolulu Academy of Arts Purchase, 1992 (7065.1) ▪ Page 68, Wayne Levin Page 71, Wayne Levin ▪ Page 76, Paul Chesley ▪ Page 82, Wayne Levin ▪ Page 91, Wayne Levin

MAUI: VALLEY ISLAND
Page 106, Corbis ▪ Page 125, Wayne Levin ▪ Page 142, Paul Chesley

LANAI: PRIVACY ISLAND
Page 155, Lanai Image Library ▪ Page 156, Oakland Museum of California Page 162, Paul Chesley ▪ Pages 166-67, Lanai Image Library ▪ Page 169, Wayne Levin ▪ Page 172, Arnold Sarrann/Lodge at Ko'ele

MOLOKAI: LONELY, FRIENDLY ISLE
Page 175, Wayne Levin ▪ Page 176, Hawaii State Archives ▪ Page 185, Paul Chesley ▪ Page 190, Paul Chesley

HONOLULU & WAIKIKI: DIAMOND HEAD AND PEARL HARBOR
Page 199, Hulton-Deutsch ▪ Collection/Corbis ▪ Page 206, Hawaii State Archives ▪ Page 209, Wayne Levin Page 212, Paul Chesley ▪ Page 216, Paul Chesley ▪ Page 220, Mission Houses Museum Library ▪ Page 222, Photodisc Page 226, Hawaii State Archives ▪ Page 228-29, Library of Congress Prints and Photographs Division ▪ Page 231, Paul Chesley ▪ Page 232, Paul Chesley ▪ Page 236, Wayne Levin ▪ Page 237, Library of Congress Prints and Photographs Division

GREATER OAHU: GATHERING PLACE
Page 250, Hawaiian Historical Society Page 259, Paul Chesley ▪ Page 266, Wayne Levin

KAUAI: GARDEN ISLAND
Page 279, Wayne Levin ▪ Page 280, Bancroft Library, University of California, Berkeley ▪ Page 282, Bancroft Library, University of California, Berkeley ▪ Page 286, Wayne Levin ▪ Pages 302-03, Paul Chesley

FLORA AND FAUNA
Page 320 (top and bottom), Paul Chesley Page 325, Wayne Levin ▪ Page 333, Wayne Levin ▪ Pages 334-36, John W. Perry ▪ Page 338, Wayne Levin ▪

SURFING
Page 340, Oakland Museum of California ▪ Page 346, Bancroft Library, University of California, Berkeley

■ About the Author

A resident of Honolulu, **Moana Tregaskis** wrote regularly on Hawai'i for the *New York Times* Sunday travel section. Before concentrating on the curiosities of travel, she spent years as a correspondent traveling the Pacific and high mountain areas of Asia. Trained in war coverage by one of America's famous war correspondents, Richard Tregaskis, she covered wars on the Indian subcontinent and in Southeast Asia for news services and is a member of the Overseas Press Club of America. Moana is a Fellow of the Royal Asiatic Society and the Royal Society for Asian Affairs. She lives in Honolulu with a view overlooking Waikiki.

■ About the Photographers

Greg Vaughn is a freelance photographer specializing in travel and nature. His award-winning imagery has appeared in such magazines as *Islands, National Geographic Traveler, Backpacker, Via, Travel & Leisure, Sunset,* and *Destinations.* He provided the photography for Compass American Guides' *Pacific Northwest* and was a major contributor to several books on Hawai'i. Although Greg and his family live in Eugene, Oregon, he called Hawai'i home for more than two decades. Read more about Greg at www.GregVaughn.com.

Paul Chesley has been a freelance photographer with the National Geographic Society since 1975, traveling regularly throughout Europe and Asia. He was honored by the inclusion of his work in the Society's first major exhibition, "The Art of Photography at National Geographic: A 100 Year Retrospective" at the Corcoran Gallery of Art in Washington, D.C. Solo exhibitions of his work have appeared in museums in London, Tokyo, and New York; and his photographic essays are regularly featured in such magazines as *LIFE, Fortune, Bunte, Paris Match,* and *Connoisseur.* Over the past six years he has participated in 10 *Day in the Life* book projects.

Wayne Levin lives on the Big Island's Kona Coast. His photography has been published in many magazines and journals, including *Manoa, A Pacific Journal of International Writing,* and in the book *Kalaupapa: A Portrait. Through a Liquid Mirror,* a book of Wayne's black-and-white marine photography, was awarded the Ka Palapala Po'okela Award for the book of the year by the Hawai'i Book Publishers Association. His work has been exhibited at the Contemporary Museum in Honolulu, the Robert Koch Gallery in San Francisco, and Rosenberg & Kaufman Fine Arts in New York City. Wayne holds an M.F.A. in photography from the Pratt Institute in Brooklyn, New York.